Adventure Guide

Dominican Republic

4th Edition

Fe Liza Bencosme & Clark Norton

HUNTER

HUNTER PUBLISHING, INC,
130 Campus Drive, Edison, NJ 08818
☎ 732-225-1900; 800-255-0343; fax 732-417-1744
www.hunterpublishing.com

Ulysses Travel Publications
4176 Saint-Denis, Montréal, Québec
Canada H2W 2M5
☎ 514-843-9882, ext. 2232; fax 514-843-9448

Windsor Books
The Boundary, Wheatley Road, Garsington
Oxford, OX44 9EJ England
☎ 01865-361122; fax 01865-361133

ISBN 1-58843-402-8
© 2005 Hunter Publishing, Inc.
Manufactured in the United States of America

This and other Hunter travel guides are also available as e-books through Amazon.com, NetLibrary.com and other digital partners. For more information, e-mail us at comments@hunterpublishing.com.

Cover photo: *Playa Juanillo*, Timothy O'Keefe (Index Stock Imagery)
Other photos courtesy www.dominicanrepublic.com
Maps by Kim André and Toni Carbone © Hunter Publishing, Inc. 2005
Index by Nancy Wolff

4 3 2 1

Contents

Acknowledgments

There are several people to whom I am forever grateful for their contributions to this project. First, to my family who had no idea what they were getting themselves into when they allowed a temperamental writer into their home. I couldn't have seen this project through to the end without your patient and loving support. Tío José "Pancho" Bencosme Guzmán, your beautiful wife and my friend, María Jiménez, my cousins Juan José, Mario and María Laura, I love you all completely. Dinorah (¡karamba!), thank you especially for keeping the coffee and the fried egg sandwiches coming.

I am also grateful to Nick Bryant, the gentleman from the British Army's Middlesex Regiment – it would have been impossible to complete the North by Northwest chapter without a knight gallant such as you. Rob Hawke, you are a traveling companion extraordinaire. Thank you, too, for turning me onto the wonderful staff and resources at the Helen F. Kellogg Library, which in turn led me to Catherine Campbell who loaned me hard-to-find books that provided colorful anecdotes. Marjorie Charles carefully reviewed chapters in addition to providing substantive information where I was lacking. Carlos Batista Velázquez from the Ministry of Tourism assisted as best he could under less than ideal circumstances. Bomba, you are the best motoconchista-cum-tour guide in all of Las Galeras. And last but certainly not the least, there is my pal, Clark Norton, whose idea it was in the first place that I join him in this adventure and who now knows just how cranky I can be. You are still, however, my favorite travel writer in the whole world.

Fe Liza Bencosme

I'd first like to thank Michael Hunter for allowing us to take on this ambitious and often exciting project. Next I'd like to thank my wife, Catharine, for her never-ending patience and understanding while I'm on the road or at the computer. I could never do this kind of work without you. My children, Grael and Lia; my sister, Mary Beth Norton; and my parents, Clark and Mary Norton, also offered valuable support and encouragement. And finally, I'd like to thank my intrepid co-author and friend Fe Bencosme, who never tired of seeking out adventures off the beaten path and whose insights into Dominican culture never ceased to fascinate me (and, I hope, the reader).

The authors would also like to thank the following people who were very generous with their time and assistance: Mara Sandri, owner of the Fior di Loto Hotel and unofficial mayor of Juan Dolio; Ralf Biegel, for his help on the south coast diving sections; Kim Bedall, founder of Victoria Marine/Whale Samaná; Jean-Philippe and Brigitte Merand, owners of Tropical Lodge Hotel in Samaná; Dagoberto Tejeda Ortiz, director of the Instituto Dominicano de Folklore; Juan Barsey of Apple Vacations; Salvatore Lobuono, owner of Hostal Primaveral La Mansión in Santo Domingo; Lory at Campo Las Palmas, the Los Angeles Dodgers training camp; the Rev. Elíardo Escoto Veloz of the Iglesia Evengelica Dominicana in Samaná; Kate Wallace of Tody Tours in Santo Domingo; Cheryl Andrews and the staff at Iberostar Punta Cana; Tomás Hungría, the general manager of the Guavaberry Golf Resort and Country Club in Juan Dolio; the staff at Sosúa Bay Hotel; the staff at Motorbike Safari Z & M; the staffs at Rancho Baiguate and Maxima Aventura; the staff at Villa Serena in Las Galeras; the staff at Trewe Tours; and the staff at the Playa Colibrí Hotel, especially Marlene at the front desk.

And to all the wonderful people we met along the way who are too numerous to mention, we won't forget you.

Clark Norton

Preface

When I was age five and living in the Virgin Islands, my mother sent me to the Dominican Republic to spend a summer with my father's side of the family – a boisterous array of grandparents, aunts, uncles, cousins, and neighbors so close that they seemed like family. As an aunt told me many years later, my mother wanted me "to know my people and culture."

More than 30 years later, I still recall that visit with the vivid clarity of the Caribbean's crystalline waters. I remember my grandparents' *bohio*, a typical rural Dominican home where I lived in the village of Juan López in Moca in the Cibao Valley – and where every other resident, it seemed, shared my otherwise unusual last name (Bencosme). I remember the Spanish-language romantic ballads that wailed incessantly from the neighbors' radios, the acres of plantain and yucca fields that served as my makeshift playgrounds, and the excitement that erupted at the dinner table over who would be among the lucky few to savor the *con-con*: burned rice scraped from the bottom of the pot, a much-treasured delicacy of Dominican cuisine.

The Dominican Republic of my early childhood was a largely rustic, burgeoning nation emerging from a turbulent political past. Then, the primary mode of transport for a family of four was typically a *motoconcho*, a motorbike in which the dad might steer with one child nestled in front of him and the mom might hang on behind with another child and a bag of groceries on her lap. And, while this scene remains a common sight in rural areas across the country, today you might see the same family cruising around in a late-model luxury four-wheel drive – a result of one of the fastest growing economies in the Western Hemisphere, including an explosion in tourism, which rocked the country during the late 1990s. (Meanwhile, many of those new tourists now prefer *motoconchos* to more comfortable rental cars as their own choice for getting around – a fact that arouses sheer bewilderment among many Dominicans.)

In the subsequent years, as I have made frequent pilgrimages to my second home, I have witnessed exponential – and sometimes unsettling – growth on the island (called Hispaniola, which the Dominican Republic shares with the much poorer Republic of Haiti). In Cabarete, a seaside resort along the country's north coast, where I went on holiday with my family in 1991, I could count on one hand the number of hotels that stretched along the lonely highway. Today, there are perhaps two dozen and twice as many restaurants, souvenir shops, tour operators, and other travel-related services and businesses – to the point where you can no longer see the beach from the roadside. Cabarete is now a center for 24-hour fun, where a mostly young, international crowd takes to windsurfing all day and partying all night.

For the visitor, this rapidly expanding tourist industry means a constantly increasing number of options for relaxing and/or exploring. The Dominican Republic offers an abundance of sun-drenched white-sand beaches where the palm trees almost seem to sway to the rhythm of a merengue beat, as well as a wealth of natural and historic attractions, vibrant nightlife and cultural activities, and a host of adventurous pursuits – including scuba diving, snorkeling, whale-watching, windsurfing, horseback riding, mountain trekking, jungle hiking, canyoning, and whitewater rafting.

If you're an independent-minded traveler, you'll find lodgings that range from luxury to low-budget, atmospheric restaurants with wonderful local food, and the chance to meet some of the friendliest people in the world. If you prefer an all-inclusive stay at a full-service resort, the country has one of the widest selections in the Caribbean – at prices sometimes startlingly low.

Although much has changed, the Dominican Republic of my childhood still exists in the warmth and hospitality of its people. For a truly memorable experience, be sure to venture into the countryside and visit with a Dominican family, who will greet you with open arms and, in all likelihood, a large plate of food (as an honored guest, you won't have to jockey for the *con-con*).

This is the Dominican Republic that I know today and continue to explore, along with my co-author, Clark Norton, who discovered the island later in his life but who has come to love it no less than I do. We hope your memories of the Dominican Republic will linger as long as ours.

Fe Liza Bencosme & Clark Norton

Introduction

History

 The Dominican Republic has a long and turbulent history, with enough milestones to make for a crowded holiday calendar and enough "firsts" to fill a page in an almanac. (Among them is having the first European settlements in the New World, established by Christopher Columbus and his brother Bartholomew.) The island has played a pivotal role in the development of the Caribbean for more than five centuries, with ample amounts of blood and treasure spilled along the way. The Dominican national character has been shaped by centuries of colonialism, political and economic turmoil, outside invasions, civil wars, and racial divisions. Remarkably, the country has now entered a phase of comparative stability.

■ Pre-Columbus

 The earliest Amer-Indians to have settled what is now Hispaniola are believed to have come from two different directions. The first migrated from the west around 2,500 to 3,000 years ago (probably from Yucatán in current-day Mexico, possibly by way of Florida and the Bahamas). These were eventually absorbed by several new waves of immigrants who came from the south, starting 2,000 years ago or more. The latter, of **Arawak** descent, originated in the Amazon and made their way north through modern-day Venezuela and the Guyanas before crossing the Caribbean via dugout canoe. Around 600 to 800 AD, the **Tainos**, one of the Arawak groups, arrived in Hispaniola and became the dominant people there. The Tainos called the island Quisqueya ("Greatness") or Haiti ("Rugged Mountain").

Another Arawak group, the **Caribs**, arrived on Hispaniola several centuries later, after populating the Lesser Antilles, the smaller islands to the east. At the time of Columbus' arrival, the Caribs' presence on Hispaniola was limited mostly to the area around present-day Samaná. The Caribbean took its name from the Caribs, as did the word "cannibal," since the Caribs were once called Canibas. While it's unproven that they actually practiced cannibalism, the Caribs were known to be much fiercer warriors than the Tainos, and had pillaged Taino villages both on neighboring islands and on Hispaniola itself.

The Tainos – whose name in Arawak dialect meant "good," "friendly," or "noble" – were believed to have been a largely peaceful, agrarian, family-oriented society, who survived by fishing, eating fruit, and growing such staples as yucca, corn, peanuts, sweet potatoes, cassava, and tobacco on communally owned plots of land. They were organized into at least five separate tribes, each headed by a cacique, or chief. As Christopher Columbus would later write, the Tainos were a strong and handsome people, and they had the most sophisticated culture in the Caribbean, rich in artistic and religious traditions. Skilled artists, sculptors, and craftsmen, they made boats, pottery, baskets, hammocks, and gold jewelry.

While the Taino people have long since disappeared, Taino culture is still much in evidence in the Dominican Republic in a number of prime archeological sites. Dozens of caves are decorated with pictographs and petroglyphs (rock art), which may be found along the southeastern Caribbean coast, the southwest, the far west, the north coast, and other areas of the country. By 1492, as Columbus' ships approached from Spain, Tainos numbered anywhere from several hundred thousand to one million or more.

■ Columbus' Arrival

Christopher Columbus, an Italian admiral in the employ of Queen Isabela of Spain, arrived in the Caribbean in the fall of 1492 with three ships, the *Niña*, *Pinta*, and *Santa María*, and his Spanish crews. They had crossed the Atlantic from the Canary Islands in about five weeks, believing they had found a shortcut to the Asian East Indies. After scouting out parts of the Bahamas and Cuba, they arrived along the northern coast of the island Columbus called Hispaniola ("little Spain"), where he made note of the exotic beauty of the mountainous landscape, the luxurious plants, and the tropical fish, as well as the friendly and docile nature of the inhabitants. Columbus wrote that the Tainos "ought to make good and skilled servants" and good converts to Christianity.

The natives threw feasts for the Europeans and indicated that Columbus and his men could find gold and other treasures in the island's interior. Columbus gathered up sample gold ornaments, plants, spices, dyes from trees, herbal medicines, plus a few native people and animals, and prepared to head back to Spain to show off the "riches of the Indies." But on

Christmas Eve, 1492, the flagship *Santa María* ran aground on a reef and wrecked near present-day Cap Haitien in Haiti. Columbus was forced to leave 39 men behind at a settlement he called La Navidad, in honor of Christmas. The men erected a fort from the salvaged remains of the ship.

Upon his return the following year with another 1,500 men, Columbus found La Navidad burned to the ground and the 39 settlers all dead. Some had died of disease and in-fighting; the rest had been attacked and killed by a local chief, Caonabo, after the Spaniards had raided and looted Taino villages. Columbus founded a new settlement farther east, along the north coast in the present-day Dominican Republic, calling it La Isabela after the Spanish queen. Although more than a third of its settlers fell ill within the first week, La Isabela survived four years, from 1494 to 1498, long enough for the Spaniards to establish a strong foothold in the area and exploit the Tainos for slave labor, women, and gold.

■ The Fate of the Indians

The Tainos were no match for the Spaniards, who brought iron weapons, armor, horses, and dogs. Caonabo, the Taino chief who had led the attack on La Navidad, was captured and killed, as was his widow, Anacoana, and almost all other Taino chiefs. European diseases for which they had no immunity – especially smallpox, influenza and measles – took a huge toll on the Tainos, as did brutal forced labor on plantations, in mines, and in construction projects. The Tainos were forcibly removed from their villages, causing their social structure to collapse and their crops to go untended. Spanish-imported cattle and pigs also ravaged their fields, resulting in widespread famine. Mass extinction followed. (The Tainos "repaid" the Europeans in part by introducing them to syphilis, the first case of which appeared in Spain in 1493.)

Within 50 years, all but a few hundred Tainos had been wiped out. No full-blooded indigenous peoples remain in the Dominican Republic today, although intermarriage with Spaniards has produced a substantial number of Dominicans of mixed "Indio" race. The only remaining full-blooded Amer-Indians in the Caribbean are about 2,000 Caribs who have survived on the island of Dominica, not to be confused with the Dominican Republic. Their original culture, though, has disappeared.

Only one Taino cacique, Enriquillo, successfully resisted the Spanish. From 1820-33, Enriquillo led a revolt from his base in the mountains of the southwest, near present-day Lake Enriquillo, where he and his men conducted raids against the Spanish and managed to elude capture. Eventually, the Spanish negotiated a settlement, and Enriquillo and his followers were allowed to live peacefully on a reserve. The author Jesus Galvan told the story of Enriquillo in his 1882 novel of the same name.

■ Expansion of Empire

 In 1498, Bartholomew Columbus, facing insurrection from Spanish settlers in La Isabella, founded the settlement of Santo Domingo along the southern coast, near the Ozama River. Santo Domingo grew to become the first permanent European city in the New World and the capital of the emerging Spanish Empire in the Caribbean. Christopher Columbus himself suffered a humiliating setback in the year 1500 when he was led back to Spain in shackles, accused of ruthless treatment of natives and colonizers alike, and of trying to usurp authority from the Spanish crown. Although he was soon released and continued exploring America, he never again wielded his previous clout in the new colony. He died in 1506, convinced he had been wrongly deprived of his rewards for discovering a new route to "Asia." As he wrote in his will, "I presented [to Spain] the Indies. I say presented, because it is evident that by the will of God, our Sovereign, I gave them, as a thing that was mine."

Columbus' successor, **Nicolás de Ovando**, shown above, appointed governor of the colony in 1502, became the driving force behind the construction of Santo Domingo. By 1503, the first city walls began to arise. Within the next few years, building would begin on the first fortress, first hospital, first church, first monastery, first stone house, and first paved road in the Americas. The first cathedral, university, and convent would follow. Explorers and conquistadors used Santo Domingo as a base for expeditions to Mexico, Peru, Cuba, Colombia, and Jamaica, all of which were claimed for the Spanish Crown.

Ovando also founded the north coast settlement of Puerto Plata in 1502, which served as a supply stop for Spanish galleons hauling silver from Mexico to Spain. To the west of Santo Domingo, Azua de Compostela was founded in 1504 and served as home for a time to such future conquistadors as Diego Velázquez (who conquered Cuba), Hernán Cortés (who conquered Mexico), and Juan Ponce de León (who later went off in search of the Fountain of Youth in Florida). By 1508, Ponce de León had constructed (using Indian labor, to be sure) a fortress-like house near the far southeastern tip of the island. The Spanish set up sugar plantations and cattle ranches in the area.

As the Indians succumbed to disease and harsh treatment, the Spanish began importing African slaves to Hispaniola to replace them; the first arrived around 1503. Some of these, called *cimarrones*, later escaped to live in the wild mountain valleys of the western part of the country, where many became small farmers. A number of their descendants survive today in outlying areas, especially near the Haitian border.

The Columbus family returned to power in 1509, when the admiral's son, Diego, was appointed governor of the colony to succeed de Ovando. To keep Diego's authority in check, however, the Spanish established the powerful Audiencia Real, a panel of judges that functioned as the unquestioned Supreme Court for the entire West Indies and Caribbean basin. The Audiencia was based in Santo Domingo, but the city's glory days were short-lived. Mexico and Peru, rich in silver and gold, became far more precious to the Crown than Hispaniola, whose stores of mineral wealth never met expectations. Diego and his family eventually returned to Spain, while colonists who remained increasingly turned to growing sugar, raising livestock, and supplying provisions to the Spanish ships that passed by the island on their way to the richer colonies. By 1520 or so, both Santo Domingo and Puerto Plata were already in steep decline.

A series of natural and man-made disasters – earthquakes, hurricanes, and raiding parties – also befell the colony. In the early 1560s, Santo Domingo and Santiago were severely damaged by earthquakes. Then, in 1586, the English buccaneer Sir Francis Drake, right, pillaged and burned much of what remained of Santo Domingo. And as the 16th century ended, much of the north coast had become a haven for smugglers and pirates. Many residents turned to trading illegally with English privateers, in direct defiance of the Spanish crown.

■ The 17th Century

Fearing that its colony was slipping out of its control, Spain decided to destroy its north coast settlements, torching Puerto Plata in 1605 and forcing its residents to relocate to the south near Santo Domingo. The Spanish also razed Montecristi, a town in the far west (near the present-day Haitian border) that was founded around the same time as Puerto Plata and had enjoyed some level of prosperity on its own. For all practical purposes, Spain abandoned the area for the next century and a half. The shock waves were felt throughout the colony, whose economy was in shambles, its people often on the brink of starvation.

In 1655, the English returned to Santo Domingo in the form of an invasion force led by William Penn – an attempt that was beaten back by the Spanish. But by then, Santo Domingo had become a virtual backwater. In 1697, under the Treaty of Ryswick, Spain ceded the western third of Hispaniola to France (present-day Haiti), while retaining control of the eastern two-thirds, the present-day Dominican Republic. France's colony, called Saint-Domingue, grew rich with an economy fueled by sugar cane and huge numbers of African slaves to work the plantations.

■ The 18th Century

Concerned about increasing French prosperity and inroads into the eastern section of Hispaniola, Spain paid renewed attention to its colony. In

1737, the Spanish imported Canary Islanders (off the west coast of Africa) to resettle Puerto Plata on the north coast, and did the same when establishing the northeastern settlement of Santa Bárbara de Samaná in 1756. Within another few decades, the north coast had become a center for the mahogany trade, exporting valuable tropical woods to Europe that had been harvested from the rainforests to the south. By the 1780s, about 150,000 settlers occupied the colony, with Spanish-ancestry settlers outnumbered nearly three to one by African slaves and mixed-race or black freemen.

In 1791, with imported Africans facing torturous conditions on the sugar plantations, a slave uprising broke out in French Saint-Domingue, led by **Toussaint L'Ouverture** (above). With the plantations burning and fearing for their colony, France abolished slavery there in 1794. L'Ouverture consolidated his base and prepared to declare an independent state called Haiti.

■ The 19th Century

The first 10 years of the 19th century saw a complicated type of military and diplomatic chess game waged among France, Spain, and the newly empowered ex-slave army in Haiti. In 1801, L'Ouverture marched into Santo Domingo and took the city virtually unopposed. The Haitians were now in effective control of the entire Spanish colony; one of L'Ouverture's first acts was to free the slaves there. In France, Napoleon Bonaparte dispatched his brother-in-law, General Leclerc, to quash the slave rebellion. The French drove the black army back to the west, and Spain ceded its territory in the east to the French in exchange for land that Napoleon had captured in Spain. L'Ouverture officially established the Republic of Haiti on the western third of Hispaniola in 1804, which remained independent. But France ruled the eastern part of the island until 1809, when a force of Dominicans drove them out and reincorporated with Spain. Meanwhile, slavery had been reinstituted in the colony, making the Haitians nervous about their own security.

In 1822, Haitian forces once again invaded the Spanish colony and regained control, abolishing slavery again and ruling over the entire island for the next 22 years. By the 1830s, a resistance movement among white property owners was brewing in the east, led by **Juan Pablo Duarte**, a young nationalist who had studied in Spain. In early 1844, Duarte and two other conspirators – **Ramón Mella** and **Francisco del Rosario Sánchez**, known as the Trinitarians – successfully led a revolt against the Haitians, resulting in the founding of the new Dominican Republic. Dominicans still celebrate February 27, 1844, as their Independence Day. And Duarte, Mella, and Sánchez have remained national heroes. The nation's first constitution was signed in San Cristóbal in 1844.

In a preview of the political instability that was to follow, the Trinitarians ruled only briefly before themselves being ousted. For the rest of the century and into the next, the country was ruled by a succession of *caudillos*, military strongmen who grabbed control from each other and ruled with iron fists. Corruption and repression reigned, as the *caudillos* rewarded their cohorts and families with the spoils of power and brutally suppressed their opponents. The country remained roiled in turmoil, with periodic coups, outbreaks of civil war, and economic crises alternating with all-too-short periods of relative peace and prosperity.

In 1861, as a means of consolidating his own power, one *caudillo*, **General Pedro Santana** (the same man who had earlier ousted the Trinitarians), invited the Spanish to annex the country. Spain sent in troops and issued new laws, spurring rebellion and civil war in 1863. Independence was restored in 1865 when Dominicans drove the Spanish out for good in the War of Restoration. (August 16, Restoration Day, is another national holiday.) Less than two decades later, another tyrant, **General Ulises Heureux**, overthrew a relatively liberal government to initiate his own reign of corruption from 1882 to 1899, when he was assassinated.

The 19th century also brought American influence to the Dominican Republic. First to arrive were two shiploads of freed American slaves, who settled in Santa Bárbara de Samaná during the 1820s. By mid-century, then-US Secretary of State William Seward was coveting the Samaná Peninsula for a naval base (Santana had offered to sell him the territory). Charges of corruption helped sink that deal, and later led to the 1870 US Senate defeat of President Grant's scheme to annex the entire country.

Some aspects of the Dominican economy did improve in the latter decades of the 19th century. Sugar, timber, tobacco, coffee, and bananas all emerged as important export crops, and the north coast towns of Puerto Plata and Sosúa both became prosperous shipping ports.

■ The 20th Century

In the early 20th century, the sugar industry became an increasingly vital part of the Dominican economy, attracting sizeable American investment. The US government negotiated a deal to take control of Dominican customs offices, and became progressively more involved in Dominican government affairs as the country devolved into civil strife and a succession of assassinations, coups and counter-coups. Finally, concerned about the political and economic stability of the country and rising German influence in the region just before World War I, the United States responded by sending in the Marines in 1916, occupying the country for the next eight years. While the US was there largely to safeguard its own interests, the occupiers did build new schools and roads. The military administration also squashed much of the domestic political violence that had torn the country apart for decades.

When the US occupation ended in 1924, Dominican democracy appeared ready to take hold. The freely elected new president, **Horacio Vásquez**, worked to improve the country's economy and infrastructure, but a new force had emerged on the scene: **Rafael Leonidas Trujillo**, a one-time telegraph operator who had commanded the US-created Dominican National Guard (police force). Trujillo staged a coup and won a trumped-up election in 1930 (claiming 95% of the vote) and quickly established an iron-fisted grip on the country.

■ The Trujillo Era

An avowed admirer of fascist Spanish Generalissimo Francisco Franco, Trujillo (left) proved to be one of the 20th century's most repressive dictators, unleashing a reign of torture, spies, intimidation, and assassination that eliminated his opponents and created a climate of fear in the general population. Confiscating most of the country's chief industries and a good deal of its land, he enriched himself and his cronies with the proceeds. In a monumental show of ego, he even changed the name of the historic capital from Santo Domingo to Cuidad Trujillo: Trujillo City.

Rumored to be part-Haitian himself, but expressing disdain for the black republic, Trujillo inflicted some of his greatest atrocities on his island neighbors. In 1937, Trujillo ordered his secret police to massacre all Haitians found on the Dominican side of the traditionally porous border. With thousands of Haitians living and working in the DR, the bloodbath was immense – an estimated 20,000 Haitians were slaughtered by Trujillo's henchmen.

Having courted American business investment with favorable economic terms, and serving as an anti-Communist bulwark in the region, Trujillo received support from the US government for much of his reign. (As President Franklin Roosevelt once famously remarked, "He may be a son of a bitch, but he's our son of a bitch.") But Trujillo was so unpopular in his own country that in the late 1950s, the Eisenhower Administration feared the Dominican Republic might be ripe for a Castro-style Communist takeover. After Trujillo unsuccessfully tried to assassinate the president of Venezuela, the Organization of American States (OAS) imposed diplomatic sanctions on the DR. On May 30, 1961, Trujillo met his own violent death, ambushed and assassinated in his automobile on a country road; the CIA was suspected of engineering it. When he died, Trujillo was one of the richest men in the world, with a personal fortune of at least

US$500 million, built by turning much of the country's economic sector into his own personal fiefdom.

■ The Post-Trujillo Era

After the assassination, Trujillo's son took power for several months, just enough time to murder all the suspected plotters and loot the public treasury one last time. He fled the country in November 1961, as his father's former vice-president, **Dr. Joaquín Balaguer**, briefly took over. In 1962, **Juan Bosch** of the leftist Dominican Revolutionary Party was elected president in the country's first free elections in 38 years, only to be overthrown by a military coup in 1963. (Again, the CIA was implicated.) In 1965, Bosch supporters launched a counter-coup. Four days later, US Marines landed again, intervening against pro-Bosch forces under the pretext that they were Communists.

In what was widely regarded as a rigged election, Balaguer was elected president in 1966, beginning an on-and-off reign of 30 years, marked by widespread corruption and repression. His next two election victories, in 1970 and 1974, were also considered tainted. In 1978, Balaguer was finally defeated by **Antonio Guzmán**, though not before Balaguer's supporters tried to steal back the election. The international community, led by then-US President Jimmy Carter, successfully pressured Balaguer to concede defeat. But Guzmán, himself corrupt and who committed suicide under a cloud of suspicion before his first term ended, and his successor, Salvador Jorge Blanco, who faced his own charges of corruption (and was later convicted of it), paved the way for Balaguer's return. With the country racked by rising prices, riots, and scandal in the mid-1980s, Balaguer won back the presidency in 1986. The DR's economic slide continued, marked by soaring inflation, currency devaluations, frequent shortages of basic services including water and electricity, and a nationwide workers' strike in 1989.

Despite it all, and with the help of some old reliable vote fraud, Balaguer was reelected in 1990, proceeding to spend freely, if not wisely, on elaborate public works projects. The most notable, and controversial, was the construction of a hugely expensive concrete lighthouse in Santo Domingo, the Faro de Colón, in 1992 to commemorate the 500th anniversary of Columbus' arrival. In protest of the cost, massive demonstrations followed, disrupting the inaugural ceremonies. Balaguer's subsequent reelection in 1994 was once again tainted by charges of voter fraud. Though he took office, he agreed to step down in two years rather than finish out the regular four-year term. In 1996, **Leonel Fernández Reyna**, who attended high school in New York City, was elected to succeed him, on a platform of economic and judicial reform.

■ The 21st Century

In May of 2000, Hipólito Mejía, the left-leaning Revolutionary Democratic Party candidate, was elected president, defeating two other candidates (including the aging Balaguer). And in May of 2004, after the country suffered a severe economic slide, Mejía was in turn soundly defeated by ex-president Fernández.

In the game of presidential musical chairs, the DR keeps soldiering on, ever more democratic but still fighting ingrained corruption and cronyism. Still, the country's elections are now reasonably free and democratic, political violence has been kept to a minimum, and the country's long history of repression is fading into the past. Serious economic and social inequities remain, but the Dominican Republic may finally be on the path to a more stable and prosperous future.

Government & Economy

■ Government

As its name suggests, the Dominican Republic (*República Dominicana*) is a republic (or "representative democracy," as the US State Department calls it). The country first gained its independence in February of 1844, when it broke away from Haiti, and officially regained it – after one of its leaders gave it back to Spain – in 1865. Its first constitution was formally adopted in November 1844, and subsequently revised at least two dozen times, as the country suffered through a century of political instability followed by dictatorship. The DR's current constitution (with later modifications) was adopted in 1966 after several years of political turmoil and civil war and a US military intervention following the 1961 assassination of dictator Rafael Trujillo.

Under its constitution, the Dominican Republic is governed by three independent branches, much like the United States: an executive branch (consisting of an elected president and vice president and a cabinet appointed by the president); a legislative branch with an elected bicameral Congress (consisting of the 32-member Senate and the 150-member Chamber of Deputies); and a judicial branch with judges chosen by the Senate. The Judiciary is headed by the Supreme Court of Justice, a 16-member body appointed by a bipartisan National Judicial Council.

The country is divided into 31 provinces and the National District of Santo Domingo, the capital, where the president's official residence is the National Palace.

Each province is headed by a governor appointed by the country's president. There are also 124 municipal districts governed by elected mayors and municipal councils (as is the National District).

Elections

The major political parties are the **Social Christian Reformist Party (PRSC)**, the **Dominican Revolutionary Party (PRD)**, the **Dominican Liberation Party (PLD)**, and the **Independent Revolutionary Party (PRI)**. Voting is both universal and compulsory, for those aged 18 and over or those married at any age. (Members of the armed forces and police, however, can't vote.)

The president and vice-president run on the same ticket and are elected by direct vote to four-year terms. (Presidential elections are held in years evenly divisible by four, while congressional and municipal elections are held in alternate even-numbered years.) In the most recent presidential election, in May 2004, Leonel Fernández, a member of the PLD, defeated Hipólito Mejía, a member of the PRD. (Mejía had succeeded Fernández four years earlier.)

Presidential election politics have traditionally been "highly spirited" (sometimes violent) and elections have frequently been marred by irregularities, though the last few have run comparatively smoothly. Much of Dominican politics is based more on family ties and associations and on the country's social hierarchies than on formal institutions of government. Old rivalries and friendships often play a decisive role in who gets rewarded with government jobs and money, paving the way for corruption.

The National Flag

The Dominican national flag, whose design is said to have been conceived by Juan Pablo Duarte, the 19th-century hero of Dominican independence, is made up of alternating blue and red corner squares divided by a white cross in the middle. In the center of the cross is the Dominican coat of arms. The blue squares represent the ideals of progress and freedom, while the red squares represent the blood spilled by liberators. The cross symbolizes the fight for freedom, while the white color stands for civil peace and union. The flag was sewn by María Trinidad Sánchez, who was a member of the Trinitarian movement with Duarte. She was later accused of sedition and hanged; the story goes that she asked for her skirt to be tied down at her hanging so that it wouldn't blow up as she dangled from the noose. The flag made its debut on February 27, 1844, recognized as the national day of independence.

■ Economy

 The Dominican economy has been on something of a roller-coaster ride since the late 1980s, when the Gross Domestic Product (GDP) dropped sharply even as consumer price inflation spiraled out of control. In the 1990s, the DR enjoyed the opposite: several years of moderate to high growth with declining inflation. In the latter half of that decade, the country led the Western Hemisphere in GDP growth.

After slowing in 2001, the GDP bounced back in 2002 – but so did inflation, rising more than 10% that year. Prompted in part by a massive bank failure, the economy then went into recession in 2003, while inflation jumped an astonishing 27%. After enjoying several years of relative stability, the Dominican peso lost much of its value, with the exchange rate going from 18.6 to the US dollar in 2002 to 46 to the dollar in February 2004. The rate became so volatile that many restaurateurs stopped posting prices on their menus.

While the favorable exchange rate boosts tourism and is generally good news for foreign travelers (though, since many tour operators and hotels charge in dollars anyway, it doesn't always help), Dominicans have been hard hit by price hikes. About a quarter of the population still lives below the poverty line, and the unemployment rates often hovers around 15%. The uneven distribution of income is also pronounced, as evidenced by the fact that Santo Domingo has the highest number of Mercedes, per capita, of any city in the Western Hemisphere – while much of the population still depends on overcrowded *guaguas* (vans) and *motoconchos* (motorbikes) to get around. Literacy is estimated at 83%, despite only six years of compulsory education. Life expectancy is about 71 years for men, 75 years for women.

Engines of the Economy

Even with the recent downturn, the country still has the largest economy in the Caribbean, with a labor force of around 2.5 million. Its three biggest economic sectors are government and services (especially tourism and transportation), industry (sugar refining, textiles, pharmaceuticals, cement, construction, light manufacturing), and agriculture. The service sector is the leading employer (primarily due to growth in tourism, telecommunications, energy, and Free Trade Zones). But agriculture is still the top sector in terms of domestic consumption and ranks second in export earnings behind mining (mainly of nickel and gold, silver and bauxite).

Sugar is the leading agricultural export, followed by coffee, cocoa, tobacco, bananas, plantains, oranges, pineapples and other fruit. Also grown are staple crops such as corn, rice, potatoes, beans, manioc, and cotton. Raising livestock (primarily cattle and pigs), dairy production, fishing, and cultivating flowers for export remain important. The United States is by far the biggest export (and import) market, followed by Canada and Western Europe; the DR runs a trade deficit of some $3 billion per year.

Nearly half of the Dominican population still live in rural areas, many of them small landholders. More than four-fifths of Dominican farms have an area of cultivable land below 15½ acres (6.3 hectares), which in most cases provides only enough land for subsistence farming. Near the coasts and in the fertile valleys, it's much more common to find large-scale farms and huge state-owned sugar plantations.

The steady growth of tourism provides one of the country's best hopes for economic recovery. In 1970, the tourism industry generated just under 5,000 jobs; in 1990, the number had jumped to more than 114,000 jobs; and by 2004, more than 770,000 were employed in tourism. To enhance the industry's prospects, the government has been expanding the country's infrastructure and its parklands.

Other recent moves to bolster the economy have included liberalizing trade, increasing foreign private investment, privatizing state-owned firms, and modernizing the tax system. US firms – mostly clothing, shoe, and light electronics manufacturers – account for much of the foreign private investment. Dominicans living abroad, especially in the United States, also provide a sizeable economic boost. It's estimated that remittances from the one million or so Dominicans living in the US (the majority in New York City) total nearly $2 billion per year, helping to prop up the country's foreign exchange balance. An estimated 60,000 US citizens, in turn, live in the Dominican Republic, many dual nationals.

Geography

The Dominican Republic occupies the eastern two-thirds of Hispaniola, the second-largest island in the Caribbean after Cuba. The separate nation of Haiti, with which it shares a 170-mile frontier, occupies the western third of the island.

Situated about midway between North and South America, Hispaniola is sandwiched between the Caribbean Sea to the south and the Atlantic Ocean to the north. Jamaica and Cuba are to the west, while Puerto Rico lies east across the 70-mile Mona Passage. The DR is about 600 miles southeast of the southern tip of Florida.

Shaped like an irregular triangle, with its short side as the Haitian border and its two longer sides as coastline, the Dominican Republic has a

The Caribbean

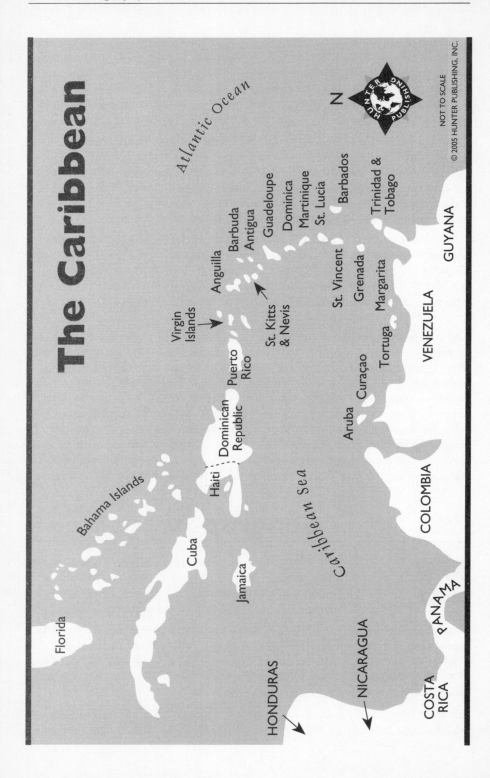

land area of about 18,700 square miles, making it about the size of the states of New Hampshire and Vermont combined. With a population of nearly 9 million as of 2004 (the second highest in the Caribbean after Cuba), the DR has a population density of 480 per square mile. About two-thirds of its people now live in cities, including more than 2,600,000 in the capital city of Santo Domingo and 800,000 in Santiago de los Caballeros. Ethnically, 16% of the country's population is classified as white, 11% black, and 73% of mixed race.

Most of the rural population still makes its living from subsistence farming. State-owned sugar plantations provide the major agricultural export. Other important crops include corn, rice, cotton, coffee, cocoa, tobacco, and fruit. Key natural resources include nickel, gold, silver, and bauxite.

■ Diverse Terrain

The country has some of the most varied terrain in the Caribbean, including the region's highest point (**Pico Duarte**, 10,128 feet, 3,087 meters) and its lowest point, **Lake Enriquillo**, which averages more than 140 feet (44 meters) below sea level. (The elevation differential is the greatest in the world within such a short distance, just 53 miles.) The DR has nearly 1,000 miles of coastline, featuring some 300 miles of white- or golden-sand beaches. The country also has arid deserts, lush rainforests, thick dry forests, and five major mountain ranges separated by a series of fertile valleys and lowlands. There are also several smaller mountain ranges. The country's dramatic elevation changes have resulted in at least 20 different climatic zones, with much wider variations in temperature and rainfall than in most other parts of the Caribbean (for more detail, see the *Climate* section).

A number of small islands lie off both the north and south coasts. The two largest are **Isla Saona** in the southeast and **Isla Beata** in the southwest. Other islands include **Catalina**, near Isla Saona; **Alto Velo**, near Isla Beata; several islets off Montecristi in the northwest; a number of small islands in Samaná Bay, most notably **Cayo Levantado**; and three inland islands within the shores of Lake Enriquillo.

Depending on the elevation and rainfall, vegetation ranges from tropical ferns, orchids, palms, and mango trees to pine trees to cacti. Estimates are that only about 15% of the country's original virgin forests remain, though much of that is now protected within the national park or scientific reserve system, which constitutes about 12% of the country's land. Over the past several decades, the government has taken steps to ward off the kinds of severe soil erosion and deforestation problems that have

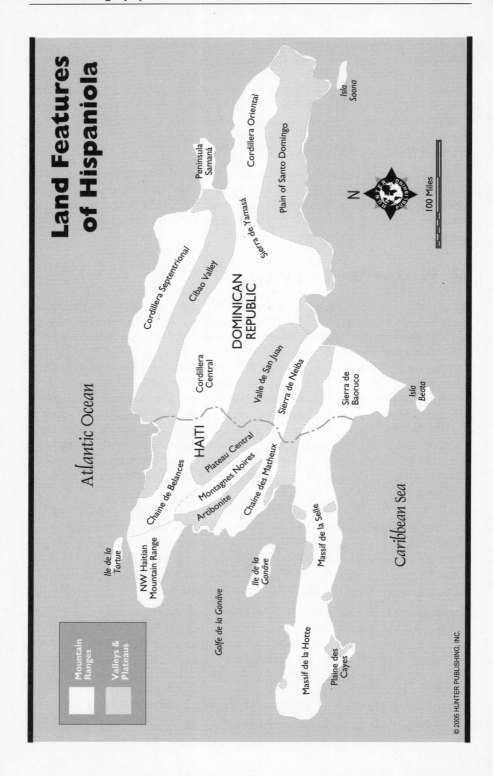

Land Features of Hispaniola

plagued neighboring Haiti, and secondary-growth forests now blanket several protected mountain regions.

The Mountains

 About four-fifths of the country is mountainous. The DR's four highest mountain ranges dominate the western part of the country, running roughly parallel to each other from northwest to southeast. The most northerly is the **Cordillera Septentrional** (Northern Range), which stretches from Montecristi in the far northwestern corner of the DR to the lowlands west of the Samaná Peninsula in the northeast. Its highest mountains rise to more than 3,000 feet.

The Cordillera Septentrional runs parallel to the Atlantic Ocean, separated from it by a fairly slender strip of coastal plain, where a number of north coast beach towns are located. Just south of the Cordillera Septentrional is the fertile **Valle de Cibao** (Cibao Valley), the nation's breadbasket and home to Santiago, the country's second largest city. About 10 to 30 miles wide, the Cibao extends 150 miles from the northwest coast east to the Bahía de Samaná.

South of the Cibao is the **Cordillera Central**, the country's highest and most rugged range. Crossing through the heart of the nation, it extends east from Haiti (where it's called the Massif du Nord) before turning south to the Caribbean and ending in the area of San Cristóbal, just west of Santo Domingo. The Cordillera Central includes not just Pico Duarte, the Caribbean's highest mountain, but the next three highest peaks as well. Known locally as the Dominican Alps, the mountain range defies tropical stereotypes by featuring sometimes freezing temperatures in winter, especially at night in the highest elevations.

Most of the country's major rivers have their headwaters in the Cordillera Central. The most important, the 184-mile-long **Yaque del Norte**, rises near Pico Duarte at an altitude of nearly 8,500 feet and runs west through the Cibao Valley till it empties into the Bahía de Montecristi on the northwest coast. The second most important river is the 114-mile-long **Yaque del Sur**, which rises to nearly 9,000 feet in the southern Cordillera Central and runs to the Bahía de Neyba on the southern coast.

South of the Cordillera Central lie two smaller and drier but still muscular mountain ranges, which make up much of the southwestern portion of the country. The **Sierra de Neyba**, the more northerly of the two, extends from Haiti 60 miles to the Yaque del Sur river northwest of Barahona. Its highest peaks top out around 6,500 feet. The **Sierra de Bahoruco** runs 44 miles from Haiti to the Caribbean, with three peaks surpassing 6,500 feet.

The Sierra de Neyba is separated from the Cordillera Central to the north by the **Valle de San Juan**, a semi-arid valley that runs 60 miles from Haiti to the Bahía de Ocoa along the Caribbean. To the south of the Sierra de Neyba is the **Enriquillo Basin** (also called the Valle de Neyba), site of the below-sea-level **Lago Enriquillo**, the country's largest inland body of water. (Composed of saltwater, it was once part of an ancient inland channel that connected it to the current Baie de Port-au-Prince in Haiti.) The 12-mile-wide Enriquillo Basin, which stretches some 60 miles from Haiti to the Caribbean, is largely arid and desert-like. It also includes the **Laguna Rincón**, the country's largest freshwater lake.

The smallest of the DR's five main mountain ranges, the **Cordillera Oriental** (Eastern Range, sometimes called the Sierra de Seibo), lies in the eastern part of the country southeast of Samaná Bay. The Cordillera Oriental runs parallel to the northeast coast and its southern foothills form a northern flank to the eastern portion of the Caribbean coast. North of Samaná Bay, the **Samaná Peninsula** – a thumb-like appendage jutting east from the north coast – is itself fairly mountainous, with some elevations reaching nearly 2,000 feet. Another smaller mountainous area, the **Sierra de Yamasa**, runs roughly east from the Cordillera Central to the Cordillera Oriental. Its highest peaks are nearly 3,000 feet.

The Lowlands

The Caribbean coastal plain, a six- to 25-mile-wide and 150-mile-long lowland that runs from the mouth of the Ocoa River west of Santo Domingo to the Coconut Coast on the far eastern end of the island, is the country's major population center. Since the arrival of the Europeans 500 years ago, much of this land has been used for livestock grazing and sugar cane growing. It's bordered on the north by the southern fringes of the Cordillera Central, the Sierra de Yamasa, and the Cordillera Oriental.

To the west, along the Haitian border, the land alternates between rugged mountainous terrain and arid, desert-like plains, characterized by dry scrub and cacti. This is the most sparsely populated region of the country.

All of Hispaniola is an active seismic zone, with periodic earthquake activity. The DR has suffered at least 10 major quakes since the 16th century, and several cities and towns have been reduced to rubble more than once. The last major quake (6.5 magnitude) was in September 2003 on the north coast, causing at least three fatalities and damaging buildings in Puerto Plata and Santiago.

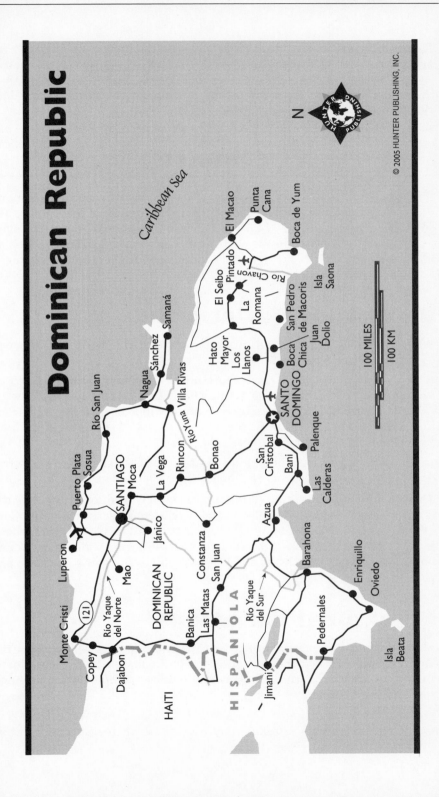

Though Hispaniola was once an active volcanic area (with many of its mountainous areas composed of ancient volcanic rock), no volcanic activity has been recorded in recent geological times. Scientists believe that the island broke off from Cuba tens of millions of years ago and has slowly moved eastward ever since.

Climate

 The Dominican Republic enjoys a mostly tropical climate year-round, with temperatures in most parts of the country averaging around 77-85°F (25-29°C). Expect year-round averages of 73°F (23°C) in the early mornings that rise to 90°F (32°C) at noon, then fall to 68°F (20°C) in the evenings. Humidity can be very high, though frequent trade winds provide some relief from the heat.

■ Altitude Variations

Where there is significant variation in temperature, it tends to be more by altitude than by season.

Beachgoers on the coast can expect fairly consistent temperatures of around 84°F (29°C) during the day and 68°F (20°C) at night, usually with extended periods of sunshine (and warm Caribbean waters). An exception can be the north (Atlantic) coast in winter, when cooler air and winds sometimes move in from the north.

In the low-lying deserts and valleys in the western parts of the country, daytime temperatures can reach more than 100°F (38 to 40°C).

The mountainous interior, by contrast, is often considerably cooler, with highs averaging about 75°F (24°C); the average temperature in the Cordillera Central resort town of Constanza is 61°F (16°C). On the highest mountain peaks, such as Pico Duarte, below-freezing temperatures are not uncommon, especially at night. Frosts and even snow sometimes appear.

■ Seasonal Variations

There are only minor temperature variations by season, which can be divided roughly into "summer" and "winter" (though by typical North American standards, the DR is mostly endless summer, with perhaps some spring tossed in).

Summer runs approximately from May to October, with August the hottest month on average. Summer daytime temperatures vary between 80 and 95°F (27° and 35°C) and average around 87°F (31°C), while night-time temperatures average about 72°F (22°C). And with the high humidity and intense sunshine that accompany this season, temperatures usually feel even hotter.

Winter runs from November to April, with temperatures somewhat milder and humidity lower. Nights can be blissfully breezy. January and February are the coolest months, when it can get quite chilly at night, even along the coast.

■ Rainfall

 Rather than changes in temperature, the major seasonal variation between summer and winter tends to be in the amount of rainfall.

In most of the country, including Santo Domingo and the Caribbean coast, May through November is the rainy season, with May and November the wettest months. The dry season generally runs from December through April, with March the driest. (Along the northern coast, however, the rainy and dry seasons are more or less reversed, so visitors to Puerto Plata, Cabarete, Sosúa, and Samaná should plan accordingly.)

"Rainy" and "dry" seasons can be misleading, however. Even during the rainy season, rain often comes in tropical-style bursts that often last a half-hour or less and then give way to sunshine. Sometimes weeks may pass with little or no rain, regardless of the season, or rain will fall fairly steadily for a few days at a time. And certain atmospheric effects, such as El Niño and La Niña can also result in changeable rainfall from year to year.

Rainfall also varies by region. Some of the DR is virtual desert, while other sections are rainforest and extremely wet. As a whole, the country averages about 55 to 59 inches (140 to 150 centimeters) of rain per year, but this ranges from a low of about 14 inches (35 centimeters) in the desert-like Valle de Neyba of the southwest to around 100 inches (254 centimeters) or more in Samaná on the northeast coast and in the Cordillera Septentrional and Cordillera Oriental mountain ranges. In general, the north and east of the country gets more rain than the south and west, with the far west being the driest of all. The mountains, in turn, tend to be much wetter than the lowlands.

■ Hurricanes & Tropical Storms

 Perhaps the biggest weather concern for visitors (and residents) is hurricane season, which typically begins in June and continues through November. Most of the biggest and longest-lasting storms, however, come through between August and October, with September being prime time. The last monster storm, Hurricane Georges, which tore through the island causing more than a billion dollars in damage and taking nearly 300 lives, hit in September 1998. Hurricane David, which slammed into the island in August 1979, was even more destructive, killing more than 1,000, leaving 10,000 homeless, and doing comparable property damage.

Major tropical storms, including hurricanes, now hit the DR on an average of once every year or two; the worst can produce violent winds, huge waves, and torrential rains and floods. The biggest hurricanes can achieve widths of hundreds of miles and sweep across much of the region with enormous force. The southern half of the country is the most vulnerable. Hurricane winds begin at 74 miles per hour (119 km per hour) and may reach 120 miles per hour (200 km per hour) or more, with rainfall sometimes topping 20 inches (50 centimeters) in 24 hours. Waves, floods, and mudslides, in fact, often cause more death and destruction than wind damage here.

The "good" news is that the DR usually gets two or three days' warning before hurricanes (which tend to form off the coast of West Africa) make landfall on the island. Tropical storms are often unpredictable, however, gaining or losing strength and changing course as they cross the ocean.

AVERAGE MONTHLY TEMPERATURES		
	Minimum	Maximum
January	66°F, 19°C	84°F, 29°C
February	66°F, 19°C	84°F, 29°C
March	66°F, 19°C	84°F, 29°C
April	70°F, 21°C	84°F, 29°C
May	72°F, 22°C	86°F, 30°C
June	72°F, 22°C	88°F, 31°C
July	72°F, 22°C	88°F, 31°C
August	73°F, 23°C	88°F, 31°C
September	72°F, 22°C	88°F, 31°C
October	72°F, 22°C	88°F, 31°C
November	70°F, 21°C	86°F, 30°C
December	66°F, 19°C	84°F, 29°C

Flora & Fauna

With the exception of the country's botanical gardens, zoos, and commercial wildlife parks, the most likely places to see the plants and animals of the Dominican Republic are in its many national parks, scientific reserves, and other protected areas (see *National Parks & Scientific Reserves* section, page 30, for more detail).

■ Flora

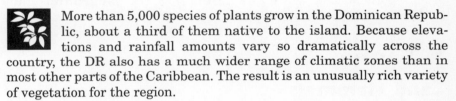

More than 5,000 species of plants grow in the Dominican Republic, about a third of them native to the island. Because elevations and rainfall amounts vary so dramatically across the country, the DR also has a much wider range of climatic zones than in most other parts of the Caribbean. The result is an unusually rich variety of vegetation for the region.

While most of the country's virgin forests have fallen to the lumberman's axe for timber or to open up land for growing crops and raising livestock, secondary-growth forests still cover nearly 30% of the country, with the largest tracts in the central mountains (now protected within Armando Bermúdez and Carmen Ramírez national parks). In the high mountains, Creole pines predominate. In the lower mountains and valley slopes, lush subtropical forests are most common, characterized by Hispaniolan mahogany, American muskwood, West Indian cedar, and several varieties of palm trees, as well as many types of ferns and bromeliads. The DR is also home to some 300 species of orchids, about half of them found in the Sierra Bahoruco range in the southwest.

The lush vegetation of the mountains and much of the eastern half of the country contrasts sharply with the large areas of arid semi-desert terrain that occupies much of the western part, epitomized by cacti, scrub trees, and low shrubs. The coastlines, in turn, are home to a number of red, white, and button mangrove swamps, which provide protection for birds and marine life. Stands of coconut palms line many of the beaches.

Notable Trees

Royal palm. Once endangered due to uncontrolled cutting for house construction, the royal palm is now officially protected in the Dominican Republic and often planted for ornamentation. The palm chat (*cigua palmera*), a native thrush-like bird, nests within it.

Coconut palm. Despite its prevalence along many of the island's beaches and its close identification with the Caribbean, this tall palm is not native to Hispaniola. One warning: it's not safe to lie directly under a coconut palm, no matter how tempting its shade. Falling coconuts can turn into dangerous missiles (especially in high winds), killing people every year in the DR. Be careful not to park your car under a coconut palm, either.

Dominican mahogany. While the practice of exporting exotic woods to Europe, beginning with the arrival of the Spanish, wiped out many of the DR's native mahogany trees, they may still be found in the subtropical forests. The mahogany is considered the national tree and is now protected from unrestricted cutting.

Also watch for such colorful trees as scarlet-flowered **flamboyants** (royal poincianas), white-and-purple-flowered **jacarandas**, and dark-green and golden **star apples**.

■ Fauna

Land Mammals

Most of the more than 30 species of mammals that inhabit the land today – including cows, pigs, boars, horses, mules, goats, sheep, dogs, cats, rats, and mice – arrived with European colonizers, starting about five centuries ago. No large native wild animals roam the DR, though you may encounter wild boar, horses, and goats in the high valleys of the Cordillera Central. All were introduced by the Spanish.

The only two remaining native land mammals – the hutia (or jutia) and the selenodon – are both highly endangered.

The **solenodon**, a dark brown, ratlike mammal that can grow up to two feet long, is the Caribbean's only remaining insectivore. Related to moles, shrews, and hedgehogs, it's now found only in Hispaniola and Cuba – and, after 30 million years on the planet, is now nearly extinct, done in by introduced predators such as the mongoose, cat, and dog. Making its home in caves and hollow tree trunks, it emerges at night to forage for insects, worms, and small animals such as lizards and frogs. You can recognize a solenodon by its long snout and tail and coarse, shaggy fur. It's also known for having a hair-trigger temper, shrieking and biting at times for no apparent reason.

The **hutia**, a rodent, shares several attributes with the solenodon: both are nocturnal, both live in caves and tree trunks, and both are facing possible extinction.

Though solenodons and hutias are said to inhabit at least two national parks (Parque Nacional del Este and Parque Nacional Los Haitises) as well as the scientific reserve, Loma Quita Espuela, your best chance for seeing either is in the zoo in Santo Domingo.

Sea Mammals

Humpback Whales

Each winter, from around mid-January to the end of March, some 3,000 to 5,000 humpback whales migrate from the North Atlantic Ocean south to the waters surrounding the Dominican Republic to mate and give birth. The DR has established a huge marine sanctuary that runs from the Silver Bank 60 miles north of the island south to the Bahía de Samaná, encompassing the northern and eastern coasts of the country. The sanctuary has become one of the best places in the world to go whale-watching. Humpbacks are active and animated at breeding time – spouting, slapping their fins, breaching (leaping out of the water), and lobtailing (beating the surface of the water with their flukes, or tail lobes) – as the males seek to establish their territory next to the females and ward off potential competitors. Male whales also sing to the females, sounds that can be heard with equipment carried on some expedition boats. Whale-watching trips range from week-long excursions in the Silver Bank to a few hours in Samaná Bay.

Manatees

Sometimes called sea cows, due to their large, oval-shaped, thickset bodies – they can weigh from 500 to 1,200 pounds and grow to 12 feet long – manatees are the only sea mammals besides whales and their own close relatives, dugongs, that spend their entire lives in water. Oddly, considering their considerable girth and generally lumbering appearance – they share a distant common ancestor with the elephant – manatees may have given rise to the mermaid myth, when ancient sailors saw them nursing their young on the surface of the water. (Perhaps when you're out at sea that long, even a gray- and rather wrinkly skinned beast with small eyes and bulbous nose and lips starts to look alluring.) They are, however, somewhat fishlike in form, with paddle-like tail fins and flipper-like forelimbs.

Manatees prefer warm, shallow, sheltered waters such as bays, estuaries and the mouths of rivers. In the case of the Dominican Republic, they are found in key habitats such as Laguna Estero Hondo, a mangrove-lined lagoon near Punta Rucia in the northwest, Samaná Bay in the northeast, and in the Parque Nacional del Este on the southeast coast. Once quite common along the shores of Hispaniola and all along the warmer eastern shorelines of the Americas, their numbers have fallen drastically over the centuries due to hunting, loss of habitat and, more recently, boating accidents (motorboat propellers are a prime culprit). Manatees are shy, slow-moving, gentle, and keep to a vegetarian diet, devouring up to 100 pounds of seaweeds and sea grasses every day. Being mammals, they have to surface for air every few minutes.

Reptiles & Amphibians

More than 1,400 species of reptiles inhabit the Dominican Republic, 83% of them native to the island. Of the many varieties of small lizards and snakes, none are poisonous. Frogs and toads are common amphibians.

American Crocodiles

 Hundreds of American crocodiles make their home in Lake Enriquillo in the southwest, one of the largest populations of wild crocodiles in the world, unique for this kind of saltwater environment. Even though the water in Lake Enriquillo is extremely brackish, the crocodiles have managed to adapt. Swimming to the mouths of freshwater rivers by day, they spend their nights on an island in the middle of the lake, where they also lay their eggs. (One of the best times to see them is early morning, when they like to stretch out on land, soaking in the sun.) Males can grow to more than 12 feet in length, while females grow to about eight feet. You might also spot crocodiles in Parque Nacional Montecristi and in Laguna Gri-Gri near Río San Juan on the north coast.

Iguanas

 Two endangered endemic species, **Ricord iguanas** and **rhinoceros iguanas**, are also found at Lake Enriquillo as well as Laguna Oviedo in the southwestern DR. Favoring arid, rocky terrain where they can dine on cacti and other desert plants, they are most common in the southwestern part of the country. Though generally shy, the iguanas at Lake Enriquillo sometimes approach visitors, hoping for a handout.

The rhinoceros iguana gets its name from the three small horns found on the snouts of the male of the species, as well as its gray color and considerable size (often from three to six feet long). The males also have a helmet-like pad on the tops of their heads, and both sexes have large throat pouches.

Sphaerodactylus Ariasae

Less than two centimeters long, this miniature gecko is the smallest reptile known to man. Its habitat is on the island of Alto Velo, south of the Pedernales Peninsula in the far southwestern part of the country.

Sea Turtles

 Sea turtles are found in tropical and subtropical waters, having adapted for life in the sea with lightweight shells and flipper-like, toeless forelimbs. While they spend most of their lives in the ocean, they come ashore to lay their eggs, and, in some cases, to bask in the sun. In the Dominican Republic, you might spot them on the offshore islands in Parque Nacional Montecristi, the shoreline of Parque Nacional del Este, and the lagoons of Parque Nacional Jaragua. All sea turtle species are threatened, however, by hunters, who kill them for their shells, hides, and oil, as well as for their meat and eggs. The largest sea turtles have already been hunted out.

Four species live off the Dominican coast. The **leatherback**, which belongs to a family separate from the other species, is the largest living turtle and has a bony, leathery skin rather than a hard shell. The brown-to-reddish-colored **loggerhead** is found both in open oceans and in shallow coastal salt marshes, stream mouths, lagoons, and bays. The highly endangered **hawksbill** (also called the tortoiseshell) is known for its yellow and brown translucent shell, which is prized for its ornamental value and has proved both its glory and its doom. The **green sea turtle**, which has a greenish-to-brownish skin and shell, is hunted for calipee, a glutinous yellow substance used to make soup.

The DR also has a variety of freshwater turtles, some of them found in Lagunas Oviedo and Rincón in the southwestern part of the country.

Fish & Shellfish

 Among the ocean fish found in surrounding waters are bluefish, tuna, king mackerel (shown at left), marlin, swordfish, sea bass, snapper, kingfish, barracuda, and grouper.

Inhabiting the offshore reefs and the mangrove swamps lining the coastlines are shrimp, conch, spiny lobsters, crabs, eels, and many reef fish, including parrotfish. The latter are parasites that specialize in grinding coral reefs into sand.

Coral

Coral reefs are complex formations produced in part by living organisms called hard corals, which absorb calcium carbonate from the water and then excrete it as limestone. Eventually the limestone creates an exoskeleton that not only encloses the animal but accumulates to form an entire ecosystem, which provides a home both for hard coral and many other forms of marine life. Soft coral (plant-like coral, such as the sea fan, that doesn't form a skeleton), algae, mollusks, sea urchins, sponges, worms, lobsters, crabs, eels, and reef fish are among its denizens. Some of these creatures help build and protect the reef, making for a nicely symbiotic relationship.

Coral reefs are found in shallow, tropical waters, such as those surrounding the Dominican Republic. Of the three types of reefs worldwide, two are found off the DR: fringing reefs and barrier (or bank) reefs. **Fringing reefs**, familiar to snorkelers, start at the mainland and are often visible at low tide just offshore. **Barrier or bank reefs** are shallow areas farther out to sea that are separated from shore by wide lagoons, and require boats to reach. These are generally richer in marine life, especially since many of the fringing reefs in the DR have been damaged by pollution and careless boating and fishing practices. However, the DR still has some areas of virtually untouched fringing reef, especially off the northwestern coast near Punta Rucia. Portions of the Samaná Peninsula in the northeast and the Parque Nacional del Este in the southeast also have thriving reef systems just offshore.

Birds

The Dominican Republic has at least 300 known species of birds, including both native species and those that migrate from the North American mainland to winter in the DR. Some 29 species are unique to the island, and eight to 10 of these are threatened with extinction. In general, the top spot for bird-watching is the southwestern part of the country; particularly rich areas include Parque Nacional Sierra Bahoruco and Laguna Oviedo in Parque Nacional Jaragua, where 130 species of birds have been identified.

Endemic (Unique) Species

Palm chat (*Cigua palmera*), shown at left. Officially designated the national bird, the palm chat is a mostly brown, thrush-like bird that builds complex nests high on the trunks of royal palm trees in coastal lowlands.

Hispaniolan parrot (*Amazona ventralis*), also called the *cottora* and nicknamed *cotica*, or "little parrot." This loquacious green parrot makes a popular (though illegal) pet. The capture and sale of parrots for pets is forbidden, but the law is rarely enforced.

Hispaniolan parakeet (*Aratinga chloroptera*), also called *perico*. The *perico* is green with red feathers and inhabits the mountains of the Cor-

Introduction

dillera Central and Sierra Bahoruco, though one flock of several hundred hangs around the Hotel Embajador in Santo Domingo.

Hispaniolan trogon (*Priotelus roseigaster*), or papagayo. A multicolored extravanganza of green, blue, red, and white, the hawk-like trogon is one of the most beautiful birds on the island, usually seen only in the mountains.

Hispaniolan lizard cuckoo (*Saurothera longirostris*), at left, or *pajaro bobo*. The endangered bluish-gray lizard cuckoo is found in the central mountains, the lowland thorn forests and even in gardens of Santo Domingo. Watch for its red eyes.

Hispaniolan woodpecker (*Melanerpes striatus*), also called *carpintero*. This endemic species is found throughout the island.

Narrow-billed tody (*Todus angustirostris*), or *chiqui*, and the **broad-billed tody** (*Todus subulatus*), or *barrancoli*. These two species, found only in the DR, are members of a family that's endemic to the Caribbean. The narrow-billed tody is bright green with white breast and favors the southwestern mountains. The broad-billed tody lives in the lowlands.

Water Birds

Around the island's lakes and lagoons and along the coast (especially the offshore islands, river deltas, and mangrove swamps), you'll find common but picturesque shorebirds such as flamingos, blue herons, great egrets, American frigate birds, brown pelicans, and glossy ibis.

Mountain Birds

In the mountains, you might spot white-necked crows, green-tailed warblers, Antillean siskins, and hummingbirds. Two new species recently found in the mountains include the **pitangua**, a night bird that nests in the ground among dry leaves, and the **white-winged crossed bill**, which lives exclusively in the pine forests of high mountains such as the Sierra Bahoruco and Cordillera Central.

One of the rarest migrating birds is the **Bicknell's thrush**, at left. After summer breeding season, it flies down from the mountains of upstate New York and Vermont to the mountains of the Dominican Republic, where it spends most of the year. The Bicknell's thrush once wintered in Haiti, until that country's severe deforestation ruined its habitat.

Flying Mammals

Numerous species of bats are found in the DR, many of them occupying the extensive cave systems around the country. Look (or look out) for them in the El Pomier Caves near San Cristóbal, in Jaragua National Park in the southwest (where there are at least a dozen species), and sometimes even in La Guácara Taina, a Santo Domingo nightclub set in a cave (after all, bats are nocturnal). Depending on the species, bats feast on mosquitoes, moths, and other insects, or on fruit. While these creatures are generally beneficial to humans, a small percentage carry rabies, so be sure to tend to any bites.

Insects

Like most tropical and subtropical regions, the Dominican Republic has countless insects. Mosquitoes and sand flies are the most noticeable – and annoying. There are plenty of spiders as well, though none are believed to be poisonous. The island's scorpions, however, can produce lethal bites.

National Parks & Reserves

Almost every adventurous traveler to the Dominican Republic will visit at least one – and most likely several – of the island's national parks and scientific reserves, which preserve and protect a growing portion of the DR's mountains, forests, deserts, wetlands, and flora and fauna. Located in every major region of the country, they range in size from less than 10 square miles to hundreds, and together total about 12% of the nation's land area. The country's highest and lowest points, its most endangered-wildlife areas, much of its remaining virgin forest and most fragile desert land, its biggest mangrove swamps, and some of its most beautiful and remote beaches all lie within the national park or scientific reserve system.

As of 2004, the country had 14 national parks and seven scientific reserves, though the parks department has been upgrading some scientific reserves to national park status, so the numbers will continue to grow. Some parks have few or no tourist facilities, or even roads. Some, such as Los Haitises south of the Samaná Peninsula, are passable only by boat, while some of the most rugged parks, such as Jaragua or Sierra de Bahoruco, can be negotiated for the most part only by four-wheel-drive vehicles. One national park (Submarino La Caleta) is nearly all water and geared to divers and snorkelers. Some others, such as La Isabela (site of the second European settlement in the New World), are of mainly historical interest.

Also overseen by the national parks department are a variety of national monuments, recreational areas, ecological corridors, and panoramic routes, totaling about 70 in all. As you travel around the country, watch for the bright yellow and green "Parque Nacional" signs. There's often a ranger station nearby, where you'll typically need to pay a fee of RD$50 to enter the park.

■ The 12 Major National Parks

Armando Bermúdez & José del Carmen Ramírez National Parks

 Located in the Cordillera Central, the DR's highest mountain region and known locally as the "Dominican Alps," these two adjacent and almost identically sized national parks together protect more than 1,500 square miles (3,885 square kilometers) of mountain territory and the rainforests and flora and fauna within. Armando Bermúdez, established in 1956, is the older of the two parks and lies directly north of Carmen Ramírez. The parks' main claim to fame is that they are home to the four highest peaks in the Caribbean, topped by Pico Duarte, 10,128 feet (3,087 meters) above sea level, followed by La Pelona, just a bit shorter at 10,112 feet (3,082 meters).

Hikers come from across the country and around the world to stand atop the Caribbean, as well as trek through unspoiled high-elevation valleys such as the Valle de Tetero and the Valle de Bao. A dozen of the country's biggest rivers (including the Yaque del Norte and Yaque del Sur) have their headwaters here as well, providing some excellent whitewater rafting opportunities. (See *Cordillera Central – The Dominican Alps*, page 283, for more on hiking, climbing, rafting, and other outdoor activities in this region.)

The parks are also known for harboring the country's largest remaining forest lands, including its surviving virgin rainforests. Park flora is a subtropical mix of tree ferns, orchids, bamboo, palms, and pine trees, depending on elevations. At the upper heights, Creole pines are predominant. Among the parks' many bird species who call the forests home are Hispaniolan parrots, white-necked crows, woodpeckers, loggerhead flycatchers, palm chats (the national bird), and Hispaniolan trogons. Mammals include wild boars and the endangered solenodons. But the weather can be anything but tropical here: On top of the mountains and even in the high valleys, temperatures sometimes drop below freezing in winter, especially at night, with a thin layer of frost covering the ground in early morning. Average temperatures, though, range from 54° to 70°F (12° to 21°C).

National Parks & Scientific Reserves

1. Reserva Científica Valle Nuevo
2. Parque Nacional Submarino La Caleta
3. Reserva Científica Laguna Rincón (Laguna Cabral)
4. Parque Nacional Sierra de Bahoruco
5. Parque Nacional Jaragua
6. Parque Nacional Isla Cabritos
7. Parque Nacional José del Carmen Ramírez
8. Parque Nacional Armando Bermúdez
9. Parque Nacional Monte Cristi (El Morro)
10. Reserva Científica Natural de Villa Elisa
11. Reserva Científica Isabel de Torres
12. Parque Nacional Cabo Frances Viejo
13. Parque Nacional Los Haitises
14. To Sanctuario del Blanco de la Plata (125km. N of Puerto Plata)
15. Reserva Científica Lagunas Redonda y Limón
16. Parque Nacional del Este

Atlantic Ocean

Caribbean Sea

N

40 MILES

Punta Cana

Higüey

El Seibo

Miches

La Romana

Isla Saona

Samaná

Sabana de la Mar

Hato Mayor

Boca Chica

San Pedro de Macorís

Sánchez

Nagua

Río San Juan

Cotuí

Santo Domingo

San Cristóbal

Baní

Sosúa

San Francisco de Macorís

La Vega

Puerto Plata

Jarabacoa

Constanza

Santiago de Los Caballeros

Azua

Barahona

Luperón

Mao

San Juan

Comenador

Pedernales

Jimaní

Montecristi

Dajabón

Isla Beata

© 2005 HUNTER PUBLISHING, INC.

Parque Nacional el Choco

Two lagoons, **Laguna Cabarete** and **Laguna Goleta**, home to thousands of birds, occupy much of this north coast park that lies between the Atlantic Ocean and the Cordillera Septentrional mountains just south of Cabarete. Other star attractions of the park are several underground caves near the lagoons that contain Taino petroglyphs and pools large enough for swimming. Some caves and parts of the lagoons aren't easily accessible, so many visitors come with guided groups or hire *motoconchos* to take them around. For more details, see the *North by Northwest* chapter, page 240.

Parque Nacional del Este

An environmental jewel, the "Park of the East" was formed to protect a large, densely forested peninsula that lies toward the southeastern edge of the Caribbean Coast. Much of the peninsula is inaccessible except by boat or hiking trail. The park also includes the smaller, though much more visited, **Isla Saona**, an island with gorgeous white-sand beaches situated south of the peninsula. Combined, the parklands harbor some 112 bird species – more than one-third of all those found in the DR. Several endangered marine species – including sea turtles (which nest along the shoreline), bottlenose dolphins, and West Indian manatees – cruise the waters around Isla Saona, while humpback whales pass by in winter. Lizards, snakes, endangered rhinoceros iguanas – and possibly even the DR's two indigenous but rare land mammals, the solenodons (ratlike insect-eaters) and hutias (foot-long rodents) – also inhabit the park.

In the interior of the peninsula, which is mainly dry forest, hiking trails lead to a number of caves containing Taino ceremonial sites, including extraordinary collections of petroglyphs and pictographs that depict historical events between the indigenous population and the early Spanish conquistadors. For details on visiting the park, see *The Caribbean Coast* chapter, page 141.

Parque Nacional Isabela de Torres

This national park encompasses (and takes its name from) the highest of the mountains to the south of the north coast city of Puerto Plata, 2,640-foot-high (805 meters) **Loma Isabel de Torres**. Though one of the country's smallest protected areas, it's also one of the most visited since it's so close to north coast resort areas. The most popular way to the top is by cable car ("Teleférico"), though steep hiking trails are also available. The reward for reaching the summit (which is flat and easy to walk around) is a panoramic view of Puerto Plata and surroundings, as well as close-ups of a statue of Christ Redeemer (Cristo Redentor) with outstretched arms. Visitors can also roam among seven acres of tropical botanical gardens, kept lush by more than a dozen subterranean rivers. See the *North by Northwest* chapter, page 240 for details on how to get there.

Parque Nacional Isla Cabritos

Lago Enriquillo, a massive saltwater lake that stretches for 26 miles near the Haitian border in the country's desert southwest, was once part of an inland channel that connected the Bahía del Neyba near Barahona to the bay of Port-Au-Prince in Haiti. Since 1974, it's been a wildlife sanctuary that roughly forms the boundaries of the Parque Nacional Isla Cabritos, named for the largest of the three islands that lie within it. Occupying a desert valley between two mountain ranges, Lago Enriquillo is the lowest point in the entire Caribbean, averaging some 144 feet (44 meters) below sea level.

Six-mile-long Isla Cabritos ("Little Goats Island"), the centerpiece of the national park, is a flat, arid, cactus-studded sanctuary in the middle of the lake that serves as a habitat for thousands of colorful tropical waterfowl and other birds. Hundreds of American crocodiles inhabit the lake as well – one of the largest such populations in the world. Two endangered endemic species, Ricord iguanas and rhinoceros iguanas (above), are among the thousands of other reptiles on Isla Cabritos. The mostly tame iguanas often approach visitors in hopes of being fed. Guided boat tours, the only way to visit the island, leave several times a day. See page 309, *The Southwest & Along the Haitian Border*, for details.

Parque Nacional Jaragua

South of Lake Enriquillo, at the tip of the Pedernales Peninsula in the far southwestern part of the country, lies the massive Parque Nacional Jaragua. Stretching over 600 square miles (1,554 square kilometers), this hot, arid, thorn-forest and cactus-filled region is mostly inaccessible. Exceptions are the wildlife-rich Laguna Oviedo and the Bahía de las Águilas, a beautiful bay with a long swath of largely deserted white-sand beaches, where sea turtles come to lay eggs. Two small islands, Isla Beata and Alto Velo, are also part of the park and (with some effort) can be reached by boat from the town of Pedernales. There are no tourist facilities to speak of within the park.

Laguna Oviedo is a stunning six-mile-long saltwater lagoon that encompasses at least a dozen small islands and is considered one of the top bird-watching spots in the entire country, including the DR's largest year-round population of flamingos. The area is also home to several species of turtles and the indigenous rhinoceros and Ricord iguanas. Visitors to the lagoon can hire local boatmen or join guided tours. The **Bahía de**

las Águilas is located west of Oviedo and southeast of Pedernales. The sand skirting the bay stretches on uninterrupted for miles.

Remote and uninhabited, **Islas Beata** and **Alto Velo** lie off the southernmost point of the Pedernales Peninsula. (Alto Velo is the southernmost point in the country.) On the south coast of Beata are a number of caves filled with Taino rock art, while both islands serve as habitat for flamingos, burrowing owls (right), and Ridgeway's hawks. Alto Velo also harbors the *Sphaerodactylus ariasae*, a miniature gecko just two centimeters long – the smallest reptile known to man. See *The Southwest*, page 312, for details on visiting the different sections of the park.

Parque Nacional La Isabela

La Isabela is one of the most historic sites in the Americas. The national park protects the remaining ruins of Columbus' second settlement in the New World, founded in 1494. Named for the Spanish queen who dispatched Columbus on his voyages of discovery, the town survived for only four years.

Unfortunately, there's not much left to see. Some of the archeological treasures were inadvertently destroyed during the Trujillo era, when the dictator ordered his men to clean up the site before an official visit; alas, overzealous workers bulldozed some of the ruins into the sea as part of the "clean up." Stones mark the outlines of several buildings, including the remnants of Columbus' house overlooking the ocean and a small church that was the site of the first Mass in the New World. A cemetery sits alongside the ruins, where scientists have unearthed the skeletal remains of perished Spaniards, some displayed in a small museum along with Spanish and Taino artifacts found in the area. The area was made a national park in 1998, and excavations continue. See *North by Northwest* chapter, page 243, for details.

Parque Nacional Los Haitises

More than 100 species of birds and mammals live in the hills, mangrove swamps, and exotic waterways of this rainforest wildlife sanctuary, including several rare or endangered species. Curious rock and coral formations host hidden limestone caves bearing pre-Columbian drawings of early Taino life. Thick with ferns, stands of bamboo, broad-leafed plants, and mahogany and cedar trees, the park has no roads and not even many foot trails into its dense interior, so it is best explored by boat. It all adds up to a popular adventure: Los Haitises, which lies along the south coast of Samaná Bay, is one of the most visited national parks in the country.

Visitors glide past islets and caves and through swamps of red and white mangroves, while colorful birds flit through the swamps and in and out of caves. Two endemic mammals, solenodons and hutias – both endangered or facing extinction – also occupy the swamps. Many of the coastal caves and grottoes have Taino pictographs etched on the walls, produced before the arrival of Columbus. See *Samaná Peninsula*, page 204, for details.

Parque Nacional Montecristi

This mostly dry, hot park is wedged between two bays in the far northwestern corner of the country just off the Haitian border. It includes a large river delta with coastal lagoons, mangrove swamps, and seven desert-like islets. American crocodiles occupy the lagoons, sea turtles lay their eggs on the beaches, and seabirds find sanctuary here. The most recognizable aspect of the park, though, is a flat-topped 778-foot (237-meter) limestone mesa named **El Morro**, which rises from the beaches and swamps on a small cape near the northern end of the park. The park service has built a set of stairs leading to the summit, but it isn't always kept open.

The national park also oversees arid **Isla Cabrita** (Goat Island), a small island marked by a lighthouse just off the most northwest point of the mainland. The beach there is prettier than any other in Montecristi, making it a popular stop with visitors. It's also a bird sanctuary harboring herons, egrets, and pelicans. Less than a mile offshore are the **Cayos Siete Hermanos** (Seven Brothers Keys), seven more sandy desert islets surrounded by reefs. Endangered sea turtles lay their eggs there, and they also serve as bird sanctuaries; pretty white-sand beaches are a lure for visitors and tour operators. The most notable of the seven is **El Atún** (Tuna), which has remarkably gorgeous flowering cacti. For details on visiting the park, see page 241 , *North by Northwest*.

Parque Nacional Sierra Bahoruco

The highlight of this vast protected area in the southwestern part of the country is its cloud-covered, heavily forested mountain range and the wide variety of bird life inhabiting it. Among some 50 species here are white-necked crows, narrow-billed todies, Hispaniolan trogons, Hispaniolan lizard cuckoos (above), and Hispaniolan parrots and parakeets – some found only in the Dominican Republic. Climbing to heights of more than 7,700 feet near the Haitian border, the park ranges from cactus-covered dry plains to mountain rainforests and pine forests and fields of broad-leafed plants and orchids (more than 160 species of the lat-

ter). But because of its remoteness and its mostly rough roads that require rugged four-wheel-drive vehicles, it's one of the least-visited parks in the country, with limited amenities for tourists. For more details on visiting the park, see page 314.

Parque Nacional Submarino La Caleta

Located about 13 miles east of Santo Domingo, this is less a formal park than a small strip of beach used as a popular launching pad for divers. The main attraction is exploring two wrecked ships, both scuttled here in the 1980s, when the park was formed. The larger of the two ships, the *Hickory*, 130 feet long, was once used to hunt treasure, salvaging sunken Spanish galleons. Over the course of the past 20 years it's become a veritable underwater museum of sea life, easily accessible to divers in the shallow waters. (Fishermen frequently provide boat rides, and organized diving tours also come here.) A coral reef with tropical fish is a big draw for snorkelers. For details, see page 138, *The Caribbean Coast.*

■ Minor National Parks

Parque Nacional Cabo Frances Viejo

This small north coast park consists of a lighthouse perched atop a majestic cliff that overlooks breathtaking coastline on the tip of a headland about halfway between Sosúa and Samaná.

Parque Nacional Nalga de Maco

Located in a remote cloud forest in the Cordillera Central near the Haitian border, this hard-to-find park contains a number of caves displaying Taino petroglyphs.

■ Major Scientific Reserves & Sanctuaries

Laguna Rincón Reserve

Also known as Laguna Cabral or the Cabral Scientific Reserve, this is the DR's largest freshwater lagoon, serving as a habitat for native turtles and several species of shallow-water wading birds, including flamingos and herons. It's at the eastern end of the Neyba Valley in the southwestern portion of the country. Guided boat tours are offered. See *The Southwest*, page 312, for more details.

Reserva Científica de Ebano Verde

This seldom-visited cloud forest reserve near Jarabacoa in the Dominican Alps protects the green ebony tree and the more than 600 other species of plants and 60 species of birds (a dozen endangered) that thrive in this area. One, *el zumbadorcito*, is the world's second-smallest bird. See *Cordillera Central – The Dominican Alps*, page 294, for more details.

Reserva Científica Lagunas Redonda y Limón

Near the town of Miches to the southeast of Samaná Bay, this nature reserve consists of two deep mangrove-lined lagoons totaling 40 square miles. They're primarily of interest to bird-watchers, who come for the chance to spot herons, great egrets, roseate spoonbills, grebes, and ospreys. The more easterly of the two, Laguna Limón, is also the more scenic and accessible. Boat tours can be arranged through the national park office there. See *Samaná Peninsula*, page 205, for more details.

Reserva Científica Loma Quita Espuela

Overlooking the rice paddies and savannahs of San Francisco de Macorís in the Cibao region, this cloud-covered protected area serves as a reserve for the country's two endangered indigenous mammals, the hutia and the solenodon. It also shelters some 58 species of birds, 18 species of reptiles, nine species of amphibians, and nine species of fish. Vegetation is lush: Gigantic trees with thick trunks are covered with moss and bromeliads, while ferns and orchids blanket the ground. An enormous waterfall feeds dozens of creeks that funnel water to cities around the region and help irrigate its fertile fields. Access to the park is via San Francisco de Macorís.

Reserva Científica Valle Nuevo

This protected alpine forest situated on a high plateau near Constanza in the Cordillera Central is noted for a stone pyramid marking the exact center of Hispaniola, and also as the source of two of the DR's biggest rivers, the Yuna and the Nizao. It's known for good bird-watching and a wide variety of vegetation, now recovering from a devastating forest fire in 1983; species endemic to Hispaniola include Creole pines and Dominican magnolias. With elevations reaching 8,530 feet (2,600 meters), temperatures sometimes drop below freezing here. The only way to get here is via a dilapidated road that can be maneuvered only by four-wheel-drive vehicle. See *Cordillera Central – The Dominican Alps*, page 293, for details.

Silver Bank Sanctuary (Santuario de Mamiferos Marinos)

Located in the Atlantic about 60 miles (100 kilometers) north of mainland DR, this huge marine reserve is designed to protect endangered humpback whales, who each winter migrate by the thousands south from the North Atlantic to breed and give birth in the waters off the east coast of the Dominican Republic. Very shallow in places, the Silver Bank contains coral reefs that have resulted in numerous shipwrecks over the centuries. (The most famous was the 1641 wreck of the *Concepción*, which sank bearing a rich cargo of silver and gold – the name Silver Bank comes from that.) Today, a limited number of tour boats are permitted to bring visitors to view the migrating whales on an up-close basis. See *Samaná Peninsula*, page 198, for more details on whale-watching trips.

For More Information

Dominican Republic National Parks Office (Dirección Nacional de Parques), Av. Máximo Gómez esq Paseo de los Reyes Católicos, Antigua Cementera, Santo Domingo DN, Dominican Republic; ☎ 472-4204, ext. 247, Spanish only; www.medioambiente.gov.do. The office is open Monday-Friday, 9 am-2:30 pm.

Culture & Customs

Visiting a foreign country can be a memorable experience in cultural exploration. It can also offer moments of temporary embarrassment as you navigate your way around an unfamiliar landscape, and stress you out from worrying about whether or not you're committing some blatant cultural *faux pas*. Are you making yourself understood, saying the right things? Did you inadvertently tell the taxi driver (in your best broken Spanish) to come back later, when you meant to say you'd be right back? While we can't begin to explain all the complexities of Dominican culture and society here, we can provide a few tips to help you move around with confidence and enhance your stay in the country.

■ Language

The official language of the Dominican Republic is Spanish. (No surprise there since the DR traces its roots to Spain.) In the tourism sectors, however, you'll find that many Dominicans speak English. In fact, you may find that your waiter also speaks French, German, and Italian – a testament to the diverse nationalities that visit (and sometimes settle in) the country. Not so surprisingly, though, you'll often find that in the countryside – and even in Santo Domingo – many residents not involved in tourism speak only Spanish.

To complicate matters further, they speak "Dominican" Spanish – which features distinct regional pronunciations and twists on otherwise universal Spanish words. For example, in some parts of the island the sound "r" is replaced by "l." And almost all Dominicans drop the middle and final "s," so that *"buenos días"* becomes *"bueno día"* and *"como estás"* is morphed into *"como tu ta."* For those who have traveled in Spain or studied Spanish in school, this can prove especially confusing – and at first you might think it's not Spanish at all that you're hearing. But the good news is that by trip's end, you may find the spirit with which *"como tu ta"* rolls off the Dominican tongue to be so ingratiating that the way you were taught Spanish in high school will never seem quite right again.

Here are some other "Dominicanisms" that will help you navigate the territory like a local:

"Chin" – pronounced "ching" – means a "little bit." Want a little bit of sugar in your coffee? Ask for *"un chin de azúcar."*

"Ahorita" may sound like the diminutive of *ahora*, which means "now" in Spanish, but it isn't. In Dominican Spanish it means "later." *"Ahora mismo"* means "right now." Confusing these two can quite understandably cause a lot of confusion.

"Ya," pronounced "jah," means a lot of things. *"Ya?"* asks, "are you ready?" At the same time, *"ya"* can also be used to say: "let's go," "enough already!" or "stop."

"Dios te bendiga" – pronounced "ben-dee-ga" – is a phrase that unaccompanied women hear a lot from men on the streets. It translates to *"God blessed you,"* and the speaker is simply complimenting the woman on her physical beauty. On the other hand, a man might also say *"bendigame"* to a woman, which means that he wants to know her in the Biblical sense of the word. Keep in mind that, while Dominican men are hopeless flirts, they're also harmless – so there's no need to take umbrage at such comments. The best response is simply to ignore it and keep walking – as Dominican women do.

"Tiene menudo?" may sound like you're asking for a bowl of tripe in a Mexican restaurant – or perhaps inquiring about a certain popular boy band of the 1980s – but it actually means "do you have any small change?" Assuming you won't be doing any panhandling, you may find this phrase most useful before getting into a taxi or mounting a *motoconcho* when the only folding money you're carrying is a large bill.

■ Greetings & Manners

Throughout the Caribbean, it's considered rude to initiate a conversation, enter public transportation or, for that matter, come within talking distance of someone without offering the appropriate spoken salutation. In the Dominican Republic, that would be *"saludos,"* although *"buenos días," "buenas tardes"* or *"buenas noches"* would work as well (though you may want to drop the final "s" in these words to fit in with the local custom). On buses and in public cars you don't direct the greeting to anybody in particular – you simply announce it as you board the bus and most everybody will respond in unison.

Kissing is another form of greeting typical in Spanish cultures. Dominicans greet each other and say goodbye by touching cheeks while making a kissing sound. Kisses are always exchanged between women and often between women and men, but only if the woman initiates it first. Dominican men are too macho to kiss each other, so they usually greet with a hug. Keep in mind that kissing isn't necessarily limited to people who know each other. Strangers might seal an introduction with a kiss if they're being introduced by a third party familiar to them both. If you make friends with a Dominican and you are introduced to another friend or a family member, don't be surprised if that person lands you a big kiss.

While it might not be politically correct to speak of a national character, Dominicans themselves will tell you that they are characterized by a gregarious spirit, tremendous patience, and a willingness to help that makes them easily familiar with one another. On the bus or waiting in line at the supermarket, Dominicans who have never met before will turn to each other and speak to one another as if they've known each other all their lives. Strangers greet each other as *"amigo"* or *"amiga." "Mi amor"* ("my love") is used commonly among men and women – even if they don't know each other – and no one takes it as sexual harassment. Dominicans also typically say *"joven"* ("young one") or *"amigo(a)"* ("friend") to get someone's attention, such as a server in a restaurant. So feel free to use *"amigo(a)"* or *"joven"* with either a young man or woman or to get your server's attention – it's expected. (*"Señor"* or *"señora"* is reserved for someone of advanced age or stature whom you would obviously defer to.)

For all their generosity and good manners, however, Dominicans aren't known for waiting their turn. Don't be surprised if you're in a shop, for example, and someone walks right up to the clerk who is serving you, says *"disculpame"* and proceeds to ask a question to the clerk – who then turns away from you to help the person who just interrupted you! Try not to be too offended or to take it personally. It's a cultural phenomenon and Dominicans don't see anything wrong with it – so getting upset or impatient doesn't solve anything.

The same holds true at fast-food restaurants. Dominicans typically walk right up to the counter (without pushing or shoving) and – as if nobody else is there – say *"joven"* and begin placing their order. The bottom line is that if you stand around politely at the empañada stand waiting for the attendant to ask for your order, you might not get your lunch till dinner time. (For whatever reason, however, lines are honored at banks and supermarkets.)

■ Dress

One's appearance is a matter of extreme pride in Dominican culture, with even the poorest person going all out to look his or her absolute best in public. No matter how intense the heat, or whether they're walking or riding a *motoconcho*, you will usually find Dominican women beautifully dressed and fully made up with their hair perfectly coiffed. Men, too, dress well, generally in long pants and a dress shirt with dress shoes and, at times, a blazer – even in daytime. (As the Dominicans say, *"La belleza antes de todo"* – Beauty before everything else.)

As a traveler visiting the country, you won't always find it practical or necessary to dress up, but there are times – such as visiting a museum, a public building, or a church – when you will be obligated to spiff up a bit. In these cases, men are required to wear long pants and a shirt with a collar, while women can dress as they please – providing they don't show too much skin. One exception to this rule is that some churches (such as the Cathedral in Santo Domingo's Zona Colonial) won't admit women wearing pants, so to prevent disappointment women might want to wear a dress while sightseeing there. But women are no longer required to cover their heads when entering a cathedral, as was the old Spanish tradition until around the 1940s or 1950s.

In the more laid-back tourist areas outside Santo Domingo, dress tends to be much more casual, and on the beach itself, just about anything goes. But residents of Santo Domingo consider wearing shorts away from the beach, especially to dinner, to be the height of tackiness and even offensive. Many top-flight beach resorts also discourage wearing shorts at dinner.

■ Music

 One thing that certainly stands out during any visit to the Dominican Republic is the population's passion for music – particularly merengue and, in recent years, bachata. Music blares from cars, corner stores, bars, restaurants – even shopping malls – at deafening levels.

Riding in *guaguas*, the crowded vans that serve as buses for most of the local populace, you will often encounter the fast-paced big-band sound of merengue, with its trademark accordions – an influence that resulted from a long history of trade between the island and Germany – or the more twangy bachata, with its honey-voiced crooners singing about unrequited love. Passengers usually sing along to themselves – when they aren't singing out loud – and someone will often yell to the driver to *"subelo"* ("turn it up") when a favorite tune is playing.

Even more popular than singing to music is dancing to it – and Dominicans, it seems, are more drawn to dance than perhaps any other people in the world. Be it at a nightclub along Santo Domingo's seaside Malecón, on a packed small-town dance floor on a Sunday afternoon, or at a baseball game – the other Dominican national passion – where pretty cheerleaders pump out dance routines to a merengue beat, it's beautiful to watch the sheer showmanship and passion of Dominicans as they dance.

■ Society

Dominican society is highly stratified, with social standing largely based on economic class, and sometimes race. Don't be surprised if you discover that in the eyes of a Dominican of modest means, you are "rich." You may be laughing and thinking: "Who me, the working stiff who saved all year for this vacation?" The answer is yes – you. For many Dominicans, the simple fact that you can afford to travel – no matter how you may have scraped up the cash or credit for it – is justification enough for the assumption. But don't be offended – the Dominican is more likely to be impressed than resentful.

Unfortunately, Dominicans as a group seem to suffer from a shame of material poverty. Both fabulous wealth and grinding poverty are on prominent display in the Dominican Republic, and the middle class has been shrinking of late. The fear of appearing poor – or, worse, being mistaken for poor – is very real here. This fear might explain at least some of the condescension many Dominicans feel toward the mostly desperately poor black Haitians who live in the DR, trying to eke out a living. You're not as poor as you think you are, the perhaps subconscious feeling seems to go, if somebody else is poorer.

It might also explain why many Dominicans – a highly creolized society composed of mixed indigenous Indian, Spanish-European and West African blood – have an aversion to being called "black." Many mixed-race Dominicans insist that they are in fact "Indio," meaning their brown complexions come from their Taino ancestors and not from the African slaves who replaced the native labor force once it had been wiped out by disease and oppressive conditions. Dominicans range from blonde-haired and blue-eyed on one end of the spectrum to dark-skinned and coarse-haired on the other. Nearly three-quarters of the population – and the most representative Dominicans – are brown-skinned and fill up the large gap in between.

■ Responsible Tourism

Responsible tourism means interacting with the local environment and culture in way that shows respect and consideration.

Throughout your adventures in the Dominican Republic you will encounter centuries-old buildings and artifacts of architectural, cultural, and historical significance. And, whether you are snorkeling in a coral reef, hiking through the rainforest, or driving through a desert, you will interact with fragile ecosystems that are hosts to a rich and diverse animal and plant life. All should be handled with care so that they will be there for others like you to enjoy for years to come. Keep that in mind while shopping, too – don't be tempted to buy items made from turtle shells, crocodile skin, mahogany, or other endangered plants and animals.

Picking up trash and not polluting natural areas should be a given. Not picking up "souvenirs" such as native plants, coral, and shells goes one step further. And not wasting limited local resources such as water and electricity shows the same kind of respect for the environment that recycling does back home.

But being a responsible traveler also means taking the time to understand the culture of the country you're visiting. Not only will you leave better informed than when you arrived, but you will be much more personally enriched for having truly meaningful interactions with the local people you meet.

In any country, the residents always appreciate when visitors try to speak the local language. If you don't already speak some Spanish, try learning some of the basics before you leave home, especially some of the local greetings that are highly valued in the DR (see page 40 for specifics). Your local library or bookstore can help; you can also check out the *Spanish Glossary* in the back of this book.

While no one expects a foreigner to behave precisely like a native during a short stay, it helps to conform a bit with local customs. Dress is a good place to start. Even the poorest Dominicans take extreme pride in their appearance. Shorts and sandals are for the beach and are not to be worn in restaurants, museums or when visiting churches, even those of historic interest. Yes, it's hot and you're on vacation, but covering up a bit is better for your skin anyway.

When taking photographs of people, be sensitive to your subjects. No one likes to be photographed as though they were exotic animals on display in a zoo. When you can, ask permission before taking close-up shots of people's faces, and respect others' right to decline if that's their choice. On the other hand, many people in developing countries can't afford cameras and love to have their pictures taken – especially if you send them a copy. Carry a pad and pen around to jot down addresses – you may make a friend out of the experience.

Above all, keep in mind that things are done differently in the Dominican Republic because, simply put, it is different. It does no good to complain how things are done "better" or faster in, say, North America. The whole point of travel is to get away from home, so relax and enjoy the slower pace and different lifestyle.

Try to keep some perspective about money as well. Some visitors will spend an entire vacation upset that they paid RD$60 for a taxi ride one day and RD$70 for the same ride on another day – a difference of perhaps 25¢. Unless someone is blatantly taking advantage of you, making an issue of it simply isn't worth the trouble. Similarly, while bargaining in the marketplace can be fun, paying a fair price doesn't have to mean haggling over every last peso. Subsidizing a small farmer or artisan to the tune of an extra dollar or two can help put food on the table for a local family.

Your ultimate responsibility as a guest in another country is not to cause problems for your hosts. Many people come to the Dominican Republic and are overwhelmed by the poverty throughout the countryside and naturally want to do something to help, and many do. But sometimes the "help" does more harm than good.

Several outfitters, for instance, sell tours of a "real Dominican campo." Monster-size safari trucks filled with tourists plow through rural villages, where children line the roads waiting for them. Why? Because many of the tourists throw candy from the trucks. You can't blame the kids – they love the candy. But long after the tourists have left, who will pay the dental bills for the poor families whose kids have toothaches? If you feel inclined to do something, consider giving something that these families can really use, such as a donation of books or school supplies to one of the rural schools. Inquire with your operator, since many of them collect such donations for the communities they work in.

Tourism is big business in the Dominican Republic, but, sadly, very little of this wealth makes its way down to the little guy. Even those staying in all-inclusive resorts can get away for a while and patronize local businesses. By doing so, you'll be contributing directly to the local economy and truly making a difference.

Practical Information

Documents You'll Need

US citizens and Canadian and British nationals may enter the Dominican Republic with an official photo ID such as a current valid passport or driver's license and the required tourist card (see below), along with a round-trip ticket to demonstrate intent to depart the country. Additional documents that serve as an official ID for American citizens include: an expired passport with a recent photo, an original birth certificate or certified copy with a raised seal, a voter registration card, or a naturalization certificate. The name on the identification documents and the airline ticket must match exactly.

Resident aliens of the United States should bring (along with the photo ID) their Alien Registration Card so that they can re-enter the United States. Legal residents of Canada and Great Britain (as resident aliens are called there) are required to have a valid passport or national ID.

While American, Canadian, or British citizens aren't required to bring a valid passport to enter the Dominican Republic, there are plenty of good reasons to carry one anyway. For starters, you'll need a passport in most cases to change money, cash traveler's checks, or make large credit card purchases. Furthermore, you also may not be able to rent a car or check into a hotel without one.

Acquiring and carrying a passport can also help insure your personal security. If you should have the unfortunate experience of losing your ID while traveling abroad, your country's embassy can confirm your identity much more easily if you own a passport. The American embassy, for example, can access the State Department's passport database to match you with the photo on file. They can't, however, access a state driver's license database or replace birth certificates. And in these days of heightened security and far-reaching anti-terrorism laws, the last thing you need is for an immigration official to doubt your identity. To be safe, always travel with a passport, and keep copies of the page with your name, picture, and number in secure places both at home and on the road as an added insurance policy if lost.

■ The Tourist Card

The tourist card is your visa, in effect, that allows you to legally remain in the Dominican Republic for up to 90 days. It can be purchased at the airport upon arrival (See *What to Expect Upon Arrival*, below, for details) and must be paid for with $10 of US currency no matter your country of origin. The tourist card is extremely important since you will be required to present it upon departure (in addition to paying a US$20 exit tax), so keep it in a safe place as you travel throughout the country. If you lose it, you'll have to buy another and pay a fine of RD$200.

■ Embarkation/ Disembarkation Cards

During your flight to the Dominican Republic, attendants will pass out embarkation/disembarkation forms. You'll need to fill these out and present them to immigration officers along with your other documentation.

■ Extending Your Stay

Many visitors come to the Dominican Republic on vacation, fall in love with the country – or with someone who lives there – and never look back. If you should decide to stay beyond the 90-day period permitted by the tourist card, you are required to visit the authorities to officially extend your stay. Overstays can incur fines up to as much as RD$200, depending on the length of the infraction. While this isn't a big expense, the red tape involved can be a huge hassle in time and energy – just ask anyone who's ever had to deal with immigration officers abroad. If, for whatever reason, you decide to remain in the DR longer than originally planned, go to any airport or immigration office and pay the nominal US$10 fee to extend your stay for three more months. The office at Centro de Los Heroes near the Malecón in Santo Domingo (☎ 534-8060) is the most convenient and efficient.

■ Traveling with Children

 If you are traveling with a child who doesn't bear your surname, you will need to carry either an original or certified copy of the child's birth certificate to prove your parentage, or a certified letter proving guardianship. Contact the Dominican consulate nearest you for further instructions on traveling with children with a different surname. Don't overlook this obligation – international child abduction laws are strictly enforced here and the Dominican authorities are vigilant when dealing with suspected kidnappers.

■ Dominican Diplomatic Representation Abroad

United States

Embassy of the Dominican Republic: 1715 22nd St. NW, Washington, DC, 20008; ☎ 202-332-6280.

New York General Consulate: 1501 Broadway, Suite 401, New York, NY, 10036; ☎ 212-768-2480, fax 212-768-2677.

Additional consular offices are located in Boston, Chicago, Houston, Jacksonville, Miami, Mobile, New Orleans, Philadelphia, San Francisco, and Puerto Rico.

Canada

Montreal General Consulate: 1470 Peel Street, Suite 263, Montreal, Quebec, H3A 1T1; ☎ 514- 284-5455/6600, fax 514-284-5511.

Ottawa Consular Services: 130 Albert Street, Suite 418, Ottawa, Ontario, K1P 5G4; ☎ 613-569-9893, fax 613-569-8673.

United Kingdom

Embassy of the Dominican Republic: 139 Inverness Terrace, Bayswater, London, W2 6JF; ☎ 7727-6285 or 7727-6214, fax 7727-3693.

What to Expect Upon Arrival

If you arrive in the Dominican Republic at Santo Domingo's Aeropuerto Internacional Las Américas, be prepared for a certain amount of chaos as you proceed through immigration formalities, luggage retrieval, customs, and into the main part of the terminal. Passengers arriving at one

Practical Information

of the country's smaller international airports will have a generally easier time of it.

> **Insider's tip:** Although airline passengers arriving at the international airport in Santo Domingo are left to their own devices to figure this out (there are no instructional signs, leading to inevitable confusion), once you have entered the terminal you will need to purchase your tourist card before reaching the immigration officer. If you haven't done so by then, you'll be sent back to get one and have to wait in line again. As you enter the terminal, look for the booths along the wall to your right and stop to buy a card before entering the immigration line. Be sure to have exactly US$10, no matter your country of origin, and a pen for filling out the card. Earlier, while still on the plane and just prior to landing, the flight attendants will have passed out embarkation/disembarkation forms. You should also fill these out before proceeding to the immigration line.

■ Immigration & Customs

 When you reach the immigration officer, present your passport or other photo ID, any visa you may have been required to obtain, your tourist card, and your embarkation/disembarkation form.

You'll proceed next to the luggage carousel for your flight. Expect to wait for a long while before being reunited with your baggage. When it (finally) arrives, head to the customs inspection line. Tourists generally clear customs with little trouble. If you are, however, singled out for questioning, it is likely that you will undergo a very thorough inspection of your luggage.

You are allowed to bring two bottles of alcohol, 200 cigarettes, and up to US$1,000 in items customs might consider gifts or resaleable. You may not enter with illegal drugs or other contraband of any kind, and getting caught attempting to do so could land you in a Dominican jail for up to 20 years – where facilities aren't nearly as comfortable as the worst cell in America.

Once past customs, you are ready to exit the terminal. Be sure to have the checked luggage receipts you were issued when you boarded your plane at the city of origin – you'll have to show them to prove ownership of the bags or you won't be allowed to leave the airport with them.

If you're booked into a nearby all-inclusive resort, a representative will probably be at the airport to meet you. Everyone else makes their way through the crowds of family members anxiously awaiting the arrival of their loved ones and the aggressive *buscones* (hustlers) offering assistance securing transportation and accommodations. While the *buscones* have a generally bad reputation among Dominicans, who view them as leeches to be kept away from tourists, most are fairly harmless freelancers who collect a commission from the hotels and car rental agencies they lead you to. (They also hope for an appreciative tip from you, or, possibly, to be hired to guide you throughout your trip.) The call is yours whether to use their services or not. Some adventurous travelers have had good experiences with *buscones* who proved to be useful guides, taking them to off-the-beaten-track places beyond the usual tourist haunts. Others have found them to be annoying, overly persistent pests and, on occasion, rip-off artists. Don't hesitate to issue a firm "no."

> **Grateful applause:** If you arrive in the Dominican Republic via a commercial airline originating out of a city with a large Dominican population, it's likely that your cabin will erupt in applause when the plane touches down on the tarmac – the Latin tradition of expressing gratitude for a safe arrival after a long journey.

Money Matters

The official currency of the Dominican Republic is the Dominican peso (RD$), circulated in one and five peso coins and in 10, 20, 50, 100, 500, 1,000, and 2,000 peso paper notes. (Technically, one peso is then divided into 100 centavos, but, although you may occasionally receive a 25 or 50 centavos coin in change or come across one lying on a sidewalk, these are now worth so little that hardly anybody bothers with them; even the most desperate panhandlers may refuse the coins as handouts these days).

EXCHANGE RATES	
US$1	RD$40-$60
RD$10	US17¢-25¢
RD$100	US$1.70-$2.50

The US dollar (US$) is widely – and warmly – accepted here. Within the tourism industry, in fact, it's often the currency of choice. You can always pay in pesos if you prefer, however. The peso floats freely against the US dollar, which means that official exchange rates can change rather drastically from day to day. Unofficial rates may vary even more, as exchange houses try to undercut the competition by offering more pesos per dollar.

As this book went to press, the peso was fluctuating daily between RD$40 and RD$60 for US$1 – a reflection of the steep devaluing of the peso in recent years (the peso had held steady at RD$12 until 2001, then started a rapid decline). This situation has made the DR an extremely cheap destination for visitors who are carrying US and Canadian dollars or euros – though it's tough on the wallets of Dominicans, who see the value of their savings dwindling as a result.

Because ATM machines are prevalent in the tourist hubs and most major credit cards are widely accepted, it isn't necessary to carry large amounts of cash or even travelers checks into the country (assuming you have ATM or credit cards). Keep in mind that your bank may charge an out-of-network fee – as much as US$5 per transaction – for using a foreign ATM. Generally speaking, though, no transaction fees are imposed in the DR.

■ Changing Money

The most competitive rates are available at the exchange houses – called *casas de cambio* – that are prevalent in tourist areas and stay open seven days a week, usually from 8 am to 8 pm You can also change money at banks (*bancos*) whose typical foreign exchange hours are Monday to Friday from 8:30 am until 6 pm. (Do not confuse *"banco"* with a *"banca,"* which is a place for buying lottery tickets and betting on baseball games – not for changing money.) Banks do not change currency on Saturdays and are closed on Sundays.

With less competition on weekends, though, some *casas de cambio* will buy dollars at less favorable rates on Saturdays and Sundays, so you may want to change enough money to carry you through till Monday. Weekends are also a handy time for visiting an ATM. (The monies you withdraw from your account back home will be deducted at the official rate no matter what day of the week it is.)

You can also exchange money at the official rate at Western Union offices, which are found in almost all tourist hubs and in some supermarkets. Your hotel may well change money, too, but you'll have to weigh the gains in convenience versus what are often much less competitive rates – at some all-inclusive resorts, for example, you might receive only half the number of pesos you would at a bank or *casa de cambio*.

When changing money and cashing travelers checks at any official outlets such as banks, Western Union offices, and *casas de cambio*, you'll need to present a valid passport. And wherever you change money, it's a good idea to ask for plenty of small bills (RD$20 notes or less), which will come in handy on numerous occasions. Don't expect taxi drivers or *motoconchistas,* for instance, to be able to make change for large bills.

Scams: No matter how great a rate you're offered, it's best to avoid money changers who operate on the street. They are often practiced scam and sleight-of-hand artists who love to prey on gullible *extranjeros* (foreigners). One notorious tactic is accepting a US$100 note, changing it into pesos, handing over the money, and then suddenly shouting, "The police are coming!" – then grabbing back the pesos and returning a US$1 bill to their unsuspecting mark before fleeing down the street. Another infamous trick involves "rolling" bills. The con artist folds the money around his finger so that what appears to be a stack of 10 or 20 bills is actually half that amount – counted twice.

■ Tipping

With so many ordinary Dominicans making a living from tips, *propina* (or tipping) is both widely practiced and widely expected, even for the smallest service performed. Restaurants automatically add a 10% tip to the check, but it's also customary to give something extra (up to another 10%) directly to the person who served you. Taxi drivers, porters, maids, other hotel staff who perform an extra service (even at all-inclusive resorts), the *motoconchista*-cum-guide who leads you to your destination when you're lost, the man on the street who helps you find a parking spot – even the kid who walks you to your car on a rainy day under the shelter of an umbrella – are all working for a *propina*. Five to 10 pesos is generally OK for a small service. How much you give beyond that is up to you.

■ Bargaining

Haggling over prices is not as common in the Dominican Republic as in some other developing countries. In fact, locals sometimes get annoyed that "rich" foreigners even bother to try to get a merchant to knock RD$100 or RD$200 off a price, when it amounts only to a few dollars. Established souvenir shops usually expect shoppers to pay the asking price, but sometimes they will reduce it by about 5% (the cost of processing a credit card transaction) if you pay with cash. More informal vendors, such as those along the streets or on the beaches, are more open to bargaining. But make sure the vendor knows you're bargaining in pesos and not dollars (or vice versa). Otherwise, a seemingly innocent bargaining session could turn into a major international misunderstanding.

Pre-Trip Planning

A good rule of thumb when getting ready for any travel experience is that for every hour spent on pre-trip planning, you can expect to save two hours or more of hassles after you arrive at your destination. Here are some things to keep in mind before you go, as well as some resources to help you in your planning.

■ When to Go

 What's the best time of the year for visiting the Dominican Republic? That depends on a variety of factors that only you can assess for yourself. When making your decision, you'll want to pay attention to the three C's: cost, crowds, and climate. Special events – such as the winter whale-watching season, February Carnaval, or the July Merengue Festival – may also influence your choice.

The island has two peak travel periods. These are December through March – when North Americans flock here to escape the cold winters – and the months of July and August, when it seems all of Europe abandons the Continent to swarm over Dominican beaches. During these six months, accommodations are much more in demand. And, of course, with scarcity comes higher prices. Air travel is much the same. During the peak winter season, major commercial carriers jack up their fares from North American hubs to Santo Domingo. (Most, though certainly not all, Europeans arrive by charter flights.)

The problem is especially acute during the month of December and throughout Easter Week, when many expatriate Dominicans return home for the holidays. At those times, commercial flights from North American cities with large Dominican populations are generally sold out far in advance, and airline rates are at a premium. So if you're looking for deals, or simply want to avoid the crowds, then avoid those peak seasons.

One added complication is domestic holidays, when Dominicans often travel with their families and may cause a run on hotel rooms at beach and mountain resorts and other desirable locations. (If the holiday falls during a long weekend, you could find yourself completely out of luck.) Even if you can find a room at those times, you may want to inquire beforehand with the hotel if you'd rather avoid crowds or children during your visit. The following is a complete list of Dominican holidays.

National Holidays

■ January

New Year's Day – January 1

Three Kings' Day (The Epiphany) – January 6

Procession of Our Lady of Altagracia – January 21

Juan Pablo Duarte Day (founding father of the Dominican Republic) – January 26

■ February

Independence Day (from Haiti, 1844) – February 27

■ March/April

Semana Santa – Holy Week

■ May

Labor Day – May 1

■ June

Feast of Corpus Christi – June 10

■ August

Restoration Day (final independence from Spain, 1865) – August 16

■ September

Day of Our Lady Mercedes – September 24

■ November

Constitution Day (signing of the first constitution, 1844) – November 6

■ December

Christmas – December 25

Events

The following cultural events also tend to draw big crowds:

Carnaval (island-wide) – entire month of February

Merengue Festival (island-wide) – last two weeks in July

Jazz Festival (Puerto Plata and Sosúa) – early October

See the *Festivals and Events* introductory section as well as individual destination chapters for more on these and other celebrations.

Practical Information

■ Climate

 Climate is the third major consideration for deciding when to visit. Perhaps the biggest weather concern is hurricane season, which typically begins in June and continues through late-November. Historically, however, there's little if any hurricane activity until August or September, when the big storms tend to come through. Recently, hurricane activity in the Caribbean has become more prevalent, so you can usually count on at least one major storm making landfall each year. Hurricane season (at least late summer) remains a peak travel period here despite September 1998's monster storm, Hurricane Georges, which tore through the island causing more than a billion dollars in damage – completely washing away one village and taking nearly 300 lives along with it. (See the introductory *Climate* section for more on hurricanes.)

The summer months also tend to bring on late afternoon thunderstorms that seem to appear out of nowhere and last only for short periods of time. During November, especially, rainfall can be heavy and can sometimes last for several days.

You can expect year-round warm temperatures to hover around 85°F (29°C) and to be able to swim any time of year in marvelously temperate Caribbean waters. (Atlantic Ocean waters along the north coast can be cooler, especially in winter, although many North American and European visitors find them perfectly comfortable for swimming in all four seasons.) Daytime temperatures in summer, however, can soar to the mid-90s (around 35°C), with sun rays so intense you may feel as if you're being fried alive. Even sunset brings little relief. Summer nights are balmy and, without air conditioning, sleep is sweat-filled. (Take note when booking a hotel room.) You'll probably want to change clothes at least once or more in daytime when visiting the DR during the summer months.

Winter, on the other hand, is more forgiving, bringing slightly cooler temperatures during the day and blissfully breezy nights.

In the Central Cordillera mountain range, temperatures are always a few degrees cooler, and below-freezing temperatures are not unheard of (many homes and the few hotels in the area come complete with fireplaces). If you're visiting the Dominican Alps, as this area is known, you'll want to pack a light sweater – and if you want to do some mountain climbing, be sure to include a coat, gloves, and hat among your gear.

■ How to Get There

 The following carriers provide direct flights to the Dominican Republic or connecting service from major North American cities through partner airlines.

Air Canada – direct service to Miami with partner airline and charter flights providing continuing service to Santo Domingo, La Romana, and Punta Caña (☎ 888-247-2262, www.aircanada.ca).

American Airlines – direct service to Santo Domingo and Puerto Plata from New York and Miami. Connecting service also available from San Juan, Puerto Rico, to Santo Domingo, Santiago, and La Romana (☎ 800-433-7300, www.aa.com).

Air Santo Domingo – daily non-stop from New York. Future flights scheduled from Miami (☎ 800-359-2772, www.airsantodomingo.com).

Continental Airlines – daily non-stop from Newark to Puerto Plata and Santo Domingo (☎ 800-231-0856, www.continental.com).

Delta – daily direct from JFK in New York to Santo Domingo (☎ 800-241-4141, www.delta.com).

Jet Blue – daily non-stop service from JFK in New York to Santo Domingo (☎ 800-538-2583, www.jetblue.com).

Lan Dominicana – Monday, Wednesday, and Friday from Miami to Santo Domingo (☎ 888-751-5263, www.landominicana.com).

Northwest Airlines – peak travel season service to Puerto Plata and Punta Caña from main hub in Minneapolis and connecting service through other major cities (☎ 800-447-4747, www.nwa.com).

Pan Am – from Boston/Portsmouth and Manchester to Orlando with connecting service to Santo Domingo (☎ 800-359-7262, www.flypanam.com).

US Airways – daily flights to Santo Domingo and Punta Caña through Philadelphia. Saturday only non-stop from Charlotte/Douglas to La Romana (☎ 800-428-4322, www.usairways.com).

■ Tourism Boards

You can visit branches in the following cities:

United States

Alaska: 1200, Columbine 3, Anchorage; ☎ 907-276-8988, fax 907-646-7937

Practical Information

Colorado: 1421 S. Pagosa Street, Aurora; ☎ 303-632-1253, fax 303-632-1103

Florida: 248 Lejeune Road, Miami; ☎ 888-358-9594 or 305-444-4592, fax 305-444-4845, domrep@herald.infi.net

Illinois: 561 West Diversey Building, Suite 214, Chicago 60614; ☎ 888-303-1336 or 773-529-1336, fax 773-529-1338, chicago@sectur.gov.do

New York: 136 E. 57th Street, Suite 803, New York City 10022; ☎ 888-374-6361 or 212-588-1012, fax 212-588-1015, dr.info@ix.netcom.com

Virginia: 14522-A Lee Road, Chantili; ☎ 703-242-3036, fax 703-378-3228

Puerto Rico: Ave. Ashford, 1452 Edifcio Ada Ligia, Suite 307, San Juan, Puerto Rico 00907; ☎ 787-722-0881, fax 787-724-7293, puertorico@sectur.gov.do

Canada

Quebec: 2080 Rue Crescent, Montreal, PQ, Quebec H3G 2B8; ☎ 800-563-1611 or 514-499-1393, fax 514-499-1393, montreal@sectur.gov.do

Ontario: 26 Wellington St. East, Suite 201, Toronto, Ontario M5E-1S2; ☎ 888-494-5050 or 416-361-2126, fax 416-361-2130, toronto@sectur.gov.do

United Kingdom

20 Hand Court, Hight Holborn WC1, London, ☎ + 44 207 24 27 778, fax +44 207 40 54 202, domrep.touristboard@virgin.net

■ Maps

Berndtsen & Berndtsen produces a detailed map of the Dominican Republic's primary and secondary roads while also highlighting the country's many natural attractions. The map is usually available at hotel sundry shops. You might also check your local bookstore before leaving home.

The National Parks Department in Santo Domingo produces an outstanding topographical map that you can have for the asking – if it's in stock. If you speak Spanish, it's best to call first (☎ 472-4202, Spanish only). The building is located north of Santo Domingo off Avenida Máximo Gómez and the intersection of Avenida Ovando (just before the overpass). Turn left onto the steep incline leading up the office, which is open Monday-Friday 9 am-2:30 pm.

■ Websites

 www.dr1.com – a heavily trafficked message board in English with lively and informative exchanges between locals and past and would-be visitors. Features a daily e-update you can sign-up for.

www.superpages.verizon.net.do – telephone directory in both English and Spanish.

www.listindiario.com (Spanish only) – the oldest and most respected newspaper in the country, an excellent source for staying abreast of local events and happenings.

www.diariolibre.com (Spanish only) – widely circulated free daily featuring short daily news briefs and good current events listing.

Accommodations

 With more than 50,000 rooms in every price range, the Dominican Republic offers some of the most affordable – and best-value – accommodations in the notoriously expensive Caribbean. Everyone from budget travelers looking for cheap-yet-comfortable abodes to well-heeled tourists who wouldn't think about staying in anything more humble than five-star resorts will find numerous options available. Accommodations vary from luxurious, often gigantic, all-inclusive chain resorts to modest pensións (private rooms in Dominican homes) – with a slew of independent hotels, apart-hotels, and guest houses falling somewhere in-between on the size and amenity scales. Where you choose to stay depends on your budget and what you hope to get out of your visit. Here are your options in brief.

■ All-Inclusive Chain Resorts

It's hard to beat the all-inclusives as a way of getting the most punch for your pesos. For one often remarkably low price, you can expect to get a beautifully appointed room on a prime beach, a host of resort-style amenities, round-the-clock entertainment, and all the food and drink you could possibly consume. The one condition for landing these great deals is that you need to set everything up before you arrive, by going through a travel or tour agency that buys in bulk or, alternatively, by shopping the different resorts yourself – the Internet is the best place to start – for the best price. (Since they're always part of larger corporate chains, you may find that several resorts are available on one website, allowing you to compare and contrast the amenities and rates.) You can also call a resort's toll-free number if it has one, though agents answering reservation lines often don't have the authority to negotiate. The worst idea is just to show up at the front desk out of the blue – in that event, you might pay as much as 75% more than guests who planned ahead.

All-inclusives can be excellent choices for families traveling with small children, since everything is conveniently located on-site, there are plenty of non-exotic food choices, and many offer supervised children's programs where kids can meet and play with others their own age. Programs usually are limited to kids aged three to 12 or thereabouts – the better ones are broken down into smaller age ranges, so that preteens aren't stuck in the same games with toddlers. Parents should also look for things such as separate swimming pools, special evening activities for kids, or babysitting services – sure signs that a resort is indeed family-oriented.

All-inclusives can also be a good option for newlyweds or any other travelers who simply want to take it easy for a few days. Even adventure travelers can use them to kick back and relax after more strenuous activities. On the other hand, for travelers who wish to get out into the countryside and sample some of the local culture and cuisine, the synthetic atmosphere behind these often walled-in compounds can grow stale fast. So you may wish to limit your stay there to just part of your trip.

For insights into other travelers' experiences at a wide range of all-inclusives across the island, check out the rave-and-rant reviews at www.debbiesdominicantravel.com and www.fodors.com.

■ Independent Hotels

One of the main differences between the all-inclusives and the independent hotels – owned not by corporate chains but by local families or other individuals – is simply size. The independents are usually a lot smaller. Other typical differences include less security (meaning they aren't walled off from the public), perhaps a smaller or lower-quality beach – and often a walk to the nearest public beach. In many cases, the hotels are closer to town and have somewhat more local atmosphere. Interestingly, however, the larger independents often retain at least some of the "everything included" concept. In other words, at least some meals (though not the glitzy entertainment) may be included in your rates. Finally, you may find lower rates at the independents – but, with fewer amenities, and sometimes lower overall value.

There's a lot of variety – both good and bad – within this category, so it helps to learn as much as you can about hotels you're considering. Along with the independent hotels we recommend, you can find out about prospective lodgings by talking to other travelers online about their experiences – for starters, try the message boards at www.dr1.com, a helpful Dominican Republic travel website.

■ Apart-Hotels

As the name suggests, apart-hotels are hotels with apartment-style rooms and, usually, kitchens – making them particularly good options for families or groups of friends traveling together. Beyond daily maid service, though, you usually won't receive the kinds of amenities you'd find at the all-inclusives or even the independent hotels. Unless you arrange for a private cook, for instance, you'll have to prepare your own meals (when you're not dining out). On the plus side, food is generally cheap to buy, so the amount you save by not going to restaurants could easily enable you to hire a local person to cook for you during your stay. If you're looking mainly for space and comfort and are willing to seek out your own food and entertainment, apart-hotels can be excellent choices.

■ Guest Houses & Pensións

The least luxurious and cheapest lodging options, typically, are the *casa de huéspedes* (guest houses, or small simple hotels), or *pensións* – usually rooms in the homes of modest Dominican families. Meals are seldom included, though breakfast may be offered for an additional price. Expect to stay in a very basic room, sometimes with a shared bath and entrance, and be prepared for cold-water showers and an oscillating fan as your only cooling device. You might also have to endure frequent power outages if the house doesn't have a back-up generator. Bring a mosquito net – you'll likely need it at night. And consider packing a small gift for your host as well. Notwithstanding mosquitoes, blackouts, and cold-water showers, staying in guest houses can be one of the best ways to meet local people – and may provide some of the most lasting memories of your trip.

Cabañas Turísticas

Around the DR you may notice lots of roadside *"cabañas turísticas"* with Vegas-style marquees touting cable TV and whirlpool baths. *"Turísticas"* is something of a misnomer or euphemism, however, since they're seldom used for purposes of tourism. Actually, these *cabañas* are motel rooms rented primarily by the hour by local couples for – well, you get the idea. But at a typical rate of RD$400 for secure parking, air conditioning, cable TV, whirlpool bath, and room service, they can also be a steal for travelers on tight budgets. Fortunately, it seems, the rooms are often unoccupied overnight after the fun couples have enjoyed their prime-time flings – so management is often willing to let them go cheap. To get the best overnight rate you usually have to check in after 11 pm and check-out by 11 am the following morning – otherwise you'll have to pay the hourly rate, making a long stay almost prohibitive.

Because *cabañas* are geared toward couples looking for privacy, guests and staff never make face-to-face contact. When you arrive at the *cabaña*, just pull your car into any open garage and close the door behind you. Enter the room through the door leading from the garage. A few minutes later, a bell will ring indicating it's time to pay. Put the money behind the little door on the wall and close it. From then on anything you need, such as food and drinks, can be obtained by picking up the phone and placing your request. Your order will be delivered via the same door. Keep in mind that the level of accommodations do vary, so if you'd like to sample a *cabaña turística* you may want to ask a local to recommend a good one in the area.

■ Camping

 There are no official campgrounds within the Dominican Republic. However, locals and some visitors do form impromptu campsites on certain beaches and park areas. If in doubt, ask permission of the local people, especially if you think you may be camping on someone's property.

On trails leading up to Pico Duarte (see *Dominican Alps* chapter, page 287), a series of cabins has been set up to shelter hikers at night. If you plan to climb the mountain, be sure to bring a sleeping bag.

■ Price Ranges

HOTEL PRICE CHART	
Rates are per room based on double occupancy.	
$	Under US$20
$$	US$20-$50
$$$	US$51-$100
$$$$	Over US$100

For each accommodation reviewed in this book, you'll find a price range marked from one to four $ signs. Price ranges are for one room based on double occupancy. At all-inclusive resorts and some other hotels and resorts, all or some meals may be included in the rates.

Eating & Drinking

 Like so many other aspects of the culture, food in the Dominican Republic is an intriguing blend of Spanish, African, and indigenous Taino elements. The result is a deliciously diverse cuisine called *comida criolla*. While it's hard to precisely define *comida criolla*, it's essentially an interpretation of standard Spanish and African dishes adapted to local ingredients, combined with some dishes that are still prepared using centuries-old Taino cooking techniques.

Because of this diverse heritage, it can be difficult to pin down what's "typical" in the cuisine. *Comida criolla* encompasses different kinds of foods prepared in different ways. It can vary by region, depending on the food culture of the particular dominant local ethnic group. It's more a *way* of cooking than a particular set of dishes, recipes, or ingredients. And it's much more spontaneous than, say, classical French cooking, where long-established rules have been laid down by masters of the art.

The one generality that (usually) applies is that Dominican *comida criolla* is based on a savory tomato-based sauce colored and flavored by an annatto-infused oil. (The annatto oil is derived from the red-orange pulp that covers the seeds of the achiote, a tropical shrub, and gives food a bright-red color and unique subtle flavor.) So there is a certain sameness amid all the diversity. In fact, you may grow tired of encountering "la bandera" (the flag) – meat or chicken with rice, beans, fried plantains and salad – that seems to appear on every Dominican menu. But Dominicans themselves never do.

■ Where to Eat Dominican Food

You can find Dominican cuisine everywhere from high-end restaurants to simple, family-operated restaurants called *comedors*. The latter are probably your best bet for exploring local foods. *Comedors* cater primarily to a local clientele, and the same grandmother or aunt has probably been cooking there for as long as the place has been in business. You can generally expect excellent food at *comedors* – especially if they're crowded with locals – and an unpretentious atmosphere where the patrons can relax and feel welcome (and where everyone knows your name).

Cafeterías are also good, casual places to try out local food. As the name suggests, customers move along a line with tray in hand as they choose from an array of prepared dishes displayed behind glass encasements. Some of the best places for visitors to try cafeterías are in supermarkets and hyper-markets (the latter including products beyond food), which tend to have nice, clean eating areas. Two chains that are especially popular with locals are the Nacional supermarket chain and the Jumbo hy-

Practical Information

per-market chain. Both are busiest during lunchtime hours and on Saturday afternoons, when Dominicans eat out in droves.

Also prevalent around the country are informal food stands found along city streets or alongside roads and highways. While some of these street carts, shanties, and holes-in-the-wall may not be as hygienic as you would wish (and should be avoided), others are merely lacking in aesthetics. So if you can look beyond their sometimes off-putting appearance, you may discover a unique aspect of the culture that few visitors experience. Among the options is the *lechoneria* (pork smoking pit), where a pig is done up in a hefty dose of oregano before it's roasted on a spigot for several hours. Another is the *chicharroneria*, where cooks are known for their preparations of thick, fried pork skins. These are particularly plentiful in the mostly rundown Villa Mella area on the outskirts of Santo Domingo, so it's mainly for the adventurous. A third type are the *frituras* – vendor carts or roadside stands that specialize in fried meat, pork and *longaniza* (home-made sausages).

■ What to Eat

Before embarking on the adventure of Dominican dining, it helps to know a few things about Dominican cuisine.

For starters, Dominicans eat a lot of meat – including beef, pork, and goat – so if you're a vegetarian, you might find yourself hard-pressed for suitable options, especially outside the city of Santo Domingo or in the big resorts. Vegetarian restaurants have recently been cropping up around the capital, however, and the massive buffets at all-inclusive resorts do feature enormous salad stations. Common vegetables include carrots, (particularly in salads), beets, eggplant, roasted yams, yucca, and broccoli.

The Dominican diet is also heavy on starchy foods such as rice, red beans (*habichuelas*), and plantains – the latter so ubiquitous that they have become part of the national identity. Other Latinos sometimes disparagingly refer to Dominicans as "*platanos*," as do self-deprecating local humorists. Dominican cuisine, with a high emphasis on fried foods, also tends to be greasy and high in salt. But recently there has been a rising awareness of eating for better health, resulting in some noticeable changes in food preparation – to the point where some restaurants now promote their new less-oil-and-salt cookery.

In the tourist hubs along the coastline you'll also find lots of fresh seafood, including excellent fish and lobster. The main non-Dominican cuisine in the resort areas is Italian – and more Italian – reflecting the large expat community that has settled in the Dominican Republic. In Santo Domingo, on the other hand, you can find everything from Arabian to Korean, Japanese to Swiss cuisines. The country's many all-inclusive resorts also often feature restaurants offering a variety of cuisines ranging from Mexican to Japanese to Brazilian. That said, resort food tends to be bland, as though aiming to please the lowest common denominator.

Must-Try Dominican Dishes

La Bandera: The most typical of all Dominican meals – meat served with rice and beans, *tostones* (fried green plantains) and a side of salad.

Asopao: Delicious soupy rice with chicken, shrimp, lobster, or octopus.

Sancocho: A hearty soup made from five different types of meat and as many potatoes and other starches; a real Dominican delicacy.

Mofongo: Mashed roasted green plantain and pork cracklings (*chicharrone*); sometimes served in a *pilon* (mortar) with a side of bouillabaisse.

Pasteles en Hoja: Mashed green plantain and yellow banana massa stuffed with meat, wrapped in a banana leaf, then boiled and served.

Mangú: A breakfast staple of mashed boiled green plantain topped with fried cheese or a fried egg. When prepared with just the right amount of olive oil and salt, this simple staple is simply outstanding.

Pescado con Coco: A delicious regional specialty of Samaná – fish served in a tomato-based coconut sauce.

Morro: A black bean and rice concoction with a hint of coconut.

Dominican Fast Food

The most popular and widely available form of *comida rapida*, as Dominican fast food is called, is *pica pollo* – pieces of fried chicken served with *papas* (French fries) or *tostones* (fried green plantain). You can try *pica pollo* at the immensely popular **Pollos Victorina** chain or at any vendor displaying a *pica pollo* sign. Meat- or cheese-filled pastry shells (*empanadas*), or smaller versions called *pastelitos*, are also popular. Dominicans eat them mostly during breakfast hours, washing them down with a cup of *café con leche*.

If you're traveling overland by bus, vendors will board just before departure to hawk *empanadas*, *pastelitos*, and other items such as fried yucca, cheese, nuts, and cakes, as well as an assortment of junk foods.

Pizza has also successfully implanted itself into the Dominican diet. **Pala Pizza** is a popular chain with locations across the island.

Practical Information

Beverages

Fruit Juices

One thing to keep in mind about Dominican food is that, if the recipe calls for sugar, you can count on there being loads of it. This is true not only for desserts but for hot and cold beverages as well. One of the favorite local beverages is the *batida,* a fruit smoothie combining sweet condensed milk with crushed ice and (of course) loads of sugar. Some of the more popular ones are: *mamey zapote,* made from a football-size fruit with a very distinct woodsy, vanilla/raspberry flavor; the pear-flavored *granadillo* (not to be confused with the *granadillo* of other Spanish-speaking countries, which is actually passion fruit); and *soursop,* which appears on menus as either *"champola"* or *"guanabana."* Pineapple (*piña*) and papaya (*lechosa*) also make tasty *batidas*, as does orange juice. For the latter, ask for a *"morir sonando,"* the name for orange juice combined with milk (but no ice). *Batidas* are available in cafeterías or any small hole-in-the-wall (*rincón*) displaying a *"batida"* sign.

If you don't want the milk with your juice, you can order up *jugos naturales* (natural juice). And if you don't want added sugar, specify *"sin azúcar."* Must-try *jugos naturales* include *chinola* (passion fruit), *tamarindo* (tamarind), *jugo de china* (orange juice), and *jugo de caña* (sugar cane). *Jugos naturales* can be purchased anywhere displaying a sign or from street vendors pushing carts brimming with fresh *chinas* or stalks of *caña.*

Coffee

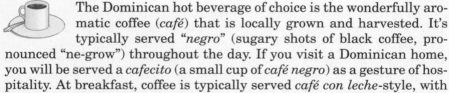 The Dominican hot beverage of choice is the wonderfully aromatic coffee (*café*) that is locally grown and harvested. It's typically served *"negro"* (sugary shots of black coffee, pronounced "ne-grow") throughout the day. If you visit a Dominican home, you will be served a *cafecito* (a small cup of *café negro*) as a gesture of hospitality. At breakfast, coffee is typically served *café con leche*-style, with about two-thirds more steamed, sweet, milk than coffee. Unless you're ordering in an upscale restaurant, you'll probably receive your coffee in a small plastic cup (and it will be automatically sweetened unless you specify *"sin azúcar."*) If you don't want your coffee too light you can specify *"mas café de leche."*

Alcoholic Beverages

 After the flag, the locally brewed Presidente beer is the national symbol of the Dominican Republic. It is served super *fría*– very cold – as the *colmados* (convenience stores) that sell the beer boast to customers (many *colmados*, in fact, rest their reputations on how cold it is). Should you choose to sit at a table in front of a *colmado* and shoot the breeze while enjoying a *fría* as locals do, demonstrate your know-how by ordering *"una fría pequeña"* (small) or the bigger and more economical *"grande"* that yields about four medium-sized plastic cups. Ask for a "Presidente" and it will be a dead give-away that you're not in the know. If the *colmado* is worth its salt, when you receive your *fría* the bottle will look as if it was pulled from the Arctic. Massage the neck of the bottle a little and then pour it slowly, or you'll end up with a cup full of ice. And, as the locals do, tilt your cup as you pour the beverage to prevent building up a head.

Brugal rum is the other alcoholic brand beverage of choice in the country. It is generally served straight but you can also have it mixed with cola (*ron y cola)* or orange juice (*ron y jugo de china*).

The other famous Dominican alcoholic beverage is *"mamaguana"* – not a brand name but the local version of hooch or home brew. It's a hillbilly/*campesino* concoction of rum, honey, several varieties of leaves and tree bark – and the *pièce de résistance*, turtle testicles – believed to have both medicinal properties and to be a powerful aphrodisiac. Sold in a variety of recycled rum bottles, *mamaguana* is readily available at roadside food stands and trinket shops, where it is said to have become the most requested souvenir of the Dominican Republic.

A final note on alcohol: At baseball games, the *colmado*, or anywhere Dominican men gather, you're liable to encounter a heavy drinking scene. While fights sometimes break out, people rarely get physical and, after a bit of verbal rough and tumble, the instigator usually simmers down or stumbles home – just to do it all over again the next evening.

Desserts

Dominican desserts are super-sweet, with the smallest taste capable of sending the uninitiated straight into sugar shock. Most common is *flan de leche* or flan made with milk and corn or coconut. *Dulce de pasta* (sweet paste) made from different kinds of fruits such as pineapple, guava, and orange are also popular. The town of Bani in the southwest is especially known for its sweets. If you happen to be passing through Bani, be sure to stop by Las Marías (on your left along Highway 2 just as you enter town) to sample the wide array of sweets, cookies, and nuts. Otherwise you can visit Casa de Dulces on Calle Arzobispo Meriño in Santo Domingo's Zona Colonial.

Service

Service Dominican-style is hospitable but often painfully slow. You'll save yourself a lot of grief (and indigestion) if you accept that fact and not try to rush through a meal. Keep in mind that your server will not bring the check until you ask for it.

Menu Prices

DINING PRICE CHART	
Price per person for an entrée, not including beverage or tip.	
$	Under US$2
$$	US$2-$10
$$$	US$10-$20
$$$$	Over US$20

Because the peso fluctuates so much from day to day, some Dominican restaurants do not post their prices. When you encounter this, don't hesitate to ask what things cost. But even if prices *are* posted, you may be charged a bit more anyway, if the peso has just lost ground against the dollar.

For each restaurant reviewed in this book, you'll find a price range marked from one to four $ signs.

■ When to Eat

For Dominicans, lunch is the big meal of the day, with many workers heading home to gather with their families around the table at the 1:30 hour. Afterwards, a short *siesta* is in order before returning to the workplace. Cafeterías and supermarkets are also busy at this time of the day. Dinner is less of an event for Dominicans. Visitors needn't worry that they won't be able to get a big evening meal, however. Dominicans eat out frequently on the weekends, when the household help is typically off. Weekends at restaurants in Santo Domingo and certain beach or mountain areas near the capital tend to be downright zoos.

Getting Around

If you arrive in the country via an organized tour you probably won't have to concern yourself much with transportation. Transfers to and from the airport and excursions are usually included with the tour package.

For everyone else, pay close attention – because getting around the Dominican Republic can be an adventure in itself, with a dizzying array of taxis, passenger cars, buses, minivans, and motorbikes competing for your business. And, of course, you can fly within the country as well. Here are your main transportation options, ranging from the quick, costly, and comfortable to the cheap, slow, and down-and-dirty.

■ Domestic Flights

Air Santo Domingo (☎ 683-8020) has regular domestic flights among the country's nine major airports. Here they are, with the main areas that they serve.

Las International Airport (east of Santo Domingo) – serves Santo Domingo, Boca Chica, and Juan Dolio

HerreraAméricas International Airport (Santo Domingo) – serves Santo Domingo with domestic commuter flights

La Romana International Airport (La Romana) – serves La Romana, Bayahibe, Higüey, and San Pedro de Macorís

Punta Caña International Airport (Punta Caña) – serves Punta Caña, Bávaro, Higüey, and nearby resorts

El Portillo Landing Field (Portillo) – serves Las Terrenas, Portillo, and northern Samaná beach areas

Arroyo Barril International Airport (Samaná) – serves Samaná, Sanchez, and Las Galeras

Gregorio Luperón International Airport (Puerto Plata) – serves north coast, Puerto Plata, Playa Dorada, Sosúa, and Cabarete

Santiago International Airport (Santiago City) – serves Santiago, La Vega, Jarabacoa, Constanza, and San Francisco de Macorís

María Montéz International Airport (Barahona) – serves southwest coast, Barahona, and Pedernales

■ Taxis

 Taxis are the most comfortable – as well as the most expensive – means of getting around, short of hiring your own car complete with chauffeur. It's safest to call the taxi company and ask for the driver to pick you up at your location rather than hail one from the streets. Otherwise, you might end up inadvertently hailing a vehicle that appears to be a legitimate taxi but isn't – you might even end up on the short end of a robbery. When you call, the dispatcher will tell you the color and number of the car as well as the fare to your destination. (Note that dispatchers seldom speak English, so if you don't speak Spanish, ask the front desk of your hotel to make the call for you.)

Taxis have no meters, so dispatchers and drivers tend to gauge fares based on distance estimates. Be sure to agree on the fare before getting into the car, or you could find yourself with an unpleasant surprise. And keep in mind that drivers don't usually speak English, so brush up on some Spanish phrases in advance. Carry exact change or a variety of bills in denominations of RD$10, $20, and $50, since taxi drivers are notorious for not having change. (This may be one way to finagle bigger tips.) Never count on drivers being able to make change for an RD$500 note or higher.

Note that taxis operating in tourist areas (such as beach resorts) tend to be much more expensive than elsewhere, but since these are usually easily walkable villages (Punta Caña/Bávaro and Juan Dolio are major exceptions), you can probably forego taxis in those places anyway. Exceptions might be getting to nearby towns for seeking out certain restaurants or beaches, or using taxis to make sightseeing excursions if you don't want to sign up for organized tours.

■ Public Transportation

Inter-City Buses

Guaguas

Technically, all buses are "*guaguas*" (gwah-gwahs) in Dominican Spanish, but when the locals use the term they're usually referring to an informal network of privately owned minibuses and vans in various stages of repair that span the entire country and serve as the lifeblood of Dominican transportation. Linking virtually every area of the island, they're especially vital in the remote countryside (as well as across the southeast) where the inter-city buses don't run. Generally speaking, they aren't air-conditioned and are often quite cramped. *Guaguas* feature both a driver and a *cobrador*, the latter a fast-talking fellow (or sometimes woman) who hangs out the door and yells out the bus' destination – don't expect to hear much English spoken. You can flag a *guagua* down on the street or highway, or you can go to the local *guagua* station to pick one up. But often you don't even have to worry about finding them – they'll find you, slowing down and trying to solicit your business as they pass.

Guaguas are invariably cheap, but to avoid being overcharged it's best to know the fare (or at least the approximate fare) before getting on. Pay the *cobrador* in small bills (up to RD$100), either as you exit or whenever he comes around to collect fares. When you're ready to get off (and when it's not a scheduled stop), shout it out to the driver ("*Dejame aquí*!) and make your way quickly to the rear. If you're going long distances, you may well have to transfer from one *guagua* to the next, often more than once. But departures tend to be frequent.

> **Insider's Tip:** Standing on a long stretch of road trying to flag down a *guagua*? Raise your hand in the air and point toward your destination to indicate you're going a long distance and to the ground for short distances. If the driver is on a long haul he may or may not stop for you.

Conchos

Sometimes also called "*públicos*," "*carros*" or "*carritos*," *conchos* are four-passenger sedans (almost invariably crammed with twice that many passengers) that run up and down the major avenues of cities such as Santo Domingo and Santiago, and also sometimes travel between cities. Before getting into a *concho*, tell the driver where you're going, because you can't count on them running regular routes or always staying on the main avenues in the way that buses do.

Once you're in the car, always say *"saludos"* as you enter and then immediately pay the *chófer* (driver) in small bills. When you're ready to disembark, just say *"dejame aquí, chófer."* If you don't know when to get out, just tell the *chófer* where you're going and he'll know where to drop you.

A Little Traveling Music...

 If you like the Latin beat you'll love public transportation in the DR, where music is always flowing from the car stereo or PA system. Passengers often coax the driver to *"subelo"* or turn up the already blaring volume on a popular tune so they can sing along.

In short, don't count on being able to snooze on the bus – or bring a good pair of earplugs.

Motoconchos

 These 125cc dirt bikes are a fun and inexpensive way to get around the countryside – and, depending on where you are on the island, may be the only way to get around. You'll see families of three or four piled on the back of these, with mom sometimes dangling a toddler in the yoke of her arm. But you won't have to ride with so many people if you don't want to. Except for Santo Domingo, where accidents are more common than in the country-side, you'll rarely see drivers or passengers wearing helmets. And *motoconchistos* (*motoconcho* drivers) – while not known for their reck-lessness – are hardly immune to taking nasty spills. So the operative phrase here is "rider beware." On the other hand, for an authentic Do-minican transportation experience, it's hard to top a scenic ride in the countryside on a *motoconcho* with the breezes riffling through your hair. On a strictly percentage basis, the odds are with you that you'll safely complete the ride. That said, getting around by *motoconcho* in Santo Domingo is strongly discouraged. Traffic is too chaotic and accidents all too frequent. *Motoconchos* do not operate at all in the Zona Colonial.

While *motoconchistas* are essentially any guys with bikes, in some towns they actually belong to organized syndicates and wear orange reflector vests, resembling school crossing guards. But you don't usually have to look very hard to find one, whatever they're wearing. In all likelihood, if you're walking along the road, standing on a corner – or even having lunch outdoors – a *motoconchista* will stop to solicit your business before you can ask for the service. Just hop on the back and straddle the driver (some women might prefer to ride side-saddle, although not all *motoconchistas* are comfortable taking passengers this way – and will tell you so). The cost of a ride depends on what village you're in and the distance you're traveling. In general, though, short rides cost anywhere between RD$10 to RD$20.

> **Note:** If you get lost while driving your own car in the countryside and ask a *motoconchista* for directions, he'll probably offer to lead you wherever you're going in exchange for a tip; RD$20 is usually appropriate. (If you get lost in Santo Domingo, pull over and consult a map.)

■ Rental Cars

Well-paved roads with excellent signage between major towns make renting a car an excellent option for exploring the island outside the city. There are five major highways in the country. Highway 1 runs through the approximate center of the country between Santo Domingo in the south and the DR's second-biggest city, Santiago, in the north. Highway 2 runs from Santo Domingo west and then northwest to the Haitian border. Highways 3 and 4 run east of Santo Domingo, connecting the capital to the popular resort areas of the southeastern part of the country. And Highway 5 runs along the north coast, from just south of Puerto Plata to Samaná. It's almost impossible to get lost in the DR if you stick to the major highways.

If you plan to do much off-road driving – say, along the Haitian border or on the Samaná Peninsula – rent a four-wheel-drive vehicle rather than a standard car, or risk getting stuck in the mud or worse. They're more expensive but well worth it. Keep in mind that you can't drive any kind of rental vehicle into Haiti.

In general, avoid city driving in favor of the countryside, where the slower pace of the pastoral communities means less stressful conditions. By contrast, Santo Domingo is a metropolis where chaos rules the road, cars jockey wildly for advantage, tailgating is a survival tactic of the fittest, and fender benders are an everyday occurrence. Major highways can also prove a challenge, with fast drivers and barreling trucks crossing lanes with abandon. There are times when you may also find cars coming at you from the opposite direction in your lane. Try to stay calm and as far to the right as possible (driving is on the right in the DR).

To rent a car you will need a credit card and a driver's license – a state or provincial license is fine, with no international driver's license required. Some companies may also ask to see your passport. Because you will be driving in a foreign country, be sure to purchase insurance coverage for liability and collision damage unless you are absolutely certain that your own auto insurance or credit card companies back home cover foreign rental cars. Read the fine print in your insurance and credit card agreements, and call the companies if you have any questions. Make sure your rental contract spells out all the charges before you sign it. Also be sure it notes all the dents or scratches already on your rental car, so you don't get charged for them when you return it. If you acquire a dent while on the road, it's usually cheaper to get it fixed by a local mechanic than return it to the rental car company for repair – their charges can be astronomical, even if you have insurance.

If you have a serious accident while driving in the DR, the local protocol is to go to the police station with the other driver to file a report. (Your car rental company might instruct you to call it first). The system is not like that in North America, where drivers typically exchange insurance and contact information and then take off. In other words, it can prove to be a time-devouring hassle. Otherwise, don't expect to have much contact with highway police – as a rule, they don't patrol the roads, though sometimes they do try to flag you down for a small bribe to let you go on your way.

Many familiar North American car rental agencies operate on the island, along with a few reliable local agencies (which tend to offer slightly better rates). Car rental agencies in the Dominican Republic include:

Alamo: ☎ 800-462-5266, www.alamo.com

Avis: ☎ 800-472-3325, www.avis.com

Budget: ☎ 800-437-9440, www.budget.com

Dollar: ☎ 800-788-7863, www.dollar.com

Hertz: ☎ 800-654-3131, www.hertz.com

Honda Rent a Car: ☎ 809-567-1015, www.hondarentacar.com

MC Auto: ☎ 809-688-6518, www.mccarrental.com

Nelly: ☎ 800-526-6684, www.nellyrac.com

National: ☎ 800-227-7368, www.nationalcar.com

 Tip: Need gas? In DR Spanish a gas station is called a *"bomba."* Ask for a gas station by any other name and it's possible no one will know what you're talking about.

Asking Directions

There are times when you'll get lost while trying to navigate your way around the DR by car or bike. Some small roads are poorly marked, wind around a lot, and sometimes even cross rivers. The best thing to do when you can't find your way is to stop and ask a local for directions. Memorize a few key Spanish phrases such as "*Dónde está* (fill in the blank)?" and you'll find that most people will be more than happy to help. Some may even lead the way for you. Don't forget to express your appreciation with a small tip, if called for.

Health Concerns

While you needn't be overly concerned about health hazards during your visit, you should be aware of what the potential health risks are and what you can do to protect yourself.

The Dominican Republic has no vaccination requirements for international travelers. However, before traveling abroad, it's always a good idea to check with your doctor – preferably a specialist in travel medicine – to see if there have been any recent contagious disease outbreaks in the areas you plan to visit, or any special precautions you need to take if you plan to venture beyond the cities and typical tourist resorts – if you plan to stay on a farm, for example, or spend much time in wilderness areas).

Just the simple act of wearing protective clothing can help prevent some of the most common health risks. Two of the most obvious are hats to ward off sunburn and shoes to avoid insect bites and contact with contaminated soils. Bare heads and bare feet invite problems.

It's also vital for everyone to keep certain vaccinations up-to-date (whether you're at home or abroad). These include shots for tetanus and diphtheria; measles, mumps, and rubella; and Hepatitis B. Your doctor can advise you whether or not you should be vaccinated for other risks such as Hepatitis A, pneumonia, influenza, rabies, cholera, typhoid, and yellow fever.

Otherwise, there are seven main health concerns to be aware of in the Dominican Republic. The first is probably the most common: **overexposure to sun**, which can lead to sunburn, dehydration, or heat stroke. The second is another frequent malady: traveler's **diarrhea** or general stomach upset from consuming contaminated water or food. The third is a serious disease: **dengue fever**, which you can get from an infected mosquito. The fourth is another serious (though rare) disease caused by mosquito bites: **malaria**. The fifth is **fish poisoning**, which comes from a toxin found in certain local seafood. The sixth is a pair of fresh-water-borne diseases: **giardiasis** and **bilharziasis** (schistosomiasis). The seventh is **HIV/AIDS** or other sexually transmitted disease, a serious concern if you're sexually active while visiting the country.

■ Sunburn, Dehydration & Heat Stroke

 In all likelihood, if you reside north of the tropics, the Caribbean sun is much more intense than what you are used to at home. Prolonged unprotected exposure to the sun can lead to a bad case of sunburn, which can be highly uncomfortable in the short term and dangerous to your health and appearance in the long term. The main risk is skin cancer, which can prove disfiguring and sometimes fatal. For the sake of your skin, it's best to avoid basking in the sun between the hours of 10 am and 4 pm – and particularly between noon and 3 pm – when harmful ultraviolet rays are at their peak. That said, if you can't imagine a Caribbean vacation without some prolonged sun-tanning and returning home with a golden glow, then be sure to use an SPF 15 or higher sunscreen. Apply it liberally and often, especially after swimming. (Don't use baby oil for sun tanning - it will block your pores and make you feel hot, to the point where you might think your skin is frying.) Wear sunscreen and take other precautions on overcast days, too – most ultraviolet radiation can penetrate the clouds.

To further protect yourself from skin damage when in the tropical sun, wear protective cover-ups as much as possible. Long-sleeved shirts, long pants, a wide-rimmed hat, and UV-protected sunglasses can all help hold off harmful rays. In the tropical heat you'll feel most comfortable in loose-fitting clothing made from natural fibers. Women might also consider protecting themselves under the shade of a parasol – that's what many of the local ladies do.

Besides thirst, symptoms of dehydration include dry mouth and nose, dizziness, muscle cramps or pain, a feeling of weakness and lethargy, and dark yellow urine. To prevent dehydration, replenish yourself with water often when you're in the sun, whether you're lying on the beach or going for a walk. It's a good idea always to carry some bottled water with you. You can also take rehydration salts, which can be purchased at Dominican pharmacies.

Heat stroke, an extremely serious condition, occurs when the body is exposed to very hot conditions for a prolonged period and overheats (much like a car engine). As the body's normal cooling mechanisms become overloaded and break down, its temperatures can reach 104° or more. Symptoms include dry, hot skin; rapid pulse and breathing; and confusion, seizures, or loss of consciousness. If emergency medical treatment isn't available, splash your skin with cool water or wrap yourself in wet towels, but don't drink anything until your body cools down.

■ Traveler's Diarrhea

While diarrhea can be related to many factors, including a rapid change in diet and overexposure to sun, it's usually the result of an infection by one of a variety of viral, bacterial, or parasitic organisms present in contaminated food and water. The safest way to avoid traveler's diarrhea in the Dominican Republic (or any foreign country) is to avoid drinking tap water or eating food washed in untreated water. Even if the water is otherwise clean, you can still become ill because your body lacks an acquired immunity to the local organisms.

By following certain basic precautions, you can reduce your risk of contracting a debilitating case. Drink only bottled water or water that has been boiled for at least three minutes, filtered, and treated with chlorine bleach or iodine tablets. Make sure that any hot food has been thoroughly cooked. Food such as meat that has been cooked and then allowed to get cold before serving might build up bacteria while sitting. Peel fruits and vegetables when possible (if they don't have a skin to peel, then they should be washed in treated water). Don't drink milk or any dairy products without boiling them first. And keep in mind that local fruit juices and drinks with ice can pose the same risks as tap water.

Unfortunately, it's next to impossible to guarantee protection against diarrhea – a fair number of travelers pick it up from the buffets at all-inclusive resorts, for example. Besides discomfort and inconvenience, the most common side-effect of diarrhea is dehydration, so drink plenty of fluids. Many hotels provide safe drinking water for you in your room. Remember that if you aren't supposed to drink the hotel tap water, don't brush your teeth in it, either. And try not to ingest water when taking a shower.

■ Dengue Fever

Dengue is a mosquito-borne illness characterized by a sudden onset of high fever, severe frontal headache, and joint and muscle pain. Many victims have nausea, vomiting, and a rash. The latter may appear three to five days after the onset of fever and can spread from the torso to the arms, legs, and face. Incidents of dengue are especially high during rainy season, when stagnant water tends to accumulate and where mosquitoes that carry dengue tend to congregate.

Your best defense against dengue is a generous application of mosquito repellent, combined with wearing long-sleeves and long pants, especially in the early morning and evening hours and when out hiking in the countryside. If you're planning on camping or sleeping outdoors, be sure to pack a mosquito net. In general, you shouldn't have to worry about dengue at large resorts since they usually keep to high standards of maintenance, including frequent sprayings against mosquitoes and diligence against accumulating stagnant water. (Exposing their guests to illness isn't good business.) Some hotels, especially smaller budget ones that aren't air-conditioned and where windows might be opened at night, provide mosquito nets or mosquito coils – but many don't. You may want to bring your own net, though a combination of insect repellent and a ceiling fan will usually do the trick.

■ Malaria

The island of Hispaniola is one of the few places in the Caribbean where malaria currently exists. That's the bad news. The good news is that the risk of contracting malaria in the DR is very small. Even so, you may still want to take precautions, particularly if you will be traveling along the rural areas of the Haitian border, where cases have been known to occur. The last reported malaria outbreak in the DR – in 1998 – was in Punta Caña on the east coast, however.

The best prevention – though not foolproof – is to guard against getting mosquito bites, particularly at dusk, and to take Chloroquine, a prescription drug that combats malaria. You need to start a regimen of Chloroquine one week before you leave home and keep taking it for four weeks after you return, so talk to your doctor about its benefits and drawbacks. Symptoms of malaria, including headaches, muscle aches, abdominal pain, fatigue, and alternating high fever and chills, may not appear until months after infection. The disease can cause severe liver and kidney damage, and can be fatal if not treated quickly.

■ Fish Poisoning

Ciguatera is a toxin produced by algae that thrive following coral reef disturbances, natural or manmade, such as hurricanes, heavy rains, or construction such as dredging. Reef fish who feed off of polluted coral or other infected fish can then become infected themselves and pass it along to humans who consume them. The most prominent symptoms of ciguatera in humans include fever-like shivering, quivering, and severe vomiting. In some cases it can produce a prickly numbness in the feet and hands, and a reverse sensitivity to temperatures – the feeling of a burning sensation, for instance, when holding a cold can of soda, or perhaps a hot shower that chills.

Since there are no outward signs of ciguatera in fish, the only surefire prevention is to avoid eating fish altogether. But, before you pass on that tasty *pescado con coco*, consider avoiding only large fish, such as snapper or kingfish, since the ciguatera build-up is more toxic in those species. Also, keep in mind that restaurants and hotels do whatever they can to keep from poisoning their customers (talk about bad for business!). They buy their fish supplies from local fishermen, who in turn can't afford to develop a reputation for selling bad fish. They know the waters they're fishing and what areas – around polluted reefs, for example – to avoid. So, while there are no guarantees, the chances of getting fish poisoning are relatively small. The decision whether or not to take the chance rests with you.

∎ Giardiasis & Bilharziasis (Schistosomiasis)

You can contract giardiasis (a parasitic infection of the small intestine) or bilharziasis (an infestation by parasitic flatworms) by swimming in or drinking water from contaminated fresh-water rivers and streams. Giardiasis can cause cramps, abdominal pain, and diarrhea; symptoms often last a week, though in some cases may persist for years. Bilharziasis can cause high fever, intestinal problems, or dermatitis, though symptoms may not appear for months or even years after infection. Both are treated with antibiotics.

∎ HIV/AIDS

Incidence of HIV/AIDS and other sexually transmitted disease is high in the Dominican Republic, so practice safe sex and bring your own supply of condoms (the quality of local condoms can be poor). The best way to avoid contracting any sexually transmitted disease is to avoid sex with prostitutes.

∎ Traveler's Medical Kit

Here are some items you may want to pack:

- ∎ Mosquito repellent
- ∎ Sun block
- ∎ Adhesive bandages
- ∎ Scissors or knife (in checked luggage only)

DR Golf Courses

1. Hacienda Golf
2. Los Mangos
3. Playa Dorada
4. Costa Azul
5. Playa Grande
6. Las Aromas
7. Jarabacoa Golf Club
8. Bella Vista

9. Loma de Chivo
10. Cayacoa Country Club
11. Santo Domingo
12. Isabel Villas
13. San Andrés
14. Los Marlins
15. Romana Country Club
16. Teeth of the Dog

17. Altos de Chavón
18. The Links
19. White Sands
20. Cocotal Country Club
21. Bávaro
22. Catalonia
23. Punta Caña

Dimivan Caracarocol, the Taino God of Scabbiness

Above: Dominican crocodile

Below: Iguana

Above: Dominican mangroves

Below: Rice fields

- Tweezers
- Antiseptic
- Anti-diarrhea medicine
- Calamine lotion (for soothing sunburn and insect bites)
- Anti-fungal cream
- Aspirin, Tylenol, or other pain killer
- Malaria pills (optional, consult doctor)
- Antibiotics (optional, consult doctor)
- Condoms

■ Traveler's Health & Emergency Insurance

If you have health insurance back home, check the policy carefully to see what it covers or doesn't cover when traveling overseas. Some policies exclude accidents that occur during certain adventure activities. You may want to look into a supplemental traveler's insurance policy that covers doctor and hospital bills while you're away.

Special policies that provide emergency medical evacuations can save you huge medical expenses in the event of an accident or other emergency. One reliable company is MedjetAssist (www.MedjetAssist.com), whose annual memberships of $195 for individuals or $295 for families include flights to the hospital of your choice anywhere in the world. One-, two- and three-week plans are also available.

Staying in Touch

 If you want to keep in touch with friends and family back home – either to gloat about the fabulous time you're having or to let them know that you didn't slip and fall into oblivion during that trek up Pico Duarte – you'll find that the Dominican Republic provides the same reliable telecommunications services you'd expect to find in North America. (We wish we could say the same about snail mail – more on that below.)

Free Internet access is a standard amenity at many of the all-inclusive resorts. Keep in mind, though, that you usually get what you pay for. Because demand for computer time is often high, you'll probably be limited to 30 minutes at one stint and you may have to wait in line for what may seem an interminable stretch. If that's the case, you may want to scoot into the nearest town, where you'll probably find any number of Internet cafes. Prices vary significantly but can be exorbitant in tourist havens such as Punta Caña and Playa Dorada.

Long-distance telephone calls can be relatively inexpensive – as little as RD$10 per minute to North America if you call from a private residence. A more likely option for a visitor is to buy a Verizon Communicard, available in denominations of RD$30, RD$50, RD$100, RD$150, RD$200, RD$250, RD$300, RD$400, and RD$500. You can buy them from gas stations, banks, supermarkets and at vending machines or over the counter in pharmacies, *colmados*, and various tourist shops. They cost about RD$12 per minute to call North America.

Less convenient but often cheaper than using a calling card is the *centro de llamada*, one of the calling centers that abound in tourist hubs. (You can easily identify them by the red-and-black "Verizon" signs or red-and-white "Tricom" signs.) Calls to North America may run as little as RD$5 per minute, or up to RD$20 per minute, depending on the location of the calling center. Sometimes you'll also find long-distance calling facilities inside Western Union offices.

Long-distance calls made from hotels are considerably more expensive, and should be your last resort, unless you're willing to pay dearly for convenience. Direct-dial rates from hotels start at around RD$35 per minute (plus access fees), but can rise astronomically. Even if you use your calling card from your hotel, you'll still have to pay the sometimes exorbitant hotel access fee.

If you use your personal calling card or any other card that you don't buy on the island, you will pay a higher per-minute charge than a locally bought card. Finally, any kind of operator-assisted call or 800-number call to North America will require an access fee if made from a hotel room or calling center. Collect calls made from private residences do not require an access fee.

> **Note:** If you're calling within the Dominican Republic, keep in mind that there's only one area code – 809. All local phone numbers in this book, with the exception of toll-free numbers, are listed without the area code for that reason. However, when calling between towns within the country, you will have to pay a long-distance rate.

Since the national postal service is unreliable, mail sent through it has a good chance of getting lost. If you want to send post cards, stamp them and drop them off at the front desk of your hotel, and they'll handle the rest. Most visitors will return home long before their post cards arrive, however.

You will find premium-priced international editions of big English-language newspapers like *The Miami Herald* and the *International Herald Tribune* available in Santo Domingo and at resort sundry shops. Alternatively, you can access round-the-clock English-language news beamed in via satellite or by cable at resorts and most hotels.

Santo Domingo

This big, sprawling metropolis of nearly three million people is the heartbeat of the Dominican Republic – its political, cultural, and economic capital and by far its largest city. Though it's situated along the Caribbean Sea, it's not the place to come if you want to lie on a beach, go swimming or snorkeling, or enjoy many of the other adventures usually associated with a tropical vacation. But Santo Domingo still offers plenty of opportunities for pulsating action.

If you're a fan of history, you will be fascinated by Santo Domingo's Colonial City, where the European development of the Western Hemisphere began more than 500 years ago at the mouth of the Ozama River. Now just one percent or so of Santo Domingo's total area, the Zona Colonial was once the seat of administration for a Spanish empire that stretched as far as Mexico and South America. Conquistadors, explorers, rogues, profiteers, and buccaneers all left their marks here in the 16th century – Christopher Columbus ("Cristóbal Colón" in Spanish), his son Diego Colón, Hernán Cortés, Sir Francis Drake, and Ponce de León among them. In 1990, the entire Zona Colonial – much of which has been restored to its original splendor – was named a UNESCO World Heritage Site.

Woven throughout the Colonial City and its more modern surrounding neighborhoods are many of the country's finest hotels, restaurants, nightclubs, museums, and cultural venues. Thousands – sometimes hundreds of thousands – of people crowd into the capital for annual music festivals and holiday celebrations. And you can hear merengue music blasting from clubs and bars any night of the week, wherever you go.

Present-day Santo Domingo has its share of problems as well: traffic, congestion, air and water pollution, street crime, rampant inflation, grinding poverty amid great wealth. At times, it can all seem overwhelming. But between stints on the beach or running the DR's wild rivers, a few days spent exploring this historic capital can be a vicarious adventure through time.

History

Santo Domingo, the first European city in the Western Hemisphere, has a turbulent history that extends more than five centuries. Founded in 1498 by Christopher Columbus' brother, Bartholomew, after earlier attempts at settlement on Hispaniola had collapsed, Santo Domingo started as a few wooden structures on the east bank of the Ozama River, where it meets the Caribbean Sea. The settlement – first called Nueva Isabela after the queen of Spain – moved to the west bank of the river after a hurricane swept through a few years later. The architect of that move, and the driving force behind the construction of the emerging new city – now called Santo Domingo – was Nicolás de Ovando, who became the colony's first governor in 1502. A year after that, the first city walls began to rise, for protection against pirate raids and other hostile attacks.

By the time Christopher Columbus' son, Diego Colón, became governor of the colony in 1509, Santo Domingo was already flourishing as the center of Spanish power in the New World. Construction had begun or would soon begin on the first fortress, first hospital, first church, first monastery, first stone house, and first paved road in the Americas. The first cathedral, university, and convent would follow. Many of these historic structures – some now restored, others lying in ruins – can still be viewed in Santo Domingo's Zona Colonial.

In the early decades of the 16th century, explorers and conquistadors used Santo Domingo as a base for expeditions to Mexico, Peru, Cuba, Colombia, and Jamaica, all of which were claimed for the Spanish Crown. The Royal Houses here held the offices of the powerful Audiencia Real, a panel of judges that functioned as the unquestioned Supreme Court for the entire West Indies and Caribbean basin, ranging as far away as Mexico and South America.

Ironically, though, these very expeditions led to Santo Domingo's rapid decline in power as the 16th century progressed. Mexico and Peru, rich in silver and gold, became far more precious to the Crown than Hispaniola, whose pomp and prominence faded with the failure to find mineral wealth there. Even the Colón (Columbus) family, whose fortunes were so intimately tied to the colony, eventually returned to Spain.

A series of natural and man-made disasters – earthquakes, hurricanes, and raiding parties – also befell Santo Domingo. After a severe earthquake ripped through the city in 1562, English buccaneer Sir Francis Drake pillaged and burned much of what remained 24 years later. Local ladies of wealth were forced to buy off Drake with a ransom of their finest jewelry.

In 1655, the English returned in the form of an invasion force led by William Penn – an attempt that was beaten back by the locals, led by Count de Peñalba. But by then Santo Domingo had become a virtual backwater. And at the dawning of the 19th century, in an event that still sticks in the craw of the national psyche, Haitian Toussaint L'Ouverture marched into Santo Domingo with an army of ex-slaves and took the city virtually unopposed. Thus began four decades in which Santo Domingo was occupied by a series of foreign powers. The French, British, and Spanish took turns over the next 20 years driving out the Haitians and each other, but, by 1822, Haitian forces had regained the upper hand throughout Hispaniola, and ruled over Santo Domingo for the next 22 years.

In early 1844, three conspirators – Juan Pablo Duarte, Ramón Mella, and Francisco del Rosario Sánchez, known as the Trinitarians – successfully led a revolt against the Haitians, which began in what is now Plaza Independencia in Santo Domingo's Zona Colonial. Dominicans still celebrate February 27, 1844, as their Independence Day. And Duarte, Mella, and Sánchez have remained national heroes.

Like the rest of the country, though, Santo Domingo remained roiled in political turmoil for another century after that, as a succession of *caudillos* grabbed power. (One, General Pedro Santana, even tried to give the country back to Spain in 1861.)

In 1936, an iron-fisted form of "stability" finally came to the capital, when Rafael Trujillo seized power. Besides brutally eliminating his enemies, the dictator changed the name of Santo Domingo to Ciudad Trujillo (Trujillo City). It remained that until 1961 – when Trujillo was assassinated. Over the next few years, a reformist government, followed by a military coup and a civil war, set the stage for a temporary American military occupation in 1965.

Politically, at least, things have been much quieter in the capital since, as a series of elected presidents have come and gone, presiding over a period of explosive growth in size and population. Most notable among them was Joaquín Balaguer, who built some of the grandest – some would say most pretentious – monuments in the city today. Industrialization, combined with economic desperation in the rural areas of the country (caused in part by a crisis in the sugar industry), have brought huge influxes of *campesinos* into the city, which is now a city both of great wealth – more Mercedes Benzes per capita than any other city in the Americas – and great poverty.

A series of 20th-century hurricanes – most recently Hurricane Georges in 1998 – has altered the modern landscape here as well. But in the midst of it all, Santo Domingo has also been busy restoring its Colonial City, giving it new life and helping to enhance its status as one of the great historic and cultural treasures of the world.

Santo Domingo

Festivals

 New Year's Eve – Santo Domingo throws one of the world's great parties every New Year's Eve, as hundreds of thousands of people crowd onto the Malecón for an all-night celebration of music and dancing.

Carnaval – The city's version of the pre-Lenten festival brings month-long costumed parades, music and dancing each February, culminating in Independence Day celebrations on February 27. On that day, marchers stream down Calle El Conde in the Zona Colonial to Plaza Independencia to re-enact the 1844 revolution that overthrew the Haitian occupation and created the modern-day Dominican Republic.

Latin Music Festival – Merengue, bachata, and salsa bands are the stars at this three-day event held each June at the Olympic Stadium.

Merengue Festival – For two weeks in late July and early August, top merengue bands from around the country and the world entertain on outdoor stages along the waterfront and in the Zona Colonial.

Restoration Festival – Along the Malecón in mid-August, Santo Domingo celebrates its (final) independence from Spain with more music and dancing, food and drink.

Getting Here

■ By Air

 Santo Domingo's **Aeropuerto Internacional las Américas** (☎ 549-0219), eight miles east of the city, is also the country's major airport. For many visitors, it's their first glimpse of the Dominican Republic – and an often chaotic and overwhelming one at that, involving sometimes long waits at immigration and baggage, and being pounced upon by a variety of *buscones* (touts) once you get past customs. Unless you want to take a chance on a *buscone* finding you a cheap hotel, rental car, or other service, give a firm "no" and move on. You'll find currency exchange windows, ATMs, rental car booths, and other services at the airport. See the introductory section on *What to Expect Upon Arrival* for more detailed information about arrivals.

Unless you rent a car or are being met at the airport, you'll probably need to take a taxi into the city (regular bus service isn't available). Reates are posted at the taxi stand to your left as you exit the airport. They run about US$25 to the Zona Colonial or the Malecón, site of most tourist hotels.

The following carriers provide direct flights to Santo Domingo or connecting service from major North American cities through partner airlines.

- **Air Canada** (☎ 888-247-2262, www.aircanada.ca)
- **American Airlines** (☎ 800-433-7300, www.aa.com)
- **Air Santo Domingo** (☎ 800-359-2772, www.airsantodomingo.com)
- **Continental Airlines** (☎ 800-231-0856, www.continental.com)
- **Delta** (☎ 800-241-4141, www.delta.com)
- **Jet Blue** (☎ 800-538-2583, www.jetblue.com)
- **Lan Dominicana** (☎ 888-751-5263, www.landominicana.com)
- **Pan Am** (☎ 800-359-7262, www.flypanam.com)
- **US Airways** (☎ 800-428-4322, www.usairways.com)

Santo Domingo's other airport, **Aeropuerto Herrera** (Av. Luperón, ☎ 567-3900), handles domestic flights only. Air Santo Domingo has regularly scheduled flights here from all other regions of the country. The airport is on the west side of the city. Taxis from here cost a minimum of US$10; but there's no set price, so make sure you establish the fare first before setting off. No regular bus service is available.

■ By Car

If you drive into Santo Domingo from the north, you arrive on Autopista Duarte (Highway 1), which becomes Av. Kennedy. From the east, you follow Highway 3 (Av. de las Américas) into the city; watch for the "Centro Ciudad" signs, which will lead you across the Río Ozama toward the Zona Colonial. From the west, you enter the city via Highway 2 (Carretera Sánchez).

■ By Bus

Caribe Tours (Av. 27 de Febrero at Navarro, ☎ 221-4422) and **Metro Expreso** (Av. Winston Churchill, ☎ 566-7126) have regularly scheduled inter-city buses that arrive in Santo Domingo from most other parts of the country.

Getting Around

■ Taxis

Taxis are the most comfortable – as well as the most expensive – means of getting around the city, short of hiring your own car complete with chauffeur (see *Rental Cars*, below). They're an especially good option at night, when pedestrian muggings are most likely to occur, and the buses stop running. To make sure you get a legitimate taxi, it's safest to call the cab company and ask for the driver to pick you up at your location rather than hail one from the streets. (Your hotel can make the call for you.)

Fares begin at RD$60 in Santo Domingo and increase in seemingly arbitrary amounts – there are no meters, so dispatchers and drivers tend to gauge fares based on distance estimates. Be sure to agree on the fare before getting into the car, or you could find yourself with an unpleasant surprise. And keep in mind that drivers don't usually speak English, so brush up on some Spanish phrases in advance. Carry exact change or a variety of bills in denominations of RD$10, 20, and 50, since taxi drivers are notorious for not having change.

Here is a short list of taxi service providers in Santo Domingo:

- **Apolo Taxi** (☎ 537-0000)
- **Taxi Anacaona** (☎ 530-4800)
- **Taxi Express** (☎ 537-7777)
- **Taxi Paraíso** (☎ 565-9595)

■ Rental Cars

You can rent cars at the airport. Try to keep your city driving to a minimum, though. Santo Domingo is a metropolis where chaos rules the road, cars jockey wildly for advantage, tailgating is a survival tactic of the fittest, and fender benders are an everyday occurrence.

Local and some North America-based agencies also offer chauffeur services that may make sense for getting around Santo Domingo without having to rent a car. As you would expect, however, the service is expensive. Try **MC Auto** (☎ 688-6518, www.mccarrental.com).

Car rental agencies with offices in Santo Domingo:

- **Alamo** (☎ 800-462-5266, www.alamo.com)
- **Avis** (☎ 800-472-3325, www.avis.com)
- **Budget** (☎ 800-437-9440, www.budget.com)
- **Dollar** (☎ 800-788-7863, www.dollar.com)
- **Hertz** (☎ 800-654-3131, www.hertz.com)
- **Honda Rent a Car** (☎ 567-1015, www.hondarentacar.com)
- **MC Auto** (☎ 688-6518, www.mccarrental.com)
- **Nelly** (☎ 800-526-6684, www.nellyrac.com)
- **National** (☎ 800-227-7368, www.nationalcar.com)

■ Public Transportation

OMSA Buses & Ejecutivos

 Riding the city-run bus system known as OMSA is a much less costly – though somewhat less comfortable and often less convenient – option than taxis for getting around Santo Domingo. The large, and sometimes rickety, grey Mercedes Benz buses do not have air-conditioning and can get quite crowded, especially during peak riding times: the morning rush (7 to 9 am), the lunch hour, and between 3 and 6 pm. The wait can seem interminable at times as well, but, if you're in no particular hurry, it's a cheap way to get around and to experience the capital like a local.

OMSA buses run up and down the city's major arteries, with general routes clearly posted above the windshield on the front exterior of the bus. Watch for "Avenida Independencia," "John F. Kennedy," "27 de Febrero," and "Máximo Gómez," which are the routes that visitors are most likely to use. The RD$5 fare is payable at the rear of the bus as you exit. The fare collector will make change for bills up to RD$100.

Alternatively, you can take the white *"ejecutivos"* for RD$10. These public buses run the same exact routes as the OMSA and can also get crowded, but are newer and air-conditioned, which can be a huge plus on a steaming summer day.

Whichever one you take, try to find a seat near the rear door so that you can get off easily. The driver will not wait for you to make your way to the exit. On the OMSA it's a good idea to tell the person collecting fares at the rear of the bus where you want to get off. This will give you time to pay your fare and make your way through the turnstile before the bus arrives at your stop.

You can download and print OMSA maps at www.omsa.gov.do/slocal.htm. (To convert the Spanish text to English, go to www.freetranslation.com.)

Here are the bus routes to Santo Domingo's major outlying attractions:

Plaza de la Cultura: Take bus marked "Corredor Máximo Gómez."

Acuario Nacional: Take eastbound bus marked "Corredor Independencia."

Las Tres Ojos: Take eastbound bus marked "Corredor Independencia."

Jardín Botanico: Take westbound "Corredor John F. Kennedy."

Faro a Colón: Take eastbound bus marked "Independencia" and exit at the last stop.

> **Tip:** The OMSA is free on Sundays – and crowded (but then, it's always crowded!).

Santo Domingo

Guaguas

When the locals say *"guagua,"* they're usually referring to a set of smaller, privately owned buses that run the same routes as the OMSA and the *ejecutivos*. These *guaguas* are manned by independent drivers who steer mini-buses in various stages of distress; a separate set of bright blue buses is run by an organized syndicate of drivers.

Both will invariably feature a fast-talking fellow hanging out the door and shouting the buses' final destination. "Duarte, Duarte, Independencia," for example, means the *guagua* is heading for the Colonial Zone via Avenida Independencia and will terminate at Avenida Duarte. These fellows – and occasionally women – are known as *cobradors* and are sometimes difficult to understand, since they speak so quickly. But you don't really need to worry about that – chances are they'll slow down long enough to solicit your business before you even have a chance to flag them down. So, do as the locals do and simply stand anywhere along the sidewalk, looking indifferent to everything, and they're bound to stop for you.

Alternatively, you may want to shout out your destination – for example, "Zona Colonial!" – and the *guagua* will stop for you if it's going in that direction. The RD$10 *guagua* fare is payable to the *cobrador* either as you exit or whenever he comes around to collect fares. It's OK to pay in bills up to RD$100.

To add to any confusion you may already have, the inter-city buses run by Caribe Tours and Metro Expreso are also *guaguas*, and locals generally refer to them as such.

Conchos

Sometimes also called *"públicos," "carros,"* or *"carritos,"* these four-passenger sedans also run up and down the city's major avenues, almost always crammed with twice as many passengers (five in the rear and three up front) than the car was designed to carry. Tell the driver where you're going before getting in, because some *conchos* turn off the main avenues and onto routes not serviced by the OMSA and other buses.

> **Tip:** If you see a driver pointing to the ground with his index finger, he's indicating that he's going through one of the city's many tunnels, while if he points in the air with his thumb, he's signaling that he's taking the road above a tunnel. Or a driver will say *"subiendo"* or *"abajo,"* which means "up" and "down" respectively – the verbal equivalent of the fingerplay.

Once you're in the car, always say "*saludos*" as you enter and then immediately pay the *chófer* (driver) RD$10. When you're ready to disembark, just say "*dejame aquí, chófer.*" If you don't know when to get out, just tell the *chófer* where you're going and he'll know where to drop you.

Orientation

 It's probably fair to say that most visitors spend the vast majority of their time in the capital either in the historic and increasingly lively Colonial City or (especially at night) along the seafront Malecón. The Malecón – site of many hotels, restaurants, dance clubs, and informal shanties for late-night eating and drinking – is officially known as Avenida George Washington and extends west for about five miles along the Caribbean from the Colonial Zone toward Río Haina.

Calle El Conde, the Colonial Zone's main strip – and a somewhat seedy one at that – is a pedestrian mall with restaurants, bars, and shopping on both sides. No matter the day of the week or time of day, the Conde is typically packed with vendors hawking a variety of touristy wares and with people strolling back and forth or hanging out on the park-style benches.

This main artery is also where you'll find most of your tourist services: Internet access, calling center, the tourist police station (at the intersection of El Conde and Calle Hostos), and a scattering of **ATM** machines inside the shops (there's one at the fast-food chain Pollo Rey, for example). If you want more ATM choices, you can head to the intersection of Calle Isabela la Católica and Calle Mercedes, where you will find yourself in the heart of the banking district, or alternatively to the banks along Avenidas Independencia and Bolivar in Gazcue. Keep in mind that after regular banking hours (6 pm during the week and 1 pm on Saturday) the only banks that provide access to their ATMs in the Zona Colonial are Banco León and Asociación Popular.

> **Tip:** Most restaurants, including fast-food chains, accept payment by credit card. In souvenir shops, you might be assessed an added 5% fee when paying by credit card.

Visitor Information

i The most accessible **tourist office** is at Palacio Borgella in the Zona Colonial (Isabela la Católica at Parque Colón, ☎ 686-3855), but, like most government-run tourist offices in the country, is not very helpful. What information is dispensed – and it's often hard to find an English speaker on site – may well be out-of-date. You may be able to find a map of the Old City here, though.

Santo Domingo

Río Ozama

Puerto Ozama

Caribbean Sea

VILLA DUARTE

LA FRANCIA

SANS SOUCI

Avenida Escopos Unidos

Avenida España

Puente Ramón Matías Mella

Calle Atarazana

Avenida del Puerto

Calle Josefa Brea

Fuerte de Santa Bárbara

SAN MIGUEL

Santa María la Menor

Convento de los Dominicanos

Calle Mercedes

Calle Arzobispo Nouel

Santa María

CIUDAD COLONIAL

Calle Hincado

Paseo Presidente Billini

C. Arzobispo Portes

C. Arzobispo Portes

Avenida Duarte

Avenida Mella

Avenida México

Calle Monte Cristi

Calle París

Calle Barahona

SAN CARLOS

Av 27 de Febrero

San Pedro

VILLA CONSUELO

Av San Martín

Av 27 de Febrero

Av 30 de Marzo

Calle Uruguay

SAN LAZARO

Ca Dr Delgado

Calle Davae

Ca Rosa Duarte

CIUDAD NUEVA

San Antonio

Avenida Independencia

Avenida George Washington

Bautista Domenicana

Calle Socorro Snachez

Avenida Francia

Avenida Ureña

Avenida México

Avenida Bolívar

EL BARRIO GAZCUE

Calle L Navarro

Calle JS Ramírez

Calle Santiago

Av Maximo Gómez

MIRA-FLORES

N

.25 Miles

.5 KM

1. Plaza de la Cultura
2. Palacio de Ballas Artes
3. Conservatorio Nacional de Musica
4. Palacio de Justicia
5. Gran Templo Nacional Masónico
6. Monumento a Fray Montesino
7. Altar de la Patria; Puerta del Conde
8. Palacio Nacional
9. La Atarazana
10. Panteón Nacional
11. Fortaleza Ozama
12. Terminal Turístico de Sans Souci
13. Academia Naval
14. Parque Mirador del Este
15. Faro á Colón
✝ Churches

The **National Park Service** (☎ 472-4204, ext. 247, Spanish only) office in Santo Domingo may be worth a visit if you're planning to do some extensive driving in the country, especially in the more remote areas of the southwest and along the Haitian border. The park service has some excellent maps for free distribution, though they don't always have them in stock, so call first if possible. You'll also need a car to get there. It's located off Avenida Máximo Gómez and the intersection of Avenida Ovando (just before the overpass); turn left onto the steep incline leading up the office. Hours are Monday-Friday 9 am-2:30 pm

The capital has five daily newspapers. The best listings for events and entertainment are in *Listin Diario* and *Diario Libre*.

Adventures

■ Zona Colonial Walking Tour

 The Old City was laid out in a grid pattern that later served as a model for many of the emerging cities of the New World, so finding your way around the Zone is fairly easy. This self-guided tour begins at Parque Colón, the epicenter of the Zone. Four of the major streets in the area border or run near it: Calle Arzobispo Meriño, Calle Isabela la Católica, Calle de las Damas, and Calle El Conde. The first three parallel each other running north and south, with Arzobispo Meriño on the west of the park, Isabela la Católica on the east of the park, and Calle de las Damas – the oldest paved street in the Americas – one block farther east toward the river. These three streets hold many of the historic sites you will visit on this tour, though you'll cover much of the rest of the Zone as well. Calle El Conde, the pedestrian throughway, borders Parque Colón to the north on its east-west journey from the Río Ozama to Plaza Independencia, bisecting the other three streets and the entire Old City along the way. Though less interesting in the historical sense than the north-south streets, it's always a lively scene and can be fun to stroll and window shop.

You could easily spend two or three days thoroughly exploring every nook and cranny of the monuments, historic houses, museums, churches, and other sights on this tour, or you could do a quick-and-dirty run-through in about a day if you're content to hit the highlights – the Cathedral, the Alcázar de Colón, the Royal Houses, the Fortress, and Plaza Independencia among them – and just admire the exteriors of some other sites. The entire Colonial Zone runs no more than a dozen blocks in any direction, with the heaviest concentration of historic sites on its eastern fringes, near the Río Ozama.

Santo Domingo

Old Santo Domingo

Ca Vicente Celestino Duarte
20
6
9
7
Ca Restauracion
10
8
Ca Emiliano Tejera

Rio Ozama

Avenida Mella
Calle Juan Isidro Perez
Calle Santiago Rodriguez
Calle Las Mercedes
Calle General Luperon
4
5
3
19
CalleSalome Ureña
21
Calle Arzobispo Merino
1
Calle Isabel la Catolica
Calle las Damas
2
Calle El Conde
Calle José Reyes
Calle 19 de Marzo
Calle Duarte
Calle Hostos
11
18
12
Altar de La Patria
Calle Arzobispo Nouel
16
Calle Padre Billini
13
14
15
Calle Palo Hincado
Calle Espaillat
Calle Santome
Calle Sanchez
Calle Arzobispo Portes
Av del Puerto
Puerto Ozama
17
Calle José Gabriel Portes
Av George Washington
22

Caribbean Sea

N
NOT TO SCALE

1. Catedral Primada del America (Santa Maria la Menor)
2. Fortaleza Ozama/Torre del Homenaje
3. Sofitel Nicolás de Ovando
4. Pantéon Nacional
5. Capilla de Nuestra Señora de los Remedios
6. La Ataranza/Museo del Jamón
7. Alcázar de Colon/Museo Maritimo
8. Casa de Colón
9. Museo Duartino
10. Ruinas de Monasterio San Francisco
11. Iglesia Convento de Santa Clara
12. Casa Tostado (Museum of the Dominican Family)
13. Convento de los Dominicanos
14. Capilla de la Tercera Order
15. Iglesia de la Regina Angelorum
16. Iglesia del Carmen
17. Puerta de la Misericordia
18. Puerta del Conde (Parque Independencia)
19. Iglesia de la Mercedes
20. Iglesia de Santa Barbara
21. Hotel Palacio
22. Monumento a Fray Montesino

When planning your walking tour, note that some attractions are closed on certain days and some keep irregular hours despite their official schedules. Try to get an early morning start in any event, so that you can take a break during the heat of midday. And, while the route isn't particularly difficult to follow, it's a good idea to bring a street map of the area to make sure you stay on track. Finally, because you'll be doing some moderate climbing and walking on cobblestones, you'll be much more comfortable if you wear a sturdy pair of walking shoes. If you want to enter the Cathedral and some of the other churches or monuments that have dress codes, avoid wearing shorts, tank tops, or other skimpy attire. Modest skirts or dresses are the safest garb for women.

> **Tip:** During your wanderings around the Zone you will no doubt be approached by a number of freelance guides offering to take you on tours of their own. Some are amateurish and overly persistent requiring a firm "no." Others are professional and knowledgeable. They can be recognized by their uniforms of khaki pants, light-blue button-down shirts, and Ministry of Tourism-issued ID tags dangling around their necks. Many speak English in addition to French, Italian, German, and, of course, Spanish. Their fees run about US$20 (in addition to the expected tip) for approximately 90-minute tours that cover the most important sites. If you do hire a guide, make sure you settle on the price in advance to avoid any misunderstandings. And remember that most all the sites on this tour are easy to locate on your own.

Parque Colón

Standing in the center of the Parque Colón is the statue of Cristóbal Colón (Christopher Columbus), pointing in the direction of Spain, with a Taino woman at his feet. If you position yourself next to the statue, you'll see the First Cathedral of the Americas to the south, and the tree-shaded café of the Hotel Conde Peñalba to the north. Two of the Zone's main arteries – Calle Isabela la Católica and Calle Arzobispo Meriño – are to your east and west, respectively.

To begin, walk south to the Cathedral.

Santa Iglesia Catedral de Nuestra Señora Santa María de la Encarnación

The construction of this, the first Cathedral of the Americas began in 1514 with Diego Colón, Christopher Columbus' son and then-governor of the Colony, laying the first ceremonial brick. But it wasn't until 1523 that

any sustained work actually began, and nearly two decades after that when the Cathedral, left, was finally completed. After the original architect deserted the project and left the island, a number of other architects took up the job and finished it over the next two decades. As a result, the facade is a mish-mash of Gothic and Renaissance styles combined with Baroque features and, for good measure, a heavy dose of Plateresque (a mingling of Moorish and Gothic styles).

In the end, the prominent Bastidas family – whose patriarch, Capitan Rodrigo de Bastidas, was the royal tax collector and mayor of Santo Domingo – saw the project through to its completion. His son, Rodrigo de Bastidas Jr., who was bishop of a diocese in Venezuela, paid for much of the work himself.

During his 1586 razing of the city, the English buccaneer Sir Francis Drake ransacked the church and stole much of its treasures. (Though he has often been given "credit" for destroying the bell tower, he couldn't have – it was never completed in the first place.) Drake and his men did burn church records, however, leaving it a mystery in many cases who is buried in the old city cemetery there. What is known is that a number of high-ranking Colonial dignitaries – including the city's first bishop, Alejandro Geraldini, and one of its earliest mayors, Capitan Rodrigo Bastidas – are interred within the church's chapels. The most famous rumored occupant was Christopher Columbus himself, said to have been buried here in 1544. But that's a matter of much dispute, especially since the Cathedral in Seville, Spain, also claims to have his remains. In any event, Columbus – or whomever – was relocated to the Faro a Colón (Columbus' Lighthouse; see *Parque Mirador del Este*, below) in 1992 during the celebration of the 500th anniversary of his first voyage to the New World. That same anniversary also prompted a major restoration of the Cathedral. (Open Mon-Sat, 9 am-4:30 pm; Sunday Mass at noon and 5 pm; free admission; proper attired required – no shorts, no pants for women.)

Walking north on Arzobispo Meriño, turn left on Calle General Luperón and follow the wall to the end of the block. The ruins of Hospital San Nicolás de Bari are on your right at the corner of Calle Hostos and General Luperón.

Ruinas de la Hospital de San Nicolás de Bari (Ruins of the St. Nicholas of Bari Hospital)

The New World's first hospital was built here around 1503 by the order of the first governor of Santo Domingo, Nicolás de Ovando, though little remains of it. Somehow surviving the onslaughts of Sir Francis Drake, earthquakes, and hurricanes, the stone structure remained nearly intact until 1911, when it was torn down out of the probably misguided fear that it might collapse on pedestrians. Today, the main threat to pedestrians are the pigeons that roost atop its huge Gothic arch (watch out for droppings), which is just about all that's left of the hospital besides two walls and pieces of Romanesque columns lying about.

The Iglesia Altagracia (Church of Higher Grace) next to the ruins was once the hospital's chapel. Inside the chapel is a bust of Dr. José Gregorio Hernandez, a physician renowned throughout Latin America for his perceived healing powers.

Casa Italia (Italian House)

Across the street from the hospital ruins on Calle General Luperón is the Italian Cultural Center, otherwise of little note except that it was the home of General Pedro Santana, the recklessly corrupt *caudillo* who annexed the country back to Spain in 1861 and was then deposed a year later. Santana shot himself in this house in 1865 when it became clear that Spain was fighting a losing battle against the Dominican rebellion for independence, and would probably not be around to cover for him.

Backtrack east to Arzobispo Meriño and continue north to Casa de la Moneda, located at Arzobispo Meriño 358.

Casa de la Moneda (House of Coins)

Little is known of this structure with the five medallions engraved in its portal. But reasonable speculation has it that it was used as a mint beginning sometime after January 1542, when Spain's Charles V ordered that all coins be minted in the colony. He often referred to the Casa de la Moneda in his written correspondence, and the street was originally named "Los Plateros" (Silversmith's Street), indicating that some kind of engraving took place here.

Continuing north, at the corner of Arzobispo Meriño and Emiliano Tejera, walk west (left) up the short hill to the ruins of the monastery called San Francisco, at Calle Hostos and Emiliano Tejera.

Ruinas de San Francisco
(The Ruins of the Monastery of St. Francis)

This site has hosted three Franciscan churches and monasteries. The first was the first monastery in America: a small wooden structure with a thatched roof built about 1502, when the Franciscans first arrived on the island. The second was constructed between 1508 and 1511 as a burial site for Don Francisco Garay, a wealthy miner who built the first stone house in the city, Casa del Cordón (see below). The third was the church whose remains still stand, albeit in poor repair.

The present construction began around 1556 and wasn't completed until nearly a century later. The church has been damaged by earthquakes and sacked by Sir Francis Drake. All that remains of the original monastery today are the impressive entrance (note the curling stone belt like that worn by the Franciscan order) and a few remnants of the original adobe walls. The Franciscan monks proselytized and educated native Tainos from this location. (Their most noted student was the infamous Taino *cacique*, Guarocuya – baptized Enrique but called Enriquillo – who would later unleash a bitter assault on the Spanish colonists.) Inside, on the walls among the ruins, you will see the shackles that kept patients in check when the monastery was used as an insane asylum in the late 19th century.

To the left of the main entrance is a Gothic portal that leads to the Chapel of the Third Order, a lay spiritual order whose members followed a faith similar to that of the Franciscans. (Monastery open daily, 10 am-5 pm; free admission.)

Walk east back down the hill to Calle Isabela la Católica and go north to Museo Duarte at number 306. The scenery begins to change here as you enter one of the poorer sections of the Old City.

Museo Duarte (Duarte Museum)

This is the site where Juan Pablo Duarte, founder of the Dominican Republic, was born. The museum here holds a sampling of personal mementos and period furnishings representative of the era. (Open Mon-Fri, 9 am-noon and 2-5 pm, Sat and Sun, 9 am-noon; RD$15.)

Continue north up the street until you arrive at a small plaza and a church at the corner of Isabela Católica and Calle Gabino Puello.

Iglesia Santa Bárbara (St. Barbara Church)

Near the old northern wall of the city, the beautiful stone church of Santa Bárbara, dating from around 1574, sits over what used to be a stone quarry. Much of the stone used to build the early Colonial structures, such as the Cathedral, the Alcázar de Colón, and the Ozama Fortress, was mined here, using Taino slave labor. After being leveled by Sir Francis Drake and a natural disaster  or two, the church was reconstructed in the 17th century. A plaque on the outside signifies that Juan Pablo Duarte was baptized here. The once-important military fortification behind the church, Fortaleza Santa Bárbara (St. Barbara Fortress), is now in ruins, but there's a nice view toward the river from here. (Open daily, 8:30 am-7 pm.)

Now turn back and head south on Isabela la Católica to the Casa del Cordón at Emiliano Tejera and Isabela la Católica.

Casa del Cordón (House of the Cord)

 The first stone residence in the Colonial City (and the New World), this historic two-story structure was built in 1502 and belonged to Francisco de Garay, who came to Hispaniola with Columbus and later became governor of Jamaica. In 1586, the wealthiest ladies of the city brought their jewelry here as part of a ransom to buy off the rapacious Sir Francis Drake. Today it houses the Banco Popular. The house gets its name from the Franciscan cord engraved above the portal. Inside is a lovely courtyard with an Islamic-styled staircase that's open to the public. (Open daily, 8:30 am-4 pm; free.)

Continue east on Emiliano Tejera until the road ends and you are facing Plaza España. To your left is the Atarazanas – a row of 16th-century warehouses now used to house restaurants, pubs, and shops. The Museum is at Colón 4.

Museo de las Atarazanas (Atarazanas Museum)

What is now a rather pricey row of restaurants, bars, and galleries was probably originally used as warehouses or a naval yard, as the Arabic word *atarazana* suggests. At the end of the row is a maritime museum displaying coins and silver and religious artifacts – recovered treasure from the wreck of the *Guadeloupe*, which sank in the Bahía de Samaná in 1724. For whatever reason, the atarazanas was one of the few places that the marauding Drake left untouched (his reputation as a heavy drinker lends credibility to the theory that, even then, the warehouses also housed taverns). Thus, most of what you see today is the original struc-

Santo Domingo

ture, which remains remarkably intact and is considered architecturally unique for its brick foundation. (The only other intact atarazanas can be found in Barcelona, Spain.) The outdoor tables here make a nice place to stop for lunch or a drink while overlooking the river. (☎ 682-5834; open daily except Wed, 9 am-5 pm, and Sun, 9 am-1 pm; RD$15.)

The wide open space in front of you is **Plaza España**, another good place to sit and have a rest under a shady tree while enjoying views of the Alcázar and the water.

At the center of Plaza España – a river-view plaza that's home to outdoor cafes and evening cultural events – is a statue of first Governor Nicolás de Ovando, facing the Casas Reales (Royal Houses). The sundial directly in front of the Royal Houses dates back to 1753. Part of the old city wall – erected to ward off assaults from sea-borne pirates and other attackers – lies ahead of you to the east. Along the wall and down the stairs is **Puerta San Diego** (St. James Gate), used during Colonial times as the main entrance into the city from the port. Dating from 1571, it was restored in the late 20th century. Proceed to Casas Reales.

Casas Reales (Royal Houses)

The seat of administrative power during Colonial times, the early 16th-century Renaissance-style Casas Reales housed the Royal Court ("Audiencia Real"), the Treasury, and the Office of the Governor. Many of the rooms have been beautifully restored, evoking the prominence of the men who occupied them and the important functions they performed. (The Audiencia Real judges who sat here, for instance, held power throughout the West Indies, extending all the way to Mexico and South America.) The museum contains an exceptional collection of Colonial-era maps, paintings, and other treasures, some salvaged from shipwrecks of Spanish galleons. Among the better exhibits is an impressive collection of weaponry donated by 20th-century dictator Rafael Trujillo. (☎ 682-4202, open Tues-Sun, 9 am-6 p.m; RD$15.)

Alcázar de Colón (The Palace of Columbus)

This is directly across from Casas Reales and overlooking the Río Azama. Of all the historic houses in the Old City, this is the most important to visit. It was built by Christopher Columbus' son, Diego, between 1511 and 1515 when he was governor of the colony. Diego and his wife, María de Toledo (niece of the Spanish king), lived there until 1523, when they returned to Spain; successive generations of the Colón family also lived there until they left the Colony half a century later. Constructed in the Renaissance style without using a single nail, the Alcázar contains more than 20 rooms and a series of open-air loggias. Its prime river location across from the Royal Houses afforded Diego an excellent vantage point of the goings-on at his office there and of the point of disembarkation for ships arriving from Spain.

After the house fell into severe disrepair with the departure of the Colón family, it was extensively restored in the 20th century. On display inside the museum here are several valuable pieces from other Spanish palaces of the 14th through 16th centuries, along with well-preserved mahogany furniture, carpets, silverware, and a 16th-century harp and clavichord. While some of the furniture and personal items are said to have been used by Diego himself, this seems unlikely since the house was vandalized often over the centuries. (Open weekdays except Tues, 9 am-5 pm, Sat, 9 am-4 pm, Sun, 9 am-1 pm; RD$15.)

Exiting the plaza to the south, you'll come onto the cobble-stoned Calle de las Damas, the oldest paved street in the Americas and so named for the bevy of high-stature ladies, led by the wife of Diego Colón, who took daily walks along it. On your right, at Calle de las Damas 55, is the Sofitel Hotel, which houses the historic Casa de Nicolás de Ovando.

Casa de Nicolás de Ovando

The home of Nicolás de Ovando, the first governor of Santo Domingo, is among a series of structures Ovando constructed in the city with the original intent of renting them out to distinguished families. Although the exact room is unknown, it's believed that Christopher Columbus himself rested here after his traumatic voyage from Jamaica in 1504. Today the house, along with the home of another prominent family – Casa de los Davilas (the Davilas family home) – has been incorporated into the five-star Sofitel Hotel. The Gothic **Capilla de los Remedios** (Chapel of Cures) attached to the north wall of the hotel was a private place of worship for the Davilas family.

The building across the street with the honor guard in full dress is the National Pantheon, located at Calle de las Damas and Calle Mercedes.

Panteón Nacional (National Mausoleum)

Built between 1714 and 1745, this building was originally used as a church by the Jesuits until they were expelled from the island in 1767. Today it serves as a mausoleum for many of the Dominican Republic's national leaders. Among them are a succession of *caudillos* who toppled each other's governments throughout the country's turbulent political history. The story has it that 20th-century dictator Rafael Trujillo – who restored the neo-classical building and made it a cemetery for heroes –

had a tomb built for himself here, expecting a hero's burial of his own. But following his assassination in 1961, he was denied the honor.

The chandelier hanging at the center was a gift to Trujillo from Spanish dictator Generalissimo Francisco Franco. The ceiling painting – called *Ascensión a los Cielos* (Ascension to Heaven) and *El Juicio Final* (The Final Judgment) – was by Spanish artist Rafael Pellicer. The adjoining property, Casa de los Jesuitas (House of the Jesuits), functioned for some time as a Jesuit university until it was returned to the Crown. (Open Mon-Sat, 9 am-7 pm; free.)

See if you can spot the next stop on the tour, on Calle de las Damas.

Casa de las Gárgolas (House of the Gargoyles)

This distinctive house took its name from the row of gargoyle statues on display at the front. The structure has undergone multiple uses since being built in the early 1500s, but is most noted as the place where the country's national anthem took form on August 17, 1883. Emilio Prud'Homme, who penned the lyrics (and is interred next door at the Panteón), and José Reyes, who wrote the music, are remembered on a plaque that graces the house.

> **Tip:** You can hear the national anthem played every morning at 8 sharp in the parking lot of the police headquarters on Calle Leopoldo Navarro in Gazcue, just across the street from the drab grey tower housing government offices and popularly known as "Huacal" (pronounced wa – kal).

Plaza Toledo

This wide-open tiled plaza with whitewashed stone arches and named for Diego Colón's wife is situated next to the Panteón. A flea market is held here every Sunday from 9 am until 4 pm, where you can browse and bargain for antique jewelry, silverware, religious icons, and other items.

The following stops will eventually put you at the southern end of Calle de las Damas and Calle José Gabriel García before continuing back up Arzobispo Meriño. First, go south to the corner of Calle de las Damas and El Conde.

Casa Francia (French House)

Built by Governor Nicolás de Ovando in the early 16th century, this house has boasted an illustrious list of tenants. Among them: Francisco Pizarro, conqueror of Peru; Baroque painter Diego Velázquez; and Alonso de Ojeda, most noted for his exploration of Venezuela. But it's best known as the place where Conquistador Hernán Cortés mapped out his expedition to Mexico. Today the house is occupied by the French Embassy. (Open Mon-Fri, 9 am-4:30 pm; free.)

Next go a short block west to Calle Conde 60 and Isabela la Católica.

Casa de Abogados (House of Lawyers)

Before it was converted to the offices for a local lawyer's association, this building served as the old town jail.

Proceed to Isabela la Católica 103, back on the Parque Colón.

Palacio de Borgella (Borgella Palace)

The construction of this attractive palace began during the Haitian occupation by the order of then-Governor Geronimo de Borgella in 1823. It functioned as the seat of government until 1875, when it was declared the president's residence. In the late 1930s, Rafael Trujillo initiated plans to transfer the presidential palace to its current location on Avenida México. After being damaged by Hurricane Georges in 1998, the building was repaired, and the Ministry of Tourism has moved into offices on the first floor. (Open Mon-Fri, 9 am-5 pm.)

The next stop is at El Conde and Isabela la Católica.

Museo Numismático & Filatélico (Stamp & Coin Museum)

Three rooms here exhibit the evolution of currency circulated in the country from Colonial times to present. The museum includes a philatelic room containing a stamp collection dating from 1865 to 1999, as well as an exhibition on the extraction and processing of precious metals for minting. Also on display is an impressive scale model of the Rosario gold mine near Cotuí. (Open Mon-Fri, 9 am-3 pm; free.)

Proceed to Isabela la Católica and Alfáu.

Casa del Sacramento (House of the Sacrament)

The legend goes that this 1520-vintage house received its name when it was offered to the church in exchange for divine intervention. Apparently, the occupants at the time kept a pet monkey. One day when the mother was at the cathedral, the monkey swooped up her baby and headed for the roof, dangling the child from its arms until the mother got down on her knees and prayed for the baby's release. Miraculously, the monkey complied. Today, the Casa houses the Archbishopric of Santo Domingo. Also belonging to the archbishopric is Casa Diego Caballero, located a few steps down

Alfáu. Don Diego was Royal Secretary to the Colony and owner of a sugar plantation in Boca de Nigua (see *Daytrips from Santo Domingo* below) that is being added to the UNESCO World Heritage Site list.

The next stop is a block east and a bit north on Calle de las Damas.

Casa de Bastidas (Bastidas' House)

With a design uncharacteristic of a family home, Casa de Bastidas resembles a warehouse more than a residence. The reason is that Capitan Rodrigo de Bastidas, who built the 16th-century structure, was Principal Royal Tax Collector of the Colony and is said to have kept all monies collected in his home until they could be returned to Spain. Bastidas went on to become mayor of Santo Domingo and, later, commander of one of the provinces in Colombia. His son Rodrigo de Bastidas Jr. would rise to prominence as bishop of a diocese in Venezuela (and chief funding angel of the Cathedral). The house itself has an architecturally interesting courtyard and archways inside; recent excavations have uncovered original parts of the house intact. (Open Mon-Fri, 9:30 am-5 pm; free.)

Head south a short ways on Calle de las Damas.

Fortaleza Ozama y la Torre de Homenaje (Ozama Fortress & the Tower of Homage)

The oldest military building in the Americas – and most important fortress in the Colonial City – is perched on a hill overlooking its namesake, the Río Ozama, which passes below to its east. Spanish conquistadors set out from here on expeditions to expand the empire to Mexico, Cuba, Peru, Jamaica, and Colombia. The complex includes a 60-foot tower, the tallest building in the Old City, which was built in 1505 by Governor Ovando and later used as a prison. (You can climb the stairs to the top for a panoramic city view.) Inside the fortress is a small military museum and a statue of González Fernando de Oviedo, commander of the fort in the mid-1500s as well as an historian and author of the influential *General and Natural History of the Indies*. Diego Colón and his wife lived here briefly when they first arrived in the Colony, until they were forced out by Spanish officials who feared he might attempt to usurp power from the Crown. Soon after, they built and moved into the Alcázar de Colón. (Open daily, 9 am-7 pm; RD$10.)

A few more yards south and you will be at the southern end of Calle de las Damas. Turning right and walking across the small plaza will put you on Calle Isabela la Católica. Walk north one block on Isabela la Católica to Calle Padre Billini and the next stop on the tour.

La Fortaleza

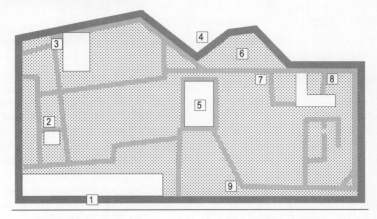

1. Carlos III Gate
2. Oviedo Statue
3. Tower of Homage
4. Tiro Bajo Platform
5. Polovorín (Gun Magazine)

6. Tiro Alto Platform
7. Ruins of original structure
8. Santiago Fort
9. Ruins of troop quarters

NOT TO SCALE
© 2005 HUNTER PUBLISHING, INC.

Iglesia Santa Clara (St. Clara Church)

The first convent in the New World (circa 1552) belonged to the Clarisas, the female branch of the Franciscan Order. The white-washed walls of this edifice stretching for an entire block give few clues of the original pretty little church, whose orchard garden once extended to the Caribbean. The church was nearly destroyed by Sir Francis Drake in 1586, and much of what you see now is the result of an extensive reconstruction financed by a wealthy money lender of the time. Whether his motives were sacred or profane is still a subject of speculation.

Continue west one block on Calle Padre Billini to Arzobispo Meriño and the next stop.

Casa de Tostado (House of Tostado)

Built sometime around 1520 by writer and scholar Francisco Tostado, this house is noted for a beautiful double Gothic window above its door. Believed to be the only one of its kind in the Western Hemisphere, it was designed in honor of Queen Isabela (a style called "Isabelina"). The house was later occupied by Tostado's son, a poet who found himself on the wrong end of one of Drake's cannonballs in 1586. It's now the home of the **Museum of the Nineteenth Century Dominican Family**, which will give you a glimpse into how wealthy Dominicans lived during the 1800s. (Open Mon-Sat, 9 am-4 pm; RD$20.)

It's a short walk south from here on Arzobispo Meriño to Calle José Gabriel García and the next stop.

Colegio de Gorjón (Gorjon School)

Construction of this building began in 1538 with the backing of Hernando Gorjón, a colonist who made his fortune cultivating sugar cane in Azua, west of Santo Domingo. He wanted to establish a school (*colegio* in Spanish), and by 1547 the institution was providing classes in grammar and logic. Some years after his death, the school was incorporated into the Archbishopric of Santo Domingo, where it became part of a theological seminary and, eventually, the second university in the New World. The building now houses a cultural institute, the **Centro Cultural de España**. (Open Mon-Fri, 9 am-5 pm, Sat, 9 am-1 pm.)

Walk toward the water for a short diversion along Avenida del Puerto.

Avenida del Puerto

This residential neighborhood of mostly lower-income Dominicans is pleasant to stroll around on a Sunday afternoon, when families from the area picnic near the **San José Fort**, one of several forts that once guarded the Old City. (Children use the ramp leading up to the fort to show off daring skateboarding feats.) From the ramp you can view the enormous **statue of Fray Anton de Montesinos**, a fierce 16th-century advocate for the humane treatment of the indigenous Tainos. This area also holds some of the city's more interesting bars, particularly **K-Ramba** (☎ 688-3587), located on the corner of Isabela la Católica and José Gabriel García. It comes alive on weekend nights with the sounds of merengue and rock.

From this point westward, unfortunately, Avenida del Puerto becomes quite smelly from all the garbage strewn about, amounting to a very unpleasant walk. Instead, head north up 19 de Marzo and then make a right turn onto Padre Billini. When you reach Calle Eugenio María de Hostos, on your left will be Plaza Duarte (the statue in the center is of Juan Pablo Duarte) and the doorstep to the site of first university in the New World.

La Iglesia y Convento de los Padres Dominicos (Church & Convent of the Dominican Order)

The Dominican Order arrived in Hispaniola in 1510 and immediately began construction of this, the oldest church in the Americas that still retains a sizeable percentage of its original elements. Note the stunning Islamic tilework over the main door, and, inside, the huge zodiac wheel carved into the stone vault of the Chapel of the Rosary. The church is also the original site of the first university in the New World: La Real

Pontífica Universidad Santo Tomas de Aquino, which dates from 1536. (In 1968, the university was relocated to a sprawling campus on Avenida José Núñez de Cáceres and renamed the Autonomous University of Santo Domingo – a heavily funded but dismally managed state-run institution.) On the north side of the church a small park bears a statue of **Fray Bartolomé de las**

Casas, a Dominican priest who, like his contemporary Fray Anton de Montesinos, is most noted for decrying the harsh treatment of the Tainos to the King and Queen of Spain (his petition to the Crown was called *The Devastation of the Indies*). Directly across the plaza is the **Chapel of the Third Dominican Order** where, in 1881, Eugenio María de Hostos (a Puerto Rican exile, adopted son of the Dominican Republic, and education reformer) would establish the first school for girls, and later a teacher's training school. A much-beloved poet and nationalist, Salomé Henríquez Ureña, aided Hostos in his efforts, and both are honored with busts in the little park just behind the church. (Open Mon-Fri 7-9 am and 5:30-7 pm, Sun, 7:30 am-noon and 7-8 pm.)

Continue west on Padre Billini to José Reyes.

Regina Angelorum (Queen of the Angels)

With its gargoyles, demons, and buttresses painting a somewhat menacing picture, this imposing stone structure houses a Dominican nunnery. Visitors are welcome inside to see the magnificent Baroque altar. Padre Francisco Billini, a 17th-century priest noted for his work with the poor, is interred in the marble sepulcher at the front of the church. (Open Mon-Sat, 9 am-6 pm.)

Five blocks west along Padre Billini will bring you to Calle Palo Hincado. Go south one block to Calle Arzobispo Portes for the next stop.

Puerta de la Misericordía (Gate of Mercy)

Designed in 1543 and renovated in 1980, this was the first gate in the Old City, serving as the entrance through the original western wall. It received its current name following the earthquake of 1842, when priests erected a shelter here to care for the injured and homeless. From the same spot two years later, in February 1844, Ramón Mella fired the first shot in the revolt that led to independence from Haiti.

At night, the east side of the wall has become a popular place to socialize. Dominicans buy their beer at the *colmado* across the street and then sit on Presidente crates chatting the night away.

Backtracking on Padre Billini to Calle Santomé and then north to Arzobispo Nouel will bring you to the next stop.

Iglesia del Carmen (The Church of Our Lady of Carmen)

Rebuilt in the 18th century after Drake set fire to it in 1586, this neighborhood church later served as a secret meeting place for Juan Pablo Duarte and his fellow Trinitarians, as the partners in the revolt against Haiti were called. The **Capilla San Andres** (Chapel of St. Andrews) that's attached to the church originally belonged to the Hospital San Andres, which was built with the noble intention of caring for sick Tainos. The hospital never had more than a few beds or patients at any one time, however, and was lost entirely during Drake's razing of the city. (The current Hospital Padre Billini was built in the mid-20th century.) The chapel, however, was rebuilt following Drake's rampage, and, every Ash Wednesday, the statue of the Nazarene above the altar is brought out for a processional – a tradition first begun in 1630.

Continue north on Calle Santomé one block to Calle El Conde. Turn left and follow El Conde west to Parque Independencia.

Parque Independencia

The Parque Independencia, with its stone entrance, Puerta del Conde, is the symbolic heart of the country. It was here that the Dominican flag was raised for the first time by Ramón Mella on February 27, 1844, creating an independent Dominican Republic. Mella and his fellow Trinitarians – Juan Pablo Duarte and Francisco del Rosario Sánchez – are interred in the massive marble mausoleum to the rear. Known as the **Altar de la Patria** (Altar of the Fatherland), it's open daily from 8:30 am to 6 pm. Admission is free; no shorts are allowed. Every day at 5:30 pm, two soldiers appear and lower the flag. Though it's a rather unceremonious affair with no pomp and circumstance, Dominicans in the immediate vicinity will stop whatever they are doing to stand at attention until the flag is down and folded and the soldiers have walked away.

The huge star in the center of the park is Kilometer 0, from which all distances in the country are measured. Notice what appears to be a moat surrounding the park. These are parts of the Colonial sewer system that have since been drained, and can be explored if you wish.

Returning to El Conde, walk four blocks east to Calle José Reyes, going north to Calle Mercedes and the last stop on the tour.

Iglesia Las Mercedes (Church of the Favor)

Arguably the prettiest church in the entire country, Las Mercedes has a stunning stone façade, a brilliant altar carved from mahogany, and an altar dressed to the hilt in silver. Also impressive are the eight richly decorated chapels and a stirring bell tower with striking Gothic arches. Dating from the 1530s, it's somehow managed over the centuries to weather the onslaughts of the unholy trinity of Drake, quakes, and 'canes.

From here, it's just a short walk south to Calle El Conde (and, perhaps, your hotel).

■ Other Attractions

Parks

Jardín Botánica Nacional (Botanical Gardens)

This sprawling public garden in the northwest reaches of the city has immaculately tended grounds, with more than 300 varieties of orchids and other flora (ferns, bromeliads, palms) on display – many of them indigenous to the Dominican Republic. The Japanese stone garden, complete with pagoda and a shrub maze, provides a cooling respite. You can walk the grounds or, if you prefer, ride a train trolley (RD$15) that winds through the park. Half-day guided bird-watching tours are also available here through **Tody Tours** (☎ 686-0882, www.todytours.com) for US$10.

To get here via public transportation, take the "Corredor John F. Kennedy" OMSA and exit at Km. 9. From there, take a smaller *guagua* north to the park. (Avenida Jardín and Los Proceres, ☎ 565-2860; open Tues-Sun, 9 am-5 pm; RD$50.)

Parque Mirador del Este

This giant public park on the east bank of the Ozama River contains two major tourist attractions: the Cuevas de los Tres Ojos and the Faro a Colón.

Cuevas de los Tres Ojos (Cave of Three Eyes)

The "three eyes" here are actually three lagoons of incredibly blue water, occupying a huge underground limestone cave once inhabited by Tainos (one of many caves and sinkholes in the park). Of varying depths, the lagoons were once used as bathing holes. There are walkways, but the most interesting of the three lakes is set way in the back of the cave and can be reached only by small boat (RD$10) that ferries passengers across the narrow channel. The jungle-like setting, enhanced by the lagoons and stalactites and stalagmites, has drawn a number of film companies here to shoot scenes for Tarzan-style adventure films.

Be sure to wear good shoes since you have to negotiate a steep set of rock steps down into the cave. To get here by public transportation, take the

"Corredor Independencia" OMSA to the park and then cross Avenida Las Américas by foot to enter the caves from the parking lot. (Avenida Las Américas, open daily, 9 am-5 pm; RD$50 adults, RD$30 children.)

Faro a Colón (Columbus Lighthouse)

Also set in Parque Mirador del Este, this massive cross-shaped stone structure – nearly 700 feet tall and the length of several football fields – was built to commemorate the 500th anniversary of Columbus' arrival in the New World. The lighthouse's powerful beacon shines in the sky in the shape of a gigantic cross, and is especially visible on cloudy nights. (It's only used at certain times, though, in order to save electricity.) Built during the regime of Joaquín Balaguer, the controversial project – many say grandiose boondoggle – was decades in the making, cost upwards of US$200 million, and displaced thousands of area residents when it was built. Local protests at the time kept many of the invited dignitaries from attending the inaugural ceremonies.

Inside, a museum displays exhibitions about Columbus from around the globe as well as paintings of the Virgin mother from around Latin America. The enormous and elaborately detailed marble mausoleum in the center is reputed to hold Columbus' remains – although, like the lighthouse itself, the explorer's final resting place has been the subject of much controversy. Spain, Italy (and, recent rumors have it, Columbus, Ohio) also claim to have him. To get there by public transportation, take the OMSA "Independencia" to the last stop. (West end of Parque Mirador del Este, Villa Duarte, ☎ 592-1492; open daily, 9:30 am-5:30 pm; RD$60; no shorts allowed.)

Parque Mirador del Sur

This four-mile-long expanse of greenery in the southwestern neighborhood of the same name is a favorite haunt of joggers, cyclists, and in-line skaters. There are a number of limestone caves here as well, two of which have been turned into a popular nightclub (See *Nightlife*, below) and a well-known restaurant (see *Places to Eat*, below). The best way to gain access to the park is from the east side of Av. Winston Churchill (which is officially named Jiménez Moya south of Avenida 27 de Febrero).

Family Attractions

If your kids are tired of sightseeing all those "old stones" in the Colonial Zone, you might try some of these outlying attractions on for size.

Acuario Nacional (National Aquarium)

Yet another ambitious and expensive Balaguer undertaking, this one has real merit – in fact, it's the premier aquarium in the Caribbean. Star of the show is a Plexiglas tunnel tank that visitors walk beneath while sharks, barracuda, and moray eels swim overhead. You can see a manatee in the aquarium as well, and there are petting pools where kids can come up close with turtles and other amphibious reptiles.

The aquarium is on the east side of the Río Azama. To get there by bus from the west side, take the eastbound city-run OMSA marked "Corredor Independencia," which stops right in front. (Avenida España, ☎ 592-1509, open Tues-Sun, 9 am-5:30 pm; RD$10.)

Agua Splash

Located, appropriately enough, right across from the National Aquarium, this water park is a good place to bring the kids on a hot day to enjoy the water slides and pools. The park is enormously popular with local families on weekends, so if you're looking for fewer crowds and shorter lines, it's best to visit here during the week. The city-run OMSA bus ("Corredor Independencia") stops in front of the aquarium. (Avenida España, ☎ 591-5927; open Tues-Sun, 10:30 am-5 pm; RD$60, children under 12 RD$40)

Parque Zoológico Nacional (National Zoo)

The 320-acre National Zoo, one of the largest in Latin America, is unusual for a Caribbean island, since many of the animals you see here are ones you might expect to find instead on a Kenyan safari: tigers, rhinos, chimps, and hyenas among them. But there are also intriguing tropical creatures such as crocodiles, flamingos, and what may be your one chance to view the endangered solenodon – a shrew-like animal found only on Hispaniola. Since the zoo is hard to find, especially by public transportation (though the "Kennedy" OMSA does go to the neighborhood), a taxi or private car is the best way to get here. (Expect to pay at least RD$150 each way from Gazcue or Zona Colonial for a taxi.) It's located north of the city, east of the Botanical Gardens. (Paseo de los Reyes Católicos and Avenida José Ortega y Gassett, ☎ 563-3149; open Mon-Fri, 9 am-5 pm, Sat & Sun, 9 am-5:30 pm; RD$15.)

Participant Sports

Despite Santo Domingo's location along the Caribbean Sea, you won't find much in the way of watersports. The sea is too polluted to swim here (the nearest nice beach is at Boca Chica, about 20 miles east), and, while there are three rivers either within or surrounding the city, you never see anyone kayaking down them. However, there are a few ways to get active in the capital:

Cycling – You can ride for several miles along **Parque Mirador del Sur**, a long expanse of greenery in the city's southwest. Ambitious cyclists make the 20-mile ride east to Boca Chica along the shoulder of Highway 3, the Avenida de las Américas.

Running – Two public parks, Parque Mirador del Sur and (to a lesser extent) the much larger **Parque Mirador del Este** (on the eastern side of the river), are popular with runners and joggers.

Spectator Sports

■ Baseball

Attending a *beisbol* game in the capital is a blast. If you're at all a fan of the game – or even if you aren't – you're likely to find it an engaging spectacle. Baseball is still king here, the national sport rivaled only by cockfighting (below).

Since the Dominican professional season extends from mid-November to early February, Major Leaguers who labor in the US from spring to October can (and often do) play in the Dominican leagues in winter. Expect a raucous atmosphere with plenty of cheering, jeering – and betting. Santo Domingo's two professional teams play at the Estado Quisqueya (Av. Tiradentes and San Cristóbal, ☎ 540-5772). Check local newspapers for schedules. Tickets can be purchased in advance or at the game, though many are sold out, so get to the box office early (evening games start at 7:30). You might be able to purchase a ticket from a scalper outside the stadium, though you'll pay several times the face value of the ticket.

■ Cockfighting

The **Club Gallistico** (cockfighting arena) in Santo Domingo is at Coliseo Gallistico de Santo Domingo (Av. Luperón, south of Av. Las Palmas, ☎ 565-3844), on the west side of the city. Matches are on weekends only, mostly Sunday afternoons. Unlike most arenas in the country, you have to buy a ticket (US$2) here to attend.

Museums

■ Museums of the Zona Colonial

For more information on some of the following museums and the Old City, see *Zona Colonial Walking Tour*, above.

Museo de las Atarazanas (Atarazanas Museum)

This maritime museum displays recovered items – including valuable coins and bars of silver – from the 16th-century Spanish galleon, *Guadeloupe*, which sank in Samaná Bay during a hurricane. (Colón 4, ☎ 682-5834, open daily, 9 am-6 pm; RD$15.)

Museo del Banco de Reservas (Banco Reservas Museum)

The enormous painting by José Vela Zanetti gracing the lobby is the sole display in this "museum," but it's well worth a stop. Zanetti, a social-realist painter and severe critic of the Spanish Civil War, lived in exile in the Zona Colonial until he was exiled from here, too – reputedly for portraying *campesinos* with sad faces in a painting commissioned by Trujillo (which Trujillo interpreted as criticism of his regime). Further works by Zanetti can be seen at the Museo Bellapart (see below), the cathedral in San Cristóbal (west of Santo Domingo), and – although now badly defaced – among the ruins of Trujillo's former hilltop palace in San Cristóbal. (Isabela la Católica 201 and Calle de las Damas, ☎ 227-2277; open Mon-Fri 10 am-6 pm; free.)

Museo de las Casas Reales (Museum of the Royal Houses)

The 16th-century building that once served as the seat of administration for the Spanish Crown in the New World now houses a museum exhibiting Taino artifacts and other relics of the Colonial era, including a rickshaw that ferried officials around the Old City and a re-creation of a 16th-century apothecary. A second-floor room houses an extensive and impressive collection of weaponry donated by Rafael Trujillo. (Plaza España, ☎ 682-4202, open Tues-Sun, 9 am-6 pm; RD$15.)

Museo Duarte (Duarte Museum)

Juan Pablo Duarte, revered by Dominicans for bringing about the country's independence from Haiti and forming the Dominican Republic, was born in this house. While it's not worth a special trip, you may want to

Santo Domingo

stop in if you're in the neighborhood. (Calle Isabela la Católica 38 and Restauración; open Tues-Fri, 8:30 am-2 pm, Sat, 8:30 am-noon; RD$20.)

Museo de la Familia Dominicano Siglo XIX (Museum of the 19th-Century Dominican Family)

The museum inside the Casa de Tostado – one of the most prominent homes in the Old City – provides a glimpse into how well-to-do Dominican families lived during the early 19th century. Besides being decked out in beautiful antique furnishings, a stunning mahogany staircase spirals to the roof, where you can catch views over the city. (Calle Padre Billini and Calle Arzobispo Meriño, ☎ 689-5057; open Mon.-Fri. 9 am-4 pm; RD$20.)

Museo Numismático & Filatélico (Stamp & Coin Museum)

An extension of the country's Central Bank, this museum displays the largest stamp and coin collection in the entire Caribbean. Two rooms are dedicated to the permanent display of Colonial-era coins and stamps and those in use since the late 19th century until today. A third room hosts rotating related exhibits. Also interesting is the scale model of the Rosario Gold Mine that lured early settlers from the La Isabela outpost to the south side of the island. (El Conde and Isabela la Católica; open Mon-Fri, 9 am-3 pm; free.)

Museums Outside the Zona Colonial

Museo Bellapart

Though housed on the second floor of a Honda dealership, this private art collection near the Botanical Gardens is worth seeking out. On display are the works of several 20th-century Dominican artists as well as the series by Spanish exile and social realist José Vela Zanetti called *La Vida de los Campesinos*. Since the exhibits rotate often (and the museum closes temporarily when they do), it's best to call ahead before making your way out here to the northwestern reaches of the city. (Avenidas John F. Kennedy and Dr. Luis Lembert Pequero, ☎ 541-7721; Mon-Fri, 10 am-6 pm, Sat, 9 am-noon; free.)

Museo Faro a Colón (Columbus Lighthouse Museum)

Several rooms here are dedicated to interpretations from around the world of Columbus' voyages to the Indies. You'll also find a permanent exhibit of paintings of the Virgin mother, done by artists from around the Americas. (West end of Parque Mirador del Este, ☎ 595-1218; open daily, Mon-Fri, 9:30 am-5:30 pm; RD$60.)

Palacio Nacional (National Palace)

The splendid neoclassical National Place, office of the country's president, dates from the Trujillo era and extends for the better part of a block. While it isn't a museum as such, its contents – a hall of mirrors with 44 sculpted Caryatids, huge epic murals, and miles of marble, mahogany, crystal, and gold inlay – are worthy of one. While there are no regularly scheduled tours, visitors are sometimes afforded one if you call for an appointment two days or more in advance. At the very least, you can admire the structure's pink exteriors, fashioned from Samaná marble. (Avenida México and 30 de Marzo, ☎ 686-4771, ext 340.)

Sala de Arte Pre-Hispánico – Fundación García Arévalo, Inc.

This private collection of Taino artifacts maintained by the philanthropic arm of the Pepsi-Cola Corporation rivals or even surpasses that of the Museum of Dominican man (below). Beautifully displayed ceramics, jewelry, ceremonial artifacts and statues of Taino gods trace the culture of the indigenous Indians from their beginnings in Venezuela to their migration to, and presence in, the Dominican Republic. (San Martin 279 and Lope de Vega, ☎ 540-7777; open Mon-Fri, 9 am-5 pm; free.)

Plaza de la Cultura

Encompassing an entire city block in northern Gazcue, this multi-building center dedicated to high art and to the cultural and intellectual development of Dominicans was initiated by then-President Balaguer in the early 1970s. The complex houses four important museums, the National Theater (for performing arts), the National Library, and a cinema. To enter any of these buildings, women and men must be properly attired – meaning no shorts or bare arms. To come here by public transportation, take the OMSA bus marked "Corredor Máximo Gómez." (Avenida Máximo Gómez and Pedro Henríquez Ureña, open Tues-Sun, 9 am-5 pm.)

Here are the four museums found within the complex:

Galeria de Arte Moderno (Gallery of Modern Art)

The permanent collection on the second and third floors here represents the country's best and most influential 20th-century and contemporary artists, including Cándido Bidó (known for his distinctive paintings of *campesinos*), Guillo Pérez, Silvano Lora, Alberto Bajo, and Clara Ledesma. The other floors rotate the works of various up-and-coming artists. (☎ 685-2153; RD$20.)

Santo Domingo

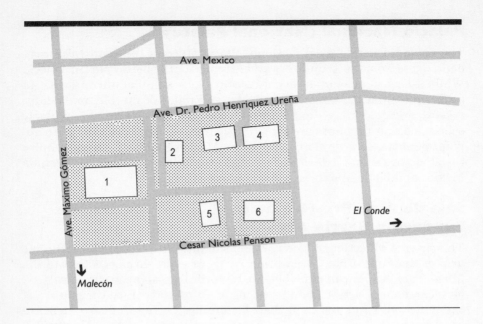

Cultural Plaza

1. National Theater
   (Teatro Nacional)
2. Modern Art Museum
   (Galeria de Arte Moderno)
3. National Museum of History & Geography
   (Museo Nacional de Historia y Geographica)
4. Museum of the Dominican Man
   (Museo del Hombre Dominicano)
5. Museum of Natural History
   (Museo Nacional de Historia Nacional)
6. National Library (Biblioteca Nacional)

NOT TO SCALE
© 2005 HUNTER PUBLISHING, INC.

Museo del Hombre Dominicano (Museum of the Dominican Man)

The barren appearance of the first floor of this outstanding museum gives little indication of the treasures on display upstairs, especially on the third and fourth floors. Climb up to the third floor to view a magnificent display of pre-Columbian Taino sculptures, jewelry, tools, pottery, and ceremonial pieces. The fourth floor focuses on the influences of the African slave trade, emphasizing religious practices, music, and carnaval traditions. There's also an excellent exhibit on Dominican peasant life, including a re-created dwelling. The building is fronted by three statues: an African, a Taino, and Fray Bartolomé de las Casas, the 16th-century friar who petitioned the Spanish Crown for the humane treatment of the Tainos. (☎ 687-3623; RD$20.)

Museo de Historia y Geografía (Museum of History & Geography)

This museum's collection spans two centuries of Dominican history. One room houses a smallish collection of historic memorabilia pertaining to the 19th-century Haitian occupation of the DR. A second room is dedicated to the eight-year American occupation of the country (1916-24); one particularly noteworthy item on display is an electric chair used to torture Dominican nationalists who were opposed to the intervention.

But the most compelling and extensive exhibit displays uniforms, medals, toiletries, and other personal effects depicting the vainglory of former dictator Rafael Trujillo, including makeup that he applied to disguise his part-Haitian ancestry. Alongside are examples of Trujillo portraits that once hung in every Dominican home, as well as public signs thanking the "Benefactor" for improving the lives of the citizenry. A final ironic exhibit is a bullet-riddled car from the motorcade in which he was assassinated. The museum's gracious director, fluent in English, is a good resource for history buffs. (☎ 686-6668; free.)

Museo de Historia Natural (Museum of Natural History)

The least noteworthy of the four museums may interest children the most. The first floor displays an enormous skeleton of a humpback whale, among other whale exhibits. There are also well-done display boxes depicting (stuffed) endemic species of the various regions of the country in their natural environments. Kids may enjoy playing with the huge lightboard that highlights the locations of the country's larimar, gold, and other geological deposits, as well as explaining the fossilization process of amber. The planetarium is the coolest (literally and figuratively) room in the museum, featuring a 25-minute audio and laser presentation of the galaxy. (☎ 689-0106; RD$20.)

■ Cultural Venues

In the Colonial Zone

Centro Cultural de España (Cultural Center of Spain)

You can view Spanish cinema here in addition to other scheduled cultural events. (Arzobispo Meriño and Arzobispo Portes, ☎ 686-8212; open Mon-Fri, 10 am-7 pm, Sat, 10 am-2 pm.)

Teatro las Máscaras (Theater of Masks)

Located in the Zona Colonial's upscale residential district, the Theater of Masks presents experimental theater productions. (Arzobispo Portes No. 52, ☎ 687-9788; Fri and Sat, 8:30 pm, Sun, 6:30 pm; RD$200.)

Santo Domingo

Outside the Colonial Zone

Instituto Cultural Dominico Americano (Dominican American Cultural Institute)

Cultural events are held regularly in the Patrick N. Hughson Auditorium at this educational institution that offers primary through graduate-level bi-lingual education. (Avenida Lincoln 21, ☎ 535-0665, fax 533-8809, www.icda.edu.do.)

Instituto Dominicano de Folklore (Institute of Dominican Folklore)

This government-run institute is dedicated to preserving the culture of everything folkloric in the Dominican Republic. Three rooms in the modest building hold a fascinating display of carnaval masks and customs from around the country. The amiable and informative director of the institute has written several books on folkloric culture and usually is on hand to give Spanish-language tours of the exhibitions. (Avenida Presidente Francisco Caamaño Deñó and Juan Parra Alba, ☎ 685-6325, fax 682-3819, folklorisimo@hotmail.com; open Mon-Fri, 9 am-5 pm; free.)

Palacio de Bellas Artes (Palace of Fine Art)

The DR's answer to New York's Lincoln Center for the Performing Arts resembles an Egyptian temple, with an engraved stone facade and high-reaching pillars. Scheduled performances include classical music and ballet as well as classic merengue acts, which are extremely popular among the local population. (Avenida Máximo Gómez and Avenida Independencia, ☎ 682-1325 or for tickets ☎ 687-3300.)

In the Plaza de la Cultura

The following four institutions, all found at the Plaza de la Cultura in Gazcue, offer regularly scheduled special events highlighting art, culture and history. Call or visit for a calendar. Proper attire is required. To come here by public transportation, take the OMSA bus marked "Corredor Máximo Gómez." (Avenida Máximo Gómez and Pedro Henríquez Ureña.)

Teatro Nacional (National Theatre)

This state-of-the-art 1,700-seat auditorium mounts ballets, plays, international festivals, and experimental theater productions. (☎ 687-3191, ext 241-239; scheduled events Tues-Sun.)

Museo Historia y Geografía
(Museum of History & Geography)

The museum hosts in-depth, reasonably priced monthly cultural, historical, and nature tours to different regions of the country. They are, however, in Spanish only. (☎ 686-6668, open Tues-Sun, 9 am-5 pm.)

Cinemateca Nacional (National Cinema)

This venue highlights the film culture of various countries through "mini" festivals. Past entries have included China, Mexico, Italy, Haiti, and Russia. (☎ 685-9396; Thurs-Sun, 8 pm; RD$20.)

Biblioteca Nacional Pedro Henríquez Ureña
(Pedro Henríquez Ureña National Library)

Regularly scheduled cultural events are held in the various salons situated throughout this massive building. A searchable database at www.bnrd.gov.do holds a wealth of books on Dominican and other Latin American topics for serious researchers. A free Internet salon is also available, though you may have to compete with a string of other would-be users. (☎ 688-4086; open Tues-Sun, 9 am-5 pm.)

Other Libraries

Helen F. Kellogg Library

A dedicated staff of expatriate and Dominican women lovingly looks after this extensive collection of books that includes a significant section on Dominican literature and non-fiction written in English. Anyone with more than a fleeting curiosity about the country's history will find this an extremely useful resource. The library is located behind the Iglesia Espicopal de la Epifania (Episcopal Church of the Epiphany), a mission-style building set a few yards off from the main street – making it easy to miss if you're not familiar with the surroundings. (Independencia and Osvaldo Báez, Gazcue, no phone; open Wed-Sun, 9-11 am, Tues and Wed, 3-5 pm.)

Spanish Classes for Foreigners

Centro Cultural de España
(Cultural Center of Spain)

Ideally located in the Zona Colonial, the Cultural Center of Spain offers intensive Spanish classes here. The downside is that they are offered less frequently than at the two schools listed below. (Arzobispo Meriño and Arzobispo Portes, ☎ 686-8212, www.enel.net./cce/, open Mon-Fri 10 am-7 pm, Sat, 10 am-2 pm.)

Instituto Cultural Dominico Americano (Dominican American Cultural Institute)

The larger and less intimate campus of one of the city's most highly regarded bi-lingual schools also offers intensive Spanish classes, though it's less conveniently located than the Centro Cultural de España if you are staying in Gazcue or the Zona Colonial areas. (Avenida Lincoln 21, ☎ 535-0665, fax 533-8809, www.icda.edu.do.)

Universidad APEC Escuela de Idiomas (APEC University School of Languages)

This intimate urban campus near Plaza de la Cultura offers several levels of intensive Spanish-language courses for non-native speakers in 12-week increments. (Avenida Máximo Gómez 72, ☎ 686-0021 ext 2269, www.unapec.edu.do.)

Art Galleries

Galeria de Arte Nader

Though situated in a residential district northwest of the tourist zone, this is still the place to go for the most comprehensive selection of contemporary Dominican art. Some of the biggest names in Latin American art in general also adorn the walls and floors of this enormous gallery. (Calle Rafael Augusto Sánchez 22 and Geraldino, Ensanche Piantini, ☎ 544-0878, www.fnader.com.do; open Mon-Fri, 9 am-6 pm, Sat, 9 am-noon.)

Galeria Cándido Bidó

This beautifully restored early 20th-century Gazcue residence serves as the exhibition studio of Cándido Bidó, the country's most celebrated artist, best known for his representations of campesinos and the pastoral life. It's hard to miss the brightly painted house with the larger-than-life statue of a musician in front. In addition to Bidó's paintings, visitors may also view his sculptures and works in metal. (Dr. Báez 5 off Bolívar, Gazcue, ☎ 685-5310, open Mon-Fri, 9:30 am-12:30 pm and 3 pm-6:30 pm, Sat, 9:30 am-12:30 pm.)

Galeria Elín

Some of the biggest names in contemporary Haitian art – Fritz Cedon and Ernst Joassaint among them – can be found here among the stacks of paintings covering the walls and floors of this gallery in the Zona Colonial. (Arzobispo Meriño 203 and El Conde, ☎ 688-7100, open daily, 9 am-6 pm.)

■ Day Trips from Santo Domingo

East of Santo Domingo

Campo Las Palmas

Primarily a training facility for up-and-coming Los Angeles Dodgers rookies, Campo Las Palmas also serves as a general tryout camp for Latin American players aspiring to join the Major Leagues. (And so far, dozens have done just that – including Boston's superstar pitcher Pedro Martinez.) Management welcomes visiting sports fans for tours of the facilities and lunch with the players when training sessions are in progress (generally year-round except for the Christmas and Easter holiday seasons). Since the camp is in the town of Guerra about 15 miles northeast of the city, you will need a private vehicle to get here – though there's been talk of providing a shuttle service from the capital. Call at least 24 hours in advance for reservations. (Guerra, East Santo Domingo, ☎ 591-8413.)

West of Santo Domingo

Ingenios (Sugar Mill Plantations)

West of Santo Domingo are the remains of four 16th-century *ingenios* (pronounced: in-he-nee-os) – sugar mill plantations that are being added to the UNESCO World Heritage Site list in 2005. (A similar fifth site, Ingenio Duquesa, is north of Santo Domingo and is also being added to the World Heritage list.) As yet, none are well marked or particularly well maintained, though that may change with their new designation. If you get lost trying to find them, don't hesitate to stop and ask a local for directions.

■ Ingenio Palavé, Manoguayabo

Palavé is the most extensive of the four sites, with the original walls and beams that supported the split-level plantation mansion still largely intact. To get here, take Highway 1 (Autopista Duarte) west to the exit for the town of Manoguayabo. Take the first left after the exit sign until you come to the fork in the road just past town. Go right and follow the road to the shack selling a rose-colored liquid in plastic bottles (kerosene). Turn left here and follow the road a short way to the ruins.

■ Ingenio Engombe, Haina

Located on the Río Haina, this was the leading area sugar plantation during the 16th-century sugar boom. Beyond the brush covering the former estate are the remains of a two-story mansion with walls, portals, and an enormous staircase still intact. The chapel next door features a beautiful Moorish-tiled roof. To get here, take Carretera Sánchez (High-

Santo Domingo

way 2) west toward San Cristóbal. Just before the Haina River is a right-hand turnoff that leads to the ruins. But the route is tricky, so you may need to ask locals for help finding them.

■ Ingenio Nigua, Boca de Nigua

This plantation was the site of a major slave rebellion in 1796 that is commemorated the last weekend of October each year during the fiesta of Nigua's patron saint. Here you can view the remains of the slave quarters and an enormous pot inside the boiling room where juice was extracted from cane. To get here, take Highway 2 west toward San Cristobál. Make a right-hand turn toward Nigua along Calle Ingenios (again, it's safest to ask a local to point out the direction for you). Once on Calle Ingenios, make a left turn. After about a five-minute drive you will come to Calle Lemba (and a single modest house on the corner). Turn left here and follow the road to the ruins.

■ Ingenio Diego Caballero, Boca de Nigua

If you managed to find Ingenio Nigua, backtrack toward Carretera Central (the main throughway in Boca de Nigua). From the church, drive west for about a mile to the ruins of the mill once owned by Diego Cabellero, former secretary of the Audiencia Real (and whose Santo Domingo home is noted on the walking tour of the Zona Colonial).

Cuevas del Pomier

The three huge caves here contain the most extensive collection of Taino drawings in the country, and perhaps the entire Caribbean. Experts believe that some date back to the time of Christ. There are also some interesting geological formations to see, and possibilities to do some rappelling deep into the caves. Wear sturdy shoes and bring a flashlight in any event.

El Pomier recently underwent a major renovation that upgrades the entrance from a hole in the ground to an attractive and more comfortable entryway that enables children, the elderly and the disabled to visit the site. To get there, take Highway 2 west toward the town of San Cristóbal. Once you enter San Cristóbal (about 20 miles west of Santo Domingo), the route to El Pomier is well-marked by signs. (Open daily 9:30 a.m-5 pm, RD$100.)

Places to Stay

Visitors to the capital city have three options for a base camp: the seaside Malecón, lined with five-star hotels overlooking the Caribbean, and one of the capital's top nightlife centers; Gazcue, a quieter, tree-lined residential neighborhood that be-

gins one block north of the Malecón and
starts just west of the Colonial city (its
main throughways are Avenida
Independencia running one-way from
west to east and Avenida Bolívar in the
opposite direction); and the compact
Zona Colonial, with its dazzling display
of 16th-century architecture. All three
lie within a short walk of each other,
providing excellent options from which to visit any part of the central
city.

HOTEL PRICE CHART	
Rates are per room based on double occupancy.	
$	Under US$20
$$	US$20-$50
$$$	US$51-$100
$$$$	Over US$100

Most visitors, however, choose to stay either along the Malecón or in the
historic Zona Colonial ("The Zone," as it's known among the expat community). Of the two, The Zone provides more sense of place. It's a lively
mix of foreign and local residents – many of the Dominican families have
lived there for generations – augmented by a daily influx of visitors from
around the world. The area's hotels – many housed in restored Colonial
structures – are among the most charming in the capital. Its restaurants
rank high in ambience, variety, and quality. And as the site of the majority of the city's more fashionable bars and nightclubs, the Zona Colonial
is also a big draw among the *uber*-chic partying set. On the other hand, if
high-rise casino hotels are your preference, the Malecón (also home to
many top restaurants and clubs) makes sense. Both offer nice strolling
opportunities.

■ Zona Colonial

Sofitel Nicolás de Ovando (Calle Las Damas, ☎ 685-9955, fax
686-6590, www.sofitel.com) $$$$

Sofitel has transformed the former home of Nicolás de Ovando, Santo
Domingo's first governor, into the prize hotel of the Colonial City (diehard
fans of the Hotel Francés, Sofitel's other hotel in the Zone, may disagree.)
This five-star hotel (formerly the Hostal Nicolás de Ovando) opened in
2003 with 104 rooms offering both contemporary and Colonial decor, as
well as a gym, library, valet parking, business center, and a top-notch restaurant. The beautiful, lush gardens overlooking the Caribbean feature
the Zone's only swimming pool. You will pay for what you get here.

Antiguo Hotel Europa (Arzobispo Meriño and Emiliano Tejera,
☎ 285-0005, fax 685-1633, www.puertomerengue.com) $$$-$$$$

After years of neglect, this three-story building underwent a major reno-
vation and re-opened in 2004 as a boutique hotel. A total of 58 standard
and superior rooms (and two junior suites) offer air conditioning, cable
TV, and telephone. The rooftop **La Terraza Restaurant & Bar** features

a "Creative Caribbean Cuisine" menu for dinner, while the bar offers live nightly entertainment. Meanwhile, the attractive lobby with appealing bar has become a hit with chic Santo Domingo residents.

Hotel Francés (Calle Las Mercedes and Arzobispo Meriño, ☎ 685-9331, fax 685-1289, www.sofitel.com) $$$-$$$$

Situated in a restored 16th-century building brimming with old-world charm, this is Sofitel's second and much more intimate Colonial Zone property. While the 19 rooms are tastefully decorated in period furnishings that conjure up the past, modern amenities such as air conditioning and cable TV quickly bring you back to the 21st century. An open-air courtyard showcases an excellent French restaurant and bar that are popular with the local community.

Hodelpa Caribe Colonial (Isabel la Católica 159, near Plaza Colón, ☎ 688-7799, fax 685-8128, www.hodelpa.com) $$$

This 54-unit boutique hotel screams "Miami Beach" – from its Art Deco-inspired décor to the circa-1950 Cadillac parked in front. Rooms are a bit small – also like Miami Beach hotels – but sufficiently tasteful to overcome this shortcoming. The heart-of-the-historic-district location, private balconies, and very exclusive atmosphere are all pluses.

Hostal Nicolás Nader (Luperón 151 and Duarte, ☎ 687-6674, fax 535-5142, www.naderenterprises.com) $$$

Though constructed in 1502 for the explorer Roberto Alvarado, he never resided here because of his duties as governor of the Central American colonies. In 1516 the building became a Jesuit convent and later was the residence of the poets Salomé Ureña and Pedro Henríquez Ureña, as well as the dictator Ulises Heureaux. In 1973 it was renovated and turned into a 10-room hotel. You'll find the same level of service and amenities as at the Nicolás Ovando, but in a far more intimate setting. The **Don Roberto bar** here is a popular gathering spot with well-heeled locals.

Hotel Conde El Peñalba (El Conde and Arzobispo Meriño, ☎ 688-7121, fax 688-7375, www.condepenalba.com) $$$

Location is the best feature of this Colonial-style hotel, which shares the same plaza as bustling Parque Colón and overlooks the cathedral in the heart of the Old City. If you like being in the mix, it doesn't get much better than this. Despite a major renovation (including the addition of air conditioning, cable TV, and telephone), the décor has retained the flavor of an old European hotel.

Hotel Palacio (Calle Duarte 106 and Salomé Ureña, ☎ 682-4730, fax 687-5535, www.hotel-palacio.com) $$$

This converted 17th-century mansion was once the home of 19th-century President Buenaventura Báez. Today the 40-room palace features well-appointed rooms – some with iron balconies – decorated with period furnishings and an impressive collection of portraits of Santo Domingo's early upper crust.

Hotel Mercure Commercial (Calle El Conde and Calle Hostos, ☎ 688-5500, fax 688-5522, www.accor-hotels.com) $$$

Located dead smack on lively Calle El Conde, this spiffy modern hotel with front-porch café tables is ideally situated for checking out the strolling pedestrian traffic. Inside is a sprawling lobby with bar and restaurant featuring French and Creole cuisine. The 96 rooms all have air conditioning, cable TV, and direct-dial phone.

Bettye's Exclusive Guest Quarters (Calle Isabel la Católica 163 and Plaza Toledo, ☎ 688-7649, fax 221-4167, bettyemarshall@hotmail.com) $$

This quirky little guest house comes with private and dormitory-style rooms that are simple yet charmingly decorated with Haitian art and furnishings – all of which are for sale through the owner's gallery across the plaza. The rooms are a little expensive considering the lack of amenities – no air conditioning, no TV, and no in-room phone – but it is well-situated a short walk from Plaza España and much of the Zone's nightlife.

Hotel Aida (El Conde and Espaillat, ☎ 685-7692) $$

Backpackers continue to flock to the Hotel Aida despite the availability of Bettye's Exclusive Guest Quarters nearby and much better budget options in Gazcue as well. Chances are that the Calle El Conde locale, with balconies overlooking the pedestrian mall, is enough to overcome its shortcomings. Rooms here are very basic, offering only cold-water showers. All are non-smoking. A shared kitchen enables travelers on tight budgets to prepare their own meals.

■ Gazcue

While the following hotels aren't what most people look for when vacationing in the Caribbean, they're perfectly nice options if you're on a tight budget or you'd prefer to stay in a quiet residential district rather than the bustling Zona Colonial.

Duque de Wellington (Independencia 304 and Pasteur, ☎ 682-4525, fax 688-2844, www.hotelduque.8K.com) $$

This small, quiet hotel lies in the center of what little action there is in Gazcue. The 22 rooms and eight suites vary dramatically, so ask to see a few before making your final decision. All rooms include air conditioning, cable TV, and phone. An on-site restaurant also offers à la carte service from 7 am to 11 pm, though the cafeteria **Hermarnos Villar** just a few steps down the street is a better choice.

Hotel Residence Venezia (Independencia 45, ☎ 682-5108, fax 682-5285, www.residence-venezia.com) $$

Conveniently located just a few blocks from Parque Independencia and the Colonial Zone, this immaculately kept hotel is an excellent find for budget travelers. Rates include telephone, cable TV, and 24-hour security.

Hostal Primaveral La Mansión (Dr. Báez 1, off Bolívar, ☎ 686-5562) $

Though the rooms here aren't as spiffy as those at Hotel La Danae, they offer good value, considering that they come with air conditioning, cable TV, and in-room phone. The on-site restaurant serves a decent enough breakfast on a pleasant front porch, though you may want to look elsewhere for dinner. Farther up Báez is a magnificent view of the presidential palace.

Hotel La Danae (Danae 18 and Independencia, ☎ 238-5609) $

This is a very good deal for the price. Rooms are a bit of a tight squeeze, but the super-cold air conditioning, cable TV, and hot-water showers are all pluses. A shared kitchen allows guests to prepare meals.

La Grand Mansión (Danae 26, off Independencia, ☎ 689-8758) $

While it's certainly nothing to write home about, bargain-basement prices make this hotel a popular choice among backpackers. Ask for a room on the second floor or away from the front desk, which tends to get noisy with staff watching TV at obnoxiously loud levels. With a little balcony facing the street, room number five is the best of the lot.

The Malecón

Several five-star high-rise hotels line the Malecón (officially Avenida George Washington). These three are the best situated – near restaurants, nightlife, Gazcue, and the Zona Colonial. Keep in mind, though, that while you may have sea views, these aren't beach resorts – the water here is too polluted for swimming. (Not to mention that there's no sand for laying out a towel.)

Hotel Meliá Santo Domingo (Malecón 365, ☎ 221-6666, fax 221-1673, www.solmelia.com) $$$$

The 245 rooms here are lavishly appointed – most with balconies and views of the Caribbean, as well as individual climate control, satellite TV, direct-dial phone, mini-bar, and luxurious marble bathrooms. Other amenities include four restaurants (including a 24-hour café), swimming pool, tennis courts and gym, plus a popular casino and discothèque.

Hotel V Centenario Intercontinental (Malecón 281, ☎ 221-0000, fax 221-1196, www.santo-domingo.intercontinental.com) $$$$

Another luxury establishment, this one offers 232 air-conditioned rooms and suites with balconies all overlooking the Caribbean, several on-site restaurants (including one on the rooftop, with killer views), swimming pool, disco, casino, and a shopping arcade.

Renaissance Jaragua Hotel & Casino (Malecón 367, ☎ 221-2222, fax 686-0575, www.renaissancehotels.com) $$$$

The best of the Malecón properties, the 300-room Jaragua provides everything you would expect from a luxury hotel, including large, well-appointed rooms, beautiful grounds with tennis courts, several on-site restaurants and bars, spa facilities, and excellent service. The hotel's Vegas-style casino and two nightclubs are especially popular with locals, drawing big crowds on weekends and for special events in the various salons.

Places to Eat

■ Zona Colonial

La Residencia (Calle de las Damas near Plaza España, ☎ 685-9955) $$$$

This elegant restaurant attached to the Sofitel Nicolás de Ovando Hotel consistently produces excellent Mediterranean-style food, beautifully presented with impeccable service.

DINING PRICE CHART	
Price per person for an entrée, not including beverage or tip.	
$	Under US$2
$$	US$2-$10
$$$	US$10-$20
$$$$	Over US$20

Caribbean Blue (Calle Hostos 205, ☎ 682-1238) $$$

You'll find New World cuisine – creative Dominican staples served up with an inordinate amount of panache – in an Old World setting here. The atmosphere in this restored 16th-century mansion is among the hippest and choicest in town. On weekend nights the second floor becomes a trendy bar.

Coco's (Calle Padre Billini 53, ☎ 687-9624) $$$

This intimate restaurant is run by longtime (and very hospitable) British expatriates. The tiny dining room has a British parlor feel to it, and you can have pre-dinner drinks in a little courtyard that's open to the sky. The extensive menu spans several cuisines, incorporating Dominican, British Empire, and Continental elements; the result is such creative entrées as yucca pancakes served with sour cream and caviar. The curry and tandoori dishes are also quite good.

Santo Domingo

La Bricola (Arzobispo Meriño 152, ☎ 688-5055) $$$

Situated in a beautifully restored 16th-century house, La Bricola special-
izes in excellent Milanese cuisine, with an emphasis on pasta and sea-
food. The attentive staff and romantic surroundings make this a nice
choice for couples.

Dar Valencia (Arzobispo Portes 255, ☎ 686-5213) $$$

More popular for its setting than for its food – though you can get a good
couscous here – Dar Valencia is a Moroccan fantasy complete with flowing curtains, water fountains, and hookah pipes. (Thankfully, it spares
you the Dominican version of belly dancing, which is about as authentic
as Egyptian merengue.) For an exotic experience that's not in a cave, this
is near the top of the list in Santo Domingo.

Le Patio (Las Mercedes and Arzobispo Meriño, ☎ 685-9331) $$$

The French cuisine here is served in an intimate and extremely elegant
courtyard restaurant attached to the Sofitel Francés Hotel.

Pat'e Palo (Atarazana 25, near Plaza España, ☎ 687-8089) $$$

You can choose between air-conditioned seating inside a beautifully restored warehouse or on the front patio overlooking the sea and Alcázar
Colón at this chic European brasserie. An inviting raw bar and a full liquor menu are added attractions.

Cafeteria Peñalba (El Conde and Arzobispo Meriño, ☎ 688-7121) $$

Part of the Hotel Conde El Peñalba, this popular café on the northwest
corner of Parque Colón is a popular meeting point and a place where lo-
cals and visitors alike chat it up at the tables or simply watch the crowds
wander past. An extensive menu features everything from Dominican
staples to burgers, pastas, and salads.

Restaurante La Masia (Arzobispo Portes 116, between 19 de Marzo
and Eugenio María de Hostos, ☎ 687-4233) $$

This Spanish *arroceria* and *marisqueria* fashions an excellent paella
Valenciana from the fresh seafood brought in daily. Another plus is its location in an upscale residential district in the Zone. After dinner, stick
around for the live guitar music or stroll the short strip where you can
visit other neighborhood bars.

La Cafeteria (El Conde 253 and Duarte, no phone) $

At this watering hole for the Zona's intellectual leftists and artists, coffee
and a selection of rums are served at the counter, to be consumed along
with passionate doses of social and political commentary of the day.

La Casa de los Dulces (Arzobispo Meriño and Calle Emiliano Tejera,
☎ 685-0785) $

This sweet shop – emphasis on the sweet – just down the hill from the ruins of the San Franciscan Monastery offers up just about every kind of

*Above: Casa de Juan Viloria (Governor under Diego Colombo),
Santo Domingo, built before 1525*

Below: Malecón, Santo Domingo

Above: Cave of Caño Hondo in Los Haitises where Taino pictographs can be seen

Below: Frogs carved from larimar

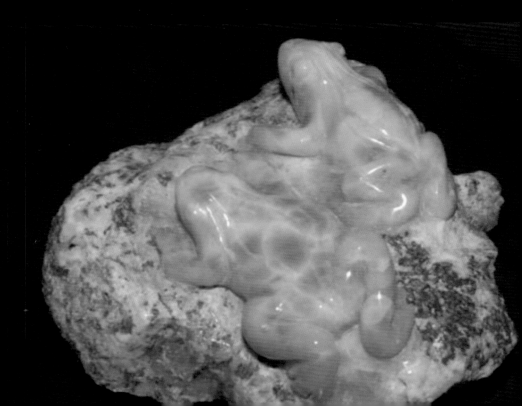

Above: Santa María de la Encarnación Cathedral, Santo Domingo
Below: Detail from Santa María de la Encarnación

Above: Calle Conde, Santo Domingo

Below: Isla Saona

Dominican dessert. Be sure to try the *pastas de dulce* (sweet pastes) and the delicious *coco horneado*, shredded coconut done up in lots of – what else? – sugar.

Nancy's Snack Bar (Emiliano Tejeda 51 along the Ataranzana, ☎ 685-1933) $

Of all the budget-priced places to eat in the Zone, this one wins out for its combination of good food, service by amiable owners, and, most all, location – on the south end of La Atarazana with a nice view of the river. The plate of the day (*la bandera*) runs about RD$65, a bargain compared to the other restaurants lining this generally pricey row.

■ Gazcue

Don Pepe Restaurant (Avenida Pasteur 41 and Santiago, ☎ 686-8481) $$-$$$

This long-standing and relatively swanky Spanish restaurant is frequented mostly by businessmen for lunch and a discerning Gazcue crowd in the evening. The menu is mostly seafood – starring lobster and giant crab – but also features a few other entrées such as roasted piglet. You won't find any lowbrow *plato del día* here. Reservations are required.

Restaurant El Conuco (Casimiro de Moya 152, ☎ 686-0129) $$-$$$

This kitschy theme restaurant aims to bring the culture of the fertile Cibao Valley to the masses. ("*Conuco*" means a small plot of land where a *campesino* grows staple foods such as yucca, corn, coffee, and plantains.) A live stage show during dinner features *perico ripiao* bands and bottle dancing (in which performers actually dance on an upright Brugal bottle). The service staff speak in the dialect of the Cibao, and a small gift shop strategically placed near the exit features *munecas* (faceless dolls), *guiros* (instruments used in folk merengue bands), and other items typical of this northern agricultural region. Popular with the tour bus crowd, the food is only so-so. You'll do best if you avoid the buffet and order from the à la carte menu.

Villar Hermanos (Independencia and Avenida Pasteur, ☎ 682-1433) $-$$

At this overwhelmingly popular Dominican cafeteria in the heart of Gazcue, you can get a takeout *plato del día* for RD$65 or for nearly double the price if you're served by a waiter. Inside around the back is the air-conditioned part of the restaurant, where you can order deli sandwiches and select a bottle of wine from a long list. A popular on-site *reposteria* (bakery), which gets pretty crowded in the evenings, serves an excellent – and unexpected – seafood salad.

■ Malecón

Adrian Tropical Food (Malecón and Máximo Gómez, ☎ 221-1764) $$

This is the outstanding flagship location of an otherwise modest chain built around the Dominican staple, *mofongo* (mashed roasted green plantains and fried pork rinds with garlic). The two-story building with a bright and airy décor is ideally situated right on the sea (tables on the lower outside deck offer the best ambience). The menu also features grilled sandwiches and what may be the best hamburger in the entire country. Evening hours usually bring on the crowds, while lunchtime tends to be less hectic.

La Parrilla Steakhouse (Malecón 515, ☎ 688-1511) $$

This popular steakhouse is actually situated on the north side of the boulevard a bit away from the water, but the open-air dining still offers plenty of ambience and great sea views. Expect excellent cuts of perfectly grilled steak served with a not-to-be-missed *chimichurri* sauce.

Vesuvio and Trattoria del Vesuvio (Malecón 521 and Máximo Gómez, ☎ 221-1954) $$-$$$

Vesuvio is one of the city's most highly regarded restaurants. Expect excellent Italian food and impeccable service, including valet parking. The adjacent trattoria, also of high quality but more casual and less expensive, serves sandwiches, salads, and pizza as well as a few pasta dishes.

■ Beyond the Tourist Zone

El Mesón de la Cueva (Parque Mirador del Sur, ☎ 533-2818) $$-$$$

Housed in a natural cave, complete with stalactites and stalagmites, this steak and seafood restaurant takes "atmosphere" to a new level (whether it's higher or lower depends on your feelings about caves). The food isn't great, but you can come for a drink at the bar and the music and dancing, if you wish. Or, if you want to make it an "all-cave" evening, head over to nearby La Guácara Taina (see *Nightlife*, below) after dinner.

Nightlife & Entertainment

■ Colonial Zone

Balcón Habanero (Arzobispo Portes 10, between 19 de Marzo and Eugenio María de Hostos, ☎ 682-5672)

This small Cuban bar in an upscale residential district has lots of atmosphere and live entertainment on Saturday evenings.

Casa de Teatro (Arzobispo Meriño 110, ☎ 689-3430)

Musical artists from the island and around Latin America make nightly appearances here in a courtyard setting.

K-Ramba (Isabel la Católica, ☎ 688-3587)

From rock to merengue, this neighborhood bar near the San José Fort blasts it out until 3 am nightly.

Proud Mary (Calle Duarte and Arzobispo Portes, ☎ 689-6611)

Run single-handedly by a Spanish proprietor everybody calls María, this popular bar combines low-lights, American pop tunes, and an interesting mix of expats and Dominicans.

Puerta de la Misericordía (Palo Hincado and Arzobispo Portes)

Not a commercial establishment, this is an informal al fresco gathering spot on the west side of the Gate of Mercy. Patrons buy their cold Presidente from the *colmado* across the street, where they also grab Presidente crates that serve as seats and tables. It is wonderfully atmospheric and even more so when wandering *perico ripiao* bands stop to belt out a few tunes and Dominicans give in to the rhythm to dance.

■ Malecón

Along the Malecón are several places where you can take in the pulsating nightlife of Santo Domingo, either at a disco in one of the top hotels or along the boulevard and east of El Obelisco (a monument erected in 1936 to commemorate the city's re-naming as Ciudad Trujillo).

Mauna Loa Night Club & Casino (Calle Héroes de Luperón and Malecón, ☎ 533-2151)

An evening at this Havana-style nightclub and casino should be on every visitor's not-to-be-missed list. Along with an enormous dance floor, you'll be treated to old-style Latin entertainment, varying from stand-up comedy acts to classic vocalists and merengue orchestras that display brilliant showmanship. Men will be most comfortable in a blazer and women should dress to kill. Cover charge is RD$100.

La Parada Cervecera (Malecón, east of Avenida Máximo Gómez)

This popular spot on the waterfront attracts adult couples looking to sit back and enjoy a few drinks – just don't expect quiet conversation. Although the live entertainment is always of good quality, the volume is turned up to excruciating levels. Dress is casual, and there's no cover charge.

Renaissance Jaragua Hotel & Casino (Malecón 367, ☎ 221-2222)

You can expect a super-lively scene any night of the week at this, one of the city's longest-standing hotels – and, in the minds of many Dominicans, *the* place to go for an evening out. Crowds flow in and out of the casino (no cover) between visits to **Jubilee** (RD$100), the high-tech disco spinning Latin and popular American and European dance tunes, or the **Merengue Bar** (no cover), where nightly live merengue pulls in big crowds. Dress is club chic, no jeans.

■ Beyond the Tourist Zone

These places are situated away from the center of the city, but are worth a special trip. Taxi drivers should know where to find them.

El Monumento del Son (Avenida Charles de Gaulle, ☎ 590-3666)

This popular *son* (jazzlike Cuban music, which Dominicans claim to have invented themselves) dance hall is best visited on Sunday evenings, when older men in wing-tipped shoes and guayaberras display amazing agility on the dance floor with their equally deft dance partners. Dress is elegant casual. No cover charge.

La Guácara Taina (Avenida Mirador del Sur, ☎ 530-2666)

In years past, this famous nightspot – located in a huge and very real underground cave – was the top place in the city for Dominicans to go for serious merengue dancing. Now, its enormous dance floors – capable of holding up to 2,000 people – cater to a mostly cruise-ship crowd who are bussed in on "Santo Domingo Nights" tours. Still, even if it's become something of a tourist trap, it remains an incredible setting (complete with real stalactites and Taino pictographs). Its live acts rival the most entertaining ones in the city. Dress: club chic. Cover charge is RD$100.

Eclipse (Avenida Venezuela, Zona Oriental)

Located on the "other side of the bridge," the eastern side of town sees few tourists, except for the intrepid ones who want to venture beyond the tourist zone. Both sides of the bustling strip along Av. Venezuela are lined with clubs fronted by enormous statues of pharaohs and sphinxs, glittering lights, and nattily dressed Dominicans. Saturday and Sunday nights draw huge crowds (most clubs are closed on Monday). Eclipse is the hottest club on the strip. Expect very loud merengue, bachata, and salsa. Should you go, take a taxi (about RD$200 each way). Dress is casual. Cover charge is RD$100.

Eagle (Avenida San Vicente, Zona Oriental)

In a country where merengue and bachata reign, there are few places in the city where you can listen and dance to salsa (Puerto Rico's national dance) except in a handful of clubs along Av. San Vicente. Some weeknights, in fact, there's nothing but salsa here. Eagle is one of the best salsa clubs (but be sure your taxi driver doesn't mistake it for the Eagle Cabaña, a quickie sex motel nearby.) Dance contests are held frequently, and even if you don't dance they're still fun to watch. Dress is casual; cover charge is RD$100.

Shopping

Santo Domingo offers by far the greatest selection of shopping opportunities in the country. Among the items to look for here are jewelry made from amber (fossilized tree sap that produces a yellow or golden gem) and larimar (a blue semiprecious stone found only in the DR), as well as local handicrafts and artworks, Latin music CDs, and, if you smoke them, cigars. The oldest shopping street in the city is **Calle El Conde**, the lively pedestrian-only street in the Colonial Zone, lined on both sides with jewelry, music, cigar, and other types of shops. The shopping experience not to miss is **El Mercado Modelo** on Avenida Mella just north of the Colonial Zone; it's open daily and filled with stalls where you can bargain for handicrafts and many other items. You can find more upscale shopping at **La Ataranzas**, the row of converted Colonial-era warehouses in the Old City. (See *Zona Colonial Walking Tour*, above.)

∎ Amber

Museo de Ambar

Set in a Colonial-era structure along El Conde, this "museum" has second-floor exhibits about how amber is formed. But the first floor is devoted to sales of good-quality (and fairly expensive) amber and larimar jewelry. Some of the more interesting amber items have ancient insects trapped within the petrified tree sap. (Calle El Conde 107 at Parque Colón, ☎ 221-1333)

Museo Mundo de Ambar

Like the Museo de Ambar, this Colonial Zone shop lures tourists in with museum-style exhibits on how amber is formed and made into jewelry, then tries to sell you the finished products – nothing wrong with that, as long as you know what to expect. Also, as in the other "museum," the jewelry is high quality, but a bit pricey. (Calle Meriño 452 and Restauración, ☎ 682-3309)

 Santo Domingo

Swiss Mine

Don't buy amber or larimar elsewhere until you check out the selection at this popular El Conde shop, where the prices tend to beat the competition. (El Conde 101)

■ Larimar

Museo Larimar Dominicano

You'll find out how larimar is mined in the southwestern Dominican Republic in the second-floor museum here, then have ample opportunities to buy the jewelry in the first-floor shop. (Calle Isabela la Católica 54, ☎ 689-6605)

■ Music

Musicalia

You can find all the merengue, bachata, and salsa music you want here. (El Conde 464)

■ Cigars

Cigar King

Dominican cigars rival Cuban cigars as the best in the world. You'll find both here – but you can't bring the Cuban ones back legally to the US (Calle El Conde 208, ☎ 686-4987)

■ General

Columbus Plaza

You'll find a wide range of items in this Colonial Zone gift store, from handicrafts to jewelry, artworks, and cigars for sale. (Calle Meriño 204, ☎ 689-0565)

La Sirena

This department store sells clothing and handicrafts among many other items. (Av. Mella, ☎ 682-3107)

The Caribbean Coast - Boca Chica to Boca de Yuma

Starting just beyond the hustle and bustle of Santo Domingo, and continuing east almost all the way to the southeastern tip of the island, lies what most visitors come to the island for – a taste of the idyllic Caribbean.

Referred to locally as the Costa Caribe (Caribbean Coast), the southeast coast of Hispaniola, with its sparkling white sand and translucent, tranquil waters, boasts a number of the Dominican Republic's top-rated beaches. Two of the best are the world-renowned **Boca Chica** and the less celebrated – though no less beautiful – **Bayahibe**. Also on the south side are several prime dive spots, including a spectacular coral reef off a small island and a number of underwater caves that have become increasingly popular with extreme divers in recent years. Baseball fans often like to make pilgrimages to the city of **San Pedro de Macorís**, which has produced a remarkable number of Major League stars, including slugger Sammy Sosa of the Chicago Cubs.

But perhaps the crowning glory of the Caribbean Coast is the **Parque Nacional del Este**, a 172-square-mile habitat for bird and plant life. The park is also the site of fascinating cave complexes housing Taino drawings that depict historical events between the indigenous population and the early conquistadors.

History

 Once inhabited by large numbers of Taino Indians, whose culture is still visible here in a number of prime archeological sites, the Caribbean Coast was one of the first settled by the Spanish after the arrival of Columbus. By the early 16th century, just a few years after the explorer first landed on Hispaniola, the

Spanish authorities were already going about the business of systematically subduing – effectively exterminating – the native inhabitants. By 1508, one of the most famous of the conquistadors, Juan Ponce de León, had constructed (using Indian labor, to be sure) a fortress-like house near the far southeastern tip of the island. The Spanish set up sugar plantations and cattle ranches, and the land has remained mostly rural and poor ever since (though the sugar and cattle barons have prospered).

In recent decades, baseball talent – best represented by the port city of San Pedro de Macorís and nearby areas – has replaced sugar as the region's most famous export. And over the past 30 years or so, tourism has come to the Caribbean Coast in a big way, with sprawling resort developments lining some of the nicer beaches, championship golf courses being built, and hordes of package tourists being ferried out to idyllic strands of once-remote islands. But the government has also moved to protect some especially vulnerable wildlife and plant habitats by creating national parkls, and – though the former seaside fishing villages are fast being swallowed up by mega-resorts – you can still find isolated pockets of the old ways of life here.

Festivals & Events

 Semana Santa (the Christian Holy Week in March or April) is celebrated with colorful Haitian-style carnaval parades, music, and religious processions in and around the city of San Pedro de Macorís.

San Pedro Apostol in San Pedro de Macorís is a festival in the tradition of the Cocolos (black English speakers who were brought to the DR from the British Virgin Islands in the 19th century to work the sugar fields), featuring their unique mummers' costumes, *guloya* music, and dancing. It takes place in late June.

Boca Chica's **Merengue Festival**, initiated to draw some crowds away from Santo Domingo's wildly popular Merengue Festival, is catching on in its own right each July.

Getting Here & Getting Around

 For Caribbean Coast sites closest to Santo Domingo, you can fly into the capital's **Aeropuerto Internacional Las Américas**, served by many daily flights from the US, Canada, Europe, and other Caribbean islands. At the airport, you can rent a car or take a taxi to Boca Chica, Juan Dolio, or other nearby resort areas.

For more easterly destinations along the coast, you might opt to fly into the relatively newer **Aeropuerto La Romana**, located about five miles east of La Romana (68 miles east of Santo Domingo). This airport serves the Caribbean Coast with daily commercial flights from Miami and San Juan, Puerto Rico, as well as from Santo Domingo and other domestic locations. It's also a popular destination for charter flights from Europe. The airport has taxis available, though if you're booked into a local resort, the hotel will most likely arrange pick-up service. (The huge Casa de Campo resort near La Romana has its own airstrip.)

Highway 3 (also known as Autopista Las Américas) is the main route leading from Santo Domingo toward the Caribbean coast. Small roads run south off the highway to connect to coastal locations such as Boca Chica and Juan Dolio. After Juan Dolio, Highway 3 runs through the city of San Pedro de Macorís and crosses over a bridge before turning into **Highway 4**, which runs east to La Romana and then turns north to Higüey and Punta Caña. You can reach far southeastern destinations such as Bayahibe, Boca de Yuma and Parque Nacional del Este via roads leading south from Highway 4.

Guaguas frequently ply the route from Santo Domingo to Boca Chica, Juan Dolio, and beyond. They leave from the southeast corner of Parque Enriquillo (Ave. José Martí and Calle Duarte), which is north of the Zona Colonial in Santo Domingo.

Information Sources

■ Tourist Offices

Boca Chica: Plaza Boca Chica, ☎ 523-5106

La Romana: ☎ 550-3242

Adventures

■ Beaches

Beaches are listed in geographic order from west to east (from closest to Santo Domingo moving to the farthest away):

Playa Boca Chica

Located about 20 miles east of Santo Domingo, this is the most famous and popular beach on the south coast. It's hard to know which lures more crowds to Playa Boca Chica: the incredibly crystal-clear calm waters and wide palm-lined beach for sunbathing, or the town's reputation for hard partying. On Sunday afternoons, especially, Santo Domingo residents and other Dominicans pour onto the *playa* to drink and dance merengue until the sun goes down. (And when the sun goes down, the really hard partying begins – accompanied by flagrant solicitations by prostitutes of both sexes.)

The strip facing the beach is jammed wall-to-wall with bars and restaurants, and when you tire of the waves of hawkers and hustlers that haunt the area, you can escape to the gentle waves of the Caribbean for some watersports, which are also present in abundance. The options are enough to make your head spin, including swimming, snorkeling, water skiing, kayaking, jet skiing, sailboarding, paddleboating, catamaraning, Hobie Cat sailing – even trolling across the water four at a time on a "banana boat" – an inflated raft that does indeed resemble a banana. You can rent equipment for all these sports from a number of outfits along the beach, at prices ranging from about US$30-75 per hour.

To reach Boca Chica, follow Highway 3 east from Santo Domingo (see *Bases for Exploration, Boca Chica*, below, for more details on how to get there.)

Playa Caribe

Local families flock to this popular beach, especially on Sunday afternoons. Intense waves also make it a hot spot for boogie boarders. You'll have to bring your own board, though, since there are no rentals available here. Playa Caribe is a few miles east of Boca Chica along Highway 3, about halfway to Juan Dolio.

Playa Juan Dolio

With its rocky, coral-laced shoreline, the swimming is less than ideal here, but this long hotel-laden stretch of beach starting about 10 miles down the road from Boca Chica is less frenetic than the latter and attracts a loyal contingent of adherents. Plenty of restaurants, bars, and resorts line much of the beach, but you won't find the types of hawkers, hustlers, and sex-for-sale pests that plague Boca Chica. (See *Bases for Exploration, Juan Dolio*, below, for more detail.)

Playa Bayahibe & Playa Dominicus

These beaches in the Bayahibe resort area southeast of La Romana combine gorgeous coastline with powdery white sand and warm turquoise waters. Much of the beach has been taken over by all-inclusive resorts, but even if you aren't staying at one you can still enjoy some nice stretches of *playa*. (See *Bases for Exploration, Bayahibe*, below, for more detail.)

Isla Saona

The most accessible beaches in this "protected" national park (part of the Parque Nacional del Este) in the far southeast of the country are overrun with package tourists. (The 50-square-mile Isla Saona draws far more visitors than the larger mainland section of the park to its north.) Still, its famously idyllic, palm-lined beaches rank among the most beautiful in the area, and you can find solitude if you search out the more remote stretches of the island.

Tip: If you want some relief from the crowds, walk over to the Club Viva Dominicus and take the unmarked foot path (a local can point it out for you) behind the restaurant, where a short hike leads through some brush. You might even catch a glimpse of the local Hispaniolan parrot there.

Though sparsely inhabited and part mangrove swamp, the island is a hugely popular stop with cruise ships and local tour operators. You know the island is geared toward package tourists when you encounter the dozens of tour buses that are typically stacked up in the parking lot at Playa Bayahibe (the same lot where you pick up boats for the mainland section of the park).

From the parking lot, speed boats and catamarans fill up with passengers before shuttling them to the island on 45-minute crossings. Most boats go to moderately developed beaches on the southwest side of the island. Expect to share the sands with both crowds of tourists and lots of hawkers and vendors. These rides cost US$75 round-trip and include a not-very-good buffet lunch (complete with rum drinks) on the island. Independent travelers might want to pack a lunch since the island eateries cater mostly to package tourists.

Good value: To visit Isla Saona on your own, and save some money in the process, first stop at the National Park office just in front of the parking lot and pay the RD$50 permit fee, then see at the dock about joining up with an independent boat headed for the island. Expect to pay about RD$500 round-trip per person. If you'd like to find some solitude, ask the boat captain to take you to one of the more remote beaches away from the heavily touristed part of the island.

The Caribbean Coast

Playa Borinquen

You'll need to hire a boatman, then climb and hike a ways to reach this secluded beach in Boca de Yuma on the bay just east of Parque Nacional del Este. But there are few better places to escape the crowds along this stretch of coastline. (See *Bases for Exploration, Boca de Yuma*, below.)

■ On Water

Diving & Snorkeling

The diving and snorkeling opportunities along the southeast coast are among the best in the country, with coral reefs, sunken ships, and sea caves among the attractions. Some sites are geared toward veteran divers only, while others are ideal for novices. Several of the large all-inclusive resorts along the coast include beginning scuba lessons in their rates, and some have certified dive shops on premises. The recommended sites below are listed from west to east (from closest to Santo Domingo to farthest from the capital).

> **Tip:** If you don't have your own diving gear or simply want the convenience of going with a group, you might consider joining a guided tour from nearby Boca Chica for about US$65. One good outfitter is **Treasure Divers** (☎ 523-5320, fax 523-4819, www.treasuredivers.de), which you can find on Playa Boca Chica just in front of the Don Juan Hotel on Calle Abraham Nunez.

Parque Nacional Submarino La Caleta

Located about 13 miles east of Santo Domingo, this is less a formal park than a strip of beach used as a popular launching pad for divers. The main attractions are two wrecked ships, both scuttled here in the 1980s, when the park was formed. The larger of the two ships, the *Hickory*, 130 feet long, was once used to hunt treasure, salvaging sunken Spanish galleons. Over the course of the past 20 years it's become a veritable underwater museum of sea life, easily accessible to divers in the shallow waters. A coral reef with tropical fish is another big draw.

To get to La Caleta on your own from Santo Domingo or any of the bases along the south coast, take Highway 3 (east from Santo Domingo or west from other locations) and follow the signs toward Aeropuerto Internacional Las Américas. The park is just west of the airport. Turn south toward the sea onto Route 66 and after going a short distance you will see a sign on your right indicating the entrance to La Caleta.

Park anywhere you find a space – in front of the small museum exhibiting local Taino artifacts is a good spot – and negotiate the 25-minute boat ride to the dive site with any of the fishermen who frequent the waters. Expect to pay about RD$800 to do this on your own.

Juan Dolio

Numerous deep dive sites are situated in this area, where you can explore sea channels, coral reefs, and some of the long chain of sea caves that border the south coast of the island (the latter for experienced divers only). Ralf Biegel (www.scubconsult.net or ralfbiegel@verizon.net.do), a German expat, has been diving the caves around Juan Dolio for nearly a decade and knows them very well. If you give him some advance notice, and you're a well-qualified diver, he'll put together a personalized cave diving tour for you. **Treasure Divers** (Playa Boca Chica, ☎ 523-5320, fax 523-4819, www.treasuredivers.de) also leads cave tours.

Isla Catalina

This little island's magnificent coral reef makes it the single most impressive – and popular – dive and snorkeling spot in the region. The highlight for experienced divers is a 130-foot dropoff known as The Wall, which is home to a remarkable underwater world of coral and brightly hued tropical fish.

Several tour operators run trips to Isla Catalina, which is just off the coast southwest of La Romana. One of the best is **Casa Daniel**, based in Playa Bayahibe (☎ 833-0050, fax 833-0010, www.casa-daniel.de, casa-daniel@gmx.net), which charges about $75 for half-day tours, lunch included. Casa Daniel also runs tours to other dive and snorkel locales in the area.

If you're staying at the Casa de Campo resort just across the bay, you can get shuttled back and forth to Isla Catalina for free. The resort's **Circe WaterSports** (☎ 813-2001; www.circewatersports.com) operates scuba tours there, as well as to other area locations.

Isla Saona

This beautiful island (see *Beaches*, above) is part of the Parque Nacional del Este (see *Eco-Travel*, below) and commonly reached by boat from Bayahibe. **ScubaFun** (Calle Principe 28, ☎ 833-0003, scubafun_de@yahoo.com), on the dock in Bayahibe, runs small group or individual snorkeling and diving tours to Isla Saona that cost about US$75. Participants can explore the nearby coral reef and have a chance to spot dolphins, manatees, and (in winter) humpback whales.

The Caribbean Coast

Other Watersports

Most major beach resorts in Boca Chica, Juan Dolio, and Bayahibe, as well as Casa de Campo near La Romana, offer extensive watersports programs that are often included in the rates. Kayaking, windsurfing, and boating are among the typical offerings.

Riverboat Tours

Río Soco & Río Chavon

You can travel both of these stunningly scenic but mild and slow-paced rivers via *African Queen*-style riverboats. The tour boats slowly make their way up and down the rivers, stopping at choice spots for lunch and swimming. The swimming holes include opportunities to swing like Tarzan from hanging vines before splashing down into the river.

Both the Río Soco and Río Chavon have their headwaters in the Cordillera Oriental mountain range, then flow south into the Caribbean. The Río Soco intersects the coastal highway just a few miles east of San Pedro de Macorís, while the Río Chavon is farther east, between La Romana and Bayahibe. But the tours are widely advertised in Boca Chica and Juan Dolio as well, and hotel pick-ups are available there. **Trewe Tours** (☎ 526-1211) is one of the better operators. The day-long trips cost about US$65, lunch included.

■ On Foot

The best hiking opportunities are in the Parque Nacional del Este, where you can trek along trails through lush tropical foliage to remote caves containing ancient Taino drawings and carvings. (See *Eco-Travel*, below, for details.)

■ On Horseback

The famous **Casa de Campo** resort (☎ 523-3333, fax 523-8548; www.casadcampo.com) outside La Romana offers guided trail rides for RD$400 per hour.

The **Crazy Horse Ranch** in Boca Chica (☎ 523-4199) features two-hour trail rides for US$40.

The recently opened **Guavaberry Equestrian Center** at the Guavaberry Golf & Country Club (☎ 333-4653, www.guavaberrygolf.

com, guavaberrygolf@verizon.net.do) in Juan Dolio offers one-hour trail rides six times daily (for ages 10 and up) at US$25 per person.

Rancho Cumayasa, north of La Romana (☎ 556-1606) has public trail rides that cost US$25 for one hour.

■ On Wheels

You can bike all the way from Santo Domingo to Boca Chica along Highway 3 (Autopista las Américas), about 20 miles. The route is generally flat and safe for cyclists, who can ride on the shoulder of the road.

■ Eco-Travel

Parque Nacional del Este

This massive and mostly inaccessible park was formed to help protect a densely forested peninsula that lies toward the southeastern edge of the Caribbean Coast. The park also includes the smaller **Isla Saona** situated across a channel south of the peninsula (see sections on *Beaches* and *Diving*, above, for more on Isla Saona). The Park of the East, as it's known in English, harbors some 112 bird species – more than one-third of all those found in the DR. And, of those, eight are found only on the island of Hispaniola, including the white-headed dove, the Hispaniolan lizard cuckoo, and the ashy-faced owl. A wealth of marine life also occupies the area. Several species of sea turtles nest along the shoreline, while bottlenose dolphins and manatees swim the waters around Isla Saona. (You might also spot humpback whales in winter.)

In the interior, hiking trails lead to a number of caves containing Taino ceremonial sites, including extraordinary collections of petroglyphs and pictographs that show meetings between the early Spanish conquistadors and the indigenous population. Some of the drawings may even represent Columbus himself. You'll have to work to reach them, however: The most extensive glyphs can be found inside three caves (**Cueva del Puente**, **Cueva José María**, and another near **Penon Gordo**), which require hiking several hours inland from the coast of the peninsula.

First, however, you need to get to the park, and that generally involves going by boat, since there are no roads. You have a few options. The most convenient, but also most expensive, is to book a guided tour. Two outfitters based in Playa Bayahibe, **Casa Daniel** (Calle Principe 1, ☎ 833-0050) and **ScubaFun** (Calle Principe 28, ☎ 833-0003) run daily trips to Cueva del Puente and Cueva José María for about US$40, boat and lunch included.

> **Caution:** The entrances to these caves are merely holes in the ground made slippery by the bat guano that covers the edges. Take your time when entering them. Wear sturdy hiking boots or shoes that grip well, and a long-sleeve shirt and pants to protect you from mosquitoes as well as from nicks, scratches and the inevitable bloody elbow should you take a spill. By all means bring insect repellent, water, and a flashlight, but pack light – these treks can be grueling in the heat.

You can also travel independently. Go to the large parking lot at the west end of Playa Bayahibe that adjoins the boat docks, where you'll find the small national park office (open 9 am-noon, daily) and where you can pay the RD$50 permit fee needed to enter. (Try to get an early start, both to allow plenty of time and to beat the heat of midday.) You'll also encounter a number of boat captains who make regular runs to the park. You can bargain with the captains, but expect to pay around RD$500 round-trip for the rides. At the park entrance you'll need to hire a ranger to accompany you for another RD$150, a park requirement. Some of the rangers do speak good English, but if your Spanish is rusty, it's a good idea to check first. Alternatively, you can skip the boat ride altogether and hike into the park by following the coastline east for about a mile and a half until you get to the park entrance. You must still, however, hire a park ranger to enter the park itself.

Once in the park, you can reach Cueva del Puente and Cueva José María along the same hiking trail. The former comes first (after about a two-hour hike), but the latter (after another hour or so) contains the more spectacular glyphs. Cueva del Puente is also known for its stalagmites and stalactites. Reaching the cave near Penon Gordo requires a separate boat trip and a hike of a bit over a mile following a two-hour boat trip.

> **Tip:** You can also access the park from the east side of the peninsula, in the tranquil village of **Boca de Yuma** (see *Bases for Exploration*, below), but the most accessible cave from that point, Cueva de Bernardo, is of less interest than the other sites. However, the 45-minute boat ride there is about RD$200 less than the one from Playa Bayahibe. Watch for the bright yellow and green signs pointing the way west from the center of the village to the park.

■ Golf

In Juan Dolio, the 18-hole par-72 course at **Guavaberry Golf Resort** (Autovia del Este, ☎ 333-4653, www.guavaberrygolf.com, guavaberry golf@verizon.net.do) is open to the public daily; call for reservations.

On-site is an excellent restaurant, a swimming pool with children's area, and an impressive billiard room displaying memorabilia of Gary Player and other famous golfers.

Nearby, the 18-hole par-72 **Los Marlins Golf Course** at the Metro Country Club (Las Américas Highway, Juan Dolio, ☎ 526-3315) is a bit shorter and less expensive than the course at Guavaberry.

> **Inside advice:** If you're staying in the Juan Dolio area and want to play a round at either Guavaberry Golf Resort or Los Marlins, call the pro shop for either and a complimentary shuttle will pick you up and deliver you back to your hotel.

Three 18-hole championship golf courses at Casa de Campo (☎ 523-3333, fax 523-8548; www.casadcampo.com), the famous resort near la Romana, were designed by Pete Dye, one of the best in the business. **Teeth of the Dog**, which features several holes set along the dramatic seafront, has been ranked among the number one course in the Caribbean. **The Links**, which extends inland, and the newest course here, **Dye Fore**, are also among the top courses on the island.

■ Historic Sites

Casa Ponce de León

This fortress-like two-story house built of stone and mahogany was the home of the 16th-century Spanish explorer Juan Ponce de León, best known for seeking the Fountain of Youth. (He later governed Puerto Rico and, eventually, tried to find the elusive fountain in Florida, where he died at the hands of natives.) Built in 1508 and beautifully restored by the park service, the house contains items that are said to have belonged to the conquistador himself, such as his suit of armor and a huge treasure chest. One fascinating aspect of the house is that it has only one exterior door and very small windows – too small for a person to fit through – all in the name of self-protection. (And safer than Florida, it seems.)

The Caribbean Coast

The site is looked after by an elderly gentleman who gives informative tours – in Spanish only – from 8:30 am to 4 pm every day except Sunday. Admission is RD$50, plus a tip for the guide. To get there, head south off Highway 4 toward Boca de Yuma. (The highway itself swings north toward Higüey at this point.) The house is located in the village of San Rafael de Yuma, a few miles north of Boca de Yuma and the coast. It's about half a mile down an unpaved road that goes off to the left (near the cemetery and a school) as you're driving south through town. The house itself isn't marked, but look for it on the right side of the road, down a long driveway.

Cuevas de las Maravillas

Once used by Taino Indians for religious ceremonies, the "Cave of the Wonders" got its moniker from the abundance of crystallized minerals found within. The big attraction for visitors, though, is a wealth of petroglyphs – some 500 in all – etched into the walls by the long-ago native inhabitants. The Dominican authorities recently invested large sums of money to install lights, ramps, and an elevator to make the 82-foot descent into the system easily accessible to the disabled, small children, and senior citizens.

Cuevas de las Maravillas (☎ 696-1797) is within view of Highway 4 about 2½ miles after the town of Río Soco, which is a few miles east of San Pedro de Macorís; watch for the bright yellow and green National Park signs north of the highway. The cave is open Tuesday to Sunday, 10 am – 6 pm, with an RD$100 admission fee for adults (RD$30 for children under 12).

Bases for Exploration

■ Boca Chica

Orientation

Just 20 miles east of Santo Domingo and a short 10-minute ride from Aeropuerto Las Américas is Boca Chica, a funky little resort town known for its beautiful beach by day and spirited bar and nightclub scene by night. Most of the action takes place on or alongside the bar-and-restaurant-lined beach, a wide, sandy, palm-fringed stretch of golden white sand where you will find people sunbathing, splashing in the calm, shallow waters, or perched at tables overlooking the action. The local color includes a lively – and persistent – mix of bands, vendors, and other entrepreneurs who hawk everything from a song to hair-braiding… or even themselves. Boca Chica can make a great day-trip from Santo Domingo or Juan Dolio on a Sunday afternoon when Dominicans from the city drive in for the party.

Since gaining popularity in the 1970s, however, Boca Chica has unfortunately become known for a much seedier side as well. At night its main strip, Calle Duarte, becomes an open-air brothel, with male "sanky pankies" and female "putas" out aggressively stirring up business among the crowds of tourists, many of whom visit the area for the explicit purpose of hooking up with prostitutes. Unless you're actively looking for that type of thing, it can make for a very uncomfortable, even sordid atmosphere.

Calle Duarte, which roughly parallels the sea, is also the place to find shopping and tourist services such as bank ATMs, money changers, calling stations, Western Union, Internet cafés, markets, and medical facilities. There's a government tourist information office at the Plaza Boca Chica (☎ 523-5106) on the corner of Duarte and Caracoles.

Getting Here & Around

Getting to Boca Chica either by car or public transportation is easy as long as you know the ropes.

By car, take Highway 3 (or Autopista Las Américas) east in the direction of Aueropuerto Internacional Las Américas.

Caution: Be sure to stay to your right, or you might end up in the lane for the Tunel Marginal, which will temporarily subject you to a dusty and pothole-ridden auxiliary road running alongside the highway, prolonging your drive to Boca Chica by at least another 20 minutes.

After driving for about 15 minutes, you will come to a toll booth, where the fee is RD$15. If you don't have exact change, take the lane marked *cambio efectivo* (change cash) where the attendant will make change for you. Approximately five miles after the toll on the right-hand side of the road you will see a Shell gas station as well as a huge sign indicating the turnoff to Boca Chica. Make this right turn and follow the road – Calle Caracol – all the way to the end. When the road bears right (as you near the water), you will be on Calle Duarte.

Guaguas to Boca Chica leave from the southeast corner of Parque Enriquillo in Santo Domingo (Calle Duarte and Ave. José Martí), charging RD$30. Cyclists can also make the ride from Santo Domingo along the well-paved and scenic Autopista Las Américas (Highway 3). Once in Boca Chica you probably won't need transportation, since everything is within walking distance. But should the need for wheels arise, plenty of *motoconcho* drivers are in sight, and there's a taxi stand on the corner of Calle Duarte and Hungria.

Places to Stay

Boca Chica sports three top-end resorts and a slew of budget- to mid-range accommodations.

Don Juan Beach Resort (Calle Abraham Nunez; ☎ 800-820-1631 in US or 687-9157; fax 688-5271; www.caei.com) $$$$

More like a village within the village of Boca Chica, this 224-room all-inclusive resort has artfully blended its facilities with the existing environment. Easy access to a lively beach – as well as a dive center and a watersports center offering a full menu of activities such as windsurfing and sailboats – add to its allure. You'll also find supervised kids' activities, a freshwater pool, tennis, bike tours, three restaurants, four bars, and nightly entertainment.

Hamaca Coral by Hilton (Calle Caracol, ☎ 523-4611, fax 523-6767; www.coralbyhilton.com) $$$$

This sprawling 598-room all-inclusive resort is on the eastern end of the beach and separated from everything – and everyone else – by a wall of security guards, who maintain a strict boundary between guests and

Boca Chica

1. Mesón
2. Hamaca Coral Resort
3. Pequeña Suiza Bar/Pensión
4. Hotel Europa
5. Discoteca Cosmos
6. Route 66 Rock Café
7. Police
8. Church
9. Central Park/express bus stop for Santo Domingo
10. McDeal Rent-a-Car
11. Don Paco Guest House
12. Post Office
13. Western Union
14. Don Juan Beach Resort
15. Hotel-Supermercado Don Emilio
16. To Andrés (Boca Marina Yacht Club, DeMar Beach Club, Pop-Eye Fisherman Club, Club Nautico)
17. Condominios Las Kasitas Del Sol
18. Alpha 3000 Auto Rental
19. Supermercado Santa Fe
20. Hotel Magic Tropical

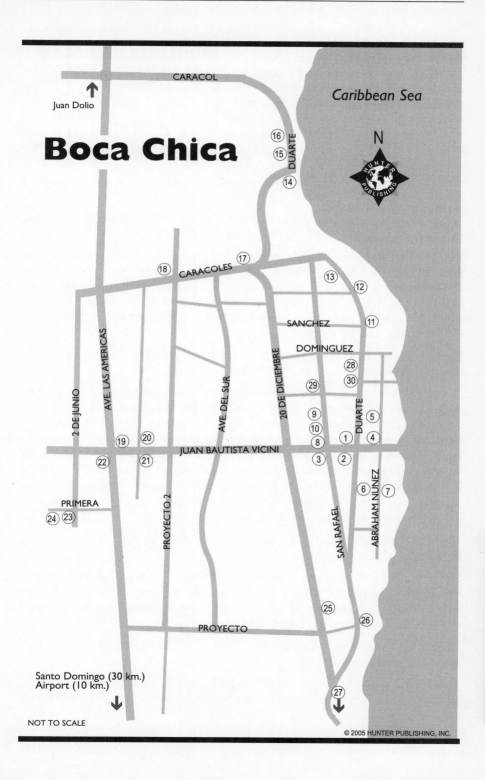

non-guests. In addition to the usual resort amenities one might expect – including four pools (two for kids), tennis, casino, disco, supervised kids' programs, and five restaurants – Hamaca has exclusive access to the best part of Boca Chica beach (which may explain why they guard it so jealously). Beach

HOTEL PRICE CHART	
Rates are per room based on double occupancy.	
$	Under US$20
$$	US$20-$50
$$$	US$51-$100
$$$$	Over US$100

activities are a flurry of non-stop action, from kayaking and paddle boating to windsurfing and beginner's diving lessons.

Hotel Dominican Bay (Juan Bautista Vicini & Calle 20 de Diciembre; ☎ 412-2001, fax 412-0687; www.hotetur.com) $$$$

This 437-room all-inclusive complex offers much of what one might expect to find at a fine resort: beautiful grounds, pool, watersports and other games, four on-site restaurants, four bars, nightly entertainment, children's activities. It is, however, two blocks from the beach – but that might be a good thing if you prefer to be away from the raucous nighttime clatter along the waterfront.

Hotel Don Emilio (Duarte 74, ☎ 523-5270, fax 523-5690, don.emilio@verizon.net) $$$-$$$$

The art deco styling, elegant common areas, and spacious rooms – some with stunning views of the beach – offer loads of panache for the money and make this the best alternative in Boca Chica to an all-inclusive resort. All rooms have cable TV, air conditioning, and mini-bar. The beachfront rooms ending in 09 also feature private Jacuzzis and floor-to-ceiling windows that stretch from wall to wall overlooking all the action on Playa Boca Chica. The ground-floor patio dining room is another good spot for people-watching. The hotel is adding a rooftop dining room and ground-floor swimming pool as well.

Hotel Europa (Calle Dominguez and Duarte, ☎ 523-5721, htleuropa@verizon.net) $$$

Until the Don Emilio (see review above) came along, Hotel Europa was considered the best on the beach. Large, clean rooms, a very accommodating staff and the few steps' walk to the beach still make it a good choice. No credit cards are accepted.

Hotel Zapata (Calle Abraham Nunez, ☎ 523-4777, fax 523-5534, zapata@verizon.net.do) $$$

This small, quiet, family-run hotel is right on the beach, with a spacious, private bar area where you can relax under a thatch umbrella while sipping a piña colada. All rooms have cable TV, air conditioning, and private balconies that either face the beach or the garden. A front door that remains locked 24 hours a day keeps hawkers and solicitors at bay.

Don Paco (Calle Duarte 6 and Vicini, ☎ 523-4816) $$

Though located on Calle Duarte, this pleasant budget hotel is away from the prostitutes and johns farther down the road and is also near the water, making for an easy walk to the beach. The rooms are clean, the garden setting is relaxing, and the owners friendly. Non-registered guests are not allowed.

Magic Tropical Hotel (Calle Arismendy Valenzuela, ☎ 523-4254, fax 523-5439) $$

Although some might find its location away from the beach a disadvantage, this hotel is an excellent value. It's run by a hip young multilingual Romanian woman, along with her brother and an elderly uncle, who looks after maintenance. The exceptionally clean rooms have fans but no air conditioning. Amenities include a pool and charming thatched-roof common area with small bar and billiard table. Non-registered guests are not allowed.

> **Warning:** Choose carefully, because there are huge gaps in the level of facilities and amenities in the less expensive categories. Once you arrive, if you don't like your accommodations for whatever reason, finding another hotel – particularly in summer, on weekends, and around Merengue Festival time in July – may be difficult. And checking into an all-inclusive resort as a last-ditch plan will cost you dearly, since the best deals are packages bought in advance. Links to the independent hotels recommended here can be found at www.bocachica.net.

Places to Eat

You won't be hard-pressed for dining options in Boca Chica: both the beach and Calle Duarte offer lots of choices. For cheap eats, you'll find a number of local ladies selling fried fish and *tostones* on the beach end of Calle Juan Bautista Vicini.

> **Tip:** Some of the establishments along the beach charge more than RD$100 for the use of a table and chairs – though they won't charge a peso if they think you've spent enough (check first so you won't be surprised).

DINING PRICE CHART	
Price per person for an entrée, not including beverage or tip.	
$	Under US$2
$$	US$2-$10
$$$	US$10-$20
$$$$	Over US$20

Da'Nancy Trattoria (Calle Duarte 16, ☎ 523-4376) $$

The Italian food at this beachfront restaurant is top-notch (it's one of the few places in town where you can get a good steak). And, with a back porch looking onto Playa Boca Chica, the setting is delightful, making it a fine spot for a lunch of light pasta or fresh seafood.

Hexxenkessel Restaurant (Calle Duarte at Plaza Isla Bonita, ☎ 523-4027) $$

If your hotel doesn't include breakfast, come here for awesome toast and eggs with bacon. It's also a good place to grab a burger, some soup or a sandwich, or just to shoot the breeze at the bar and watch the passing parade go by on Calle Duarte.

Neptuno's (Calle Duarte 12, ☎ 523-4703) $$

Neptuno's, whose outdoor deck extends over the sea, offers up the best seafood on this side of the island. The annoyance is trying to get there. Though it's within easy walking distance of town, the Hamaca Coral Resort (see above) won't let non-guests cross its beach to get to it – thus forcing most customers to go about four miles out of the way to reach a place that's otherwise within a stone's throw. Once you alight from your vehicle, though, you'll find the grilled seafood platters and lobster and shrimp dishes to be first-rate. Drinks are also good here, which helps draw crowds of visitors on Sunday afternoons. Be sure to make reservations – you wouldn't want to waste the cab ride over.

Pequeña Suiza (Calle Duarte, ☎ 523-4619) $$

Despite its Swiss-sounding name, the Suiza serves up mostly (very good) Italian food. It does, however, have a cheese fondue specialty that's popular with the local expat crowd, who come here to escape the madness in the streets.

Nightlife & Entertainment

Nightlife in Boca Chica is centered around the bars and dance clubs lining both sides of Calle Duarte. Among the more popular ones are **Route 66** and **Cosmos** (although the constant heavy soliciting by male and female prostitutes can be mightily off-putting). You'll find a less intrusive atmosphere at **Mundo Center**, a local dance club in the nearby village of Andres just to the west (best reached by taxi or one of the *guaguas* heading back toward Santo Domingo), an impoverished area and home to most of the people who work in Boca Chica hotels. The **Hamaca Coral** features your run-of-the-mill resort disco that will occasionally admit non-guests for a steep price, depending on hotel occupancy at the time. Otherwise, you can pass the night away at **Hamaca Casino Boca Chica** (which isn't nearly so choosy about admitting non-guests), where gamblers drink, snack, and smoke for free, with transportation to and from your hotel included.

■ Juan Dolio

Orientation

 Beginning about 10 miles east of Boca Chica along Highway 3 is the sprawling beachside resort area of Juan Dolio, a lengthy stretch of hotels, restaurants, and beach homes whose eastern end has been transformed over the past two decades into an all-inclusive haven known as Villas del Mar. Its western end, meanwhile, has remained a quiet seaside village. In the early 1990s there were plans to extend development to the west as well, but the arrival of Hurricane Georges in 1998 caused extensive damage and put at least a temporary end to them. The shells of several abandoned hotel projects survive to give the area something of a low-rent, depressed feel.

Despite this less-than-appealing façade, and a rather rocky, coral-strewn shoreline that makes for some unpleasant swimming, the village of Juan Dolio remains a second home of sorts to the many visitors who have been spending their vacations here for years. Many Santo Domingo residents own beach homes on the village's short strip (which takes all of 10 minutes to walk down), and you quickly get the sense that you are almost joining a big family when you come to stay here. Even in the resort enclave of Villas del Mar, the atmosphere is much different from Boca Chica: less crowded, less frenetic, less beset by all the hustlers and hawkers.

> **Inside advice:** If you're staying in a guest house along the western strip and don't have access to a phone, you can head to the Fior di Loto Hotel, whose owner operates an ad hoc tourism office for visitors (there's no official one in Juan Dolio). She also sells calling cards and can put you in contact with local diving and tour operators.

You'll find a number of good, small, restaurants on the village strip, but many more options abound in Villas del Mar, which is just a short walk from the eastern end of the strip. Villas del Mar is also where you'll find local tour operators, ATMs, calling stations, and most other tourist services.

The Caribbean Coast

Caution: While the western and eastern sections of Juan Dolio are near each other, consider taking a taxi between the two since the area has occasionally been plagued by robberies, even in daytime. (Some hotels also offer shuttle service.)

Getting Here & Around

The closest airport to Juan Dolio is **Santo Domingo's Aeropuerto las Américas**. Taxis and rental cars are available from the airport to Juan Dolio.

Guaguas stop at Juan Dolio from Santo Domingo and Boca Chica. Whether taking public transportation or driving, you'll follow Highway 3 eastward from Boca Chica. A few miles after the village of Guayacanes, watch for a Shell gas station on your left and a *comedor* on your right; the corner immediately after is the short road leading to the village of Juan Dolio. Turning right, proceed to the end of the road, where you'll see the Fior di Loto Hotel.

Tip: If you miss that turn (or if your *guagua* driver fails to stop), you can still access the strip from the next corner. (Be sure to tell the driver, *"dejame aquí!"*)

If you continue along Highway 3, you'll soon reach the resort area of Villas del Mar in eastern Juan Dolio. You'll know you've arrived once you see all the hotels and restaurants on both sides of the road.

Places to Stay

The following four Barcelo hotels are grouped near each other on Villas del Mar beach:

Barcelo Capella Beach Resort (Villas del Mar, ☎ 526-1080, fax 526-1088, www.barcelo.com, h.capella@verizon.net.do) $$$$

HOTEL PRICE CHART	
Rates are per room based on double occupancy.	
$	Under US$20
$$	US$20-$50
$$$	US$51-$100
$$$$	Over US$100

This five-star all-inclusive resort features 500 rooms with all the trimmings, catering to honeymooners and families alike (a supervised children's program keeps the kiddies quiet for adult relaxation). Opportunities for watersports abound – from swimming in the five pools to scuba diving, windsurfing, kayaking, and catamaran rides in the sea. One downside is that, for the money you're spending, the stretch of beach here is less appealing than those in Boca Chica or Bayahibe.

Barcelo Colonial Tropical (Villas del Mar, ☎ 526-1660, fax 526-2538, www.barcelo.com, h.capella@verizon.net.do), $$$$

The smallest of the four nearby Barcelo properties, this colonial-style hotel has just 40 rooms and suites. Guests have access to the facilities at the much larger Barcelo Capella next door. All-inclusive plans are available but optional here.

Barcelo Naiboa Caribe (Villas del Mar, ☎ 526-2009, fax 526-2310, www.barcelo.com) $$$$

Geared to young people (meaning those in their 20s and 30s), this 440-room all-inclusive is the least expensive of the four Barcelos. There's a heavy emphasis on entertainment here and round-the-clock action on the beach.

Barcelo Talanquera (Villas del Mar, ☎ 526-1510, fax 526-2408, www.barcelo.com, h.talanquera@verizon.net.do), $$$$

The 437-room Talanquera courts the family trade with plenty of beach activities and five swimming pools amid landscaped grounds. A certified dive center is located at the watersports center.

Coral Costa Caribe (Las Américas Highway, ☎ 526-2244; www.coralbyhilton.com) $$$$

The rooms are small at this rather mediocre 492-room all-inclusive resort, which probably explains the 24-hour sports bar. When guests tire of the beach, the claustrophobic rooms, and round-the-clock entertainments, they can drink themselves into oblivion.

Guavaberry Golf Resort (Autovia del Este, ☎ 333-4653; www.guavaberry.org) $$$$

Management has recently pulled together a villa rental program from among the multi-million dollar homes that dot the golf course here. Suitable for large families or groups of friends, the villas are over 4,000 square feet and all have kitchens and three bedrooms. Besides the proximity of golf, there's an excellent on-site restaurant and a swimming pool with children's area. Meals aren't included in the rates, but you can have room service or groceries delivered to your villa. While the resort is removed from the beach, a complimentary shuttle service runs to and from the Guavaberry Beach Club during the day – while another shuttle ferries you to a nearby casino in the evening, if you like.

Meliá Juan Dolio (Boulevard Villas del Mar, ☎ 526-1521, fax 526-2184, www.solmelia.com)

This all-inclusive resort has 270 rooms and suites and a sizeable spa that includes saunas, steam rooms, Jacuzzis, and a gym. A pool rests in a tropical garden, the tennis courts are lit for night play, and there are two restaurants and a karaoke bar.

Hotel Coop Marena (Calle Central, ☎ 526-2121, coopmarena@verizon. net.do) $$$-$$$$

Nicely located in the quieter western part of Juan Dolio, just across the road from the beach, this 213-room independent all-inclusive resort caters mostly to groups and conferences, though individual travelers are certainly welcome. (Families will appreciate the good children's programs.) The hotel maintains a nice pavilion where guests can relax around the pool overlooking the ocean while the staff entertains guests with all-you-can-stand activities and drinks. Shuttle rides are provided to the Villas del Mar area.

Embassy Suites Hotel (Las Américas Highway, ☎ 688-9999; www.losmarlins.embassysuites.com; judol_embassy@hilton.com) $$$

The Embassy Suites, also known, rather confusingly, as Metro Country Club (and a Hilton to boot), has 126 two-room suites with either king or double bed and an additional sofa bed in the living room. Guests receive complimentary breakfast and use of the 18-hole golf course (guests also have access to the 18-hole Guavaberry course across the highway), as well as a swimming pool and tennis court. The downside is that you are nowhere near the beach, but the hotel does provide complimentary shuttle service there.

Playa Esmeralda (Las Américas Highway, ☎ 526-3434; www.hotel-playaesmeralda.com) $$$

In terms of facilities, this is – hands down – the best hotel in the area. The beautiful rooms and the grounds alike are immaculately maintained, and it's set along a nice stretch of sand. The only downside is that it's on Highway 3, a bit removed from the rest of Juan Dolio – but the comfort, service, and better beach make up for the out-of-the-way location.

Fior di Loto Hotel (Calle Central, ☎ 526-1146, fax 526-3332; hfdiloto@verizon.net.do) $-$$

This simple but inviting hotel takes the top prize locally for atmosphere. While the 22 rooms are pretty basic, the Italian owner, Mara Sandri, who divides her time between the Dominican Republic and India, has incorporated Indian touches into the décor. The hotel also offers free yoga classes, a gym, a private sundeck, and a popular restaurant (see below). Rooms are fan-cooled, and have hot water, and cable TV. The long list of repeat guests from all over the world testifies to its popularity, much of it thanks to Mara Sandri's hospitality.

Don Pedro Guest House (Calle Central, ☎ 526-2147) $

You'll find basic rooms available here on the second and third floors of the owner's home. (At times the place may appear closed, but there's always someone around.) It's conveniently located directly across the road from the entrance to the beach and the Bar Trapiche (owned by the Don Pedro), where you can get cheap eats.

Places to Eat

Since Juan Dolio is a haven for expat Italians, just about all of your dining options will be pasta and pizza – or pizza and pasta. There is also one very pleasant local *comedor*, **El Rincón** (☎ 860-8336), next to the Oasis Bar on the strip (see *Nightlife* below), where you can get one-quarter of a succulent rotisserie chicken and a healthy serving of tasty potatoes for about RD$70.

DINING PRICE CHART	
Price per person for an entrée, not including beverage or tip.	
$	Under US$2
$$	US$2-$10
$$$	US$10-$20
$$$$	Over US$20

Also in Western Juan Dolio

Bahía del Duque Marina Club (Calle Central, ☎ 526-1311) $$

A very nautical-looking seaside establishment characterized by prominent blue awnings, this restaurant has an extensive Italian menu including carpaccio, lobster by the pound, and octopus entrées.

El Sueno (Calle Central, ☎ 526-3903) $$

The longest-standing restaurant in western Juan Dolio, El Sueno has earned a solid reputation for consistently fine Italian food and service. Open-air seating in a lush garden setting and reasonable prices make it the kind of place that patrons like to return to again and again.

La Grotta Azzura (Calle Central, ☎ 526-2031) $$

There's not much atmosphere here to speak of – from Calle Central, the restaurant appears nothing more than a small windowless room with a glass door facing the street, though just around the corner of the building is an outdoor setting – but the high-quality pizza makes it a worthwhile stop, and you can get it to go.

Fior di Loto (Calle Central, ☎ 526-1146) $-$$

On most nights, the restaurant at the Fior di Loto Hotel serves up a variety of very good pastas, salads, and *comida criolla*. Once a month, during the hotel's full-moon cultural nights, you'll be treated to Northern Indian cuisine (with recipes gathered by owner-chef Mara Sandri on her frequent trips to the Subcontinent). But if you don't happen to be there then, call the hotel and request an Indian meal at least 24 hours in advance, and Sandri will try to accommodate you.

The Caribbean Coast

In Villas del Mar

Guilia's Café & Sports Bar (Boulevard Villas del Mar, ☎ 526-1492)

Without doubt the most popular eatery in all of Juan Dolio, Guilia's main draw is a giant-screen TV that lures sports fans on big-game nights. Sandwiches, burgers, and lots of cold beer make up the usual sports café fare.

Las Palmeras (Boulevard Villas del Mar, no phone) $$

Though unglamorously located in the center of Plaza Colonial Tropical shopping mall, Las Palmeras' al fresco dining and good pasta, pizza, and international dishes make for a winning combination.

Le Pam Pam (Boulevard Villas del Mar, ☎ 869-0310) $$

This French fish and seafood restaurant across the road from Hotel Playa Real does a wonderful grilled lobster special. Reservations are recommended.

In Guayacanes

Deli Swiss (Calle Central, Guayacanes, ☎ 526-1226) $$-$$$

Run by Walter Kleinert, a retired chef to UN dignitaries (who previously owned a restaurant in Boca Chica "when it was nice"), Deli Swiss is worth a trip to the nearby quiet village of Guayacanes when you want a completely different atmosphere. Kleinert's fresh fish and pasta entrées and desserts are creative both in flavor and presentation. His extensive wine list has won plaudits from *Wine Spectator* magazine, and his Scotch and cigar collections draw businessmen in from Santo Domingo on the weekends, when they puff on stogies, sip single malts, and sit on the patio admiring a gorgeous strip of beach. Deli Swiss is a few miles' drive back west toward Santo Domingo (watch for the prominent road signs announcing Guayacanes).

Nightlife & Entertainment

Juan Dolio is relatively quiet at night except for the **Oasis Bar** along the strip, where you can hear live music on the weekends. On the eastern (Villas del Mar) side, check the **Las Palmeras** restaurant, which presents live music on Wednesday nights with a regularly changing roster of artists. The **Coral Costa Caribe** resort sells passes to unregistered guests for RD$250, which includes admission to its dance club and drinks.

■ San Pedro de Macorís

Orientation

 This industrial port city 40 miles or so east of Santo Domingo isn't much to look at – poverty-stricken and neglected, it's suffered from the lagging fortunes of the local sugar industry and from severe damage by Hurricane Georges in 1998. But San Pedro is of interest to avid baseball fans who like to pay homage to the place that has produced a remarkable number of Major League stars such as Sammy Sosa, Rico Carty, George Bell, Julio Franco, Joaquín Andujar, Juan Samuel, and Tony Fernandez. (While known as the "City of Shortstops," its output has embraced every position of the game.)

To take in a *beisbol* game (best in winter, November through January, when professional Dominican League games are played that often feature Major League players), head to the Estadio Tetelo Vargas (Av. Circunvalacion and Carretera Mella), located in the center of town along the main road from Juan Dolio. The stadium is home to the Estrellas Orientals (the Eastern Stars), who have been playing in San Pedro for nearly a century. Local fans take the game seriously, and you can expect raucous crowds cheering on their favorites. Check schedules in the local newspapers (including those in Santo Domingo); tickets cost around RD$100. Games are usually played in the evenings; Major League teams sometimes work out local prospects in the stadium during the day. You can sometimes visit the various training complexes in the area run by Major League and Japanese teams, with a host of young prospects competing in the summer leagues here.

When you're not at a game, you can spend time strolling along the city's engaging Malecón, a wide seaside boardwalk with public beaches and vendors selling various types of tasty street food. The clapboard houses you see from here (and on the outskirts of town) produced many of the Major League baseball stars we know today and who have become local royalty here.

Places to Stay & Eat

In Town

 Howard Johnson Hotel Macoríx (Malecón at Av. Deligne, ☎ 529-2100, fax 529-9239) $$$

This is the best – and really the only good – lodging in town, with 170 rooms, a swimming pool, three restaurants, and a raft of other amenities.

Outside Town

Santana Beach Resort and Casino (☎ 412-1010, fax 412-1818, www.santanabeach.com, h.santana@sympatico.ca) $$$$

If you want to combine your baseball watching with the all-inclusive resort life, the sprawling Santana Beach resort, located about three miles east of town, has a setting on a nice stretch of beach, with 400 rooms and a casino. The shallow waters are good for kids to swim in, and lots of watersports are available, ranging from windsurfing to diving. Restaurants are mostly buffet-style. Because of the resort's rather secluded location, you should have your own vehicle if you want to spend any time away from it.

Dominican Baseball Invasion

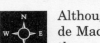 According to a recent survey by ESPN, the cable sports network, one of every seven players in the Major Leagues as of 2004 – about 100 players in all – was born in the Dominican Republic. (The list includes some of the top players in baseball, such as Sammy Sosa of the Chicago Cubs and Pedro Martinez of the Boston Red Sox.) And that number is bound to grow, since nearly one-third of all current minor league players were born in the DR. The Dominicans' astonishing success is attributed to a number of factors: the popularity of baseball in the country, the view of local youngsters that a professional contract is the surest way out of grinding poverty, the nearly two dozen training camps that have been set up here by Major League and Japanese teams, and – not to be overlooked – an abundance of talent and hard work.

■ La Romana

Orientation

Although La Romana, located about 24 miles east of San Pedro de Macorís along Highway 4, is one of the wealthier towns in the area, there's little of interest here for visitors. The main reasons to come are to access the nearby airport or to stay at or visit Casa de Campo, a mega-resort that's one of the finest in the country. You can even bypass the ATMs in town by using those at Casa de Campo (which you can visit even if you aren't a guest).

Places to Stay & Eat

Casa de Campo (☎ 523-3333, fax 523-8548; www.casadcampo.com) $$$$

HOTEL PRICE CHART	
Rates are per room based on double occupancy.	
$	Under US$20
$$	US$20-$50
$$$	US$51-$100
$$$$	Over US$100

This massive 7,000-acre resort complex six miles east of La Romana was built by the Gulf & Western Corporation in the 1970s on the site of a former sugar plantation. (It's now owned by Premier World Marketing.) Probably the most glamorous resort in the entire country, it has hosted such celebrity guests as Elizabeth Taylor, Bill Clinton, Madonna – and Michael Jackson and Lisa Marie Presley on their wedding night. Home-grown fashion designer Oscar de la Renta maintains one of the 150 private villas here, and the 300 luxurious hotel rooms, mostly situated within two-story casitas, are set amid manicured grounds and gardens.

The "absolutely fabulous" amenities include a private airstrip, polo grounds, three 18-hole golf courses designed by Pete Dye (including the famous oceanfront "Teeth of the Dog"), and a skeet-shooting course that ranks among the best in the world. Both the golf courses and skeet-shooting course are open to the public. Of course, all the usual resort amenities you might expect are here, too, only more so: multiple swimming pools (including a dual-level pool), day and night tennis courts, a highly regarded dive center, horseback riding, 10 restaurants, children's programs, and cabaret entertainment among them. Full meal plans are available, but you do have to pay separately for several of the more high-end activities. Grounds are so large that guests have to be shuttled around the property (including to the beach), unless they have a car at the resort.

The resort's Playa Minitas, while relatively small, is still a gorgeous stretch of sand. Among the watersports available here are snorkeling at the offshore coral reef, windsurfing, paddleboating, and sailing. You can also make arrangements to go deep-sea fishing for marlin and kingfish, and make diving excursions to Isla Catalina, which lies a bit over a mile south of La Romana surrounded by the turquoise waters of the Caribbean.

Adjacent to Casa de Campo is **Altos de Chavon**, a shopping, dining, entertainment, and museum complex that does a booming tour-bus business.

Situated on a hilltop overlooking the Río Chavon gorge, it's built to resemble a centuries-old Mediterranean village, complete with cobblestone streets and Italianate villas. Altos de Chavon features both high-quality artisans' and jewelry shops and lower-brow souvenir shops – some find

The Caribbean Coast

the overall effect kitschy, others charming. Even if you're among the former, it's worth a visit to check out the Museum of Archaeology here, which displays Taino artifacts collected in the area.

> **Tip:** The 5,000-seat open-air amphitheater at Altos de Chavon is a pleasant place to catch a stage show or concert (Julio Iglesias and Carlos Santana are among big name performers who have appeared). You'll find numerous restaurants scattered throughout the complex as well, most run by Casa de Campo and serving cuisines ranging from Italian to Mexican.

Rancho Cumayasa Eco Resort (Km 14, Highway 4, ☎ 757-0535, fax 757-3150; ranchocumayasa@yahoo.com) $$

This set of 10 cabins run by an Ecuadorian man and his American-educated daughter is a real find. Located near Cuevas de las Maravillas (see *Eco-Travel*, above) on a site once occupied by Tainos, it's about nine miles (watch for the 14-kilometer road marker) west of La Romana. The camp is ideally situated on lush, bougainvillea- and flamboyant-filled grounds alongside the Cumayasa River (whose brackish water means no mosquitoes – though the beds are equipped with mosquito netting, just in case).

Rates include all meals – Rancho Cumayasa is known for its freshly prepared Dominican dishes – and the use of canoes and paddleboats for exploring the river. The Hurricane House, a novelty structure on the property where water runs uphill and everything is topsy turvy, is a big draw for kids, while couples can dance to merengue or bachata music by the riverside plaza. Horse-drawn wagon rides or horseback rides though the countryside are available for an extra charge.

> **Inside advice:** Even if you're not staying at Rancho Cumayasa, you can make use of the facilities by purchasing a day pass for US$25 per adult, US$18 per child aged six to 12. The pass includes an hour's horseback riding, use of canoes and paddleboats, admission to Hurricane House, and lunch.

■ Bayahibe

Orientation

 Ten years ago there wasn't much to this tiny seaside fishing village. Independent travelers who did come here took rooms in the homes of local families or in a handful of cabañas to use as a base camp for exploring the wildlife preserve and extensive cave system in nearby Parque Nacional del Este (see *Eco-Travel*, above). Upscale hotel chains have since discovered the gorgeous coastline of calm waters and powdery white sand, and today the area has been divided into two parts: **Playa Bayahibe** – which remains a haunt for independent travelers – and **Playa Dominicus**. The latter, about three miles east of Playa Bayahibe, has been cleverly renamed by developers and marketed to a more upscale crowd as an all-inclusive resort haven. As you might suspect, Playa Dominicus has the better beach of the two.

Either spot will almost certainly result in what locals like to call a "no hassle" vacation. Those who come here for diving may prefer to stay in Playa Bayahibe, where Casa Daniel (see *Places to Stay*, below) runs well-organized trips to Isla Catalina across the bay (see *Diving and Snorkeling*, above).

FBI FREDDY

While the fact that the all-inclusives have taken over most of the playa has stirred up a bit of resentment from the locals, at least one resident, a toothpick-thin Dominican man who bills himself as FBI Freddy, has decided to fight back with a bit of humor. Freddy walks the beach wearing a ridiculously exaggerated security guard's uniform that comes complete with a toy gun tucked in his waist, a hibiscus flower above his name tag, and handcuffs that look more like hula hoops against his thin frame. Freddy reminds beachgoers that he's there to keep them safe from the "bad element" and implores them to stay safe during his frequent beer breaks, which he announces through a bullhorn. There's method to his madness: His aim is to poke fun at the absurdity of the security officers who patrol the beaches of the resorts, keeping locals away (even the water is cordoned off so Dominicans can't swim among resort guests). Freddy is a personification of the good-humored Dominican saying: "*Al mal tiempo; buena cara*," which means "maintain a good face even in bad times." And he puts on the best show in all of Playa Dominicus.

If you do choose to spend your time in Playa Bayahibe, take a good stash of cash with you, since there is no ATM in the area and most of the hotels and restaurants do not accept credit cards. But you can always hop a *guagua* to Playa Dominicus, where you'll find a Banco Popular ATM and Western Union across from the Viva Dominicus resort. On the same street are also two *casas de cambio*.

More downscale Playa Bayahibe, meanwhile, does have a medical center and pharmacy (just behind Cafeteria Julissa), and a laundromat, Lavanderia Nueva Generacion. And most of the restaurants and cabañas in Playa Bayahibe have installed at least one computer terminal with Internet access. You'll find a few more terminals (as well as international calling and fax service, if you need it) at B@y@hibe Telecom in the brightly painted house across from the parking lot.

The all-inclusive resorts have usurped most of the shoreline. Everybody else is forced to use a small strip of sand just east of the Casa del Mar resort in Playa Bayahibe or another short strip of Playa Dominicus between the Coral Canoa and Viva Dominicus resorts, known as Playa Libre (Free Beach). Playa Libre must accommodate both the local population and guests of the independent hotels who have not purchased beach privileges from Viva Dominicus.

> **Directional info:** To get from Playa Bayahibe to Playa Libre, follow the footpath leading along the water from behind Casa Daniel. At some point it may become impassable, however, if it rained the night before. If so, turn south a few yards and then make the 50-minute trek over the rocky bluffs – but be sure to have good walking shoes. The walk is considerably longer and more difficult than the regular path.

Getting Here & Around

 If you're arriving in Bayahibe via Aeropuerto La Romana and staying at one of the resorts, your package will most likely include airport transfers. If you're going the independent route you can rent a car at the La Romana airport at the desks inside the terminal or take a taxi from the airport for about US$25.

Guaguas are available from Santo Domingo to La Romana (RD$65); you'll then need to transfer to another *guagua* for Bayahibe (when you get to La Romana, ask the driver to drop you at the *"parada para Bayahibe"*). *Guaguas* stop both in Playa Bayahibe – watch for Cabañas Trip Town on your right as you enter the village – and in Playa Dominicus by the Eden Village complex. The fare from La Romana is RD$25 for either trip.

Driving from Santo Domingo or other points east, just follow the well-marked Highways 3 and 4 in the direction of La Romana. About eight miles east of La Romana, road signs will lead you southeast to Bayahibe. The entrance to Bayahibe is hard to miss: there's a 20-foot-high steel arch bearing the town's name as well as advertising for the various tourist facilities in the area.

Places to Stay

Casa del Mar (Playa Bayahibe, ☎ 221-8880, fax 221-2776; www.sunscaperesorts.com) $$$$

This 568-room all-inclusive resort sits on the choicest stretch of Playa Bayahibe. You'll find watersports, a pool, beach bar, three restaurants, a disco, and horseback excursions here. All rooms are spacious, well-appointed, and feature poolside terraces or balconies. Though it advertises itself as being located in La Romana, it's actually in Playa Bayahibe.

Casa Daniel (On the footpath to Playa Dominicus, ☎ 833-0050, fax 833-0010; www.casa-daniel.de, casa-daniel@gmx.net) $$

These very basic accommodations with community bathrooms are mostly intended for divers, but could be a saving grace in a pinch since none of the other budget hotels in the Playa Bayahibe area accept credit cards. It's about a five- minute walk away from the center of town along an unlit footpath (there are lights on nights when there's a game at the nearby baseball diamond, however). Since crime against tourists is virtually non-existent in Playa Bayahibe, the unlit path isn't a real problem.

Hotel Bayahibe (Calle Principe, ☎ 707-3684, fax 556-4513) $$

This is an extremely good deal considering the location of this hotel – right in the center of town and just a short walk to the beach – and room amenities such as balconies, TV, and hot-water showers. Rooms are fan-cooled.

Cabañas Trip Town (Calle Principe, ☎ 833-0082, fax 883-0088); Hotel Llave del Mar (Calle Principe, ☎ 883-0081, fax 224-6270); Cabañas Francisca (Calle Principe, ☎ 883-0016) $

Nothing really distinguishes these three lodgings from each other. All are run by local families, all are located within close proximity on Calle Principe, and all offer similar accommodations: squeaky-clean rooms with fans and hot-water showers. They even look the same from the outside except for variations in the exterior paint.

Places to Stay in Playa Dominicus

Even though some of the resorts listed below bill themselves as located in La Romana, they are actually in Bayahibe.

Iberostar Hacienda Dominicus (☎ 888-923-2722, www.iberostar.com, reservations@iberostar-hotels.com)

Opened in 1991, this 496-room resort spreads back from the beach with two buildings surrounded by tropical gardens. Four restaurants include one buffet-style and three à la carte (featuring Mexican, Japanese, and steak). Kayaking. catamaraning, sailing, windsurfing, and swimming in

HOTEL PRICE CHART	
Rates are per room based on double occupancy.	
$	Under US$20
$$	US$20-$50
$$$	US$51-$100
$$$$	Over US$100

three pools are among water activities; you can get your scuba certificate here, too, for an extra charge. A kids' club watches over children aged four to 12.

Viva Dominicus Beach and Viva Dominicus Palace (☎ 800-898-9968 or 686-5658, fax 687-8583, www.vivaresorts. com) $$$$

The all-inclusive Viva Dominicus Beach, with 530 rooms, and Viva Dominicus Palace, with 330 rooms, are situated next to each other on a beautiful stretch of beach, with guests of one able to share facilities of the other. (Guests of some other nearby hotels also have beach privileges here.) Windsurfing, canoeing, sailing, snorkeling, and introductory diving are among watersports included in the rates; guests can earn their scuba certification for an extra fee. The "Beach" property has three fresh-water pools, two theaters (one for live stage shows, the other for movies), a disco, a supervised kids' club, and four restaurants, two buffet-style and two à la carte (of the latter, one is Mexican, the other a pizzeria). The "Palace" property has a full service spa and fitness center.

El Eden Village (Avenida La Laguna, ☎ 688-1856, fax 688-2485; www.santodomingovillage.com, edencxa@hotmail.com) $$$

This all-inclusive vacation village spread across a full block offers three types of accommodations: two-bedroom villas, two-bedroom apartments, or basic rooms with king-size or double beds. All are cooled by air conditioning and feature both hot and cold showers. A pizzeria adds variety to the cuisine, which includes burgers and local dishes, and the karaoke bar and billiards table make it a lively place in the evening hours.

Residencial Boca Yate (Calle Principe, ☎ 688-6822, www.hotel-bocayate.com) $$$

This is by far the best option for independent travelers in upscale Playa Dominicus. The small, basic but tastefully decorated rooms here are clustered around a well-maintained courtyard and have loads of charm. Showers are cold water and rooms are cooled by fans, but the good Italian restaurant, lively bar, and short walk to the beach helps make up for those shortcomings. The hotel also runs excursions to nearby attractions.

Cabaña Elke (Calle Principe, ☎ and fax 689-8249; www.viwi.it) $$

While not nearly as charming as Residencial Boca Yate, these basic cabañas are slightly more upscale, with hot-water showers and an onsite swimming pool. A screened-in sitting area is another nice touch, even though it faces the wall of the Viva Dominicus complex across the road. Guests here also have access to the Viva Dominicus beach and restaurants. Additional amenities include a bar and an Italian restaurant.

Places to Eat

 There aren't many options for dining out in Playa Dominicus beyond the all-inclusives. Both Cabaña Elke and Residencial Boca Yate have small restaurants that serve mainly Italian cuisine. Playa Bayahibe, on the other hand, has a number of restaurants lining the waterfront along Calle

DINING PRICE CHART	
Price per person for an entrée, not including beverage or tip.	
$	Under US$2
$$	US$2-$10
$$$	US$10-$20
$$$$	Over US$20

Segunda and Calle Principe. Unless you have a car, though, you will have a hard time finding transportation between the two sides after dark, when *guaguas* stop running.

Big Sur Café (Calle Principe, Playa Bayahibe, ☎ 248-2462) $$

The Big Sur is hard to miss, just across from the parking lot for the boats to Isla Saona, where upwards of 20 tour buses are parked at any given time during the day. In addition to the customary lobster and fish you'll find fajitas on the menu here. Prices are geared toward the heavy tourist traffic in the area, so expect to pay a bit more for the location.

Casa del LangosTa (Calle Principe, Playa Bayahibe, no phone) $$

Overlooking the bay, this is a pleasant choice for lobster as well as good Italian dishes.

Restaurant El Bahía (Calle Principe, Playa Bayahibe) $$

This is an inviting thatched-roof open-sided establishment that opens right onto the water. An extensive menu features meat, poultry, and seafood prepared four ways: *parilla* (grilled), *guisado* (slow-cooked), *encebolla* (smothered in onions), or *frito* (fried). It is one of the few establishments here that accepts credit cards, though only with an RD$300 minimum (which isn't posted anywhere).

Barco Café (Calle Principe, Playa Bayahibe) $

On the east end of the road, this café does a good European-style breakfast and has a popular bar, which was fashioned from a discarded boat that gives the establishment its name.

Cafeteria Julissa (Calle Segunda, Playa Bayahibe) $

While this casual eatery isn't much to look at, you can stop in here for a good cup of strong coffee and cheese-filled empan*adas for breakfast. Lunch is the usual Dominican fare of rice and beans with either chicken or meat for about RD$80. You can get fresh fish here, too, at prices generally lower than in nearby restaurants.

The Caribbean Coast

Nightlife & Entertainment

 Playa Bayahibe doesn't have much in the way of nightlife. Once the sun goes down the streets clear out, except for weekend nights when very loud merengue blaring from the *colmado* on Calle Principe draws a heavy drinking crowd. On the water's edge in the center of town and directly across from Restaurant Casa del LangosTa is a small *comedor* that remains lively day and night with customers waiting for take-out portions of whatever the cook has prepared that day.

More options abound in Playa Dominicus, where the resorts offer high-glitz, albeit kitschy, Vegas-type floor shows and discos spinning Top 40 American tunes. Unless you're a registered guest, though, you'll have to pay a cover charge in the neighborhood of RD$600. Otherwise, head over to El Eden Hotel for free-of-charge karaoke as well as disco, billiards, and slot machines.

■ Boca de Yuma

Orientation

 A small, idyllic seaside village set on the edge of ocean-pounded cliffs with a majestic view of the Caribbean, Boca de Yuma is the kind of place you don't want to tell anybody about. The extremely congenial villagers rarely ever see visitors during the week, except for the few who pass through on their way to Parque Nacional del Este and Cueva de Bernardo (see above). On Sunday afternoons, Dominicans often drive in from La Romana and San Pedro, literally clogging the one little main street on their way to **Café de las Brisas**, an extremely popular dance spot on those days.

In front of the café and overlooking the bluffs is a small park frequented by local families, containing remnants of a wall and cannon that protected this charming hamlet in the days of the conquistadors. North of town, you can visit the **Casa Ponce de León**, the onetime house of one of the most famous of the Spanish explorers. (See *Historic Sites*, above.)

The pleasant and secluded **Playa Borinquen** can be found on the other side of the slip of land jutting out into the sea at the east end of town. You'll have to pay a fisherman about RD$20 each way to row you there (10 minutes), then climb the steep steps up before making the short 15-minute hike to the beach on a well-traveled foot path.

> **Tip:** En route, ask your boat guide to make the quick diversion into the cove (ask him to show you the "*cueva pirata*"). The scenery is stunning and the ride quite peaceful. (Reward him with an additional RD$50 or so for the added hard work.)

Facilities on Playa Borinquen are mostly lacking except for a pleasant local lady who sells cold refreshments from a makeshift stand in front of her modest house at the top of the stairs. To return, you can either ask the boatman to come back for you at a designated time or simply stand on the shore and wave to the other side to indicate you need a pick up. Someone will row over in your direction.

Getting Here & Getting Around

From La Romana, take Highway 4 east for about 40 minutes until you see the sign for Boca de Yuma, then turn southeast and continue for another 11 miles or so until you reach the magnificent bluffs and can only turn either left or right. You also can't miss the bright yellow and green National Park signs, pointing the way to an entrance for Parque Nacional del Este (see *Eco-Travel*, above).

Rental cars are available at La Romana Airport. You can also rent a vehicle from El 28 (see *Where to Stay and Eat*, below) once you arrive, but taxis from the airport are expensive. *Guaguas* also ply the route from La Romana directly to Boca de Yuma.

> **Warning:** If you decide to stay in Boca de Yuma, bring plenty of cash since the closest ATM is in La Romana to the west or Higüey to the north – up to an hour's drive away in either case.

Where to Stay & Eat

El 28 (Calle Duarte, ☎ 476-7680) $$

Named for the psychiatric hospital located at KM 28 on Highway 1 (where patrons of the owner's version of *mamaguana* are purported to end up), El 28 is your one option for accommodations here. The few rooms are basic but comfortable, with air conditioning and hot showers. There's also a pool. The on-site Italian restaurant serves up excellent homemade pasta prepared by the owner's mama.

The Coconut Coast

Best known around the world as "Punta Caña," the Coconut Coast is nothing less than central casting's vision of a Caribbean beach resort. All the superlatives – and all the clichés – are here along this 30-mile stretch of powdery white-sand beaches, swaying palm trees, and crystal-clear blue waters. What's more, the climate is as near-perfect as you can find: year-round sunshine, cloudless skies, and warm temperatures cooled by soft ocean breezes.

Not surprisingly, the beaches are lined by dozens of mega-resorts positioned like dominoes along the sands, which help make Punta Caña both one of the most internationally celebrated corners of the Dominican Republic as well as one of its least "authentic." Located on the eastern tip of the island about 125 miles from Santa Domingo, Punta Caña is virtually a world unto itself – more like an international enclave than an integral part of the country.

With few exceptions, you won't find atmospheric seaside villages here, or much in the way of natural adventures. There are few local restaurants or small charming hotels undiscovered by the masses. Punta Caña is where the masses come to soak up the sunshine, swim in the sea, quaff exotic drinks, fill up on massive (if mostly generic and often bland) buffets, and, for the most part, commune with other tourists. For many Punta Caña vacationers, the most contact they'll have with Dominicans outside the airport is with the waiters who serve them their piña coladas by the pool or the maids who fluff their pillows at night.

Serving the influx are many of the finest accommodations available in the country – some 20,000 rooms and growing – overwhelmingly in all-inclusive resorts. While many, if not most, Punta Caña visitors make the resort life here the focus of their entire stay in the country, there's no law that says you can't use it for re-charging your batteries after a daunting climb up Pico Duarte or a challenging cross-country bike ride – which is exactly what some adventuresome travelers do. The atmosphere at these huge palaces is downright indulgent. Besides the all-you-can-eat buffets and free-flowing drinks, you can expect to find non-stop activities – ranging from beach sports to discos, casinos to Vegas-style entertainment – in a setting that's reminiscent of the Nevada gambling mecca (except that here there are waves lapping the sands).

There is a downside to all the indulgence, however: the potential impact of rapid development on the local environment. Over-use of natural resources has caused some erosion of the very attractions that draw people here, particularly the beaches and offshore coral reefs. Some of the criticisms by environmentalists and a rising awareness of the need to have sustainable programs in place have led many resort and tour operators to begin promoting environmental awareness by educating and training their staffs. Few resorts, however, have gone beyond that to implement real steps toward control, such as investing in reusable resources or – the most obvious but least likely – scaling back on the number of visitors. You may want to keep environmental policies in mind when deciding where to stay. **Green Globe 21** is a worldwide certification program that facilitates sustainable tourism. For more information and guidelines on "green hotels" visit their website at www.greenglobe21.com.

History

 Barely more than 25 years ago, Punta Caña was a mostly deserted stretch of superbly scenic coastline. That all changed when Dominican pilot and businessman Frank Rainieri and New York labor lawyer, environmentalist (and *Earth Times* magazine founder) Theodore Kheel flew over the area searching out locations for possible resort development. That trip eventually led to what became the Punta Caña Group, a coterie of developers that includes not only Kheel and Rainieri but celebrity partners such as designer Oscar de la Renta and singer Julio Iglesias. (These and other luminaries such as Mikhail Baryshnikov have prime beachfront vacation homes at the Punta Caña Resort and Club, one of the first and finest resorts in the area.)

Punta Caña took off as an international destination when Rainieri used his own money to construct a nearby airport, eliminating the need for a long, bumpy bus ride from Santo Domingo. Europeans started arriving in droves by charter flight, North Americans followed later, and today Punta Caña has become one of the hottest destinations in the entire Caribbean, second only to Puerto Plata as an all-inclusive haven in the Dominican Republic.

Festivals

 Each January 21, thousands of religious pilgrims make their way to Higüey's Basilica de Nuestra Senora de la Altagracia to celebrate the **Procession of Our Lady of Altagracia**, the holiday recognizing the country's patron saint. It's one of the largest annual religious processions in the country.

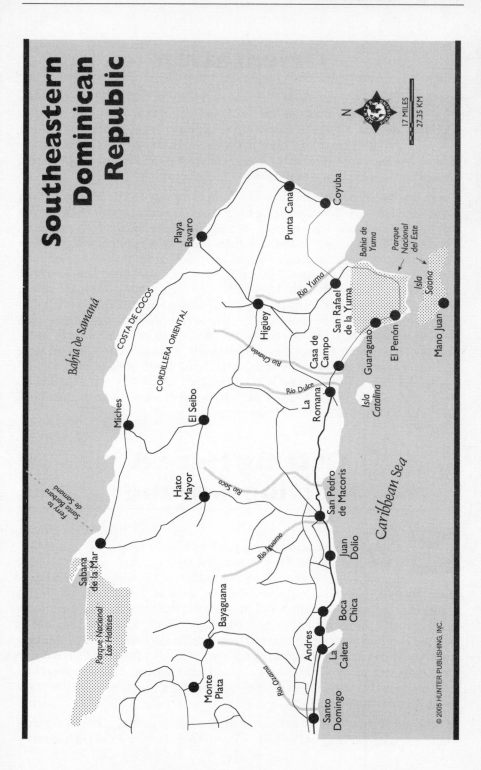

Southeastern Dominican Republic

N

17 MILES
27.35 KM

Punta Cana
Coyuba
Playa Bavaro
Bahía de Yuma
Parque Nacional del Este
Isla Saona
Río Yuma
San Rafael de la Yuma
Casa de Campo
Mano Juan
Guaraguao
El Penón
Higüey
Río Chavón
Bahía de Samaná
COSTA DE COCOS
CORDILLERA ORIENTAL
Río Dulce
La Romana
Isla Catalina
El Seibo
Miches
Río Soco
Hato Mayor
San Pedro de Macoris
Ferry to Santa Bárbara de Samaná
Caribbean Sea
Sabana de la Mar
Parque Nacional Los Haïtises
Río Iguamo
Juan Dolio
Bayaguana
Boca Chica
Monte Plata
Andres
La Caleta
Río Ozama
Santo Domingo

Orientation

The Coconut Coast is one long strip with hubs at either end: Punta Caña at the south end and Bávaro to the north. The seaside village of **Cortecito** – a funky little hangout for independent travelers – lies in between. To the far north lies the village of **Macao**, where miles of deserted beaches and rocky roads await adventurous travelers – and possible future development.

There are two shopping malls away from the resort strip, **Plaza Punta Caña** and **Bávaro Shopping Center** (see *Shopping*, below), where you can browse souvenir shops or sip on a drink while taking in the scenery. **TropiCall**, located in the Plaza Punta Caña, is a comfortable place to make long distance phone calls and enjoy a cool drink. If the lines for your hotel computer access get too long, you can also surf the Internet here. Keep in mind, though, that at US$10 for an hour, Internet prices are high. Also in Plaza Punta Caña is a Western Union office, bank ATM, and several currency exchangers. You are better off changing money here than at your hotel, since the hotels buy dollars at an exorbitantly unfavorable rate (unfavorable to their customers, that is). The main *guagua* station is located closer to the southern (Punta Caña) side of the strip opposite the Palma Real Villas Golf & Country Club. Although *guaguas* do make stops along the beach, you may choose to disembark at the terminal and take a taxi (☎ 522-0617) from there.

Getting Here & Getting Around

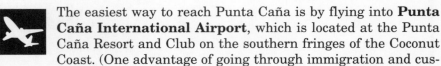

The easiest way to reach Punta Caña is by flying into **Punta Caña International Airport**, which is located at the Punta Caña Resort and Club on the southern fringes of the Coconut Coast. (One advantage of going through immigration and customs formalities here is that you can bypass the chaos at Santo Domingo's international airport.) In summer, Punta Caña's airport hosts more than a hundred international flights per week, and in winter, about 250 per week. Commercial carriers serving Punta Caña include **American Airlines** (with non-stops from New York and Miami), **US Airways** (with non-stops from Charlotte, NC), and **Air France**. US Airways offers very competitive vacation packages, such as a six-day/five-night vacation (with air) for under US$800.

If you visit the Coconut Coast via an all-inclusive package, it's likely that your resort will arrange transportation to transfer you from the airport –

The Coconut Coast

but check with your travel agent to make sure this is included in your package. Otherwise, you will have to take an expensive taxi (average US$25) to your hotel. Car rentals are available at the airport through several reputable agencies including **Avis** (☎ 688-1354) and **Dollar** (☎ 687-5747). Renting a vehicle is the best way to explore the area on your own. Taxis in Punta Caña/Bávaro are extremely expensive – averaging about US$30 one-way – and *guagua* service, while available, is not as extensive as needed to reach many points on the strip.

If you arrive on the Coconut Coast by bus from other parts of the country, you will likely do so via **Expreso Ejecutivo Bávaro** (☎ 682-9670), which leaves daily at 7 am and 4 pm from Juan Sanchez Ramirez and Máximo Gómez in Santo Domingo (RD$160). En route the bus makes brief stops at the stations in San Pedro de Macorís, La Romana, and Higüey, so you can also board at those locations.

> **Inside advice:** It's best to take the morning bus if possible since the afternoon bus doesn't arrive in Punta Caña until 9 pm, when it's already dark. This can be a problem if you're trying to spot your hotel along the dark road and the driver neglects to announce stops. (If possible, sit up near the front and let the driver know your destination in advance.) The bus will let you off in front of your resort's main gate, which means you'll have to carry your luggage to the reception area yourself. If you can't manage that, ask the security guard at the gate to call the front desk for a bellman to come down and meet you (he'll probably arrive via a golf cart). If this sounds like an unglamorous way to arrive at a resort – and you care about such things – you can get off the bus at the entrance to Bávaro (Cruce de Vernon, marked by a police station and Shell gas station) and take a taxi from there.

Adventures

With few attractions available in the area outside the resort complexes, you may find little reason to leave them during your stay. But if the Disney-like resort atmosphere gets to be too much, some of the following activities will offer a change of pace and scenery.

■ On Water

 Virtually every all-inclusive resort along the Coconut Coast features an extensive watersports program, with many of the activities included in the rates. Offerings typically (though not always) include snorkeling, beginning diving lessons, sailing, waterskiing, kayaking, canoeing, fishing, and windsurfing – not to mention the chance to swim in the sea and in multiple pools. Individual resort reviews below provide more details.

- **Group Snorkeling & Waverunning Tours** – You can sign up for these or similar tours at most of the major all-inclusive resorts. (Tour operators often set up displays there.)
- **Bávaro Splash** – Dash along the Bávaro coastline on a two-person waverunner. Participants must be at least 18 years old (US$60).
- *Kon Tiki* – This 60-foot party-raft cruises along the Punta Caña shoreline to a snorkeling spot dubbed "Buccaneers' Reef." Free-flowing rum punch, Caribbean music, lunch and snacks are included (US$53).
- *Marinarium* – This excursion includes sightseeing up and down the Punta Caña coast in a craft that's a cross between a catamaran and a glass-bottom boat. It includes stops for snorkeling, all equipment, lunch, snacks on board, and entertainment (US$75).

■ On Wheels

Free as a Bird Motorbike Tours (☎ 221-6500 ext. 694 or 1-223-8980 (cellular)

If you're at least 21 and a licensed driver, you can set off on an all-day, 75-mile guided tour of the countryside aboard your own 125cc motorbike. The adventurous trips – offered only at Iberostar Hotels – cross over two shallow rivers, through fruit and cocoa fields. A traditional lunch with a Dominican family in included and the day ends with a swim at beautiful Macao beach (US$65).

Outback Jungle Safari (☎ 552-1573)

These tours, most appropriate for families with kids aged 12 and up, will take you through the nearby countryside on the back of an enormous pick-up truck. The tour begins with a visit to a Dominican home and cocoa farm, then ends with a stop at a beautiful beach for boogey-boarding. If your kids are younger than 12, make sure they're strong and independent enough to climb in and out of the truck by themselves and can secure themselves during the rough ride (US$75; US$35 for kids 12 and under).

Parranda Caribena

Drive and sightsee around Punta Caña/Bávaro aboard this yellow school bus transformed into a thatch hut on wheels, while whooping it up to Caribbean music and filling up on rum punch (US$85).

The beach at Isla Saona

Above: Bayahibe

Below: Sailing offshore of the Parque del Este

Above: Las Terrenas

Below: Playa Bonita

The Coconut Coast

Tropical Racing (Bávaro, ☎ 707-5164)

Teenagers, especially, may enjoy this go-kart racing track, located at the first Bávaro turnoff and open daily from 4 to 10 pm. Cost is US$15 for a 20-minute spin.

■ In the Air

Helidosa

Be whisked away to a deserted island, go whale watching, or just enjoy a leisurely tour of the magnificent Punta Caña/Bávaro coastline by helicopter. Contact the tour operator at your hotel for specifics.

■ Independent Family Activities

Punta Caña Lanes (Bávaro, ☎ 959-4444)

You can bowl here on 18 lanes, play billiards, hit the video arcade, or surf the Net. A cafeteria and ice cream shop are on premises. Open Monday to Friday, 4 pm to midnight, Saturday and Sunday, 1 pm to midnight.

Manati Park (Bávaro, ☎ 552-6100, www.manatipark.com)

This sprawling eco-themed – but environmentally controversial – wildlife park exhibits animals including iguanas, caimans, flamingos, tropical birds, snakes, sea lions, and parrots. An exotic array of orchids highlights extensive garden displays. You can also take in a dancing horse show or swim with dolphins here, both for considerable additional fees. The swimming-with-dolphins option has been the most controversial aspect of the park: several of the first group of dolphins here died prematurely, and animal-rights advocates have been critical of their habitat and treatment. Regular admission is US$25 for adults and US$15 for children, which includes hotel pick-up.

■ Tours Out of the Region

You can also sign up at many resorts for full-day tours that will take you beyond the Coconut Coast. If your main destination is Punta Caña and you won't have a chance to otherwise explore the Caribbean Coast or Santo Domingo, these tours could provide a handy way to do so. (Of course, you pay for the convenience.) Prices quoted are for one adult; children 12 and under pay half-price unless otherwise stated. They include transportation to and from the hotel and lunch; some include drinks.

Isla Saona

This idyllic 50-square-mile island is part of the Parque Nacional del Este (see Caribbean Coast chapter), with beaches that are some of the most beautiful in the country (US$75). The tour includes a boat trip to the island along with chances for swimming and sunning.

Altos de Chavon & Isla Saona

Altos de Chavon is a medieval-themed shopping and museum complex that's part of the world-renowned Casa de Campo Resort, a favorite haunt of big-name celebrities (see Caribbean Coast chapter). The tour then stops at Isla Saona (see above) for lunch and sunning on the beach (US$85).

Fly-Fishing Isla Catalina

Barracuda and marlin are just two kinds of fish you might catch on this excursion that takes you off the southeastern coast near Isla Catalina (see Caribbean Coast chapter) for some serious deep-sea fishing (US$90).

Santo Domingo City Tour

Colonial Santo Domingo is the focus of this tour to the country's capital, including visits to the first cathedral in the New World, the ruins of the first university and the first hospital, as well as the home used by Christopher Columbus' brother Bartholomew, Santo Domingo's first governor (US$60).

■ Cultural Excursion

About an hour's drive west of the Coconut Coast, the city of **Higüey** makes an interesting daytrip if you have your own vehicle. While most of the city itself is concrete sprawl, Higüey has a huge draw in the unusual **Basilica de Nuestra Senora de la Altagracia**, whose enormous spire dominates the city's skyline. Variously viewed as a masterpiece – or monstrosity – of modern architecture, it's well worth a look to decide for yourself.

Each January 21, one of the country's largest religious processions takes place in Higüey, the Dominican Republic's equivalent of a holy city. Thousands of Catholic pilgrims make their way to the basilica to pay homage to what they believe are the miraculous healing powers of the Virgin de la Altagracia, the country's patron saint. The faithful wait in line for hours to visit with Tatica, as she is called, where they pray to her portrait enclosed in a glass case. The story goes that the 13 x 18-inch 16th-century portrait of the Virgin Mary gazing at baby Jesus arrived on the island sometime around 1502 and was eventually donated to the parish in Higüey. Originally enshrined in the Iglesia San Dioniso just off the parque central, it was moved in 1971 to what was then the newly built basilica. The gold and silver tiara above the image was placed there by Pope John Paul II during a visit in 1979.

After visiting the basilica, **Don Silvio Grill** (Gral. Santana 20, ☎ 544-4309) is a good open-air place to enjoy a tasty local lunch. If you're traveling with kids you might want to head over to the "Boulevard," also known as Calle Duarte, where you can enjoy simple take-out while the tots romp around the little playground. Not far from Don Silvio's, **La Nancy Bar** (Agustin Guerrero, 50), a popular watering hole, is an entertaining place to cool off with a cold Presidente beer and shoot the breeze with some very colorful characters and the *motoconcho* drivers waiting for fares under the shady tree out front.

Shopping

Bávaro Shopping Center & Plaza Punta Caña. You can hop any *guagua* plying the road up and down the Punta Caña/Bávaro strip to Bávaro Shopping Center, an open-air mall near the Fiesta Palace Resort where you can wander around the shops and haggle with super-eager store clerks. Directly across the street is the somewhat more charming Plaza Punta Caña, a marketplace with rustic stalls and open-air environment. The clerks tend to be just as enthusiastic as at Plaza Bávaro, and they all sell the same kitschy souvenirs. Bargaining here can be part of the fun.

Fabrica de Sillas de Montar Rondon (Calle Agustin Guerrero, 41, Higüey, ☎ 554-3276). This low-key, family-run business has been churning out beautifully hand-crafted riding saddles from the same modest location in Higüey for the last 60 years. The young man currently running the store has been hanging around the shop since before he could walk and is now carrying on the family tradition.

Bases for Relaxation

With packages typically including room, entertainment, all meals and drinks, often even airfare – usually at very competitive prices – the Coconut Coast's all-inclusive mega-resorts can be an extremely attractive value. Owned by various international (mostly European) chains, they're able to attract the kind of volume necessary to offer deep discounts and keep the customers flowing year-round.

While there's a certain cookie-cutter quality to many of the resorts (which in turn resemble many other such resorts found in tropical locales around the world), the level of amenities does vary. One small example: "All-you-can-drink" might mean no-frills local brands versus a good premium label. More significantly, the quality of food can differ quite markedly, room service may or may not be part of the package (if this is important to you), and the resort may place limits on which of its restaurants you can dine in – you may be limited to the buffets, for example, and have to pay extra if you want to eat in the à la carte restaurants.

You'll also find variations in distance to the beach, the amount of English spoken by the staff (this can be more of a problem in resorts that cater mainly to say, Germans or French), and the types of activities emphasized – some being stronger on watersports, for instance, others on entertainment. Sometimes there may even be significant differences within the same chain or even within the same resort complex – as in the case of the five adjoining Barcelo hotels all marketed under the name "Barcelo Bávaro Beach Resort" (see below).

Putting such individual differences aside, however, you can be pretty sure you will enjoy the types of settings their brochures invariably promise: "spectacular white-sand beaches" and "lush tropical gardens" among them. You can also expect a well-appointed room with air conditioning and cable TV, an enormous pool or two (or more), numerous restaurants, often a theater and disco, boutiques, maybe an on-site casino – and more than enough staff to cater to your every whim (assuming it's legal). As one chain touts, these complexes do offer literally "almost everything under the sun."

To get the best deals, check with tour operators or a travel agent. Individual hotel or chain websites are good places to check for last-minute deals. While all fall into the $$$$ price category, keep in mind that all or most of your food and entertainment is included, which can amount to spectacular values.

Barcelo Bávaro Beach Resort (☎ 686-5797 or 800-227-2356 in US and Cañada; fax 656-5859; www.barcelo.com, sac5@barcelo.com)

This mega-resort complex operated by Barcelo Hotels and Resorts consists of five adjacent hotels – one five-star property (the **Bávaro Palace**) and four four-star properties (the **Bávaro Beach**, the **Bávaro Caribe**, the **Bávaro Golf**, and the **Bávaro**

Casino). Stretching along a mile and a half of white sand beach on Playa Bávaro, and with nearly 2,000 total rooms, it's the largest resort complex on the Coconut Coast. Differences in the properties lie largely in where the hotels are situated – their proximity to and views of the beach, gardens, or golf course, for instance. (The Bávaro Palace, the newest and most expensive, has a prime beach location.)

Bávaro Palace

All the hotels are connected by a mini-train system and share a wealth of facilities, including 14 restaurants, 16 bars, nine tennis courts, and five pools, some reserved for children or adults only. The two largest hotels, the Bávaro Palace and Bávaro Beach, have about 600 rooms each, followed in descending order by the Bávaro Caribe, Bávaro Casino, and Bávaro Golf. Rooms all have tropical décor and balconies or terraces; 1,600 rooms are on the beach, while the rest are a five- to 10-minute walk away.

You can be active from sunup long past sundown here. There are three watersports centers, one specializing in dinghy sailing, another in windsurfing, and a third offers kayaking, water-skiing, scuba diving, reef snorkeling, glass-bottomed boat tours, and fishing trips (some of these activities cost extra, however). Also not included in the "all-inclusive" rates are greens fees at the 18-hole, par 72 golf course, except for guests at the Palace, who get three free rounds per week. Nor are all 14 restaurants included – though the nine that are (12 for Palace guests) may be enough to satisfy most tastes. Nightly entertainments include a casino, three discos, three theaters, and the Tropicalisimo Show, a Caribbean review. Some entertainments are also staged on the beach.

Barcelo Villas Bávaro Beach Resort (Playa Bávaro, ☎ 221-8555, fax 221-8556, www.barcelo.com)

This beach resort complex consists of three more Barcelo properties, known as **Barcelo Villas Bávaro**, **Barcelo Bávaro Village**, and **Barcelo Bávaro Ocean**, all situated next to each other along Playa Bávaro. The three properties total 632 rooms, with Bávaro Ocean the smallest (156) and Villas Bávaro the largest (262). There's not much to distinguish among them, and all three share the same facilities. Those include five restaurants (three buffet, one à la carte, and one beach grill), several bars, a wide variety of watersports activities (windsurfing, dinghy sailing, snorkeling, kayaking and more), three tennis courts, three pools (one for kids), and lots of entertainments, ranging from dancing to parties to glitzy live stage shows with Caribbean themes. You can count on round-the-clock activity here for both kids and adults – much like a cruise ship on land. Rooms are decorated in tropical style with balconies and terraces and are situated in villas or two- and three-story buildings.

Breezes Punta Caña Resort, Spa & Casino (☎ 412-8782 or 877-467-8737, www.superclubs.com)

The largest resort in the SuperClubs chain, the Breezes Punta Caña offers up 735 rooms and suites with balconies or terraces, with views of ocean, gardens, or the free-form Olympic-size pool. Watersports included in the rates include introductory scuba lessons, kayaking, windsurfing, and sailing at the hotel beach. On land, you can try the rock climbing wall, check out the circus trapeze, play tennis, even ice skate. You have six restaurants to choose from here, including TexMex, Japanese, French, and Italian, as well as an al fresco buffet and a beach buffet. The five bars include a swim-up pool bar and a 24-hour beach bar. A disco features rock music, while the amphitheater stages nightly Caribbean shows and the casino stays open till 3 am. The Miniclub for kids is for ages 4 to 12.

Carabela Bávaro Beach Resort (☎ 221-2728, fax 221-2631, www.vistasolhotels.com, carabela@vistasolhotels.com)

Situated next to the little village of El Cortecito (see page 188), the early-90s vintage Carabela Bávaro has 350 double rooms, 25 split-level family rooms, and 24 junior suites on Bávaro Beach. All rooms have terraces, while junior suites also have Jacuzzis. Three restaurants feature a combination of buffet and à la carte service; theme nights range from Mexican and Chinese to Spanish and Dominican. There are also five bars, two pools, a children's miniclub and kiddie pool, a late-night disco, evening stage shows, and plenty of free watersports (scuba diving and deep sea fishing are extra). It all adds up to a well-run resort.

Catalonia Bávaro (☎ 412-0000, fax 412-0001; www.cataloniabavaro.com, hcbavaro@catalonia.com.do)

Owned by a Spanish hotel chain, Hoteles Catalonia, the Catalonia Bávaro is one of the newest and nicest resorts along the Playa Bávaro, with comfortably spacious and colorful but tastefully decorated rooms, a clean stretch of white sand beach, exceptional landscaping with open-air architecture, a huge pool (with separate kids' pool), and good food served in a variety of theme restaurants including Italian, Tex-Mex, French, and Japanese. There's also an ice cream and crêpe parlor open from late afternoon on, and free snacks and drinks available by the pool all day and in the disco at night. Although the resort has more than 700 units, they're nicely situated around the grounds in some 30 three-story villas. Watersports include catamarans, kayaks, scuba lessons, snorkeling, sailing, and windsurfing. In the evening, you can learn to dance merengue or attend live music and stage shows. There's also a well-managed kids' mini-club here.

Club Med Punta Caña (☎ 888-932-2582 in US, 686-5500, fax 565-2558, www.clubmed.com)

Club Med, a pioneer in the all-inclusive concept, was one of the first resorts in Punta Caña, dating from the early 80s. And it is showing its age a bit compared to the newer resorts up the coast. Still, with 75 acres of gardens and coconut groves and a half-mile-long stretch of gorgeous white sand beach to play on, you won't feel overly crowded here. The curving, bending swimming pool seems to stretch on forever as well. Club Med has more than 500 rooms housed in bungalows, along with two restaurants. Unlike some Club Meds, this one is family-friendly, with an extensive kids' program for ages two to 17 that includes a circus school. And, like all Club Meds, it has something of a summer camp atmosphere, with exuberant "GOs" (staff) leading "GMs" (guests) in scads of potential activities, from salsa dance classes to hip-hop lessons. Windsurfing, kayaking, sailing, and snorkeling are among the watersports options.

■ Fiesta Hotels & Resorts

These three hotels, all owned by the Fiesta chain, are next to each other on Playa Bávaro:

Bávaro Palladium Grand Resort and Spa (☎ 221-8149, fax 221-8150, www.fiesta-hotels.com, bavaro@fiesta-hotels.com)

The most lavish of the three Fiesta resorts, the Bávaro Palladium has 636 rooms in bungalows and villas spread over huge acreage shaded by scores of coconut palms and other tropical vegetation. With a gorgeous white-sand beachfront – complete with coral reef just offshore for snorkeling and diving – a host of water- and land sports, two pools, six restaurants (including beach and poolside eateries), five bars, a casino, a disco, gym, shopping center, and 24-hour medical service, all that's missing is someone to lather on your sunscreen (you'll have to arrange that yourself). And if you tire of the international buffets, Tex-Mex food, and pizza at this resort, you can head over to the other two Fiesta resorts (see below) to try out their restaurants and bars, all included in the rates.

Fiesta Beach Resort & Spa (☎ 221-3626, fax 221-3832, www.fiesta-hotels.com, bavaro@fiesta-hotels.com)

Much smaller than the Bávaro Palladium Grand, the Fiesta Beach has 327 double rooms and a dozen junior suites, set amid coconut palms and tropical gardens. There are three bars and two restaurants here, one Italian and the other with international cuisine and Caribbean specialties. (You can also dine at the other two Fiesta resorts.) Watersports include windsurfing, kayaking, and catamaran sailing. Or you can lounge around a big pool, play tennis, or hit the beachside spa with gym, sauna, and steam baths. Entertainment for all ages flows both day and night, with a supervised club for kids and a disco and casino for adults.

Fiesta Palace Resort & Spa (☎ 221-0719, fax 221-0819, www.fiesta-hotels.com, bavaro@fiesta-hotels.com)

The smallest of the three Fiesta resorts, the Fiesta Palace has 264 double rooms and eight junior suites set in villas surrounded by gardens. If the three restaurants here – an international buffet, a Mediterranean à la carte, and a beach/poolside grill – aren't enough, guests have dining privileges at the other two neighboring Fiesta resorts. And if the proximity of water makes you thirsty, you can swim up to the pool bar or visit two other bars on the white-sand beach. Watersports include windsurfing and kayaking, and there's a beachside spa with sauna, steam baths, Jacuzzi, and gym. The well-supervised children's program, Fort Fiesta, caters to kids ages three to 12.

■ Iberostar Hotels & Resorts

Iberostar Bávaro (☎ 221-6500, fax 688-6186, www.iberostar.com)

 The biggest and best of the Iberostar resort complex – which also consists of Iberostar Dominicana and Iberostar Punta Caña (see below), with which it shares beach and facilities – Iberostar Bávaro has 590 comfy junior suites spread over 74 two-story bungalows. You'll find all the usual resort amenities here, from palm-fringed Playa Bávaro to a big swimming pool, a spa and fitness center, entertainment center, separate commercial center with casino, disco, and shops, and a collection of restaurants and bars. Dining options range from steak house to Mediterranean to Japanese, though the quality and variety of the food doesn't match that of some other area resorts. Kids ages four to 12 have their own mini club, mini pool, mini disco, and mini shows – sorry, kids, no mini casino.

Iberostar Dominicana and Iberostar Punta Caña (☎ 221-6500, fax 688-9888, www.iberostar.com)

Oriented toward families, with lots of supervised children's activities (for ages four to 12) and a separate pool for kids, these adjoining resorts share facilities with each other (the larger Iberostar Bávaro, see above, is nearby). Each hotel has 346 standard rooms and junior suites ensconced in four-story buildings. A buffet restaurant, a daytime beach restaurant, and four specialty restaurants – including Caribbean and Mexican food as well as steak – satisfy most chow hounds. Guests have use of a casino, disco, fitness center, and spa, as well as a beautiful stretch of Playa Bávaro. A few sports activities have additional fees. Service generally wins high marks.

Meliá Caribe Tropical (☎ 221-1290 or 800-336-3542 in US; fax 221-6638; www.solmelia.com, melia.caribe.tropical@solmelia.com)

Technically, this is two hotels – the Caribe and the Tropical – the former catering more to business travelers and conferences (and, among leisure travelers, couples seeking a quieter environment), while the latter is designed more for families, with kids' pool and supervised activities. But for all practical purposes the two comprise one mega-resort, located within a short distance of each other and sharing facilities. A total of 1,044 good-sized junior suites are divided among 44 two-story bungalows, with lush gardens, palms, and landscaping throughout. The beach, Playa Bávaro, is a nice stretch of white sand, while the swimming pools are lavish. No fewer than a dozen buffet-style and à la carte restaurants offer everything from gourmet French cuisine to buffet Mexican dishes. There are nine bars to wash down the food. You can sweat or pound out your over-indulgences in the spa and gym, or get your exercise on the tennis courts or at a nearby golf course, where guests have free play in summer. At night, you can hit the casino or the disco or attend cabaret shows.

Natura Park Eco-Resort & Spa (☎ 221-2626; fax 221-6060; www.blau-hotels.com; hotel.natura@verizon.net.do)

While billing itself as an eco-resort, it's hard to pin down the environmentally friendly aspects of Natura Park beyond the lack of air conditioning in the restaurants (you may want to carry one of those little portable fans to dinner) and the use of biodegradable soaps in the rooms. Still, it does have a lovely and rather isolated natural setting, with acres upon acres of tropical gardens, coconut palms, and mangroves – good for nature walks – and a typically white sand beach along Playa Bávaro (which is plagued by seaweed at times, however). The 490 rooms and 20 suites are good-sized, nicely decorated in island style, and set in 13 two-story buildings, which take up only about a tenth of the total property here. All rooms are air-conditioned and have either balconies or terraces. Since opening in 1997, it's drawn mainly a European clientele, so the staff isn't terribly well-versed in English. But you will find the usual wide variety of watersports, nightly entertainments, a well-stocked health and beauty spa, kids' activities, a swimming pool (with children's pool as well), four restaurants and four bars.

Occidental Allegro Punta Caña (☎ 687-5747 or 800-858-2258 in US and Canada, fax 687-1381, www.occidentalhotels.com)

After closing for renovations, this 540-room resort reopened in 2003 completely repainted, repaired, and refreshed, from room décor to restaurants, swimming pool to garden walkways. (The resort's beach – an exceptional stretch of powdery white sand – didn't need refurbishing, though it does frequently get cleaned by the maintenance department.) Rooms all have private balconies, some with ocean views, and are divided among nine three-story buildings. The six restaurants include a poolside grill, a beach buffet, and another that serves Caribbean specialties; two snack bars and six regular bars round out the eating and imbibing opportunities. Sports included in the rates range from tennis and horseback riding to non-motorized watersports (kayaking, windsurfing, snorkeling) and scuba lessons in the pool. There are supervised activities for kids and nightly entertainment for adults, including free entrance to the Mangú Disco. In sum, you'll find just about all you could ask from an all-inclusive here.

Occidental Grand Flamenco Punta Caña (☎ 221-8787 or 800-858-2258 in US and Canada, fax 221-8790, www.occidentalhotels.com, ohfbav.ventas@verizon.net.do)

Located along a beautiful stretch of Playa Bávaro, this huge resort has 873 rooms and suites and eight restaurants (seven of them included in the rates). There are also three pools and plenty of watersports along the white-sand beach, as well as supervised kids' activities and nightly entertainment for adults. Those who feel a bit like herded cattle in such an environment can check into the Royal Club, a "hotel within the hotel" with 51 rooms and suites. The Royal Club features restricted access and a number of private services not available to the hoi polloi.

Ocean Bávaro Spa and Beach Resort (☎ 221-0714 or 888-403-2603 in US and Canada, fax 221-0814, www.oceanhotels.net, info@oceanhotels.net)

With waving coco palms, sparkling clean white-sand beach, lush vegetation, winding walkways, thatched-roof buildings, and flamingos strolling the grounds, the Ocean Bávaro fulfills all the fantasies of a prototypical tropical resort. You can choose among 739 rooms and suites here, as well as three swimming pools and a variety of watersports activities: beginning scuba lessons, windsurfing, sailing, snorkeling and kayaking among them. Also part of the all-inclusive package here are five à la carte restaurants (including Mexican, Brazilian, and seafood) and three buffets – along with two snack bars, one open 24 hours. You may need the late-night snacks to fortify you for choosing among 14 different evening shows, a disco, or five bars.

Paradisus Punta Caña (☎ 687-9923, fax 687-0752, www.solmelia.com, paradises.punta.cana@solmelia.com)

Owned by Spain's giant Sol Meliá hotel chain, the Paradisus Punta Caña is five-star quality and service all the way, with the operative theme of "the more, the better." The 1996-built resort sports 542 spacious suites (each with recently refurbished island décor and balcony or terrace) spread out among nearly three dozen bungalows, surrounded by tropical gardens and bordering a mangrove forest. There are also 11 restaurants, ranging from Spanish to Japanese, French to Mexican, with plenty of options for grilled seafood and local specialties. You'll have an equal number of choices of how to spend your time at the beach – another Playa Bávaro white-sand beauty – from kayaking to windsurfing, snorkeling to water bikes and glass-bottom boat rides. When you're tired of that, you can head to an enormous pool, four illuminated tennis courts, a fitness center, horseback riding facilities, casino, theme dinners, nightly shows, merengue dancing classes, and six bars. And oh yes, a nice big bed when you're ready to collapse at night.

Punta Caña Resort and Club (☎ 888-442-2262 or 959-2262, fax 687-8745, www.puntacana.com, reservas@puntacana.com)

With three miles of white sand beach, a championship golf course designed by P.B. Dye, and its own marina and airport (now used by everyone else in the area), the Punta Caña Resort and Club is one of the classiest along the Coconut Coast. Its 420 rooms are located in three-story buildings or villas along the ocean or surrounded by gardens; some villas were designed by resort resident Oscar de la Renta. Eight restaurants range from formal to casual (only breakfast and dinner are included in the rates, however). Besides golf – greens fees are additional, though discounted for guests – activities include swimming in two pools, scuba diving, tennis, horseback riding, windsurfing, snorkeling, sailing, kayaking, and waterskiing. There's a kids' club and a petting zoo here, too.

Punta Caña, designed as a low-density resort, prides itself on its environmental awareness. Its co-developer, Frank Rainieri, is president of the Punta Caña Ecological Foundation and chairman of the Caribbean Association for Sustainable Tourism. The resort practices recycling and irrigates its gardens with purified wastewater. The Punta Caña Nature Reserve, which harbors a variety of plants, birds, and fresh-water springs, begins at the resort's beach and is open to guests for nature walks.

Riu Hotels and Resorts (☎ 888-666-8816 in US, 866-845-3765 in Canada, 221-7575, fax 682-1645, www.riu.com)

Five Riu resorts with a total of 1,800 rooms occupy a spectacular stretch of sands in the northern reaches of Playa Bávaro. **Club Hotel Riu Bambu** is the newest, biggest, and most luxurious of the chain, with 560 rooms. **Hotel Riu Melao** is the smallest with 244 rooms, while the **Hotel Riu Naiboa**, **Hotel Riu Palace Macao**, and the **Hotel Riu Taino** have between 360 and 372 rooms each. While the Bambu is loaded with amenities, the Macao oozes faux-Asian atmosphere, and the Taino is infused with charm, the Melao and Naiboa are less enticing (the Naiboa is a bit of a walk to the beach, while the Melao has fewer facilities than the others). Still, this is a professionally run set of resorts, with perfectly decent food, good service, and lush, well-kept grounds. One possible downside for English-speakers is that, with guests drawn heavily from Germany, not much English is spoken here.

Secrets Excellence Punta Caña (☎ 685-9880 or 866-467-3278, fax 685-9990, www.secretsresorts.com, info@secretsresorts.com.do)

This 446-room Colonial-style resort, surrounded by thousands of palm trees and lying along a white-sand beach, is geared toward romantic couples and honeymooners. (Don't even think of bringing the kids here.) Suites have private Jacuzzis for two, private balconies, and 24-hour room service; some feature special swim-out access to the pools (you can swim right up to the pool bars if you like). Seven restaurants offer a variety of cuisines such as Italian, Mexican, and Chinese, and there's a classy spa where you can indulge in massages, hydrotherapies, and mud therapies. After-dinner activities include live stage shows and a casino.

Sirenis Cocotal and Tropical Resort (Playas Uvero Alto-Macao, ☎ 688-6490, fax 688-7999, cocotal@sirenishotels.com)

Situated on the northern fringes of the Coconut Coast at unspoiled Macao beach, this new resort complex comprises the **Sirenis Cocotal Beach Resort** (with 427 rooms) and the **Sirenis Tropical Suites** (with 389 rooms). Some of the facilities here have daily time limits. Included in the rates are an hour of windsurfing, canoeing, and snorkeling a day, and a half-hour a day of catamaran use. The Jacuzzi and sauna are also on the stopwatch. But you can stay as long as you want in the disco and casino (natch) and you can nibble on 24-hour snacks between buffet or à la carte meals (with Mexican, steak, and seafood among the choices). When your time is up in the Jacuzzi, you can head to separate pools for adults and kids.

Sunscape Punta Caña Grand (☎ 686-9898 or 866-786-7227 in US, fax 686-9699, www.sunscaperesorts.com)

With 346 rooms and eight suites, all with balconies or terraces, this midsize all-inclusive is popular with English-speaking families, who like the American, Tex-Mex and Italian food – strong on snacks like pizza, hot dogs, and nachos. The kids' activities include Disney movies and pool games. Most of the staff speaks English. The dining room air conditioning also wins high praise here, as does the energetic staff, always ready to lead an activity at beach or pool. At night, live entertainment is presented on the resort stage.

And finally, one resort that is not all-inclusive:

Los Corales (Playa Bávaro, El Cortecito, ☎ 221-0801, fax 552-1262, www.los-corales-villas.com, corales@verizon.net.do)

Los Corales is really a small collection of rental villas, rather than a typical Punta Caña resort. It's the place to come if you're looking for some quiet and relaxation away from crowds and the frenetic atmosphere of the all-inclusives, plus a bit of local atmosphere away from the super-luxurious international scene nearby. The first five villas were built here in 1993 by an Italian developer, and 30 more have been added since. The two-floor villas, with separate apartments on each floor, are on or within 100 yards of Playa Bávaro and surround a small plaza with a few shops, a pizzeria, a beach bar and restaurant, another bar that also serves light meals, and an ice cream parlor. Other restaurants are within walking distance. Each apartments has a bedroom, living room, small kitchen, a small balcony or patio, and both ceiling fans and air conditioning. The beach has safe swimming, with a coral reef offshore keeping away big waves and undertow. There's also a small swimming pool. At night, if you want more action, you can head to the nightclubs and casinos at nearby resorts.

■ Nightlife & Entertainment

Disco Mangú at the Occidental Allegro Punta Caña Hotel (see above) is *the* place in Punta Caña for nightlife. If you're a woman traveling alone or with girlfriends, you can expect an inevitable invitation from a local guy to take you there. The dance floor is always jammed with vacationers and locals getting down to American and European tunes as well as Latin and reggae beats. The super-size television screen is a hit with the sports-loving crowd. Cover charge is US$10 for non-guests.

Karaya Club features a colorful Vegas-type show, *Caribe Caliente,* set inside a cave and touting famous performers from the Dominican Republic, Venezuela, and Cuba. The action starts at 9:45 pm, Thursday through Monday. Tickets are US$45.

Jelly Fish (in Bávaro next to the Meliá Tropical employee entrance, ☎ 623-0231) is where Punta Caña/Bávaro hotel staff members go to chill out. There is no merenque or bachata in sight here, just the lucid tones of down-tempo lounge music in a very contemporary setting. The two-story building combines an excellent seafood restaurant on the first floor (you might want to check it out if you tire of the buffets at your all-inclusive) with an old fishing boat serving as a deck over the beach. The top floor offers hammocks and comfortable sofas for quiet conversation.

El Cortecito

On the beach at Cortecito

This funky, tiny seaside village is popular with independent travelers. The commune's only street is about the length of a basketball court, with the beach and Posada de Piedra (Stone House) on one side and Cortecito Inn on the other. On the same side of the street and right next door to Posada de Piedra is the popular Capitan Cook restaurant (see *Places to Eat*, below). At the entrance to El Cortecito is an informal *parada* selling crafts and an assortment of *motoconshistas* looking for fares returning to Punta Caña/Bávaro. Independent travelers also tend to gather here.

You can catch a *guagua* (RD$10) or a *motoconcho* (RD$20) to Cortecito by standing in front of the Fiesta Hotels & Resorts billboard just behind Plaza Bávaro. Cortecito is a short ride from either Punta Caña or Bávaro, but you could miss it if you blink – so stay alert and watch for the turnoff from the main road.

■ Places to Stay

Cortecito Inn (Playa Cortecito, ☎ 552-0639, www.hotelcortecitoinn.com, cortecitoinn@verizon.net.do)

While this hotel is a bit on the shabby side, it's just across the road from the beach and comes with air conditioning, TV, pool, and a restaurant (see *Places to Eat*, below). It is also the fanciest of your two options for accommodations in El Cortecito. Room rates include breakfast. It also offers an all-inclusive dinner for RD$100.

La Posada de Piedra (Playa Cortecito, ☎ 221-0754, www.laposadapiedra. com, laposadapiedra@hotmail.com)

This charming two-story home directly on the beach has two small rooms with a lovely private balcony on the second floor (a very elegant Peruvian woman and her family live below). Four cabañas on the beach offer more rustic accommodations. If you don't need anything too fancy, the posada's beachfront location makes it an excellent choice of accommodation while in Cortecito.

■ Places to Eat

El Capitan Cook Restaurant (Carretera Cortecito, ☎ 552-0645)

With its house specialty of grilled seafood and lobster platter for two – which includes a fabulous salad, dessert, and cocktail for RD$1,000 – this restaurant is wildly popular. Capitan Cook does a bustling business with busloads of group tours from the all-inclusives in Punta Caña/Bávaro, so be prepared for a wait. Reservations are recommended.

Langosta del Caribe Restaurant (Carretera Cortecito, ☎ 552-0774)

If the scene – or the wait – gets to be too much at Capitan Cook's, this is a nice alternative right next door. The menu here features similar fresh seafood and grilled lobster, although the service staff isn't nearly as animated as that at Capitan Cook. For a low-key lunch, this is a fine choice.

Restaurant Le Surcouf (Carreterra Cortecito, ☎ 552-0639)

The none-too-exciting restaurant at the Cortecito Inn has RD$150 nightly dinner specials that include an entrée, salad, and coffee.

The Coconut Coast

Samaná Peninsula, Bay & Surroundings

Poking out like a thumb on the far northeastern corner of the Dominican Republic, away from the crunch and bustle of big cities and tourist hordes, the 30-mile-long Samaná Peninsula is known for its natural beauty and a host of adventurous ways to enjoy it. Its long white-sand beaches, fringed by coconut palms and lapped by turquoise waters, offer remarkable solitude for such picture-postcard settings. Away from the coast, by contrast, the peninsula is mostly wild – a tropical tangle of lush forests, waterfalls, and deep green mountains. Yet there are plenty of creature comforts to ease the hard edges. The main town, Santa Bárbara de Samaná (more commonly known simply as "Samaná"), offers up a range of tourist amenities along the southern tier of the peninsula, while two atmospheric little beach resorts on its north coast, Las Galeras and Las Terrenas, serve up just the right mix of local fishing-village color and ron-y-cola infused nightlife.

Along with its beaches, Samaná is best known for its world-class wintertime whale watching in Samaná Bay and environs, perhaps unsurpassed in the world. Other adventures include scuba diving and snorkeling amid coral reefs, sailing and swimming in the clear ocean waters, and hiking and horseback riding along the beaches and through jungles. But, if you're so inclined, you can also stretch out on a swath of powdery sand, soaking up sun or resting in the shade of a palm tree, gazing at the sky and sea. Nowhere else in the Dominican Republic are the chances for pulsating action and glorious inaction married so effectively.

History

 When Christopher Columbus first landed at Playa las Flechas on the Bahía de Samaná in 1493, the local natives greeted him with a fusillade of arrows ("*las flechas*" in Spanish). That set the tone for another five centuries of somewhat turbulent history. The Samaná Peninsula has been fought over by great powers, used as a lair by pirates, settled by ex-slaves and African refugees, eyed by politicians as a possible naval base and, later, a mega-resort.

The Indians that Columbus first encountered were the Ciguayos, a branch of the Tainos who later joined with the European explorer to help subjugate their fellow tribesmen. That tactical error helped the Spanish remain the predominant colonial power in the region for centuries to come. The Spaniards established the settlement of Santa Bárbara de Samaná in 1756 by shipping over residents of the Canary Islands (off the west coast of Africa) to help populate it. A few decades later, they traded the land off to Napoleon Bonaparte for some French-controlled territory back in Spain. The French, in turn, later were forced out by separate forces of British and Haitians.

Meanwhile, colonial-era pirates infested the area and plundered whichever ships were present and vulnerable at any given time. Until the 19th century, a narrow channel separated the peninsula from the mainland, making it an ideal spot for the small pirate vessels to evade the larger Spanish galleons and French or British merchant ships and warships. (By the time accumulations of sediment fused the channel to the mainland – turning the former island into a peninsula – the pirates had largely faded into the history books.) The pirate heritage is commemorated, among other ways, in the names of islands that frame Samaná Harbor – known, after a 17th-century brigand, as the Banister Cays.

The 19th century brought American influence to Samaná. First to arrive were two shiploads of freed American slaves, who settled in Santa Bárbara de Samaná during the 1820s. Their legacy remains even today in the city's contingent of native English-speaking residents, many of whom still sport English last names. By the 1850s, the powers-that-be in Washington were coveting the area for a naval base. But, after the US Senate rejected annexation of the Dominican Republic, the Americans diverted their interest to Cuba's Guantanamo Bay. Until World War I, that is, when the US occupied the island to keep the Germans from gaining a foothold there.

Today, the Germans are back in Samaná – along with French, Italians, Spanish, British, Swiss, and other Europeans – in the form of hotel and restaurant owners, tour operators, and, of course, the tourists they cater to. Strolling along the waterfront here, you might hear references to *la playa*, *la plage*, *la spiaggia*, and *der strand* – as well as *the beach*.

Yet for all the multicultural mix, the peninsula retains the feel of the Dominican countryside. The grandiose plans of former Dominican President Joaquín Balaguer, who back in the 1970s dreamed of creating one of the world's great resort complexes at Samaná, eventually came to naught. But for independent-minded and adventurous travelers, at least, that's probably all to the good. While the area has certainly become much more developed in the past 15 years or so, Samaná is still remote enough to retain the natural beauty and tranquil charm that make it one of the most alluring corners of the Dominican Republic today.

Festivals

Both Protestant **Harvest festivals** and the Catholic **San Rafael** observance are held in the town of Samaná each fall, ending in late October. Watch for *bambula*, a traditional Dominican dance kept alive mainly on the peninsula.

The **Santa Bárbara Fiesta Patronal** is celebrated in the town of Samaná in early December, with more *bambula* music.

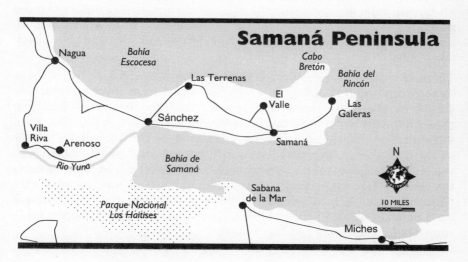

Getting Here & Getting Around

Scheduled domestic flights operated by **Air Santo Domingo** leave from Santo Domingo or Puerto Plata for the small Portillo airstrip near Las Terrenas. The new "international" airport at Arroyo Barril, 10 miles west of the town of Samaná, is operating at limited capacity for Air Santo Domingo domestic flights; the runway is too short to accept large international flights.

The most direct way to Samaná by public transportation is either by **Metro Expreso bus** or **Caribe Tours**. Caribe Tours buses connect Puerto Plata on the north coast of the country to Samaná along Highway 5 via Sosúa and Cabarete, while both Metro Expreso and Caribe Tours connect Santo Domingo daily to Samaná, a 150-mile, four- to five-hour journey over a succession of roads. (Talk of a new highway from Santo Domingo to Samaná is so far just that – but if and when it's built, it should improve the ride.) Both Caribe Tours and Metro Expreso have offices on the Malecón in Samaná. Some travelers also arrive by ferry from the town of Sabana de la Mar, located on the southern edge of Samaná Bay, a potential option for anyone arriving from the eastern part of the country. The 45-minute ferry ride can be choppy at times, however.

Once you arrive, *motoconchos, guaguas*, and regular taxis are readily available, either for travel within towns or between towns on the peninsula. Rental cars can be hired in the towns of Samaná, Las Galeras, and Las Terrenas. If you're planning to drive extensively and explore some of the area's more remote beaches and waterfalls, it's best to rent an all-terrain vehicle, which will allow you to navigate the peninsula's more primitive roads (some barely worthy of the name). Many are little more than rutted paths that require four-wheel-drive vehicles and good shock absorbers.

There are just three paved roads on the peninsula, and only two of those in good condition. Highway 5, which leads east from Puerto Plata, also serves as the main connecting route across the peninsula, running through the town of Sanchez as it heads east to the town of Samaná. Once it leaves Samaná, the same road – now known as Carretera Las Galeras – continues east and then swings north to Las Galeras at the northeastern end of the peninsula. The peninsula's other well-paved road connects the town of Samaná with the resort town of Las Terrenas on the northwestern coast. A third paved, but heavily potholed, road heads north from Sanchez about 11 curvy, hilly miles to Las Terrenas. No direct route connects Las Terrenas and Las Galeras.

Information Sources

■ Tourist Offices

Las Terrenas: Carretera Las Terrenas, ☎ 240-6363

Samaná: Calle Santa Bárbara, ☎ 538-2332

Adventures

■ On Water

Beaches

Along with its palm-covered terrain, the Samaná Peninsula is best known for its spectacular beaches – one of them rated among the best in the world. With most of the finest beaches located along the northern edges of the peninsula, **Las Galeras** is the best jumping-off point for visiting many of them. Several can be reached by the combination fishing boats and informal ferry service based in front of the food kiosks on Las Galeras' main beach (RD$300-400) or by four-wheel bikes – known as quads – that can be rented from **Xamana-Rent-Moto** (☎ 538-2380) on the road running parallel to the same beach. **Rancho Thikis** (☎ 223-0035) runs guided horseback tours to many of the area beaches and other points of interest for around US$40.

The first group of beaches are arranged in geographic order from the town of Samaná heading east and then north up the coastline to Las Galeras.

Beaches Samaná to Las Galeras

■ Playa Las Flechas

Playa Las Flechas (also known as Anacaona) not only serves up sun and sand, but a history lesson, too. According to local lore, the beach is named "The Arrows" after an aggressive encounter between Christopher Columbus and the Tainos who inhabited the area when he arrived; it's believed to be the site of the first confrontation between Europeans and natives in the New World. Today it's a cozy beach that faces Cayo Levantado and is a good place to spend the afternoon after a morning of whale-watching. A small bar and restaurant, called the Anacaona, serves up good Dominican food. (On Friday nights the bar features music and an interesting mix of visitors and locals.) The beach is about three miles east of Samaná and is accessible via a dirt road just behind the Gran Bahía Hotel (see *Places to Stay, Samaná*, below); watch for the "Anacoana" sign. From Samaná the *guagua* ride runs about RD$35.

■ Cayo Levantado

With its gleaming white-sands, swaying coconut palms, and glistening blue waters, this small island – once celebrated in Bacardi commercials as the ideal Caribbean paradise – features the most beautiful beaches in the near vicinity of the city of Samaná. But paradise, in this case, includes sharing the sunshine with hordes of daytrippers, who are ferried onto the island from town daily – and facing constant hassling by vendors, along with tourist-trap food and beverage prices. In short, you can do much better than this at other, less readily accessible beaches on the peninsula. If you do go to Cayo Levantado and want to escape the crowds, look for the short footpath that starts to the right of the ferry dock. The path will lead you to the quieter side of the island, where the beaches are more deserted. To get to Cayo Levantado, you can take a ferry from the docks at Samaná (about US$20 each way), or, from the beach at Las Flechas (just behind the Gran Bahía Hotel on Carretera Las Galeras).

> **Good value:** Less expensive ferries are available in the pueblo of Las Cacaos farther up the *carretera*. Whale-watching tours sometimes include a stop on the island following the main event.

■ Playa Fronton

This spectacular beach on the tip of Cape Samaná, just northeast of Las Galeras, is lined by a seamless stretch of palm trees. While its reef-protected lagoon makes for good snorkeling, a slight undercurrent could pose a danger to inexperienced swimmers. The bigger draw here, however, is the 300-foot rock face rising from behind the palm thick. Several rope routes with various overhangs, ledges, and footholds make this an especially popular spot for rock climbers from across the island. (See *Rock Climbing*, below, for more information.) If arriving on your own, you can reach Playa Fronton by following the directions from Samaná to Boca del Diablo (see *Off the Beaten Path*, above), or by ferry from Las Galeras (unless the waves are too rough).

■ Playa Madama

A small isolated beach with crystal-clear water, Playa Madama is surrounded by interesting rock formations and caves with Taino drawings for exploring. Afterwards, you can buy refreshments and light eats at a beach bar. Reach it in 30 minutes by ferry (RD$300) from Las Galeras main beach or in an hour and a half by horseback (see *Horseback Riding*, below).

■ Playa Cala Blanca

Accessible by a 10-minute walk east along the Las Galeras beachfront to just before the Casa Marina Bay Hotel (see *Places to Stay, Las Galeras*, below), this public beach is blessed with fine sand and calm waters. With its proximity to town and shallow, reef-protected swimming, it's another favorite with families.

■ Playa Galeras

This half-mile horseshoe-shaped beach is remarkably beautiful, especially considering that it lies just off the main road in town. Calm, shallow water makes for good swimming. During your stint on the sand, you might want to grab a bite – the fresh seafood is locally caught – at one of the casual thatched-roof eateries lining the entrance to the beach. Or you can hop on a boat here to reach other area beaches.

■ La Playita

This small sandy beach near town is just a short walk west of Hotel Villa Serena (see *Places to Stay, Las Galeras*, below), and offers excellent reef snorkeling in calm, shallow waters. The safe pool-like environment makes it a great spot for kids to have their first go at donning mask and fins.

■ Playa Colorado

This golden-sand beach, set in lush surroundings, fronts a planned residential community that consists mostly of expats. You're likely to have this quiet beach much to yourself, except for area residents or the occasional visitor who arrives on horseback. (The horseback trip takes about an hour and costs US$40; see *Horseback Riding*, below.) You can also reach it in 20 minutes by boat from Las Galeras main beach (RD$300).

■ Playa Rincón

The prize of the peninsula, and a strong contender for the finest beach on the entire island, isolated Playa Rincón has won plaudits from top travel magazines as one of the world's best beaches. Located at the base of the 2,000-foot mountains at the west end of Bahía del Rincón, whose turquoise waters are crystal-clean, Playa Rincón offers nearly three miles of uninterrupted white sands and lush palm groves – which all adds up to an idyllic backdrop for an island castaway experience. To add to local flavor, Dominican families run makeshift kitchens on either end of the beach, selling excellent grilled fish and lobster dishes. There's also a small waterfall forming a refreshing pool at its base on the west end across from the picnic tables.

You can get to Rincón via a 30-minute ferry ride from Las Galeras main beach (RD$400). You might also hook up with a quad-bike excursion or make the drive on your own. If so, you will need four-wheel-drive to navigate the long, rough, bumpy road comfortably. Get to Playa Rincón via the well-marked route from Carretera Las Galeras near the entrance to town. The total drive usually takes from 45 minutes to an hour.

> **Tip:** Future plans may include a major all-inclusive resort to be built at Playa Rincón, so this beach falls into the "see it now" category.

Samaná Peninsula

Beaches North of Samaná

■ Playa El Valle

Because of its isolation and the rough, hazard-strewn road leading to it, this is a little-visited beach, tucked into a cove that dips down from the north shore. But, assuming you have four-wheel drive, the trip may be worth it just for the gorgeous scenery en route. The beach itself is framed by lush tropical vegetation and a river that runs parallel to it (surfacing from May to August, when tides are lower). Since the beach borders an unprotected reef, you'll often find big waves and rough ocean waters here, which can make it dangerous for swimming. Some people have been caught in the undertow and drowned here, so never swim alone.

To get to Playa El Valle, follow the marked sign just east of the town of Samaná on the road to Las Galeras. Turn left (north) at the sign. You'll have to ford two small rivers along the way, while passing fruit trees, cacao, and cattle farms. The arduous seven-mile drive takes about 30 minutes from the highway with four-wheel-drive; without it, you could get stuck in mud for hours.

Beaches in & Around Las Terrenas

■ Playa Bonita

This gorgeous eight-mile stretch of mostly undeveloped beach caps the west end of Las Terrenas. Development in this area is mostly sprawling beachside homes owned by expatriates, along with a small handful of hotels, and you'll typically encounter few other people. Playa Bonita is easily accessible by foot from Las Terrenas if you walk the length of the beach west until you get to the little footbridge. Cross this and then continue along the path through the trees, taking the road that bears to the left.

■ Playa Coson

Coson is another stretch of beautiful sands, even less populated than Playa Bonita. It begins north of Playa Bonita and continues for another four miles and change before ending at the base of rugged cliffs. You can walk there from town (heading west along the water) in about an hour and a half, or take a *motoconcho*.

Whale Watching

The Bahía de Samaná, part of a marine mammal sanctuary that encompasses the northern and eastern coasts of the Dominican Republic, is one of the best places in the world to go whale-watching. Each winter, from around mid-January to the end of March, some 3,000 to 5,000 humpbacks migrate from the North Atlantic Ocean south to the waters surrounding the DR to mate and give birth.

This is the perfect time to observe the whales at their most active, because breeding season is when the males – as eager to impress females as those beach boys back at the piña colada bars in town – are the most animated, aggressive, and playful. (Humpbacks are known as the most frolicsome of whales, though when it comes to mating, they aren't fooling around.) Opportunities abound to watch them spout, slap their fins, breach (leap out of the water), and lobtail (beat the surface of the water with their flukes, or tail lobes), as the male whales seek to establish their territory next to the females and ward off potential competitors. With the right equipment, which is provided on some whale-watching vessels, you can also hear them sing to attract female mates. (Some critics have described the "singing" as more like moaning, but to the whales it's no less romantic.) You might also spot recently born calves, the result of the previous year's mating (and moaning) season. If you come to the Dominican Republic in winter, you aren't likely to regret making the trip to Samaná for this incredible natural spectacle.

Several companies offer whale-watching excursions from Samaná, mostly on the Bahía de Samaná. You can book daily whale-watching tours through many Samaná area hotels or local travel agencies. **Victoria Marine/Whale Samaná** (Malecón, ☎ 538-2494, kim.beddall@usa.net), run by a Marine biologist from Canada, is the oldest and probably still the best and most environmentally sensitive whale-watching outfit in town. Half-day trips cast off twice daily (9 am and 1:30 pm from Samaná and 9:30 am and 2 pm from Cayo Levantado, an island in the bay; see below) aboard 50-foot motor vessels equipped with bathrooms, snack bars and hydrophones for listening in on the male singers. Adults pay US$45, while children under 10 are half-price.

Alternatively, you can simply venture down to the dock in Samaná and make your own arrangements with one of the independent boat captains who run small excursion boats. While these trips will no doubt be cheaper, you probably won't find the same level of scientific expertise as you would from the organized outfitters. Also keep in mind that boat captains must follow strict rules designed to protect the whales. For example, no more than one large boat and two smaller ones may be in the vicinity of any group of whales at one time, and even then must stay at least 165 feet away (and another 100 feet farther if there's a whale calf in the group). A boat may remain with one group of whales for a maximum of 30 minutes. Boats must also slow down or stop when they encounter whales in the bay, and not permit any passengers to swim with the whales. If your boat captain violates any of these rules, don't be afraid to speak up.

Longer excursions, lasting one week and costing about US$2,500, run up to the Silver Bank Marine Sanctuary, a 1,158-square-mile area, 60 miles north of the peninsula. **Aquatic Adventures** (☎ 954-382-0024,

Samaná Peninsula

www.aquaticadventures.com), based in Florida, runs naturalist-led excursions to the Silver Bank aboard 18-passenger, 120-foot vessels, equipped with hydrophones for listening to the whales sing. You'll have opportunities for "soft in-water encounters" with the whales on these trips. As Aquatic Adventures defines them, they're not scuba diving or aggressive swimming but passive floating at the water's surface in mask, fins, and snorkel, intended to let humans and whales interact in a non-threatening way. No Ahab wannabes need apply.

> **Tip:** To learn more about the whales, you may want to visit the Center for the Conservation and Eco-Development of Samaná Bay and its Surroundings (**CEBSE**), located on Av. La Marina (Malecón) in the town of Samaná (☎ 538-2042, www.samana.org.do), a non-profit organization committed to sustainable tourism in the area. The CEBSE office in Samaná is open to the public and offers free information on the whales such as vital statistics, migration activity, and breeding habits.

WHALE ARIAS

Recent research has shown that humpback whale singing is much more prevalent than previously believed, and that the male whales sing not just during mating season in the Caribbean, but also during spring feeding season back in Atlantic waters off New England. In addition, their singing range is much wider than scientists had known – ranging over eight octaves, from a low bass to a high soprano. Their songs are often highly structured and repetitive, almost like choruses in popular human music, and can last up to a half-hour each – but they sometimes involve improvisation, much like jazz riffs. Along with wooing females, the singing is believed to help establish hierarchies among the males, explaining why they continue to sing after mating season ends. Or, scientists speculate, maybe they just like showing off.

Diving

The north coast of the Samaná Peninsula offers some of the best dive sites on the island for both recreational and experienced divers. The areas around Cabo Cabron near Las Galeras and El Portillo near Las Terrenas feature a mixture of shallow and deep dive sites, including coral reefs, sea caves, tunnels, and, with the right equipment, an opportunity to listen in on singing male whales that frequent the area from January through March.

Two good outfitters, **Dive Samaná** (at Casa Marina Bay Resort in Las Galeras, ☎ 538-0210) and **Stellina Dive Centre** (at the otherwise closed-down Hotel Cacao Beach in Las Terrenas, ☎ 240-6000) organize trips down under to various points around the peninsula.

Of the 23 named dive sites in the area, these are the most popular:

Plaza Helena, a sloping reef with depths of 32 to 48 feet and a bright array of marine life.

Plaza Monica, an advanced 100-foot dive with beautiful coral formations and a variety of big reef fish.

Punta Pidi, a 70-foot-deep reef that drops off to 130 feet and features a beautiful coral landscape.

Bajo de las Pescadores, an 80-foot dive site populated with large coral formations and big fish.

Cabo Cabron, a 150-foot-high cliff off the Bahía de Rincón and the point of the peninsula that juts out the farthest into the Atlantic; it continues downward to depths of 140 feet, with coral-covered walls and caves below, and offers chances to hear whales singing as they migrate south.

Punta Tibisi, another rock cliff that plunges 130 feet into the sea and contains underwater terraces with caves that serve as hideouts for barracudas and sea turtles.

The Tower, a giant rock formation off Cabo Cabron and the most spectacular of all sites on the peninsula (the top of this mostly submerged mountain sticks out about 15 feet above water, but for 165 feet beneath the surface it houses an amazing marine community replete with coral, fans, and sponges as well as lobster, crabs, and a variety of pelagic fish).

Las Ballenas (The Whales), three small islands resembling humpback whales off Las Terrenas, which offer a vast collection of cave and tunnel formations between depths of 30 and 50 feet.

La Catedral, a huge underwater cave popular for its big air pocket.

Fishing

Make arrangements with one of the local boat captains at Las Galeras main beach to go in search of grouper, snapper, and kingfish.

Snorkeling

Snorkeling is excellent in the shallow waters near Las Galeras, especially at La Playita and around Playa de Rincón (see *Beaches*, above).

Dive Samaná (located at Casa Marina Bay Resort, ☎ 538-0210) offers snorkeling excursions in the area.

■ On Foot

Hiking

Hike to the tip of Cape Samaná for a swim at Playa Fronton (see above). The path that leaves from the Boca del Diablo (see *Off the Beaten Path*, above) takes about an hour to the beach.

You can also hike two miles or so to El Limón waterfall from one of the entry points off the road connecting the town of Samaná with Las Terrenas, in lieu of taking a horse there.

Rock Climbing

The top place for rock climbing is Playa Fronton (see *Beaches*, above), on the southeast side of Cape Samaná. A bonus: If someone in your party isn't interested in climbing, he or she can simply enjoy this spectacular stretch of beach. **Caribbean Bike & Adventure Tours** (☎ 571-1748, www.caribbeanbiketours.com) offers rock climbing tours for US$65.

■ On Horseback

Rancho Thikis (Las Galeras, ☎ 223-0035) leads guided horseback rides to Playa Rincón and other isolated beaches around Las Galeras. Prices run about US$40 for half-day trips.

You can also join makeshift horseback or muleback trips to El Limón waterfall run by local residents (see *Eco-Travel*, below).

For horseback riding excursions from Las Terrenas, check with **Rancho La Isabela** (along the beach, ☎ 839-2683).

■ Eco-Travel

Salto de Limón (El Limón Waterfall)

Of the many waterfalls on the Samaná Peninsula, El Limón is the most spectacular. Nestled deep in thick palm forest, it rises 900 feet above sea level, and cascades 150 feet into a deep pool of water. In fact, of all the waterfalls to visit in the entire country, El Limón may have the most alluring combination of beauty, size, prime surroundings, and relative ease of access – though it's still something of an adventure to reach (making it all the more of a thrill when you do). Trails to the falls are lined with giant ferns and huge trees, with rivers and thatched huts adding to the tropical ambiance.

NATIVE & EXOTIC PLANTS

Along the riverbanks and trails to the waterfall you may see native tree species such as juan primero, cigua blanca, uva de sierra, cabirma, and the palma real or royal palm (left). The royal palm, once endangered due to uncontrolled cutting for house construction, is now officially protected in the Dominican Republic. The cigua palmera, a native heron, nests within it.

Cultivated native species commonly seen on treks to the falls include the guanabana or soursop, bija, and higuero, a type of gourd once used by Indians as vessels and containers, now decorated and sold as souvenirs. You'll also see coconut palm, mango, and breadfruit trees, all closely identified with the tropics and the local cuisine. Strange as it may seem, though (since it's hard to imagine traditional dishes in the area without them), none of the three are native species here. You can also see home gardens and cultivated crops such as coffee, cocoa, and groves of orange and grapefruit along the trails.

El Limón is off the road that connects the town of Samaná with Las Terrenas. You can approach it from either direction – it's roughly halfway between the two – by *guagua* or *motoconcho* if you don't have your own vehicle. Along the road are several *"paradas"* or entry points run by local families, which you'll find in the tiny pueblos of El Limón, El Café, Arroyo Surdido, and Rancho Espanol. (The route to the falls is a bit shorter from the latter two.) At the *paradas*, you can buy soft drinks and arrange for guided treks by foot or, preferably, on horseback or by mule. Since it's a strenuous 1½- to two-mile hike even for those in good shape, it's a good idea to let a horse or mule carry you at least part of the way – you have to walk up a steep incline at the end in any event. You can also arrange to have a Dominican lunch (typically meat/chicken, rice and beans, small salad, soft drink) prepared and waiting for you upon your return from the falls.

Did you know? The *paradas* work together with an the ecotourism association called **ACESAL** (The Association of Community Ecotourism of Salto El Limón; www.saltolimon.de) that aims to manage the area's natural resources wisely, while providing visitors with a worthwhile experience.

These 2½-hour tours cost about RD$500, excluding lunch, and are well worth the cost – the trained guides not only can show you the way to get there safely, but can answer your questions as well. (Be sure to request an English-speaking guide.)

> **Inside advice:** You can visit the waterfall daily during daylight hours only. Dress appropriately, including sturdy (preferably waterproof) hiking boots. If you come during rainy season (May to December), be sure to bring rain gear as well. Stick to the trails to avoid disturbing wildlife or damaging vegetation, and stay back from the top ledge of the waterfall. If you have any garbage, pack it out and leave it at the *paradas* once you return from the falls.

Parque Nacional Los Haitises

The more than 100 species of birds and mammals that live in the hills, mangrove swamps, and exotic waterways of this 83-square-mile wildlife sanctuary include several rare or endangered species. Curious rock formations – the result of 40 million years of geological upheavals – host hidden limestone caves bearing pre-Columbian drawings of early Taino life. Thick with ferns, stands of bamboo, broad-leafed plants, and other lush rainforest vegetation, the park has no roads and even few trails into its dense interior, and is best explored by boat. It all adds up to a popular adventure – Los Haitises is one of the most visited national parks in the country.

While the park lies south of the Samaná Peninsula, just below the western "throat" of Samaná Bay, most of its visitors arrive on day-trips via ferry from the town of Samaná. Ferries from Samaná leave directly across from Banco Popular on the Malecón at 7:30 am and 1:30 pm and cost RD$70. Once across the bay, the ferries deposit passengers in the dusty town of Sabana de la Mar, which lies just to the east of the park. When you step off the ferry there, expect to be met by swarms of *buscones* who are paid by boat captains to generate business for trips into Los Haitises. While it's all negotiable, the going rate is about RD$1,000 for a boat carrying up to six people. (If you're traveling by yourself or just one or two others, try to hook up with other travelers during the ferry ride across the bay.) The guide who accompanies the boat costs another RD$400, and there's a park entrance fee of RD$50 per person as well.

Caution: No matter who you travel with, dress for hot, humid weather (and, very possibly, rain) and carry insect repellent, water, and sunscreen.

Great egret

On the boat tours, which stick close to the coastal regions of the park and take about 2½ hours, you'll glide through swamps of red and white mangroves, the largest collection of mangrove rivers in the country. Along the way, you'll have a chance to spot colorful birds such as blue herons, pelicans, cormorants, grebes, roseate terns, frigate birds, egrets, and Hispaniolan parrots and parakeets. Two endemic species, solenodons (ratlike insect-eating mammals) and hutias (foot-long rodents) – both endangered or facing extinction – are also said to occupy the swamps. And you'll visit some of the coastal caves and grottoes with Taino pictographs etched on the walls. These may include Cuevas Arena, San Gabriel, Remington, and La Linea, where you can see drawings and carvings of Taino faces, hunters, gods, and whales produced before the arrival of Columbus. (The same caves later harbored notorious pirates such as John Rackham and Jack Banister.)

Time savers: If you're willing to pay more for convenience, you can book a day-tour to Los Haitises for US$45 – which includes guide, transportation, and lunch – through **Victoria Marine** in Samaná (Malecón, ☎ 538-2494). **Samaná Tourist Services** (Malecón, ☎ 538-2848) offers similar tours daily. You can also find boat tours that leave for the park daily from the port town of Sanchez to the west.

Reserva Cientifica Lagunas Redonda y Limón

This nature reserve, about 40 miles east of Sabana de la Mar and near the town of Miches to the southeast of Samaná Bay, consists of two lagoons totaling 40 square miles. They're primarily of interest to bird-watchers, who come for the chance to spot herons, egrets, and ospreys. The more scenic, accessible, and easterly of the two, Laguna Limón, can be entered from the national park station just off highway 104, which leads east from Sabana de la Mar. There you can hire a guide and a boat to take you across the water at about RD$500 for four people; the price includes boat, guide, and park fee.

The marked entrance to Laguna Redonda, also off Highway 104 but several miles west of Laguna Limón, points to a difficult road that requires four-wheel drive to negotiate, especially because of a small stream that crosses it. Keep in mind that once you arrive at Laguna Redonda there are no guarantees you will actually make it onto the water, since there is no park station here and rarely a boat captain. Still, you can do some bird-watching from the water's edge.

You can also visit the reserve by organized tour from the southeast coast of the island. **Trewe Tours** (☎ 526-1211) offers full-day trips from Boca Chica and Juan Dolio that begin with a scenic drive up and around the Cordillera Oriental mountains overlooking Miches and the two lagoons, followed by a boat trip on Laguna Limón. After a lobster lunch and a cigar-rolling lesson, the group makes a short ride on horseback to Playa Limón, a spectacular undeveloped beach where sea turtles lay eggs in spring. The trips also include a stop at a club gallistico (cockfighting arena). Although you won't see an actual fight, birdwatchers might understandably be appalled at the notion of cockfighting. Still, the visit does provide some insight into the second-most popular sport on the island, after baseball. The cost of the tour, which includes lunch, is US$99 per person.

COCKFIGHTING

As much a national spectator sport in the DR as baseball, and far older and more traditional (the Spanish are said to have introduced it here centuries ago), cockfighting can be found in just about every community in the country, from cities to small villages. Matches take place in circular arenas called club gallisticos, usually on the weekends, particularly Sunday afternoons. (And if there isn't a club gallistico, someone's backyard will usually suffice.) While many if not most outsiders view the spectacle of roosters fighting (often to the death) with spurs and fake claws attached to their feet as sheer animal cruelty, the owners of the birds themselves clearly dote on their feathered combatants, grooming them and proudly carrying them upright on their arms en route to matches. The underpinning of the "sport," though, is gambling – frenzied crowds placing wagers on their favorites. Otherwise, admission to the fights is usually free.

■ Off the Beaten Path

These off-the-beaten-path adventures can be done on your own for free and offer intriguing alternatives to what everybody else may be doing.

Boca del Diablo (Devil's Mouth)

The aptly named Devil's Mouth is a blow-hole gouged out of the rocks that roars when it spouts water, sometimes up to 150 feet high. It's situated on a cliff overlooking Cape Samaná, the eastern tip of the peninsula. It's a good place to kick back and, in winter at least, watch migrating whales go by.

To get there from the town of Samaná, take Carretera Las Galeras (this is the road leading east from Samaná). About six miles after the pueblo of Las Cacaos, watch for a dirt road that goes off to the right and is marked by the club gallistico (cockfighting arena). Follow the dirt road east until it ends. The blow-hole is just before the thicket of trees obscuring a downhill footpath to Playa Fronton (see *Beaches*, above) and directly across from Cueva de los Mulcieglos (see below).

Cueva de los Mulcieglos (Bat Cave)

 This enormous cave at the base of a marble mountain lies directly across from Boca del Diablo (see above). A wide opening makes the cave easy to enter and explore, but be sure to carry a flashlight since it gets darker the farther you venture in. A 20-minute hike into the cave leads to a frigid freshwater pool where you can cool off after a hike. As the name suggests, the cave is inhabited by bats (as are just about all the caves on the island). Wear good hiking shoes to protect your feet from the bat guano on the cave floor.

Pilon de Zucar

The crest of this hill 1,300 feet above the bay provides a breathtaking 360-degree view of the entire peninsula, from Samaná Bay to Cabo Cabron, Las Galeras to Las Terrenas. To get there from the town of Samaná, take Carretera Galeras east toward Las Galeras. Shortly after leaving town, watch for the El Valle marker, and go left (north). Continue on this road (crossing two small streams) until you arrive at a very small dirt path. Turn right onto the path and follow it until it comes to a small pueblo at the base of the pilon.

When you reach the pueblo, you may need to ask one of the villagers to point out the path to the top. (You'll have to hike a bit over 1,000 feet – the east side is easier to climb up than the west side.) The families who live in the area are always willing to help with directions – even cook a meal for you and have it ready when you come down, if you ask before heading up.

If you get a chance, you might also check in with Jean-Phillipe Merand at the Tropical Lodge Hotel in Samaná (see *Where to Stay*, below) before heading off. He's done this climb by a 125cc motorbike and knows the route well.

Bases for Exploration

■ Santa Bárbara de Samaná

Orientation

Santa Bárbara de Samaná is best known as the jumping-off point for whale-watching excursions in Samaná Bay. The town itself is modern and pleasant, with houses dotting the hillsides overlooking the bay, a nice seaside business area that often bustles with diners and club-goers in the evenings, and plenty of palm trees and lush tropical vegetation. Following past fires and a local version of urban renewal in the latter decades of the 20th century, however, virtually all remnants of the old 18th-century city are gone. Samaná also lacks quick access to beaches, although there are a few along the bay. For the best beaches on the peninsula, you'll need to venture to Las Galeras or Las Terrenas.

It's easy to find your way around town – Highway 5 (the main road that cuts across the peninsula) turns into Avenida La Marina (the Malecón), which runs along the waterfront and then takes off east to Las Galeras. Most everything that happens in town lies along this route or near it. Tourist services on the Malecón include an ATM, currency exchange, calling center with Internet access, pharmacy, and the Metro and Caribe bus stations. You'll also find whale-watching tours and the ferry to Sabana de la Mar there, as well as the office of **Samaná Tourist Services** (☎ 538-2740), a local travel agency that can be helpful with travel advice (and, of course, try to sell you a tour or rent you a car).

> **Tip:** If you plan to visit Samaná – or anywhere on the peninsula – during whale-watching season (mid-January through mid-March), it's wise to make hotel reservations well in advance.

Getting Here & Getting Around

The most direct public transportation to Samaná is either by Caribe or Metro bus companies. Both have offices on the Malecón, near many of the main hotels and restaurants. *Guaguas* from nearby towns stop on Calle Rosario Sanchez near El Mercado, the large city market north of the Malecón. From the market, you can easily catch a *motoconcho* or a *motoconcho*-drawn rickshaw into town.

You can rent a car or four-wheel-drive vehicle from **Samaná Tourist Services** (Malecón, ☎ 538-2740).

Places to Stay

Most lodgings in town are low-budget guest houses and pensións primarily suited to backpackers.

HOTEL PRICE CHART	
Rates are per room based on double occupancy.	
$	Under US$20
$$	US$20-$50
$$$	US$51-$100
$$$$	Over US$100

Occidental Gran Bahía (Carretera Las Galeras, ☎ 538-3111, fax 538-2764, www.occidental-hoteles.com) $$$$

This coral-colored "tropical-Victorian" resort is about a 15-minute drive east of Samaná on the way to Las Galeras. You'll know you've arrived when you come upon rows of acacia trees lining both sides of the road and then arching across it to form a shady canopy – a first indication of the beauty that awaits guests inside. After you check in, you may not want to leave. The resort is perched on a cliff with a majestic view of the ocean, while the garden-like grounds feature a dramatically situated pool, a horse stable, a patio restaurant, and a courtesy ferry to the beach at Cayo Levantado. (The hotel is also very close to Playa las Flechas; see *Beaches*, above). The 100 rooms and suites are large, air-conditioned, and decorated with island flair and light, tropical colors.

Tropical Lodge Hotel (Malecón, ☎ 538-2480, fax 538-2068, www.tropical-lodge.com. $$-$$$

With its comfortable rooms and moderate prices, the Tropical Lodge is the best all-around lodging option in Samaná. Located on a hillside on the far eastern end of the Malecón, it's away from the noise but still within a reasonably easy walking distance of the town dock, restaurants, and other tourist services. The 17 rooms have air conditioning or fans and some have balconies and cable TV. (Ask for the room facing the Malecón with the large, private balcony.) A restaurant (see *Places to Eat*, below), pizzeria, and cafeteria are on premises, and there is also a lovely pool area with a nice view of the bay that's very pleasant for passing a quiet evening with cocktails. Rates include breakfast for two but you can add dinner for an extra US$20.

> **Tip:** The hotel is run by a French couple, Jean-Phillipe and Brigitte Merand, who have been here 18 years and can help arrange just about any local tour you want. Jean-Phillipe is also a fount of information about the area, having covered much of it himself on his motorbike.

Hotel Docia (off Calle Santa Bárbara, ☎ 538-2041) $

Perched on a small hill one street behind the Malecón, this modest hotel has very basic but clean rooms and a convenient location that puts it at the top of budget options. The front porch here is nice for lounging in a chair, catching the sea breezes, and chatting with the owner or other guests.

Places to Eat

Café de Paris (Malecón, ☎ 538-2488) $$

Popular with expats, Café de Paris also garners plaudits from visitors for its pizza, crêpes, and other light fare served up in a lively (sometimes raucous) atmosphere.

DINING PRICE CHART	
Price per person for an entrée, not including beverage or tip.	
$	Under US$2
$$	US$2-$10
$$$	US$10-$20
$$$$	Over US$20

Chino (off Calle Santa Bárbara, ☎ 538-2215) $$

This Chinese restaurant sits high up on a hill overlooking Samaná Bay. Along with Chinese standards, you can get a surprisingly good version of the regional Dominican specialty, *pescado con coco*. Access is from the Calle Santa Bárbara behind the Malecón.

Le France (Malecón, ☎ 538-2257) $$

The gourmet Dominican and French entrées here make for a delightful pairing in a pleasant setting on the Malecón. You can't go wrong ordering any dish with shrimp, and their chocolate cake is renowned. Credit cards are not accepted.

L' Hacienda Bar & Grill (Malecón, ☎ 538-2383) $$

Another favorite of local expats, L'Hacienda serves up excellent steaks and grilled seafood in an outdoor café setting. Credit cards are not accepted.

Camilo's (Malecón, ☎ 538-2495) $-$$

With a nice seaside location near the parque central on the Malecón, Camilo's specializes in good Dominican food, including grilled fish and chicken *asapao*, at reasonable prices. It's also one of the comparatively few restaurants in town that opens before noon – serving breakfast as well as lunch and dinner.

Semi-Báez (Carretera Las Galeras, no phone) $-$$

Located near Playa Las Flechas where ferries leave for Cayo Levantado, this restaurant serves Dominican staples and regional specialties such as *moro de gandules con coco* and *mero el coco*. Credit cards are not accepted.

Tropical Lodge (Malecón, ☎ 240-6231) $-$$

The Tropical Lodge hotel's main restaurant serves French cuisine during dinner hours, while a patio that opens onto the Malecón is a good place for lunch. Pizzas and the *pica pollo* are excellent choices for a light meal. You can also have breakfast here.

Nightlife

The bars and late-night restaurants along the Malecón are the happening spots, with a number of rum shacks blaring merengue and bachata. **Naomi**, a disco above L'Hacienda restaurant, is the slickest nightclub in town, playing both merengue and Euro hits. Avenida Rosario Sanchez is the center of a rough-and-tumble heavy drinking scene. For a really offbeat experience, visit the "car wash" along the Calle Santa Bárbara – this is what they call the places where ordinary Dominicans go to drink and dance at night. (You'll find similar car wash scenes in other Dominican towns as well.)

■ Las Galeras

Orientation

This close-knit fishing village at the end of Careterra Las Galeras is one of the last true slices of paradise remaining in the Dominican Republic. Fronting the village is a beautiful beach with a collection of open-air shanty-cum-diner food kiosks at its center, which serves as the main gathering spot in town. Anything that happens

in Las Galeras usually takes place here where locals, the few resident expats, and visitors (who are quickly welcomed into the fold) all meet under a highly informal thatched-roof setting.

For tourist services, head to the main road (Careterra Las Galeras), where you'll find the village's only supermarket and money changer (there are no ATMs here), a Western Union office, a Verizon call center, a handful of restaurants – and its one source for entertainment: an open-air dance hall called **Indiana's** that blasts *bachata* at a typically deafening volume.

Getting Here & Getting Around

The only way to get to Las Galeras by public transportation is in a *guagua* (RD$35) from Samaná. *Motoconchos* also make the run. If you have your own vehicle, take the Carretera Las

Galeras all the way east and then north until the road deadends at Las Galeras' main beach, a one-hour, 16-mile trip. Once there, the most you'll need for getting around within the village limits are your two feet or a bicycle, which can be rented from several of the hotels. For getting outside the village, you can catch a ride on a *motoconcho* or rent your own vehicle (four-wheel-drive may come in handy). Try **Xamana-Rent-Moto** (☎ 538-0208).

Places to Stay

 For such a small, unassuming village, Las Galeras has a remarkable number of good places to stay. And, unlike some other parts of the island, the lodgings here have 24-hour electricity, vital for cooling the air in your room at night. Note that none of the hotels have, or need, addresses – standing at the food kiosks on the beach, they're all within eyesight.

HOTEL PRICE CHART	
Rates are per room based on double occupancy.	
$	Under US$20
$$	US$20-$50
$$$	US$51-$100
$$$$	Over US$100

Casa Marina Bay (☎ 538-0020, fax 538-0040, www.amhsamarina.com) $$$$

A 200-room all-inclusive resort set amid lush palm groves a bit east of the center of town, Casa Marina Bay has some rooms with beach views and others that look over garden areas. All rooms feature air conditioning, cable TV, and private balcony. Fifty split-level bungalows come with separate living room areas and kitchenette. An array of amenities include watersports, daily activities for adults, a kids' club, and nightly entertainment. Except for Playa Rincón, the stretch of beach here may be the nicest in the area, on a peaceful reef-protected bay with calm, shallow waters, generally safe for kids. But if you do want to stroll into town for a change of pace, just walk west along the beach for about seven minutes and you'll arrive at the food kiosk, where you can share laughs with some if the friendliest people around.

> **Tip:** Dive Samaná (☎ 538-0210), the top diving outfitter in the area, is based at the Casa Marina Bay. Dive Samaná also runs whale-watching trips in winter.

Club Bonito (☎ 538-0203, fax 538-0061, www.club-bonito.com, clubbonita@verizon.net.do) $$$$

This contemporary hotel is a designer gem just a stone's throw from beautiful Las Galeras beach. The 21 large rooms are tastefully decorated, and most have ocean-view terraces and air conditioning. You'll find a swimming pool and an excellent Italian seafood restaurant here (rates include breakfast), and the hotel is wheelchair accessible.

Villa Serena (☎ 538-0000, fax 538-0009, www.villaserena.com, vserena@verizon.net.do) $$$$

The most elegant hotel in Las Galeras, Villa Serena is a plantation-style mansion that overlooks beautifully maintained gardens, a gently curved swimming pool, and a picture-perfect desert island a short distance off the crescent beach. The 21 rooms all have terraces with ocean views and either air conditioning or fans. Rates include breakfast. (The excellent restaurant, open for three meals a day and serving French and Caribbean cuisine, will also serve non-guests if you call ahead.) The one downside here is the saltwater showers.

Todo Blanco (☎ 538-0201, todoblanco@hotmail.com) $$$

As the name implies, everything is done up in white to create an air of tranquility. The public areas of the hotel, particularly the restaurant and lobby lounge, are as elegant as the Italian owners. The fan-cooled guest rooms fall a bit short of that standard. Still, it's an exquisite place and its location – within a wonderful garden – is just far back enough from the shoreline to give you the sense that, when you cross the well-maintained lawn to the beach, you are crossing the grounds of your own private estate.

Juan y Lolo Bungalows (☎ and fax 538-0208, juanylolo@hotmail.com) $$-$$$$

These well-equipped and extremely well-maintained thatched-roof bungalows can comfortably sleep two to six people each. All are tastefully decorated in bright Caribbean colors with porches that are perfect for having breakfast just steps from the beach. Rooms are fan-cooled.

Casa Por Que Non (☎ 538-0011 or 514-661-9013 in Montreal, Canada) $$

This cozy B&B near Club Bonito is open only from December to May, when the French-Canadian owners winter on the island. Rates include a wildly popular breakfast served in a pleasant garden setting.

Plaza Lusitania (☎ 538-0093, fax 538-0066, www.samana.net, plazalusitania@hotmail.com) $$

Don't let the location of this hotel – above a supermarket in a commercial building – put you off. All rooms are super-clean, tastefully furnished, and offer balconies and air conditioning. And since the first floor houses a supermarket and pizzeria, you aren't likely to go hungry.

Samaná Peninsula

Places to Eat

All the following restaurants are on the Carretera Las Galeras, the main road leading in from Samaná that deadends at Las Galeras beach. The tourist season slows down tremendously after the July/August European crush, so a few of these places may be closed if you visit during the fall. The

DINING PRICE CHART	
Price per person for an entrée, not including beverage or tip.	
$	Under US$2
$$	US$2-$10
$$$	US$10-$20
$$$$	Over US$20

supermarket in the Centro Comercial building is always well-stocked, however, and local eateries such as the kiosk and *comedors* stay open year-round. In addition, **Hotel Villa Serena**, **Club Bonita**, and **Todo Blanco** all have excellent kitchens that will accommodate non-guests if you call a day ahead for a reservation.

Casa Por Que Non (☎ 538-0011) $$

Open only from December to May when the Canadian proprietors of this B&B (attached to their private home) winter on the island, Casa Por Que Non serves an excellent breakfast, open to the public.

Chez Denise (☎ 538-0219) $$

This street-side café with patio seating does great crêpes as well as fresh fish prepared in a variety of ways. A favorite hangout for local expats, it's open for breakfast, lunch, and dinner.

El Pizzeria (no phone) $$

Located on the ground floor of the Centro Comercial building, El Pizzeria serves up salads and meat entrées along with good pizza.

Galeras Beach Kiosk (no phone) $

At this collection of shacks on the beach in the center of town, you can enjoy some of the best fried fish and *tostones* (fried plantains) you may have in your life – all for about RD$100. Don't overlook this local watering hole for a casual meal while you're here.

Patiserrie (no phone) $

This small bakery tucked away in a cozy corner just off Carretera Las Galeras is a good spot for breakfast, coffee and pastries.

Nightlife & Entertainment

Most visitors end up passing away the evening hours at the kiosk on the beach, shooting the breeze with friendly locals. The more adventurous make their way to **Indiana's**, the open-air dance club along Careterra Las Galeras, just a few yards beyond the entrance of the town. The blaring merengue is hard to miss.

■ Las Terrenas

Orientation

This little town, built and run mostly by French expats, can be as lively as Boca Chica on the Caribbean Coast or Sosúa farther west along the north coast, but without the noticeable sleaze factor that plagues those other tourist hubs. The main part of Las Terrenas runs for a bit over a mile along beautiful beachfront. In the center of town stands the El Paseo Plaza, while the pueblo of El Portillo lies to the east and the lovely Playas Bonita and Coson lie to the west. The pace is more tranquil at either end of town, yet the outskirts (where most of the hotels are) are still relatively close to Las Terrenas' nightlife and restaurants. While there's a fair amount of noise from *motoconchos,* especially in the high winter and summer seasons, for the most part Las Terrenas remains uncrowded and laid-back.

All tourist services, such as an ATM, Internet cafés, currency exchange, and safety deposit boxes (the one downside to Las Terrenas is a high incidence of petty theft) can be found around the El Paseo Plaza. *Motoconchistas* also hang around the area waiting for fares. To the east of the plaza on Calle Libertad is **Sunshine Tourist Info** (☎ 240-6184), a travel agency where you can rent a vehicle, book excursions, or have just about any of your questions answered.

Getting Here & Getting Around

While there are a number of ways to get to Las Terrenas, none of them is without some degree of complication. The most comfortable, as a general rule, is to fly into the El Portillo landing strip, about four miles from town. **Air Santo Domingo** offers daily service from the capital. Once there you can hop a *motoconcho* to Las Terrenas (drivers usually can be found hanging around the airstrip waiting for passengers).

Another option is to take a **Caribe** or **Metro bus** from Santo Domingo, Puerto Plata, or other points on the island to the town of Sanchez south of Las Terrenas. There you can change for rickety *guaguas* or pickup trucks that head north from Sanchez 11 miles via a steep, narrow, winding, pothole-ridden road into Las Terrenas. These adventurous rides (even more so when it's raining) will run you about RD$100 per person – though you'll be guaranteed a visually stunning ride over the mountain.

Las Terrenas

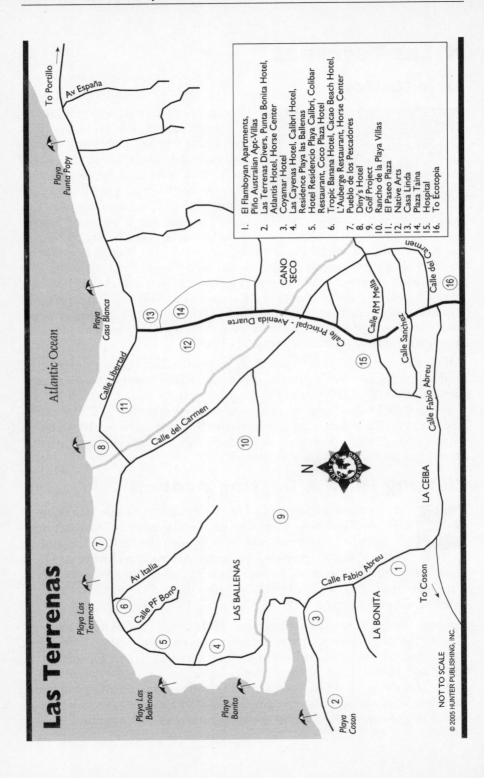

Atlantic Ocean

To Portillo

Av España

Playa Punta Popy

Playa Casa Blanca

Playa Las Terrenas

Playa Las Ballenas

Playa Bonita

Playa Coson

Calle Libertad

Calle del Carmen

Av Italia

Calle PF Bono

LAS BALLENAS

Calle Principal - Avenida Duarte

CANO SECO

Calle RM Mella

Calle Sanchez

Calle del Carmen

Calle Fabio Abreu

Calle Fabio Abreu

LA CEIBA

LA BONITA

To Coson

To Ecotopia

N — HUNTER PUBLISHING

NOT TO SCALE

© 2005 HUNTER PUBLISHING, INC.

1. El Flamboyan Apartments, Piño Australian Apt-Villas
2. Las Terrenas Divers, Punta Bonita Hotel, Atlantis Hotel, Horse Center
3. Coyamar Hotel
4. Las Cayenas Hotel, Calibri Hotel, Residence Playa las Ballenas
5. Hotel Residencio Playa Calibri, Colibar Restaurant, Coco Plaza Hotel
6. Tropic Banana Hotel, Cacao Beach Hotel, L'Auberge Restaurant, Horse Center
7. Pueblo de los Pescadores
8. Diny's Hotel
9. Golf Project
10. Rancho de la Playa Villas
11. El Paseo Plaza
12. Native Arts
13. Casa Linda
14. Plaza Taina
15. Hospital
16. To Ecotopia

A third option is to take a bus all the way east to the town of Samaná, then take a *motoconcho* or *guagua* back northwest to Las Terrenas along a flat and well-paved road. That ride, while more comfortable, is longer (about 40 minutes, in addition to the extra time required to reach Samaná by bus) and more expensive, about RD$300.

> **Tip:** Keep in mind that, if traveling some distance by *motoconcho*, you won't want to be carrying much more luggage than a backpack. (The driver may be able to balance a smallish bag or two up front.)

Once in Las Terrenas, you can rent a vehicle at **Jessie Car Rental** (Calle de Carmen, ☎ 240-6415) or from **Sunshine Tourist Info** (Calle Libertad, ☎ 240-6184).

Places to Stay

Las Terrenas has the most lodging options of any place on the peninsula. With the exception of one all-inclusive resort catering mostly to French package tourists, accommodations are either independent hotels to the west of the town center or a slew of rock-bottom budget options to the east. For the lat-

HOTEL PRICE CHART	
Rates are per room based on double occupancy.	
$	Under US$20
$$	US$20-$50
$$$	US$51-$100
$$$$	Over US$100

ter, check out the area around Ave. Emilio Prud Homme, where you can find a number of places with basic, fan-cooled rooms with cold water for about RD$400 a night. The following are nicer options on the west end of the beach.

Guatapanal Hotel and Resort (Playa Coson, ☎ 240-5050, fax 240-5536, www.guatapanal.com.do) $$$$

Situated on lovely, remote Playa Coson five miles from Las Terrenas, this 208-room all-inclusive resort is the kind of place you could settle into for several days and never leave (though if you do want to head into town, twice-daily shuttle service is available). Most rooms have balconies or terraces with sea views, and all have air conditioning, cable TV, and direct dial phones. Facilities include a swimming pool, restaurant – with much better food than the average all-inclusive – bar, watersports center, a disco, and a theater with live stage shows at night.

Hotel Bahía de Las Bellenas (Playa Bonita, ☎ 240-6066, www.las-terrenas-hotels.com) $$$$

Here you'll find 32 beautiful thatched-roof rooms arranged in clusters of four and spread across immaculately maintained grounds. The fan-cooled rooms are decorated in Caribbean, Mexican, Moroccan, or

French Provencial themes, while the large bathrooms that open up to the sky feature a water fountain and touches of lush foliage. An on-site restaurant is open until 11 pm daily, and rates include breakfast. Bahía de Las Bellenas also manages a collection of equally nice villas along Playa Bonita.

Hotel & Restaurant Atlantis (☎ 240-6111, www.atlantisbeachhotel. com) $$$-$$$$

Older than the Hotel Bahía, the Atlantis, on Playa Bonita, is filled with character. The 19 individually decorated rooms – some bigger than others, some with air conditioning and some not, but each one interesting on its own – are named after various exotic locales such as Seychelles, Grenada, and Cairo (Jamaica is fabulous). The owners, a French gourmet chef and his wife, turn out a delectable foie gras and a wonderful Caribbean dorado in champagne sauce at the hotel restaurant. Rates include breakfast.

Playa Colibri (☎ 240-6434, fax 240-6437, www.playacolibri.com) $$$-$$$$

This collection of privately owned one-, two-, and three-bedroom villas is clustered around a pool that's lively both day and night. One of the best features of this cozy resort-like establishment is the exceptionally attentive service provided by the front desk staff. Others include a cheery décor, cable TV, a restaurant, and large patios for relaxing. The split-level three-bedroom villas have a particularly luxurious feel. Playa Colibri is situated along the beach on the far west end of Las Terrenas, away from the town noise but still a comfortable stroll away from the lively nightlife scene.

Hotel Coco Plaza (Calle Francisco Bono, ☎ 240-6172) $$$

Each of the 16 extremely elegant (if little) rooms – and one enormous top-floor suite – in this small hotel comes with air conditioning and private balcony. The nice lobby bar also serves an excellent breakfast. The hotel can get noisy, sitting on the corner of a busy intersection, just across the road from L'Aubergine Pizzeria, one of the more popular dining spots in the area. The amiable live-in manager and his daughter are of East Indian origin, have lived all over the world, can hold a conversation in several different languages, and take excellent care of their guests.

Kari Beach (☎ 240-6187, www.karibeach.com) $$$

Located a few doors down from Hotel Playa Colibri, the Kari Beach (formerly Hotel Kanesh Beach) also has bright and cheery fan-cooled rooms, though not as tasteful as its neighbor. The restaurant here has traditionally been good, but a recent change in hotel management may affect its standards.

Casa Grande Beach Hotel (☎ 240-6349, www.casagrandebeachhotel. com) $$

Although the Casa Grande is more of a guest house than a hotel, it's still a pleasant, less expensive option on Playa Bonita. The basic, fan-cooled rooms are in a building that stands apart from the lobby and the restaurant, where you can get inexpensive yet elegant meals. One offbeat feature is a surfboard out front that announces the room rates.

Las Cayenas Hotel (☎ 240-6080) $$

This large plantation-style house is one of the oldest in Las Terrenas, built nearly 20 years ago when the sophisticated Swiss woman who owns it came to the island as a visitor and decided to stay. Guests often congregate on the hotel's large verandah, but also have the option of sitting on their own private balconies, which come complete with rocking chairs. Rooms are basic but comfortable and fan-cooled. Rates include American breakfast.

Diny (☎ 240-6113) $

A very popular and highly recommended budget hotel right on the beach, Diny does have one big downside: it's also dead smack in the center of Las Terrenas – at a major crossing where every *motoconcho*, it seems, drives by, especially in early morning. Ask for a room away from the street noise.

Places to Eat

Thanks to the large expatriate community, many of whom have gone into the hospitality business here, Las Terrenas offers an extraordinary number of good restaurants for such a small area. While restaurants in town come and go with sometimes alarming frequency, most of the following have weathered the test of time. Several hotels listed above also have excellent dining facilities.

DINING PRICE CHART	
Price per person for an entrée, not including beverage or tip.	
$	Under US$2
$$	US$2-$10
$$$	US$10-$20
$$$$	Over US$20

Casa Boga (☎ 240-6321) $$

The two Basque women who run Casa Boga take extreme pride in their *cocina vasca*. Because of their location in the Pueblo de Pescadores (Fisherman's Village), the owners are able to get first dibs from the local fishermen as they come in off their boats at the end of the day, and always feature fresh seafood on their menu.

Indiana Café Bar & Restaurant (☎ 886-9565) $$

One door down from Casa Boga, the Indiana also offers a wide variety of seafood, including flambé shrimp, grilled lobster, and an especially interesting entrée of grilled dorado with sea urchin crême.

L'Aubergine Pizzería (☎ 240-6167) $$

Tucked away on the far end of a tiny street just after the Pueblo de Pescadores, this unassuming pizzeria is overwhelming popular, especially with the backpacking crowd. At night it's a lively joint with very loud music, so if you want to escape the din you may want to order your pizza to go.

Restaurant Luisanne (Calle Coronel Francisco, ☎ 804-3671) $$

The young owners of this recently opened restaurant featuring French and Creole cuisine have impeccable taste and style, and their menu reflects their creativity: entrées include salted octopus, rabbit filet in thyme flower, and beef pavé with marrow.

Steakhouse Chalet Suisse (☎ 240-6162) $$

On the east end of the beach, this Swiss-style restaurant – a lively beach bar by day – is known for its excellent steaks and fondue specialties for dinner. (And don't worry – they don't haul out the cuckoo clocks at night.)

El Zapote Restaurant (Av. Juan Pablo Duarte, no phone) $

It's not easy to find good local food in Las Terrenas, where exotic (meaning foreign to the DR) cuisine abounds. But you can sample it here and, for very little money, on the front porch of a local home. A full meal of fresh fish, rice, and salad goes for a modest RD$80 or so.

Nightlife & Entertainment

Just about every restaurant in Las Terrenas has a bar, and at some point as the night wears on they usually attract small crowds and become quasi-clubs. One exception is the full-fledged disco **Nuevo Mundo** on Carretera Las Terrenas, d, where you can dance the night away to local music as well as European tunes. For kicking back to down-tempo lounge music (along with a fine bottle of wine or your libation of choice), head over to **Syroz** on Calle Libertathe only upscale bar in Las Terrenas and open every night until 4 am.

■ El Portillo

To the east of Las Terrenes lies El Portillo, site of the landing strip that now serves Las Terrenas. It was originally built, though, to shuttle in guests of the nearby mega all-inclusive **El Portillo Beach Resort** (☎ 240-6100). The resort sits on prime beach that's mostly off-limits to anyone not staying there. The area is also known for several dive sites.

North by Northwest – Río San Juan to Montecristi

The nearly 200-mile-long north coast of the Dominican Republic has been dubbed, variously, the "Silver Coast," the "Amber Coast," and the "Green Coast." Locals often just call it "La Costa" (the coast). However you choose to refer to it, the DR's northern shoreline, which fronts the Atlantic Ocean, is one of often startling beauty. (When explorer Christopher Columbus first saw it, he is said to have called His-

paniola the "most beautiful land on earth.") Some of the country's most enticing beaches and most popular resort areas lie along this stretch of coastline, which has become a playground for water lovers. The north coast presents the most varied scuba diving and snorkeling opportunities on the island and at least two of its top golf courses, as well as some of the best windsurfing in the world, propelled by afternoon breezes off the Atlantic.

Catering to visitors are a raft of all-inclusive resorts, more than a dozen of them bunched together in the walled-off compound known as **Playa Dorada** ("Golden Beach"), just outside the centuries-old city of Puerto Plata. Attracting hundreds of thousands of vacationers a year, Playa Dorada is one of the most popular tourist destinations in the Caribbean, though Punta Caña and Bávaro on the Coconut Coast have lately commandeered the title of "all-inclusive resorts capital" of the region. Still, Playa Dorada retains huge mass-market appeal, especially among Canadians and Europeans. Other north coast resort areas, such as **Sosúa** and **Cabarete**, also draw big international crowds. A beach vacation on the north coast can be an around-the-clock affair of snorkeling by day and getting snockered by night, dancing to merengue beats or perhaps hitting the roulette wheels at one of the resort casinos. Or, you can simply lie back on a beach towel or lounge chair in the time-honored fashion and take in the tropical breezes, the warming sun, and the salt air – rum punch optional.

Many visitors, alas, confine themselves only to the resorts. But those who don't venture out beyond the compounds miss out on a region of tremendous diversity that's rich in both history and natural wonders. Travelers here can visit historic parks such as La Isabela – a settlement founded by Christopher Columbus – and unspoiled eco-parks that protect wildlife, caves, lagoons, river deltas, headlands, mesas, and mangroves. The topography ranges from the green lushness of the eastern half of the region to the increasing aridity and desert-like conditions of the far northwest. Small fishing villages add touches of atmosphere and authenticity.

A trip to the north does come with some caveats. While many of the coastal beaches are sheltered by offshore coral reefs, others are not. On the latter, waves and undertow can be strong, rendering them dangerous for swimming. The Atlantic waters can also get a bit chillier in winter than the Caribbean waters along the southern coast of the island. And you run the risk as well of getting rain here year-round, especially toward the northeast, where winters can be wetter and cooler than elsewhere in the country. One piece of good weather news is that, from summer through fall, hurricanes are generally less of a threat in the north than in the south.

History

 In the autumn of 1492, while surveying the north coast of Hispaniola, Christopher Columbus himself is reported to have named this area Puerto Plata ("Silver Port") because the sun glinting off the water resembled a flotilla of silver coins. As visions of mineral treasures danced in his head, Columbus established the coastal settlement of La Isabela in January 1494, which was abandoned in 1498. In 1502, however, Nicolás de Ovando, the governor of the new Spanish colony, formally founded the town of Puerto Plata, the first permanent settlement and still the most important city along the north coast.

For its first two decades, Puerto Plata thrived as a supply stop for Spanish galleons hauling silver from Mexico to Spain. But by 1520 or so, the town was already in steep decline, bypassed by other Caribbean ports. As the 16th century progressed, the north coast became a center for smugglers and pirates (and in some cases remains a haven for shady characters to this day). Fearing that its colony was slipping out of its control, Spain did its best to destroy Puerto Plata in 1605, torching the city, deporting its residents to the south near Santo Domingo, and abandoning the area for another century and a half. The Spanish also razed

Above: Samaná Peninsula

Below: Cayo Levantado

Above: Samaná Bay (Bahía de San Lorenzo)

Below: Bahía de las Aguilas, a strip of coastline adjoining the Jaragua National Park
that has been targeted by developers

Above: Windsurfing off Playa Bávaro

Below: Baoba del Piñal, near Río San Juan on the north coast

Salto El Limón, off the road that connects the town of Samaná with Las Terrenas

Montecristi, a town in the far west (near the present-day Haitian border) that was founded around the same time as Puerto Plata and had enjoyed some level of prosperity on its own.

It wasn't until the 1730s, when Spain tried to hold off the increasing power of rival France in the region, that the Spanish regained interest in the area, importing a group of Canary Islanders to resettle

Playa Dorada golf course

Puerto Plata. Within another few decades, the north coast had become a center for the mahogany trade, exporting valuable tropical woods to Europe that had been harvested from the rainforests to the south.

A century later, during the War of Restoration in the mid-1860s, Puerto Plata bore the brunt of heavy fighting between Dominican nationalists and Spanish loyalists. After the Spanish were driven out, the city was rebuilt and blossomed again into a thriving port, this time in the exportation of tobacco, sugar, cocoa, and salt. By the late 19th century, Puerto Plata had become the Paris of the Caribbean, worldly, sophisticated, and wealthy. European merchants built fabulous Victorian mansions there, many of them still standing in the Old City. Meanwhile, Sosúa – created by the United Fruit Company down the coast to the east – developed into a prosperous port for banana exportation, and remained so almost until the onset of World War One.

But the area once again went into steep decline in the early 20th century, beset by foreign power struggles and domestic strife. When dictator Rafael Trujillo came to power in 1930 and reshaped the country's economy to emphasize south-coast sugar plantations, the north coast was left to stagnate. Trujillo did make news in 1940 when he offered refuge to Jews fleeing Nazi Germany and several hundred of them then settled in Sosúa, where they created a barrio known as El Batey and prospered in the dairy business. Today, though, El Batey is best known as Sosúa's tourism hub. North coast tourism took root in the 1970s and 1980s, with the development of the Playa Dorada all-inclusive resort complex near Puerto Plata. Sosúa, meanwhile, became a hotbed of sex tourism, luring increasing numbers of visitors from Europe and North America and setting off a hotel building spree. After a police crackdown on prostitution in the mid-1990s, Sosúa has seen a recent resurgence in it – indicative of another spate of economic hard times. Sparkling new resorts continue to spring up along the north coast, however, as Cabarete windsurfers, Sosúa scuba divers, Playa Dorada beach lovers, and a whole new wave of eco-tourists and adventure travelers continue to discover this remarkably varied stretch of coastline.

North by Northwest

Festivals

Puerto Plata and Montecristi both hold **Carnaval** celebrations each weekend during February. In Montecristi, celebrants are known for being the most aggressive in the country – separating into warring camps of "Toros" (who wear bull masks) and "civiles" and beating each other with whips. Both sides are heavily padded, but spectators should watch from a safe distance.

Puerto Plata holds a **Cultural Festival** each June, and a **Merengue Festival** and a **Jazz Festival** each October. The Jazz Festival extends to Cabarete and Sosúa as well.

Orientation

Puerto Plata – situated about midway along the north coast and with a population of about 200,000 – is the main gateway to the region. The international airport serving the north coast is 15 minutes away by taxi, and the main coastal road, Highway 5, runs through the city. Good bus connections link Puerto Plata with Santo Domingo, Santiago, and the Samaná Peninsula. Many visitors, however, skip Puerto Plata itself in favor of the Playa Dorada resort complex just to its east. Still, even if you don't stay in Puerto Plata, it has an interesting Old City – much of what's standing there dates from the Victorian era, except for a waterside fortress that survived from the colonial period – and wonderful views from the top of its backdrop mountain, Isabel de Torres.

East along the coast from Puerto Plata lie the resort areas of **Sosúa**, **Cabarete**, and the quieter but emerging beach area between **Río San Juan** and **Cabrera**, which is about halfway between Puerto Plata and the Samaná Peninsula. West of Puerto Plata are some of the most beautiful – and least visited – beaches in the country, especially at **Luperón** and **Punta Rucia**. The more remote stretches of the northwest also feature the historically significant ruins of the **La Isabela** settlement and the desert-like islands off **Montecristi**, a national park that borders Haiti. The Montecristi area rivals Sosúa for some of the best scuba diving and snorkeling on the entire island.

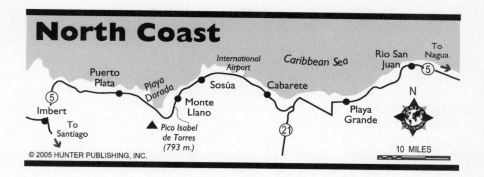

Getting Here

Gregorio Luperón International Airport, about 10 miles east of Puerto Plata on the road to Sosúa, serves the north coast. Airlines that fly here include **Air Canada** (☎ 888-247-2262), www.aircanada.ca; **American Airlines** (☎ 800-433-7300), www.aa.com; **Continental Airlines** (☎ 800-231-0856), www.continental.com; and **Northwest Airlines** (☎ 800-447-4747), www.nwa.com. If you arrive on a package tour or are booked at one of the all-inclusive resorts, you'll probably be met by a hotel shuttle bus. Otherwise, taxis, *motoconchos,* and rental cars are available at the airport. *Guaguas* run from the main highway, located just outside the airport entrance, which you can walk to if you aren't burdened by too much luggage. A currency exchange is open weekdays at the airport.

Buses operated by **Caribe Tours** (Av. Pedro Clisante, Puerto Plata, ☎ 586-4544) and **Metro Expreso** (Beller and 16 de Agosto, Puerto Plata, ☎ 586-6062) make the 3½-hour trip from Santo Domingo to Puerto Plata via Highways 1 and 5, passing through the fertile Cibao Valley and Santiago, the country's second largest city. The two bus companies also have frequent departures from Santiago, only an hour or so from Puerto Plata.

Getting Around

If you don't want to rent a car, you can rent motor scooters at many hotels in the Puerto Plata area. Meanwhile, *guaguas* run east between Puerto Plata's parque central and Sosúa, and from Sosúa to Río San Juan, though the latter trip involves at least one transfer. Going east, you'll travel along Highway 5, a nicely paved coastal road that extends all the way to the Samaná Peninsula.

Going west is more difficult. Highway 5 turns south toward Santiago at Puerto Plata, and the coastal roads west get progressively rougher and more potholed the closer you get to Haiti. (Some barely deserve the description "road" at all.) If you want to cover much ground in the northwest, especially along the coastal areas, renting a four-wheel-drive is strongly recommended. From Highway 30, which runs inland roughly paralleling the coast, you'll find turnoffs to Luperón, La Isabela, and Punta Rucia, but from Punta Rucia west to Montecristi, especially, the roads can be a real mess. The fastest way to get to Montecristi is to take Highway 1 west from Santiago and skip the coastal roads altogether. (If you're coming from Puerto Plata, take Highway 5 south to Highway 1, then go west.) If you aren't driving yourself, you can find *guaguas* plying the main routes and intrepid *motoconcho* drivers tackling some of the lesser ones.

Information Sources

There's a tourist office in Long Beach on the eastern end of the Malecón in Puerto Plata (☎ 586-3676), but unless you're just passing by, it's not worth going out of the way for.

The website, www.puertoplataregion.com, provides some background information on the coast from Puerto Plata to Cabarete, while the competing www.puertoplatainfo.com and www.puertoplata.com.do are only marginally useful.

Adventures

■ On Water

Beaches

The beaches below are listed from east to west, starting southeast of Cabrera and traveling west along the coast to Montecristi.

Cabrera to Río San Juan Area Beaches

While breathtakingly scenic and pleasant enough for spending an idyllic day on the sands, many of the beaches from Cabrera to Río San Juan are also known for powerful riptides that claim lives on a regular basis. Inexperienced swimmers should be careful and children should be watched closely. Except where indicated, the beach entrances are well marked and accessible from coastal Highway 5.

■ Playa Bonita

Considering how lovely it is, it's perhaps surprising that no hotel chain has as yet grabbed up Playa Bonita, which remains accessible to all. You'll find it a few miles north of the city of Nagua and about 15 miles south of Cabrera.

■ Playa Entrada

This long, narrow, often nearly deserted strip of sand about seven miles south of Cabrera is characterized by an abandoned village to one side and a picture-perfect island so close to shore that it's within swimming distance. Unless you're a very strong swimmer, though, don't be tempted by its idyllic allure – the waters here are unprotected and not always safe. The town of La Entrada, just to the north of the beach, has a few eating places.

■ Playa Diamante

About two miles north of Playa Entrada and a few miles south of Cabrera, scenic Playa Diamante is one of the few beaches in the Cabrera area where you can swim without fear of undertow. Its calm, quiet, very shallow waters extend well out from shore, and you can even let kids go wading there, as long as they don't stray too far out. The sandy beach faces east, so it gets good morning sun. The unpaved access road is not well marked, however, so stop at one of the *colmados* along the road to ask exact directions.

■ Playa Breton

This beach near Abreu-Breton west of Cabrera is characterized by white cliffs rising high above crashing surf, which makes for great scenery and risky swimming.

■ Playa Preciosa

A lovely, secluded strip of beach at the headland of Parque Nacional Cabo Frances Viejo, Playa Preciosa is popular with surfers and other water-loving thrill seekers. But the undercurrent is particularly strong here, so inexperienced swimmers should be very careful. It's located just east of famous Playa Grande (see below).

■ Playa Grande

Located a few miles east of Río San Juan, 1½-mile-long Playa Grande is one of the longest white-sand beaches on the north coast, and known as one of the most beautiful on the entire island. Unfortunately for the public, the Occidental Allegro resort has taken over one end of the beach, though the far end (where there are food and cerveza stands) is still open to all and draws big crowds on Sundays. There's good surfing here in winter; waves can get high.

North by Northwest

■ Playa Caleton

About two miles east of Río San Juan, 500-foot-long Playa Caleton offers shallow waters and a protected cove – a safe swimming area for children – which is unusual in this area. It also has very clear waters for snorkeling. Sandy and pretty, with white sand and framed by big rocks, it's a popular spot, particularly on weekends, when locals hawk fried fish and inexpensive Dominican food.

■ Playa Río San Juan

Though located in the front and center of the town of Río San Juan, this small strip of beach is usually deserted since Playa Caleton, Playa Grande, and other better choices lie nearby to the east.

Cabarete Area Beaches

Cabarete area beaches – which stretch almost uninterrupted for 30 miles – are best known for windsurfing and the relatively new sport of kitesurfing, though they're also very popular with surfers. June through August is prime time for breezes; surfing waves are best in March.

■ Playa Cabarete

Only about a quarter of this wide, four-mile-long white-sand beach is developed, but that stretch is solidly lined with restaurants, hotels, bars, and clubs. The waters, meanwhile, are crowded with windsurfers. Off to the sides, away from the center of the action, the beach is much quieter. Lying along a reef-protected bay, Playa Cabarete is blessed with afternoon ocean breezes that are ideal for windsurfing, especially in the summer months. (Beginners can practice in the milder morning winds.) At night, restaurants set plastic tables on the beach, and the sands become the floor for alfresco dining by the sea. Many of the bars, in turn, become discos and clubs, with music blaring long into the night.

■ Playa Encuentro

This largely undeveloped beach about 2½ miles west of Cabarete is known for its great winds and waves – meaning, in turn, great windsurfing, surfing, scuba diving, and kitesurfing. The **Delmar Ocean Experience** (☎ 360-2576) is a small surfing, kitesurfing, and diving operation based there. Take Highway 5 west of Cabarete, then go north on the unmarked turnoff. (Ask in Cabarete for specific directions.) Each March, this beach is the site of the Encuentro Classic, matching some of the world's top windsurfers and surfers.

Sosúa Beaches

■ Playa Libre

All-inclusive hotels have staked out parts of this sandy, cliff-lined cove in the El Batey section of Sosúa. With all the hotel guests, the beach can get quite crowded.

■ Playa Sosúa

This wide, crescent-shaped stretch of white sands lines a small, cliff-sheltered bay and forms a nearly perfect tropical beach, except that it does get crowded. It serves as a separation point for Sosúa's two main barrios, El Batey and Los Charamicos, and is flanked to the rear by restaurants and bars. You can swim and snorkel in clear, calm, reef-protected waters here, or just lie on the sands and watch the world go by.

■ Playa Chiquita

Expect lots of local color (including litter) at this small beach in Sosúa's Dominican barrio, Los Charamicos.

Puerto Plata Area Beaches

■ Playa Bergantín

If you're staying in Puerto Plata (or just passing through) and don't want to pay as much as US$65 for day-passes at one of the private beach resorts, then Playa Bergantín – which is just east of the Playa Dorada resort complex (see below) – makes a nice public alternative. Here, you can enjoy a relaxing day on the sands away from the noise of Puerto Plata. Amenities include lounge chairs to rent and rickety shacks selling fresh-cooked fish or lobster, pizza, hamburgers, and hotdogs, along with ice-cold Presidente beers and soft drinks.

> **Warning:** The sandflies get really bad about 5 pm, so it's best to get here earlier in the day.

■ Playa Dorada

The "Golden Beach," site of 14 all-inclusive resorts, is protected by reefs, leaving the waters mostly calm, clear, and warm. Lots of watersports are available, with much of the equipment free to hotel guests. Anyone can drive into the Playa Dorada complex, but, for non-guests, day-passes to the beach run a steep US$40 to $65, including lunch and drinks.

■ Long Beach

This is Puerto Plata's town beach, on the east end of the Malecón. While it's not the cleanest stretch of sand or an ideal spot to spend a day at the beach, it's filled with local color – residents hang out here to enjoy a few beers from one of the many shacks lining the curve. While it's fine to join in, you may have to elbow your way through some unsavory characters.

■ Costambar

Just west of Puerto Plata, Costambar has a long stretch of sand with few waves and calm waters good for kids, but this once-lively resort area has been pretty dead of late.

■ Playa Cofresí

About five miles west of Puerto Plata, gorgeous, palm-lined Playa Cofresí is popular with locals who come here on Sundays for picnicking and merengue. The water tends to be choppy, however. Two resorts have opened here to complement a number of small *pensións*, but it remains a nice spot for a quiet getaway.

Luperón Beaches

■ Playa Luperón

About 20 miles west of Puerto Plata (at least as the crow flies), Luperón has everything you'd want from a north coast beach: blue waters, white sands, palm trees, and good windsurfing, snorkeling, and diving. A marina is nearby, and you can sometimes make arrangements with boat captains for trips to offshore reefs. It's a place either to get away from it all, or to go for a day-trip or stopover from Puerto Plata. The easiest way there is to take Highway 5 south to Carretera Luperón (Highway 30), which you can pick up just north of Imbert; the road then leads west to Luperón.

El Castillo to Punta Rucia Area Beaches

This stretch of coastline about halfway between Puerto Plata and Montecristi isn't particularly easy to get to, but those who persevere are rewarded by some of the best beaches, snorkeling, and diving on the north coast.

■ Playa Isabela

This beach is just down the dirt road to the right of Rancho del Sol, the one tolerable hotel in El Castillo, and is used mostly by locals who live in the area. Tourists tend to prefer the much lovelier beaches farther west in Punta Rucia, but if you're staying in El Castillo, Playa Isabela is more convenient.

■ Playa Ensenata

About a half-hour walk along the dirt track leading east of Punta Rucia, this mile-long beach with incredibly white sand and calm, shallow blue water is one of the most beautiful on the north coast. It's also very popular on weekends with families, who play merengue and bachata at incredibly high decibels. To escape the blaring music, you'll need to head for the far western end of the beach (where you'll only be subjected to the vibration that might drift downwind in your direction).

■ Playa Punta Rucia

Just as beautiful as neighboring Playa Ensenata, Playa Punta Rucia also gets crowded – mostly with the flocks of tourists bused in by tour operators from Puerto Plata. You can always seek solitude on the far east end of the beach, where you might encounter only a few daytrippers also wandering away from the crowds. On the west end there's a restaurant/bar that caters to package tourists, and a small lagoon, good for birdwatching, which lies down a dirt path. And if you press on as far west as you can go, you will eventually come to a peaceful mangrove swamp.

■ Cayo Arena (Sand Island)

Cayo Arena, an exquisite little sand bar just off the coast of Punta Rucia, is reached by boat and is often populated with hundreds of daytrippers ferried over by tour operators from Puerto Plata. There's good swimming and a healthy coral reef for snorkeling. To visit independently, make arrangements a day in advance with one of the boat captains on the beach, who charge around US$75 per person. The all-you-can drink rum-punch concession provides little relief from the sun, so bring a protective wide-brimmed hat.

Montecristi Area Beaches

■ Playa Detras El Morro

Where the paved road ends in the Parque Nacional Montecristi (see *Eco-Travel*, below), just a few yards beyond the park ranger station, a dirt and gravel road leads to a beautiful secluded beach aptly named Playa Detras El Morro (Beach Behind El Morro, which is the huge limestone mesa that dominates the area). The beach ends at the tip just off to the north that marks the country's farthest northwest point. The pinkish-brown sand juxtaposed against intense blue waves is strikingly beautiful, but the strong undercurrent can be dangerous. For safer swimming, try Playa Juan de Bolaños (below).

■ Playa Juan de Bolaños

Named for the Canary Islands pioneer who settled Montecristi in 1533 (along with 60 other families), this beach is popular with locals and visitors – probably because of its relatively safe swimming in turquoise waters. Otherwise, it comes up short in the charm department. The beach fronts a development of vacation homes in various stages of construction and the palm trees lining the beach are too sparse to provide either beauty or shade. The beach is located a short distance outside the town of Montecristi. Take Calle Duarte past Montecristi's parque central until

North by Northwest

you come to a small bridge. Turn left at the Coco Mar Restaurant, which also marks the entrance to the beach. The national park office is at the far end of the beach.

■ Isla Cabrita (Little Goat Island)

This arid island has the prettiest beach in Montecristi, making it a popular stop with visitors. Ask about renting a boat (RD$500) at the national park station there.

■ Cayos Siete Hermanos (Seven Brothers Keys)

Pretty white-sand beaches on seven cactus-studded offshore desert islands make these Montecristi National Park spots popular with visitors and tour operators. To get to **El Atún**, the most notable beach isle, go to Playa Juan de Bolaños, where you can hire a boat for about RD$500.

■ Playa de los Muertos (Beach of the Dead)

This unremarkable beach probably isn't worth the trouble of crossing the small river (which you can do by foot or four-wheel drive vehicle) that separates it from Montecristi. But it is uncrowded, so if you'd like to seek it out, take the same route as for Playa Juan de Bolaños above – but, after crossing the bridge, turn right instead of left. The dirt road will lead you to the beach.

Diving

Río San Juan Area

The surrounding waters offer good beginning and advanced dive sites with abundant tropical fish and marine life. It's possible to see dolphins, whales (from January to March), barracudas, groupers up to four or five feet long, and many colorful reef fish. Make arrangements with **Gri-Gri Divers** across from the beach (Gaston Deligne 4, ☎ 589-2671, www.grigridivers.com). Rates range from US$65 for a resort course to full PADI certification for US$350. Single dives are US$40, with additional dives at package rates. All dives are from boats, three to 20 minutes from shore, and take place daily except Sunday at 8:30 am, 11:30 am, and 2:30 pm. Diving is good all year, but the water is warmest from April till October. The dozen or so dive sites range from 26 to 164 feet (eight to 50 meters) in depth, and are found amid caves, coral reefs, and underwater mountains. You can expect to see crabs, yellow sting rays and moray eels among many tropical fish and shellfish.

■ Dive Sites for Advanced Divers

Caves Dudu. This dive is in a freshwater lagoon in the lower range of the coastal mountains where the visibility is an astonishing 160+ feet (50 meters). It's a good spot for advanced divers to be introduced to the allures of cave diving.

Seven Hills. Three dives are required to see all of this underwater mountain of coral, which has a wall-like drop of more than 160 feet (50 meters).

Crab Canyon. Dives take you 85 feet/26 meters down through colorful coral arches.

Others: Nurse Shark Bank (131 feet/40 meters); Moray Bank (125 feet/38 meters); Slingshot Point (125 feet/38 meters); Alligator Alley (98 feet/30 meters); Eden Wall (79 feet/24 meters); and Crater (66 feet/20 meters).

■ Dive Sites for Intermediate Divers

The Boulders. 49 feet/15 meters, with cave and swim-through holes.

Chenchos Point. 46 feet/14 meters, with airlock cave and lots of swim throughs.

Cannons and Anchors. 39 feet/12 meters, with four large cannons and an anchor with coral.

■ Dive Sites for Beginners

Natural Swimming Pool. 16 to 33 feet/5 to 10 meters, with lots of fish and coral.

Cabarete Area Diving

Make arrangements with **Dolphin Dive Center** (☎ 571-0842) for underwater explorations of local reefs, walls, wrecks, and underwater caves and canyons. Depths reach 60 feet within the bay. Dives are US$28 each; a PADI course is US$299.

Sosúa Area Diving

Sosúa is the capital of north coast diving. Prime sites include a shipwreck, a canyon dive, and a wall dive. These sites are home to hundreds of tropical fish and plant life; grouper and porcupine fish are frequently spotted, as well as brightly colored fan coral. Among the habitual visitors to the area are whale sharks, manatees, and dolphins. **Northern Coast Diving** (Av. Pedro Clisante 8, ☎ 571-1028; www.northerncoastdiving.com; northern@verizon.net.do) offers a resort course for US$60 and full certification for US$325.

■ Sosúa Dive Sites

Moray eel

Wreck Dive (maximum depth 118 feet/36 meters). The sunken *Zingara*, a 148-foot (45-meter) cargo ship, is home to a six-foot moray eel that has a reputation for surprising curious divers. This dive has the additional feature of an adjacent reef wall, allowing divers the option to ascend to a shallower depth. The wall is host to numerous fan corals, whips, barrels, and tube sponges.

Octopus

Paradise Reef (maximum depth 104 feet/32 meters for advanced divers, 40 feet/12 meters for beginners). Advanced divers enjoy deep night dives here, good for spotting octopi and squid. Beginners dive along a colorful reef wall.

Chiquita Reef (maximum depth 100 feet/30 meters). Stingrays are the stars at Chiquita Reef, along with various schools of brightly colored tropical fish.

West Wall (maximum depth 100 feet/30 meters). Parallel to Sosúa beach, the West Wall begins at a depth of eight meters/ 26 feet and extends all the way to the ocean floor. Among other reef creatures living on the wall, the prickly sea urchin is particularly fond of the spot.

Airport Wall (maximum depth 80 feet/24 meters). Widely considered the best dive spot in the region, the reef wall begins at a depth of 40 feet/12 meters. The remaining 40 feet/12 meters is a maze of swim-throughs, caves, and schools of tropical fish. Inside one of the caves is a massive elkhorn coral, a rare creature that can flourish without sunlight.

Five Rocks (maximum depth 80 feet/24 meters). Suited for all levels of diving ability, Five Rocks is a bottom feeder's heaven. Lobsters, conchs, and crabs hide inside towering barrel sponges.

Sea urchin

Garden of Los Charamicos (maximum depth 80 feet/24 meters). Parallel to the Canyon, this underwater garden has spectacular sponge and coral formations, including large pink and purple fan corals and alien-looking, multi-colored barrel sponges.

Coral Gardens (maximum depth 60 feet/18 meters). Splendid outcrops of multi-colored coral rise up between patches of pure white sand. The plants that grow here attract queen angelfish.

Three Rocks (maximum depth 27 feet/8½ meters). Linked with Coral Gardens, these are three giant coral heads that span 150 feet/45 meters, hosting an incredible mix of tropical fish and plant life.

Pyramids (maximum depth 50 feet/15 meters). As a result of land eroding into the sea and chunks of the coastal cliffs falling off, the Pyramids are made up of gulleys, cliff corals, and swim-throughs.

Canyon (maximum depth 33 feet/10 meters). A split reef wall about 12 feet/4 meters high forms an underwater avenue filled with spectacular sponge life.

La Puntilla (the "little point" – maximum depth 30 feet/9 meters). Four fallen boulders have created a variety of caves and swim-throughs here. Species of particular interest are the barracuda, the spotted eagle ray, and the Jewfish.

Puerto Plata Area Diving

Contact **Caribbean Marine Diving Center** (Plaza Turisol, ☎ 261-3150) or **Dressel Divers** (Iberostar Costa Dorada, ☎ 320-1000) for diving expeditions.

El Castillo to Montecristi Diving

Fan coral

Less than a mile off the shores of El Castillo begins a large grouping of the healthiest and most intact set of coral reefs on the island, continuing on through Punta Rucia and ending at the far northwestern end of the country. There are few formal dive operations west of Sosúa, however. In Punta Rucia, check with Rainer Angermann of **Coral Reef Tours** (☎ /fax 656-0200; angermannskeet@hotmail.com) to help coordinate dive tours in that area. In El Castillo and Montecristi, ask around at your hotel or from locals if Angermann is unable to accommodate you.

Bahía de Manzanillo Diving

About 18 miles south of Montecristi, on the southern side of Parque Nacional Montecristi in the Bahía de Manzanillo, more than two dozen sunken ships await exploration. They include two Colonial-era Spanish galleons, the *Santa Catalina* and *San Jorge,* which were hauling cargoes of gold, jewels, and silver coins from Honduras when they sank during a storm. Experienced divers can explore these former treasure troves (the booty has long since been looted) with a survey team from Boston University that has been involved in an ongoing study of the wrecks. Contact info@oldship.com for information.

Snorkeling

The snorkeling is excellent at many points along the north coast, especially from Sosúa west to Montecristi, where coral reefs fringe the coastline. Most resorts can provide snorkeling equipment.

Cayo Arena (Sand Island)

Cayo Arena is an exquisite little sand bar just off the coast of Punta Rucia, surrounded by a still intact and healthy coral reef. To visit Cayo Arena independently, make arrangements a day in advance with one of the boat captains on the beach. Excursions from Punta Rucia range from US$75. Bring snacks, plenty of water, and a protective hat.

North by Northwest

Windsurfing & Kitesurfing

The Cabarete area, known worldwide for its ideal windsurfing conditions, is the capital of north coast windsurfing, though many resorts beyond Cabarete also offer windsurfing equipment and lessons, often included in the rates. The summer months – June through August – are ideal for windsurfing, when the trade winds range from 15 to 25 mph. Cabarete Bay is considered suitable for all levels, from beginners to expert. Beginners can practice inside the protective reef in the mornings, before winds pick up. Experts head out in the afternoons and venture beyond the reef, where waves can get high and the action fierce.

Kitesurfing (also called kiteboarding) is a rapidly growing sport that has held its 2003 and 2004 world championships in Cabarete. Rather than a sail, kitesurfing relies on a giant kite to catch the wind and propel riders across the ocean. Several days' lessons are highly recommended before trying it – there's a real element of danger, since riders can reach high speeds and controlling the boards requires practice. Expert kitesurfers can perform a variety of tricks and jumps, literally flying across and over the water. Inexperienced riders can find themselves propelled into risky collisions.

Windsurfing Schools

Carib Bic Center (Cabarete, ☎ 571-0640, www.caribwind.com) has several learn-to-windsurf packages available. Three-hour classes run US$100.

Fanatic Center Cabarete (Cabarete, ☎ 571-0861, www.fanatic-cabarete.com) has a number of lessons available, including US$19 for a one-hour group lesson and US$89 for five hours; the latter includes two weeks of rental equipment. Fanatic also has packages that provide accommodations and Spanish lessons.

Vela/Spinout High Wind Center (Cabarete, ☎ 571-0805, www.velacabarete.com) has two- to three-hour group lessons for US$50, or one-hour private lessons for US$45 ($55 with equipment rental).

Kitesurfing Schools

Caracol Kite Center (Cabarete, ☎ 571-0680, fax 571-0665, www.hotelcaracol.com) gives lessons for four days, two hours per day, for US$352 (private) or US$281 per person for a couple. Special packages are available that include rooms and other perks at the Apart Hotel Caracol Cabarete (see *Places to Stay, Cabarete*, below).

Kitexcite (Cabarete, ☎ 838-1225, www.kiteexcite.com) is Cabarete's oldest kitesurfing school, dating from 1999. Instructors use radio helmets to communicate with students while they're learning. Group lessons (up to three people) range from US$267 to $425; five-hour "blitz" courses are offered.

Vela/Dare2Fly (Cabarete, ☎ 571-0805, www.dare2fly.com) has three-day (nine hours) group lessons for US$330, featuring multi-lingual instructors.

Fishing

Fishing vessels go in search of grouper and barracuda in Atlantic waters. Contact **Fishing Tours** (Duarte 5, Río San Juan, ☎ 589-2753) or **Magante Fishing** (Mella 18, Río San Juan, ☎ 589-2677).

Cascading

 Iguana Mama (☎ 571-0908, www.iguanamama.com) runs guided cascading trips to the 27 waterfalls of Damajagua, a labyrinth of tunnels, caves, and natural pools. (Cascading combines hiking with sliding and jumping down waterfalls.) Although previous experience isn't necessary, participants need to know how to swim and should have decent upper-body strength. Tours leave Tuesdays, Thursdays, and Saturdays at 8 am and cost US$60 per person.

■ On Land

Golf

 Two north coast par-72 courses are ranked among the finest on the island:

Playa Grande Golf Course (Km 9 Carretera Río San Juan-Cabrera, ☎ 582-0860 ext. 27 or 800-858-2258), near Río San Juan, has been called the "Pebble Beach of the Caribbean," with 10 of its 18 holes bordering the ocean atop dramatic cliffs. Robert Trent Jones was design consultant. Make reservations in winter. Greens fees US$67 for 18 holes, caddy US$7, cart US$23.

Playa Dorada Golf Course (☎ 320-4262) was designed by Robert Trent Jones Jr. and surrounds the Playa Dorada resort complex. Greens fees US$40-$65 for 18 holes, caddy US$9, cart US$23.

Hiking

 Iguana Mama (☎ 571-0908, www.iguanamama.com) coordinates hiking treks up Mount Isabel de Torres near Puerto Plata. Prices are $65 per person for an all-day (8 am-3:30 pm,

North by Northwest

Mon, Fri, and Sun) trip. Start at sea level and finish near 2,700 feet; this is for intermediate to advanced hikers only.

Iguana Mama also runs three-hour guided hikes through El Choco National Park (see *Eco-Travel*, below). These are appropriate for all level hikers, and cost US$35 per person; they leave Wednesdays and Sundays at 8:30 am.

On Horseback

Adventure Riding Park (Abreu, ☎ 582-1170 ext. 1508) offers rides through the mountains south of the coast, starting at US$25.

Gipsy Ranch (Carretera Sosúa-Cabarete, opposite Coconut Palm Resort, ☎ 571-1373) is the largest riding stable in the region, offering one- to four-hour rides between Sosúa and Cabarete. Rates are US$22 per person for a two-hour ride.

Rancho Al Norte (☎ 223-0660) offers weekly packages with lodging and rides in the mountains near Cabarete, starting at US$690 per person, per week.

Rancho Marabel (Gaspar Hernández, ☎ 253-0954) has an all-day waterfall ride for US$60 per person; the price includes hotel pick-up in the Río San Juan area.

Rancho Montana (☎ 571-0990) takes riders along Playa Cabarete for US$25.

Rancho Sol y Mar (Cabarete, ☎ 571-0815) has riding tours departing from Sosúa and Cabarete.

■ On Wheels

Mountain Biking

Iguana Mama (☎ 571-0908, www.iguanamama.com) runs a variety of guided bike trips in the Cordillera Septentrional mountains south of the coast. The most popular is the 18-mile downhill cruise, good for just about all ages; it leaves Mondays at 8 am and costs US$85. After winding down mountain roads and a river swim, the trip includes an Indian lunch at the exotic Blue Moon Restaurant.

Another favorite (but more challenging) route is El Choco Road, once used to transport bananas to ports on the coast. The 28-mile ride includes both mountain and coastal scenery, with good views of the rural countryside near Cabarete. Half-day trips (Thursday and Saturday mornings) are US$40.

■ Organized Adventure Tours

Cafemba Tours (Calle Separación 12, ☎ 586-2177) can arrange Jeep safaris and more.

Cocotours (☎ 586-1311) offers a full range of guided adventure tours from Puerto Plata, including Jeep safaris, river rafting trips, and catamaran trips.

Freestyle Catamarans (Puerto Plata, ☎ 586-1239) runs full-day catamaran trips from Puerto Plata to Sosúa that include snorkeling for US$69.

Iguana Mama (☎ 571-0908, www.iguanamama.com) is the top adventure operator on the north coast, with mountain biking, hiking, rafting trips, and more.

Islabon Boat Jungle Tours (Sabaneta de Yásica, ☎ 696-3253) runs exotic half-day riverboat tours to a lagoon and back, passing through rainforest and mangroves.

Outback Safari (Plaza Turisol, Av. Luperón, Km 2.5, Puerto Plata, ☎ 244-4886, www.outbacksafari.com.do) offers Jeep safari tours to area beaches and into the mountains for US$69.

■ Spectator Sports

Puerto Plata's professional **baseball** team plays from November to February at José Briceno Stadium, off Aves. Circunvalación Sur and Hermanas Mirabal.

■ Eco-Travel

These parks are listed geographically from east to west along the north coast.

Laguna Gri-Gri

The parque central of Río San Juan serves as the entrance to a stunning mangrove lagoon and seabird habitat. Boats take visitors through the mangrove forests and to see caves and rocks. Most notable is the lengthy **Cueva de las Golondrinas**, formed by an 1846 rockslide and now filled with swallows. Half-day lagoon tours can be arranged either through your hotel or directly with **Campo Tours** (☎ 589-2550) for about US$20, but if you're staying in Río San Juan, you may just want to amble down to the dock and make your own arrangements with one of the fishing boat captains for about RD$500. The lagoon is open daily, during daylight hours only. The best time to spot wildlife is early morning.

Parque Nacional el Choco

This 30-square-mile park includes two lagoons – **Laguna Cabarete** and **Laguna Goleta** – that lie between the Atlantic Ocean and the hills of the Cordillera Septentrional near busy Cabarete beach. The lagoons, home to thousands of birds, are protected in large part by dense brush and are not all that easily accessible. Star attractions of the park are several underground caves near the lagoons that have large pools where you can swim and view some Taino petroglyphs. Some of the caves are more easily reached than others, so many visitors come with guided groups; organized tours, run by Iguana Mama and others, are about RD$300. You could also hop a *motoconcho* (about RD$40 plus tip) for a 45-minute ride through the brush. If you go on your own, from Highway 5 just west of town you can see the unpaved road and bulletin board indicating the entrance to the park, directly across from the Paraiso y Camino del Sol Resort. (Open Mon-Fri, 9 am-5 pm.)

Parque Nacional Isabel de Torres

Red-tailed hawk

This national park encompasses (and takes its name from) the highest of the mountains just south of Puerto Plata, 2,640-foot-high (805-meter) Isabel de Torres. Though one of the country's smallest national parks, it's also one of the most visited since it's so close to some of the main north coast resort areas. The most popular way to the top is by cable car (*teleférico*), though steep hiking trails are also available. The reward for reaching the summit (which is flat and easy to walk around) is a panoramic view of Puerto Plata and surroundings, as well as close-up views of a statue of Christ Redeemer (Cristo Redentor) with outstretched arms, similar to the more famous one on Corcovado in Río de Janeiro. Visitors can also roam among seven acres of tropical botanical gardens, where some 600 varieties of plants are kept lush by more than a dozen subterranean rivers. The gardens are also a bird sanctuary harboring nearly two dozen indigenous species, including rare Hispaniolan parrots and red-tailed hawks.

If you take the cable car, you'll have sensational views of the coast on the way up and down. Cable cars make the trip to the top Monday through Saturday from 8:30 am to 3:30 pm; the price is RD$50. The entrance is marked by a huge "*Teleférico*" sign on Avenida Circunvalación Sur west of town. A short hill (Ave. Teleférico) leads to the cable car. You can also hike up the mountain, a strenuous climb that you can do on your own on with a group. **Iguana Mama** (☎ 571-0908, www.iguanamama.com) leads guided hikes for US$65 per person.

Laguna Estero Hondo

This mangrove-lined lagoon between El Castillo and Punta Rucia is one of the last remaining areas in the country where you might catch a glimpse of the fast-disappearing manatee, which is endangered due to dwindling habitat and accidents involving speedboats. It's also a good place to spot birds, such as egrets and roseate spoonbills. Arrange excursions from El Castillo or Punta Rucia – check with **Punta Rucia Sol** (☎/fax 471-0173) – or take a four-wheel-drive vehicle, since you'll have to cross some rivers.

A MANATEE TALE

By 1875, when Samuel Hazard, author of *Santo Domingo: Past and Present*, visited the island, the number of manatees that had once inhabited the area had already significantly dwindled. In the account of his visit he retells a tale first published in 1671. The story goes that around the time the Spanish first arrived on the island, a Taino cacique kept a pet manatee in Estero Hondo. The animal had been domesticated and was so tame that when the cacique called him by his name, "Matoom," he would swim up to the cacique's home to be fed. Later he would return to the lagoon, sometimes giving rides to children on his back. One day, however, a Spaniard is said to have lashed out at him – and, as a result, Matoom would never again come out of the water if a clothed person was nearby. The manatee is said to have lived in the area for 26 years.

Parque Nacional Montecristi

This 212-square-mile park occupies the far northwestern corner of the country just off the Haitian border. Largely dry, hot, and studded with cacti, it includes two bays and a large river delta (where the Río Yaque del Norte empties into the sea), complete with coastal lagoons and mangrove swamps. Eight desert-like islets lie offshore. American crocodiles occupy the lagoons, sea turtles lay their eggs on the beaches, and seabirds find sanctuary on the islands.

The most recognizable aspect of the park, though (and sometimes referred to as a national park itself), is a flat-topped 778-foot (237-meter) limestone mesa named **El Morro**, which rises from the beaches and swamps on a small cape near the northern end of the park, near the town of Montecristi. The park service has built a set of stairs leading to the summit, but they're sometimes blocked off. Bad weather may be one reason – it can get very windy at the top. While there are no marked trails, it's fairly easy to get around El Morro on foot. Every January 21, on the national holiday of the Procession of Our Lady Altagracia, some 2,000 people make a religious pilgrimage to the top. The national park office is at the far end of Playa Juan de Bolaños near El Morro. The fee for entering is RD$50.

Great egret

Within the national park jurisdiction is **Isla Cabrita** (Little Goat Island), small, arid and marked by a lighthouse just off the northwestern point of the mainland. Though the terrain is dry, the beach is prettier than any other in Montecristi, making it a popular stop with visitors. It's also a bird sanctuary, harboring herons, egrets, and pelicans. Inquire about renting a boat from the park station at the foot of El Morro (RD$500) or on Playa Juan de Bolaños. One boat captain likes to entertain clients with tales about eating orange scrambled eggs in his youth, which he says came from the "bubi birds" that inhabit the island.

Other islands within the park are the **Cayos Siete Hermanos** (Seven Brothers Keys), seven small cactus-studded, sandy desert islets surrounded by reefs, less than a mile offshore. Endangered sea turtles lay their eggs there, and they also serve as bird sanctuaries; pretty white-sand beaches are a lure for visitors and tour operators as well. The most notable of the seven is El Atún (Tuna), which has remarkably gorgeous flowering cacti. To get to El Atún, go to Playa Juan de Bolaños (see *Beaches*, above), where you can hire a boat for about RD$500.

■ Other Outdoor Attractions

Lago Dudu

Much is made about this freshwater swimhole just off Highway 5 at La Entrada, about seven miles south of Cabrera. And, although it's every bit as idyllic as a Tarzan movie set (as it's often described), it is also tiny and ringed by lush foliage, leaving little space for sitting or even standing around. So tours and tourists usually stay just long enough to take a quick dip in the chilly deep waters before heading off. (Open daily during daylight hours only; RD$20.)

Parque Nacional Cabo Frances Viejo

This small national park features a lighthouse perched atop a majestic cliff overlooking breathtaking coastline. It's on a headland between Cabrera and Río San Juan. (Open Mon-Fri, 10 am-4 pm; RD$50.)

■ Historic Sites

Fort San Felipe

 Built in the mid-1500s, this is one of the oldest forts in the New World. On a promontory at the west end of the Malecón in Puerto Plata, it's the only remaining Colonial-era structure in the city, having survived the destruction of the city by the Spanish in 1605. In its day, the fort was regarded as impenetrable, complete with eight-foot-thick walls and a moat, all designed to keep pirates at bay. It was also used as a prison on and off for centuries, up through the time of Trujillo; among the illustrious "tenants" was Juan Pablo Duarte, the father of the country, who spent time here in 1844. A museum displays old weapons and artifacts, but the view of the coast from the turrets is more memorable. A seaside park borders the fort to the east, and an 1879-vintage lighthouse stands nearby. (☎ 261-6043; open daily 8-5; RD$10.)

Parque Nacional La Isabela (El Castillo)

This is one of the most historic sites not just in the DR, but in all the Americas. The national park protects the remaining ruins of Columbus' second settlement in the New World, founded in 1494. Technically, at least, La Navidad, which is on the Haitian side of the island, was the first settlement, though it was merely a fort constructed to house Columbus' sailors who had been stranded there when the flagship *Santa María* ran aground in late December 1492. None of the sailors left at La Navidad survived the first year. Named for the Spanish queen who dispatched Columbus on his voyages of discovery, La Isabela was also probably doomed from the start – one-third of its men took sick in the first week, and it was abandoned altogether in 1498.

Unfortunately, there isn't much left to see. Stones mark the outlines of several buildings, including the remnants of Columbus' house overlooking the ocean and a small church that was the site of the first Mass in the New World. A cemetery sits alongside the ruins, where scientists have unearthed the skeletal remains of perished Spaniards; one of them is displayed in the cemetery. A small museum containing Spanish and Taino artifacts found in the area sits nearby. Some of the archeological treasures were inadvertently destroyed during the Trujillo era, when the dictator ordered his men to clean up the site before an official visit; alas, unknowing workers bulldozed some of the ruins into the sea as part of the "clean up."

Still, busloads of visitors eager to walk in the footsteps of history continue to make the journey here from Puerto Plata and other north coast tourist centers. Even without much to peruse, the chance to stand on the same cliff that Columbus did and peer down on the bay (which probably looks much the same as it did 500 years ago) can be a memorable event. The area was made a national park in 1998, and excavations continue.

The park is an ordeal to get to on one's own, so most come by guided tour. If you do drive, take Highway 5 south from Puerto Plata to Imbert, and then Route 30 (Carretera Luperón) west to Luperón. At Luperón, follow the huge sign pointing to the Templas Las Américas (see below), a church across the road from La Isabela. (The park is also mentioned on the sign, but in smaller lettering.) The road leads west to the park.

> **Warning:** Avoid Route 29, which on maps appears to be a straight shot to La Isabela from the south. It isn't. You will make it as far as the modern town of La Isabela, but the road to the park is impassable after that. Locals will divert you east toward El Estrecho, where you'll have to traverse a long bumpy road and cross three small rivers, with the help of locals who will guide you across the shallow parts in exchange for a tip. Eventually you'll reach Route 30, the paved road that leads to the park from Luperón. Take lots of water and make sure you have sufficient gas before setting out.

If you don't have a rental car, you can catch a *guagua* from Puerto Plata to Imbert, transfer to another to Luperón, and then take a *motoconcho* to La Isabela, a two-hour trip.

While it's also possible to visit the ruins coming east from Punta Rucia, there are two small river beds along the dirt track running between the two towns that often make it difficult to pass without a four-wheel-drive vehicle. Boat captains might be enticed to make the trip from Punta Rucia – arriving by water as Columbus did does have a certain romantic appeal – but this too can be an especially bumpy ride if the waters are rough. It's also expensive, running at least RD$1,000 for fuel alone. (☎ 472-4204; open 9 am to 5:30 pm, Mon-Sat, closed Sun; park admission RD$50.)

> **Did you know?** If you're driving backroads in the Dominican Republic and have to forge a river or two along the way, keeping a light foot on the accelerator can help you from getting stuck in the rivers while trying to cross. The gas blowing out of your exhaust will prevent water from getting in and causing your car to stall. In other words, don't try to plow too quickly through the river – but don't take your foot off the accelerator, either. Continue driving slowly and steadily.

Templas las Américas

This charming and rather elegant little neo-colonial church, built in 1992 to commemorate the 500th anniversary of Columbus' arrival, is across the road from the entrance to the La Isabela ruins. Inside, the church is quite bare and austere, except for beautiful stained glass windows and brightly painted and framed stations of the cross. It's open daily from 8:30 am-5 pm, with free admission.

A MYTH & A MISTAKE

The notion that Christopher Columbus was one of the few people of his day to believe the world was round was a myth that originated centuries later. By the late 15th century, few scientists clung to the belief in a flat earth. Columbus, though, did propound a theory that Asia lay much closer to Europe than was commonly supposed. Navigators at the time knew of one sea route to south Asia: around the Cape of Good Hope, the southern tip of Africa. Columbus surmised that by crossing the Atlantic and approaching Asia from the east rather than the west, he could shorten a treacherous journey by weeks or even months. So when Columbus and crew arrived in the Bahamas after a five-week voyage from the Canary Islands in the fall of 1492, he was convinced he had found India (hence the word "Indians" for the natives). And he went to his grave in 1506 still believing he had found a new route to the Indies. By that time, ironically, a rival explorer, Italian Amerigo Vespucci, had already surveyed the coast of South America in 1499. After announcing that he had found an entirely new continent – which lay between Europe and Asia – Vespucci was immortalized for the discovery. In Vespucci's honor, a mapmaker of the day labeled the land "America." Columbus, in turn, had to settle for the country of Colombia as a namesake.

■ Cultural & Other Attractions

Brugal Rum Bottling Plant

Short guided tours show how rum is bottled at this Puerto Plata plant, located on the well-traveled road to Playa Dorada. Afterwards, tour-goers are treated to free daiquiris on the patio. (Highway 5, Puerto Plata, ☎ 586-2531; open Mon-Fri, 8-3; free.)

Museo Judio Sosúa (Hebrew Colony Museum)

Located in the old Jewish settlement of Sosúa, established by refugees from Nazi Germany in World War II, this synagogue with small attached museum has exhibits on the Jewish colony in El Batey. (Martínez and Dr. Rosen, Sosúa, ☎ 571-1386; open Mon-Fri, 9 am-1 pm and 2 pm-4 pm; RD$65.)

Museo del Ámbar (Amber Museum)

Housed in a beautifully restored Victorian mansion near Puerto Plata's parque central, the Museo del Ámbar is superior to the amber museums in Santo Domingo (which are more like glorified jewelry stores). Guided tours are given in English. A big part of its excellent collection of rare amber (which is fossilized resin) are pieces containing plants, insects, and tiny lizards that have been trapped inside for millions of years. The best amber in the world comes from the Cordillera Septentrional mountains just south of Puerto Plata, and you can buy some if it here if you wish. (Calle Duarte 61, Puerto Plata, ☎ 320-2215, RD$25, open Mon-Sat, 9-6; closed Sun.)

Museo Máximo Gómez

The Montecristi home once owned by the Dominican-born 19th-century Cuban revolutionary now serves as a museum that exhibits various personal effects, photos, and an account of his attempts to liberate both Cuba and the Dominican Republic from Spain. The chatty curator (who unfortunately speaks Spanish only) is a wealth of knowledge for anyone interested in Dominican history. (Calle Mella, Montecristi; open Mon-Fri, 9 am to noon and 2:30-5:30 pm; free admission.)

■ Family Attractions

Columbus Aquaparque

This enormous waterpark near Sosúa has 25 rides with names such as Kamikaze Slide (with a dramatic high drop), Blackhole (a wild ride through pitch darkness), Lazy River (a winding raft ride that runs the length of the park), as well as a number of restaurants, bars and souvenir shops. (Carretera Puerto Plata-Sosúa, ☎ 571-2642; open daily 10 am-6 pm; RD$200.)

Fun City Action Park

Especially popular with teenagers, this amusement park near Playa Dorada has go-karts, sprint and midget cars, grand prix cars, and bumper cars on four separate racing tracks. Admission charge includes unlimited racing, and free shuttle service is offered from Playa Dorada, Cofresí, the Riu Resort complex, and Sosúa. (Km 8 Carretera Puerto Plata-Sosúa, ☎ 320-1031, www.funcity-gocarts.com; US$15 adults, US$10 children.)

Ocean World Adventure Park

This new zoological marine park, jutting out on a point at the resort town of Cofresí west of Puerto Plata, takes animal "encounters" to a whole new level. If you've ever wanted to swim with sharks – or touch, pet, and feed them – you can do it here, in what's billed as the world's first shark interaction pool (these are the non-man- , woman- , or child-eating varieties). Perhaps you'd rather swim with tigers – you can do that here, too (though in this case you're separated by a window). You can also have close-up encounters with sea lions, stingrays, and bottlenose dolphins, in the "world's largest dolphin lagoon."

Animal rights activists and many environmentalists are highly critical of the practice of swimming with dolphins, pointing to various premature dolphin deaths in similar facilities, though Ocean World claims its trained dolphins are happy with the idea. Still, you can have fun at Ocean World without communing with Flipper. A tropical rainforest features an aviary with dozens of colorful birds. A reef pool permits safe snorkeling amid an array of exotic fish. And a swim grotto (which blends into the tiger habitat) invites swimmers to cool off against a backdrop of waterfalls and lush vegetation. None of this comes cheap – some of the animal encounters cost US$80 to $145 on top of the admission price. But for families, especially, who don't get much taste of the tropical wild outside the resort "wildlife," a day at Ocean World may be the ticket. (Cofresí, ☎ 291-1000, www.ocean-world.info; regular admission US$55 adults, US$40 ages 4-18, includes round-trip bus transport from some hotels; US$25 admission price with additional paid dolphin and sea lion encounters.)

North by Northwest

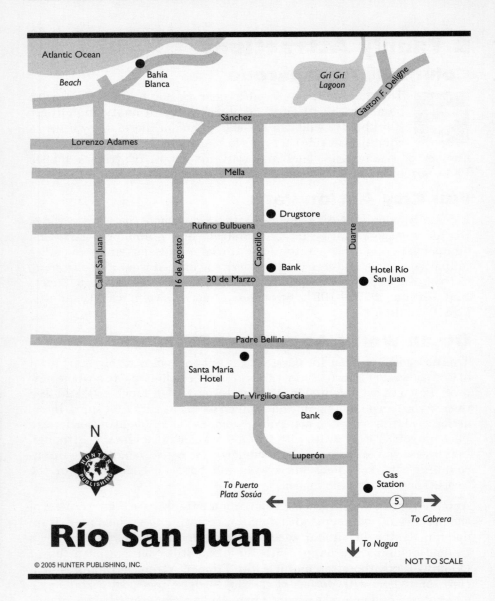

Atlantic Ocean

Beach

Bahía Blanca

Grí Grí Lagoon

Gaston F. Deligne

Sánchez

Lorenzo Adames

Mella

Drugstore

Rufino Bulbuena

Calle San Juan

16 de Agosto

Capotillo

Duarte

Bank

30 de Marzo

Hotel Río San Juan

Padre Bellini

Santa María Hotel

Dr. Virgilio Garcia

Bank

N

Luperón

Gas Station

To Puerto Plata Sosúa

5

To Cabrera

To Nagua

Río San Juan

NOT TO SCALE

Bases for Exploration

■ Río San Juan

This sleepy, quiet, small town is bordered by the thick mangrove swamps of Laguna Grí-Grí (see *Eco-Travel*, above), and, a few miles east, the glorious 1½-mile Playa Grande (see *Beaches*, above). A number of resorts in the area, which include those in nearby Breton and Cabrera, have opened here to take advantage of the beautiful beaches. Río San Juan also has a growing reputation as a diving center, with coral reefs and underwater caves and mountains to explore. Jeep safari tours also set out from here into the local countryside.

Getting Here & Getting Around

Caribe Tours offers daily direct service to Río San Juan from Santo Domingo five times a day: 6:30, 8, and 9:30 in the morning, or twice in the afternoon at 2 and again at 3:30. You can also take a *guagua* east to Río San Juan from Puerto Plata or Sosúa via coastal Highway 5, though you'll have to transfer several times along the way. *Guaguas* also ply Highway 5 east from Río San Juan to Breton, Cabrera, and Nagua regularly during daylight hours.

Rental cars are available at two hotels (contact **Lucke, S.A.**, ☎ 582-1170 ext. 1534 at the Occidental, or ☎ 226-1590 ext. 2045 at the Bahía Principe). The area's 24-hour taxi service can be reached at ☎ 589-2501 in Río San Juan, ☎ 582-1170 ext. 1536 in Playa Grande, or ☎ 589-7474 in Cabrera.

Places to Stay

Bahía Principe San Juan (Playa Escondido, ☎ 226-1590, fax 226-1991, www.bahia-principe.com) $$$$

This massive 941-room all-inclusive complex just west of town is virtually a village unto itself, complete with tropical gardens, walkways, and surrounding mangrove swamps. It's also the

HOTEL PRICE CHART	
Rates are per room based on double occupancy.	
$	Under US$20
$$	US$20-$50
$$$	US$51-$100
$$$$	Over US$100

oldest resort in Río San Juan, having started out in 1995 catering primarily to Germans. (A fair number of the former guests now live as expats in the area, partially explaining the presence of so many German businesses here.) All rooms have air conditioning, satellite TV, balcony or terrace, and telephone. The resort is set on a three-mile-long private beach sheltered by a coral reef. Amenities include seven restaurants, 11 bars, two swimming pools, watersports (including windsurfing, catamarans, kayaking), tennis, mini-golf, bicycle rentals, fitness center, merengue classes, kids' club, and daily shuttle service to Cabarete and Sosúa.

North by Northwest

Occidental Allegro Playa Grande (Playa Grande, ☎ 582-1170, fax 582-6094, www.occidental-hoteles.com) $$$$

Formerly known as Caribbean Village Playa Grande, this 300-room all-inclusive complex overlooks the choicest beachfront along this stretch of coastline, the 1½-mile-long Playa Grande. The Robert Trent Jones-designed golf course (☎ 582-0860), with 10 holes overlooking the sea, is rated one of the best in the world. The rest of the resort (such as the swimming pool) doesn't live up to the five-star standards of the beach and golf course, but you can still eat well at the Brazilian and Italian restaurants and even at the buffets.

Hostal La Catalina (Cabrera, ☎ 589-7700, fax 598-7550, www.lacatalina.com) $$$

This small hotel is out of town and a bit hard to find, but is one of the most atmospheric inns in the region. Each of its 30 rooms and apartments has its own ocean view with balcony or patio. Amenities include an excellent French restaurant (see *Places to Eat*, below), shuttle service to nearby beaches and Playa Grande Golf Course, and transfers from Puerto Plata airport. La Catalina is known for its service, and the staff can arrange diving and eco-tours, deep-sea fishing excursions, and horseback or hiking trips. Ask about the local bird-watching and waterfall excursions.

Hotel Bahía Blanca (Calle Gaston F. Deligne, Río San Juan, ☎ 589-2563, fax 589-2528) $$

This hotel has a convenient location just in front of tiny Playa Río San Juan and is a roll out of bed to the entrance of Laguna Gri-Gri (see *Eco-Travel*, above). The rooms are large and comfortable, with hot-water showers, ceiling fans, and in-room fridges. An on-site restaurant/bar with terrace overlooking the beach is a pleasant setting for dining or passing the evening.

Places to Eat

 Around the lagoon along Calle Sanchez in Río San Juan are a number of *comedors* where you can get good Dominican food for about RD$65. The following are more formal restaurants.

La Catalina Restaurant (Cabrera, ☎ 598-7700) $$$

DINING PRICE CHART	
Price per person for an entrée, not including beverage or tip.	
$	Under US$2
$$	US$2-$10
$$$	US$10-$20
$$$$	Over US$20

The French food at the restaurant attached to Hostal La Catalina doesn't come cheap, but the high quality, fine service, extensive wine list, and patio dining make it a good choice for a splurge. You'll need your own transport – it's a few miles outside town. Call ahead for reservations and directions.

Restaurant El Mangle (Laguna Gri-Gri, no phone) $$-$$$

This open-air restaurant serves pricey seafood mostly to package tourists visiting Laguna Gri-Gri. But its exotic location – tucked away in the thick of the mangroves across a suspended footbridge – helps make up for its shortcomings.

Cheo's Café Bar (Padre Billini 68, Río San Juan, ☎ 589-2377) $$

The *platos diversos* here include seafood, meats, pastas, and pizzas, served up in casual surroundings.

Pizza El Dorado (Cabrera, ☎ 589-7231) $$

Pizza, sandwiches, and salads are the fare at this popular Cabrera sports bar, which comes equipped with satellite TV for watching the big games.

Rancho Grande Bar & Grill (Mata Puerco, near Playa Grande, ☎ 343-8756) $$

Within a stone's throw of the Occidental Allegro Playa Grande, this restaurant specializes in excellent steaks and other grilled meats. It's a good option for those who want a change of scenery or who tire of the buffet lines at the all-inclusives.

Restaurant Criolla (Playa Grande, ☎ 223-0679) $$

Before or after sampling the fresh and filling Dominican food here, the owners invite guests to stroll through their large garden, featuring more than 170 types of fruits and vegetables.

Restaurante Virginia (Breton, ☎ 589-7218) $$

If you're looking for reasonably priced – and very good – seafood served by an attentive and friendly staff, this restaurant is well worth a short trip to Breton.

Nightlife & Entertainment

 Things generally slow to a crawl in Río San Juan after the Jeep safari tours return guests to their hotels, but some signs of life do crop up at the local watering holes around the lagoon, where people gather just to sit and chat for the evening. **Mega Disco**, the only formal nightclub in town, keeps an inconsistent schedule but is a fun place when it's open. It's at the east end of Carretera Sanchez, facing the lagoon.

■ Cabarete

Orientation

 Way back in the 1980s, Cabarete was a quiet fishing village along Highway 5 that literally took less than five minutes to drive by. Those who visited the town and its magnificent beach generally stayed with people they knew or rented a humble room in the home of one of the modest families who lived in the area. But those early visitors would barely recognize the Cabarete of today. The former peace and tranquility have given way to hordes of mostly young people who come from around the world for the surf, sun, and non-stop fun. To call Cabarete "lively" would be an understatement. From sunup into the wee hours of the morning, the resort is alive and jumping, with a pace that's more than frenetic and a volume that's on full blast. Picture "college spring break" 365 days a year and you've got the idea.

The main town itself occupies a strip of coastal Highway 5 that's no more than a half-mile long and no wider than a small two-lane road. On the north side of the highway is the beach – though at this point you can't see it from the road anymore since so many hotels, restaurants and shops now line the strip. (The upside to this is that those same restaurants spill onto the wide beach at night, which makes for wonderful seaside dining in the sands.) On the other side of the highway are more shops and restaurants, and just a bit farther to the south lie lagunas Cabarete and Goleta, part of El Choco National Park (see *Eco-Travel*, above).

What has made Cabarete so popular? Simply put, it's become the windsurfing capital of the Americas, widely recognized as one of the top 10 windsurfing spots in the world. Back in the mid-1980s, legendary Canadian windsurfer Jean la Porte discovered that Cabarete Bay contained ideal winds and other conditions for the sport. In 1988, Cabarete hosted the first professional World Cup of windsurfing, and it's often been held here since. To accommodate the windsurfers, hotels and adventure sports outfits have followed in their wake. The area has also become a hotbed for the more recently developed sport of kitesurfing, and has hosted world championships in that sport as well.

Getting Here & Getting Around

Cabarete is about 15 miles east of the north coast's international airport, and is easily reached by *guagua* from Puerto Plata and Sosúa, which lie to the west along Highway 5. Highway 5 also connects Cabarete to Río San Juan and the Samaná Peninsula to the east. From Santo Domingo, **Carib Tours buses** travel north to Puerto Plata, and then *guaguas* travel east to Cabarete.

Motoconchos go up and down the strip in town, though you may feel that you're taking your life in your hands to ride them.

Places to Stay

Azzurro Club Cabarete (Calle Principal, ☎ 571-4000, fax 571-4545, www.starzresorts.com) $$$$

Opened in 2004, the Azzurro Club is a colorful, eye-catching addition to the Cabarete beachfront. Positioning itself to attract a hip young sports-minded clientele, it features 108 rooms and nicely land-scaped grounds with plenty of palm trees and a beautiful pool.

Paraiso y Camino del Sol Resort (Calle Principal, ☎ 571-0893, fax 571-0892, www.amhsamarina.com) $$$$

This four-star, 189-room all-inclusive is a good choice if you'd like to stay a bit removed from the frenetic activity of Cabarete, yet close enough to take in the action when you want to – it's about two miles and a short shuttle ride away from town (provided free by the hotel). Divided into two sections – Paraiso del Sol and Camino del Sol – the resort caters to both couples and families. You can take free scuba diving lessons in one of the three swimming pools here, or get windsurfing lessons at Cabarete Beach. Three buffet restaurants, an à la carte Italian restaurant, a lunchtime pool grill, and three bars take the edge off hunger and thirst.

Viva Wyndham Tangerine (Carretera Cabarete, ☎ 571-0402, fax 571-9550, www.vivaresorts.com) $$$$

This activity-oriented all-inclusive opened in late 2003 with 222 rooms. All come equipped with king- or queen-size beds, air conditioning, satellite TV, telephone, and private balcony or terrace. Watersports (with free group instruction) include windsurfing, kayaking, sailing, snorkeling, and diving for beginners. For dining and drinking, there are three restaurants, a snack bar, and two bars; at night, the staff stages one of 14 different nightly shows, and there are also theme parties and dancing. A kids' club provides supervised activities for ages 4 to 12, and there's a mini-disco for kids as well.

Apart Hotel Caracol Cabarete (Carratera Cabarete, ☎ 571-0680, fax 571-0665, www.hotelcaracol.com) $$$

You can have all the comforts of a (very nice) home with the services of a resort here. Among the amenities are two swimming pools with Jacuzzi and swim-up bar, two restaurants (one with a live "Tropical Show"), a massage clinic, a kids' playground and babysitting service (the latter for a fee), gift shop, ice cream parlor, free Internet, business center, currency exchange, daily maid service, free parking, and beach towel and laundry service. The one- and two-bedroom apartments come with large balconies and fully equipped kitchens, while the bright and spacious studios have kitchenettes. The penthouse apartment, good for a family, includes two bedrooms and two baths and a full kitchen. Rates include breakfast.

Cita del Sol (Carretera Cabarete, ☎ 571-0720, fax 571-0795, www.citadelsol.com) $$-$$$

With 47 one-bedroom apartments equipped with kitchens, air conditioning, cable TV, daily maid service, and telephones, this apart-hotel is one of the best deals in Cabarete. It has a good location on the beach as well.

Hotel Villa Taina (Carretera Cabarete, ☎ 571-0722, fax 571-0883, www.villataina.com) $$-$$$

Centrally located and on the beach, this attractive hotel with tropical ambience offers 53 comfortable, tastefully furnished rooms. All units are air-conditioned and feature a spacious balcony or terrace, cable TV, telephone, DSL connection, mini-bar/refrigerator, and in-room safe. When it's time for action, you can hit the pool or windsurfing center. Villa Taina prides itself on ethnic touches: The lobby displays some Taino artifacts (the hotel is named for the island's now extinct indigenous inhabitants), and management has even employed Chinese *feng shui* techniques to foster a harmonious setting.

Hotel Casa Blanca (Carretera Cabarete, ☎ 571-0934, www.casablancacabarete.com) $-$$$

The two two-story buildings here are set directly on the beach and come with a combination of studios with kitchenettes and one-bedroom apartments. Accommodations are basic yet comfortable and cater to everyone from individual travelers to couples and groups vacationing together. Prices range from US$10-12 for rooms with shared baths to US$20-60 for those with private bath.

Hotel El Pequeño Refugio (Carretera Cabarete, ☎ 571-0770) $$

Complete with its own windsurf rental shop (Club Mistral), this moderately priced 40-room hotel has a nice beach location and is understandably popular with windsurfers. (As the hotel touts itself, "Only one minute from bed to board!") There's nothing fancy about the rooms, but they are clean and comfortable and have private baths with shower. A restaurant and beach bar are on premises. For those on more of a budget, its adjacent sister property, Casa Verde (same phone), offers inexpensive and very basic cold-water rooms.

Places to Eat

 When it comes to eating outside of a resort, many of the tourist hubs in the DR offer the same selection: pasta, pasta...and pasta, perhaps with a side of pizza. Cabarete is another story. The row of bars and restaurants fronting the beach reflect the diversity of the expat community that calls Cabarete home. Add to that the restaurants' nightly custom of placing tables and chairs on the sands for wave-side dining, and Cabarete's restaurants rank near the top in the country for atmosphere and variety.

Cabarete Blú (Calle Principal, ☎ 571-9714) $$-$$$

While the international fare is nothing extraordinary, the open-air patio – under the palm trees and the stars, dead-smack on Cabarete Beach – proves a memorable setting.

Chez León (Calle Principal, ☎ 571-3346) $$

This French and Belgian bistro on the main strip is a great place for breakfast and brunch; don't miss the scrumptious Belgian waffles.

El Chino (Calle Principal, ☎ 571-0972) $$

This is the spot to satisfy any cravings for Asian food. Chinese is the main cuisine, but you can also get Indonesian specialties here.

Ho-La-La Café (Calle Principal, ☎ 571-0806) $$

Seafood comes with a French twist at this cute little bistro on the strip. Portions are large considering the reasonable prices. The seafood chowder is a must and the fresh lobster is some of the best prepared in Cabarete.

José O'Shay's Irish Beach Pub (Calle Principal, ☎ 571-0775) $$

A Latino-Irish bar? In cosmopolitan Cabarete, it makes complete sense. This lively pub serves breakfast, lunch, dinner, and late-night snacks, when O'Shay's really starts hopping. (Then again, what bar in Cabarete doesn't?) If you're hankering for an American-style cheeseburger, this is the place. O'Shay's also offers nightly seafood specials along with live music and a wide-screen satellite TV for sporting events.

Miro's on the Beach (Calle Principal, ☎ 571-0888) $$

Cabarete's finest restaurant serves up "Cocina Ecléctic," an inventive (and tasty) fusion of Caribbean and North African cuisines. With its waterside locale, it's hard to top the combination of food and atmosphere here.

Schnitzel Paradise (Calle Principal, ☎ 753-7541) $$

You may never have previously contemplated patronizing a combo Austrian-Mexican restaurant – Arnold Schwarzenegger bench-pressing burritos comes to mind – but the atmosphere is so convivial here that even the thought of schnitzels with margaritas starts to make sense.

Pandería Repositera Dick (Calle Principal, no phone) $-$$

This bread and dessert bakery is overwhelmingly popular anytime of the day (except Sunday afternoon when it's closed) and is *the* place for breakfast. Inviting décor and an open-air setting on the road's edge make it a great place for people-watching on Cabarete's main strip.

Nightlife & Entertainment

You won't have trouble finding nightlife in Cabarete. Bars on the strip come alive at night, some transforming into discos and clubs, often with live music. Dance clubs include **Bambu**, **Ono's**, **Lax**, and **Crazy West**, all of which play Euro pop and American music, though some DJs spin merengue and salsa. You can also check out the **Tiki Bar** and **Café Pitu**. None of these places has an address or phone number – but you can't miss them as you cruise the strip.

José O'Shay's Irish Beach Pub (Calle Principal, ☎ 571-0775)

Live music complements the late-night snack menu at this lively Latin-accented Irish pub.

Los Brisas (Calle Principal, ☎ 571-0614)

A restaurant by day and early evening, Las Brisas becomes a popular bar and disco as midnight approaches. They're more likely to play merengue and bachata here than at some of the other clubs.

Miro's on the Beach (Calle Principal, ☎ 571-0888)

Besides being a great place to eat (see above), Miro's serves as a venue for the annual Puerto Plata Jazz Festival (which extends as far as Sosúa and Cabarete) in October.

■ Sosúa

Orientation

 Compared to spring-break-like Cabarete, Sosúa is like graduating from university and entering the "real world" – or at least a mellower world. The main strip, Pedro Clisante in El Batey, is nice for walking and is lined with shops, restaurants, and bars, which are a little more upmarket than Cabarete.

Sosúa Bay is stunningly beautiful and placid. A stroll along the waterfront around the north bend of **Pedro Clisante**, with cliffs overlooking the bay and gentle waves lapping below, is one of the most pleasant spots in the entire region. There are three beaches here, the central one being **Playa Sosúa**. On the east end of the playa is **El Batey**, the onetime Jewish barrio, first populated in 1940 by several hundred refugees fleeing from Nazi Germany; some of their descendants remain here today. Today, El Batey caters mainly to tourists, with hotels, restaurants, shops, and a variety of tourist services – banks, Internet cafes, clinics, a pharmacy, and a Western Union office – scattered amid the upscale residential areas. If you're looking for more local color, at the west end of playa is a traditional Dominican neighborhood, **Los Charamicos**, where you'll find chickens pecking amid the fruit and vegetable stands and shacks housing residents and rum houses.

If there's a downside to Sosúa, it's prostitution. After reducing its notorious earlier reliance on the sex industry in the 1990s, Sosúa has seen it return with a vengeance as a result of the severe economic downturn since 2001. About the best you can say is that the sex market has not yet reached the visibility of that in Boca Chica on the Caribbean coast.

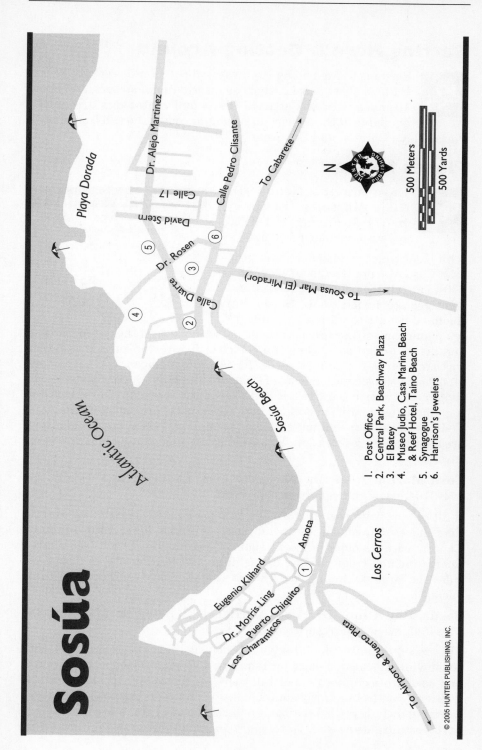

Sosúa

Atlantic Ocean

Playa Dorada

Sosúa Beach

Dr. Alejo Martinez

Calle Pedro Clisante

Calle 17

David Stern

Dr. Rosen

Calle Duarte

To Cabarete

To Sousa Mar (El Mirador)

⑤
④
③
②
⑥

Los Cerros

Amota

Eugenio Klihard

Dr. Morris Ling

Puerto Chiquito

Los Charamicos

①

To Airport & Puerto Plata

N

500 Meters

500 Yards

1. Post Office
2. Central Park, Beachway Plaza
3. El Batey
4. Museo Judio, Casa Marina Beach
   & Reef Hotel, Taino Beach
5. Synagogue
6. Harrison's Jewelers

North by Northwest

Getting Here & Getting Around

Sosúa is located along Highway 5 about 17 miles east of Puerto Plata, a short drive east of the international airport, and about 10 miles west of Cabarete. Taxis and rental cars are readily available at the airport, and *guaguas* make the run from Puerto Plata, Playa Dorada, and Cabarete.

Places to Stay

Casa Marina Beach (Dr. Alejo Martínez, El Batey, ☎ 571-3690, fax 571-3110, www.amhsamarina.com) $$$$

HOTEL PRICE CHART	
Rates are per room based on double occupancy.	
$	Under US$20
$$	US$20-$50
$$$	US$51-$100
$$$$	Over US$100

A bit older than its adjacent sister property, Casa Marina Reef (see below), this 300-room all-inclusive resort sits on a semi-private beach along Sosúa Bay. Rooms have air conditioning, cable TV, telephone, and either terrace or balcony with views of the ocean, the garden areas, or the pool. There's a choice of five restaurants (two buffet, three à la carte, including seafood, Italian, and Mexican) and seven bars, all of them shared with guests of Casa Marina Reef. Supervised kids' activities and a cash-bar disco is included in the rates, but horseback riding, nighttime tennis, and motorized watersports are extra. At the Aqua Center, snorkeling equipment, kayaks, small sailboats, and windsurfers are available by reservation. You can also arrange fishing and diving excursions.

Casa Marina Reef (Dr. Alejo Martínez, El Batey, ☎ 571-3535, fax 571-3104, www.amhsamarina.com) $$$$

Built on a private reef in 2001, the 378-room all-inclusive Casa Marina Reef shares many facilities (including restaurants, bars, disco, and Aqua Center) with its older adjacent sister, Casa Marina Beach (see above). Rooms include tropical-style furnishings and local crafts as décor. Besides one large swimming pool, there's a smaller children's pool and three Jacuzzis.

Sosúa Bay Club (Dr. Alejo Martínez, El Batey, ☎ 571-4000, fax 571-4545, www.starzresorts.com) $$$$

This recently built colonial-style all-inclusive has 193 rooms, 144 with ocean view. It's a good place for families, with supervised kids' activities and a separate children's pool, but there's plenty of activity for adults as well, ranging from nightly shows to scuba clinics in the pool. Buffet restaurants include grilled seafood, sushi, and pasta, and there are two à la carte restaurants as well. Watersports include windsurfing, kiteboarding (with instruction), kayaking, and Sunfish sailing, all part of the all-inclusive package.

Victorian House (Dr. Alejo Martínez, El Batey, ☎ 571-4000, fax 571-4545, www.starzresorts.com) $$$$

This five-star boutique hotel began life as a plantation house built by the United Fruit Company in the early 1900s as a getaway for its owners. Built on a cliff overlooking Sosúa Bay, it's now one of the most romantically situated hotels in the country, with 50 Caribbean-styled rooms, a spa with massage therapist, four restaurants, and five bars. Hors d'oeuvres are served on the terrace at sunset, and 24-hour room service picks up the slack.

Piergiorgio Palace Hotel (Calle La Puntilla, ☎ 571-2626, fax 571-2786, www.piergiorgiohotel.com) $$$-$$$$

This gleaming white, 51-room faux-Victorian hotel sits perched on a cliff 100 feet over the ocean, a bit west of the city center. Rooms are good-sized and each opens out onto a veranda for soaking up the views of water, sunsets, the pool, or Pico Isabel de Torres to the west. The tropical décor runs to rattan and colorful bedspreads. You can choose among pricing plans that include room and breakfast only, or all meals if you wish. The excellent on-premises Italian restaurant has a spectacular setting (see *Places to Eat*, below).

Hotel Yaroa (Calle Dr. Rosen 25, ☎ 271-2651, fax 271-3814) $$

Under Dutch management and just five minutes' walk from the beach, the Hotel Yaroa is known for offering good value. Rooms are best suited for two persons each (though a third person can fit) and come with air conditioning, ceiling fans, telephones, and balconies. The European-style on-premises restaurant serves breakfast, lunch, and dinner, not included in the rates. There's also a small bar, a rooftop sundeck, and a pool where you can get beginning scuba-diving instruction.

Tropix Hotel (Libre, El Batey, ☎/fax 571-2291, www.tropixhotel.com) $$

Co-owned by an American woman born in Sosúa and descended from some of the town's first Jewish settlers, the Tropix was one of Sosúa's first hotels, established in the 1980s. Casual, secluded, and with just 10 rooms (including four suites) in small two-story buildings, it's a nice alternative to the big resorts that now dominate the beaches. Rooms overlook tropical gardens and the pool; breakfast, which costs a bit extra, is served poolside. A small kitchen is available for communal use. The hotel is within walking distance of the beach, restaurants, and shops, and horseback riding excursions can be arranged.

North by Northwest

Places to Eat

La Puntilla de Piergiorgio
(Calle La Puntilla, ☎ 571-2626) $$-$$$

The restaurant at the Piergiorgio Palace Hotel (see *Places to Stay*, above) offers some of the best Italian cuisine on the north coast, especially its fresh fish. But it's most notable for its seven outdoor patios and bars that provide wonderful views of the ocean at sunset.

DINING PRICE CHART	
Price per person for an entrée, not including beverage or tip.	
$	Under US$2
$$	US$2-$10
$$$	US$10-$20
$$$$	Over US$20

Morua Mai (Pedro Clisante, El Batey, ☎ 571-2966) $$-$$$

This popular patio restaurant has a prime people-watching location on the main street in town and serves up live entertainment along with excellent surf & turf, seafood paella, charcoal-grilled lobster, and New York-style pizza. It also scores big for its Taino-themed décor and atmosphere – complete with wood, wicker, thatch, and slowly revolving ceiling fans.

On the Waterfront (Calle Dr. Rosen #1, El Batey, ☎ 571-3024) $$-$$$

Easily the finest dining establishment in Sosúa, On the Waterfront offers a romantic, open-air and clifftop setting with enchanting views of Pico Isabel de Torres by day and the setting sun at dusk. Seafood (lobster, calamari, grilled fish), steaks, fine wines, and premium cigars are on the bill of fare. It's open everyday for breakfast, lunch and dinner.

Square & Compass (Pedro Clisante, El Batey, ☎ 981-8019) $$

You can get Indian specialties every night of the week here, a nice change from the usual array of steak, seafood, and pastas. But this being Sosúa, you can get those, too.

Taino Beach (El Batey, in front of Casa Marina Beach Resort, ☎ 571-1269) $$

Styled after a traditional Taino *bohio* (a circular thatched-roof hut), this combination seafood grill, steakhouse and pizzeria makes a nice escape from the nearby all-inclusives.

Nightlife

Sosúa isn't the nightlife capital that Cabarete is, but Pedro Clisante in El Batey does have a variety of merengue bars, expat pubs, and sidewalk cafés to explore. You're likely to encounter a number of "professionals" working the bars at night.

The Voodoo Lounge (Pedro Clisante, next to the Sosúa Bay Hotel, ☎ 571-3559)

This club bills itself as a "step up" – meaning a step up from the common ramshackle *puta* (prostitution) joints – but it doesn't necessarily mean that the same hanky-panky, sankie-pankie business doesn't go on. Still, the décor is attractive, and the high-tech light and sound systems are impressive. Free shooters promotions draw a heavy partying crowd. It's open every night from 5 pm.

A Scenic Sidetrip to Santiago

Carretera Turística (Highway 25) is a scenic drive through lush mountains that ends in Santiago, the country's second-largest city. From Sosúa, go west on the Carretera Puerto Plata-Sosúa about 10 miles until you meet the little rotunda (traffic circle) in the road. Take the road to the right to meet up with Carretera Turística, which heads south 30 miles to Santiago.

Along the way, about eight miles down Highway 25, you can stop in Tubeagua at **Tropical Plantation** (☎ 656-1210, open daily from 9 am to 5 pm), where you can have lunch and tour a large tropical flower farm. The botanical garden has tropical birds, butterflies, orchids, and an animal farm/petting zoo.

Despite its 800,000 population, Santiago itself isn't a tourist mecca, with few attractions of even marginal interest. But if you find yourself spending time there, here are the main sights (most located within a few blocks of the city's main commercial street, Calle del Sol).

Monument a los Héroes de la Restauración (Monument to the Restoration): Built in 1940 on the highest point in the city and visible throughout, this tower honors the heroes who restored the country's independence during the War of Restoration against Spain in the 1860s. (It originally honored the vainglorious dictator Rafael Trujillo, but that was changed after his assassination in 1961.) If you make the somewhat arduous climb to the top, the tower offers panoramic views overlooking the city and the fertile Cibao Valley. Inside is a mural painted by the Spanish social-realist artist Vela Zanetti, who was forced into exile by Trujillo after Zanetti dared to depict peasants struggling for freedom. (Av. Monumental; open daily except Sundays, 9-noon and 2-5; free admission.)

Catedral de Santiago Apóstol: This late 19th-century neoclassical cathedral is just south of one of the city's nicer green spaces, Parque Duarte. You can stop in to see the carved altar, the stained-glass windows, and the tomb of the 19th-century tyrant Ulises Heureux. (Calles Benito Monción and 16 de Agosto, open daily; free.)

Museo del Tabaco (Museum of Tobacco): Near the cathedral, this museum traces the history of the five-century-old tobacco industry in the DR (Santiago serves as the main transport point for tobacco from the Cibao Valley, which is shipped here and then on to ports such as Puerto Plata and Santo Domingo). You can also see a demonstration of how cigars are made. (30 de Marzo and 16 de Agosto; open Tues.-Fri., 9-noon and 2-5, Sat., 9-noon; free.)

La Habanera Tablaclera (Cigar Factory): This working cigar factory offers tours where you can watch the wrapping process from leaf to label. (16 de Agosto and San Luis; open Mon.-Fri., 8:30-4:30; free.)

Centro Cultural Eduardo León Jimenes: Visual arts and anthropology are showcased at this nicely presented modernistic museum just north of downtown. The visual arts collection includes award-winning paintings, sculpture, etchings, and photographs by Dominican artists, with an emphasis on the School of Santiago. The anthropological collection contains cultural treasures spanning 5,000 years on the island. (Av. 27 de Febrero No. 146, ☎ 582-2315; open daily 9-5; free.)

Museo Folklòrico de Tomas Morel (Tomas Morel Museum of Folkloric Art): One of the best places in the country to see Carnaval masks, the collection here includes elaborate and colorful masks from Santiago and other Carnaval hotspots around the DR such as Cabral and La Vega. (Restauración 174, ☎ 582-6787; open Mon.-Fri., 9-1 and 3-6; free.)

Estadio Cibao: Santiago's stadium hosts professional baseball games from November to early February. (Av. Imbert and Domingo Bermúdez; tickets RD$150.)

■ Puerto Plata

Orientation

 Five-centuries-old Puerto Plata is a big, noisy city that appeals to a particular kind of tourist – the really adventurous kind who enjoys visiting odd cities with an alluring air beneath the surface. Puerto Plata fills that bill, with its colorful expat community and the narrow streets and gingerbread Victorian architecture of its Old City. The latter is a holdover from its heyday as a tobacco and sugar port in the late 19th and early 20th centuries, when it outshone even Santo Domingo as a wealthy enclave. Today, Puerto Plata is more industrial and traffic-choked, but worth a look around if you're on the north coast. Besides tourism, Puerto Plata's modern economy is built on sugar, tobacco, and rum – a nutritionist's nightmare but a hedonist's haven. (Perhaps attracting all those expats.)

Most visitors spend the bulk of their time along or near the Malecón, the mile-long-plus promenade that runs along the ocean. On the far west end is **Fort San Felipe**, the city's one relic of Colonial days, dating from the mid-16th century. Toward the other end is **Long Beach**, the city's public beach, where you can watch for offshore whales in winter. In between are a succession of restaurants, bars, dance clubs, and colorful shacks frequented by prostitutes. (Should you walk through at night, you may feel like covering yourself in a body condom.)

South of the Malecón, the city has a beautiful **parque central**, featuring a reconstructed two-story Victorian gazebo complete with Moorish arches. The parque central is set amid the city's oldest streets and is lined by gingerbread Victorian mansions.

Just east of the city is **Playa Dorada**, the walled all-inclusive resort compound that aims to be a world unto itself, drawing a half-million vacationers a year, many of whom fly in from Canada and Europe on value-priced package deals. Besides 14 resorts and a white-sand beach, Playa Dorada has a raft of restaurants, bars, pools, discos, casinos, and sports facilties, including an outstanding golf course that wraps around the resorts. If you aren't staying in one of the resorts, you can buy day-passes for the beach that include food and drinks.

Getting Here & Getting Around

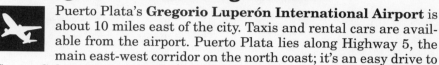

Puerto Plata's **Gregorio Luperón International Airport** is about 10 miles east of the city. Taxis and rental cars are available from the airport. Puerto Plata lies along Highway 5, the main east-west corridor on the north coast; it's an easy drive to Sosúa, Cabarete, and other north coast resorts, as well as to Santiago in the southwest (via Highways 5 and 1). Public buses and *motoconchos* leave from the parque central to go back and forth between the city and the nearby Playa Dorada resort complex. If you're willing to pay more, taxis are quicker (and generally safer than *motoconchos*). Call for a pickup or hail one at the parque central; keep in mind that there are no meters, so settle the fare in advance. The narrow streets of the old city are best explored on foot.

Places to Stay

Puerto Plata

Sofy's B&B (Calle Las Rosas, ☎ 586-6411, gillin.n@verizon. net.do) $$

This B&B is a find: three rooms in a comfortable contemporary home in a quiet neighborhood a few blocks off the Malecón. Rates include an American-style breakfast. Noelle, the proprietor, is an excellent cook who will prepare just about anything you request. Dominicans have been known to drive from as far Santo Domingo for her liver paté, and her Thanksgiving dinners are legendary. Call ahead if you'd like to try dinner there.

Hotel Castilla (José del Carmen Ariza 34, ☎ 586-7267, www.samsbar. 20M.com, sams.bar@verizon.net.do) $

One block from the parque central and popularly known as **Sam's Bar & Grill**, this American-owned hotel and bar, which occupies a rambling wooden Victorian, was the first inn built in Puerto Plata in the late 1800s. A giant wall map pays tribute to its renown with world travelers, who have stuck the map with hundreds of pins to identify their far-flung homelands. Don't expect much from the basic and rough accommodations, which are accessed by climbing a flight of rickety steps above the bar. The rate does include private bath, fan, and breakfast, and Internet access is available for a fee. An aging basset hound is the bar's namesake; Samantha's birthday is celebrated on July 16 with a huge *"Samcocho"*

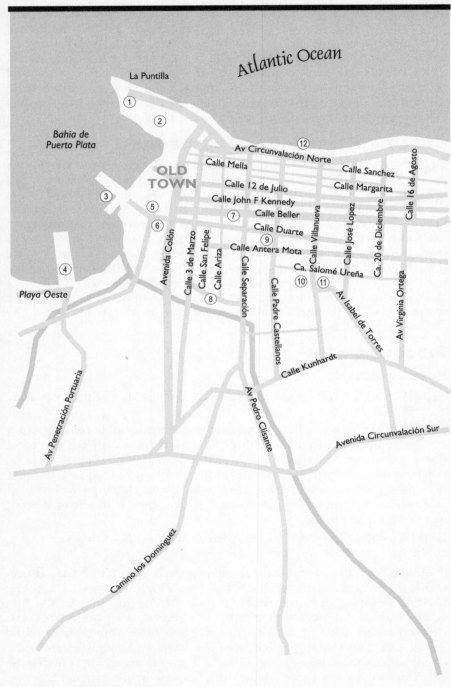

Atlantic Ocean

La Puntilla

Bahia de
Puerto Plata

Av Circunvalación Norte

Calle Mella
Calle Sanchez
Calle 12 de Julio
Calle Margarita
Calle John F Kennedy
Calle Beller
Calle Duarte
Calle Antera Mota
Ca. Salomé Ureña

OLD TOWN

Playa Oeste

Avenida Colón
Calle 3 de Marzo
Calle San Felipe
Calle Ariza
Calle Separación
Calle Padre Castellanos
Calle Villanueva
Calle José Lopez
Ca. 20 de Diciembre
Calle 16 de Agosto
Av Virginia Ortega
Av Isabel de Torres

Calle Kunhardt

Av Penetración Portuaria

Av Pedro Clisante

Avenida Circunvalación Sur

Camino los Dominguez

Puerto Plata

13

14

Hermanas Espignolio

15

16

Urb. Arenzo Hurtado

Carolina

Avenida Luis Ginebra

Calle A

Calle Presidente Vasquez

Calle Rafael Aguilar

Avenida 27 de Agosto

Calle C

Calle D

Calle B

Calle F

Avenida Circunvalación Sur

Hermanas Mirabal

17

18

To Sosúa, Playa Dorada

Calle Juan Lafitte

Calle Kunhardt

N

1000 Meters

1000 Yards

LEFT PAGE
1. Fortaleza y Museo San Felipe
2. Lighthouse, Gen Luperón Monument
3. Pier
4. Cruise Ship Dock, Customs
5. Park
6. Old Train Station
7. Central Park, Iglesia San Felipe
8. Street Market (Mercado)
9. Amber Museum
10. Cemetery
11. Mercado
12. Malecón (Oceanfront Promenade)
RIGHT PAGE
13. Malecón
14. Parque Nacional Litoral Sur
15. Puerto Plata Latin Quarter
16. Puerto Plata Beach Resort
17. Brugal Rum Distillery
18. Baseball Stadium

North by Northwest

party. (A play on words – *sancocho* is a hearty Dominican stew and delicacy.)

East of Puerto Plata

■ Costa Dorada

Costa Dorada (not to be confused with Playa Dorada, which is another couple of miles down the highway), a five-minute drive east of Puerto Plata. You can walk to the public beach here from the eastern end of Puerto Plata in about 20 minutes or less; the following two resorts face the remainder of the beach.

Coral Marien Costa Dorada (☎ 320-1515, www.coralbyhilton.com) $$$$

The 325 rooms in this all-inclusive on Costa Dorada beach are divided into six three-story buildings, set amid tropical gardens and huge freshwater swimming pools. The standard resort watersports are available, including windsurfing and beginning scuba lessons (given in the pool), kayaks and paddle boats. A spa offers several different types of massage, and a kids' program keeps the youngsters busy. The seafood grill isn't included in the rates, but other restaurants are, including Mexican and a French crêperie.

Iberostar Costa Dorada (☎ 320-1000, fax 320-2023, www.iberostar.com) $$$$

Another large all-inclusive on the beach, the Iberostar has 498 brightly decorated rooms and 18 junior suites spread across nine three-story buildings. All rooms have balcony or terrace; junior suites have sea views. Windsurfing, kayaking, and sailing Sunfish are included, but limited to one hour per day per person. Shows and disco dancing keep guests hopping at night, while a mini-club entertains kids aged 4 to 12.

■ Playa Dorada

This 14-resort walled-off tourist village comes complete with more than 4,500 rooms, a mile-long-plus white-sand beach, a championship golf course designed by Robert Trent Jones, and a parcel of casinos and nightspots open to all guests. To accentuate Playa Dorada as a "world apart," there's a 26,000-square-foot shopping mall (Playa Dorada Plaza) that includes boutiques, souvenir shops, a medical center, a department store, three cinemas, banks, a travel agency, a call center, a liquor store, an Amber "Museum," and an array of bars and restaurants.

> **Prices:** All resorts in the Playa Dorada are in the $$$$ range, but most food, drink, entertainment, and activities are included in that price. Be sure to book any all-inclusive resort in advance, preferably before leaving home, or risk paying far more than those who did.

Caribbean Village Club on the Green (☎ 320-1111, fax 320-5386, www.occidentalhotels.com)

The 336 rooms here occupy 45 two-story villas spread over 16 acres lush with tropical foliage and bordering Playa Dorada's championship golf course (greens fees not included in the all-inclusive package). The beach is a trek, however. You can get beginning scuba lessons in the pool or take clinics in several other watersports activities. Three restaurants, nightly entertainment, and a kids' club round out the offerings.

Casa Colonial Beach & Spa (☎ 320-2111, fax 320-2112, www.vhhr.com)

A 51-unit all-suite beachfront hotel that opened in 2004, the Casa Colonial is the first resort at Playa Dorada that is not all-inclusive. Aiming for five-star luxury, it comes with perks like an 8,000-square-foot spa, guest room (rather than lobby) check-in, four top-floor Jacuzzis overlooking the ocean, and even a "pillow menu" offering a selection of soft, firm, or feather. A piano bar in the lobby is open to non-registered guests.

Dorado Club Resort (☎ 320-2019, fax 320-3608, www.hotetur.com)

This all-inclusive resort near the beach has 206 rooms spaced among nine small buildings, as well as three restaurants, nightly entertainment, a kids' program, and a variety of watersports included in the rates.

Gran Ventana (☎ 320-2111, fax 320-2112, www.vhhr.com)

One of the plushest resorts at Playa Dorada, with beautiful tropical gardens, the all-inclusive Gran Ventana combines Caribbean with Victorian touches in its design, reflecting the flavor of nearby Puerto Plata. You won't be alone here – the resort has more than 500 rooms, five restaurants, seven bars (including a pool bar, a swim-up bar, and a beach bar), two pools, a kids' club and pool, and plenty of beachside activities – so you won't be bored.

Grand Flamenco Puerto Plata by Occidental (☎ 320-5084, fax 320-6319, www.occidental-hoteles.com)

This huge 16-building complex, which totals 582 rooms and good-sized junior suites, is another outstanding property (just don't expect intimacy). Eight restaurants offer plenty of variety at mealtimes, while included activities run the gamut from horseback riding to merengue classes. Kids' programs and an array of watersports, some at the beach, some at the sprawling pool, are also on the docket.

Hotel Playa Naco (☎ 320-6226, fax 320-6225)

This 326-room all-inclusive gets generally high marks for its service and all-around "fun" quotient. There's a huge pool with waterfall and kids' pool, tennis courts, and children's programs, along with the usual beach activities. Of the restaurants, the best is the Caribbean Grill; the buffets can get tiresome. The disco goes late into the night.

North by Northwest

Jack Tar Village (☎ 320-3800, fax 320-4161, www.allegroresorts.com)

Families look elsewhere – this village (with 290 rooms spread over 73 villas) is off-limits to kids. Beyond that, it has all the usual amenities, with four restaurants, nightly entertainment, two pools, and plenty of watersports – windsurfing, sailing small catamarans, kayaking, snorkeling, beginning scuba lessons – included in the package.

Occidental Allegro Playa Dorada (☎ 320-3988, fax 320-1190, www.occidentalhotels.com)

One of the better Occidental/Allegro properties here, this palm-tree-studded resort has just over 500 rooms (many with ocean views) and six restaurants. Horseback riding, scuba clinics, tennis, kayaking, and a kids' club are among the activities included.

Paradise Beach Club and Casino (☎ 320-3663, fax 320-4858, www.amhsamarina.com)

An all-inclusive with immaculate grounds and 436 rooms and suites, the Paradise Beach Club features three restaurants with top-flight food, five bars, a beachfront location, a nice selection of non-motorized watersports, and a kids' program included in the rates. Horseback riding, nighttime tennis, and motorized sports are extra.

Puerto Plata Village Resort (☎ 320-4012, fax 320-5113, www.puertoplatavillage.com)

With 400 Victorian-style villas and rooms aping the style of nearby Puerto Plata, Puerto Plata Village is home to five restaurants, four bars, tennis courts, a kids' club, and two pools (one for adults, one for kids). Windsurfing, sailing, and scuba lessons are included in the rates. It's closer to the golf course than the beach, and wheelchair-friendly.

Victoria Resort (☎ 320-1200, fax 320-4862, www.vhhr.com)

The Victoria Resort (styled with appropriately Victorian decor) has 190 rooms away from the beach, but does offer direct access to the Playa Dorada golf course. Other amenities include nightly à la carte dining, four bars, and two pools, one for adults only. Sailing, snorkeling, windsurfing, kayaking, diving instruction, tennis, and bicycling are included as well, but limited to one hour per day per person.

■ Other Resorts at Playa Dorada

Interclub Fun Royale/Fun Tropical (☎ 320-4054, www.interclubresorts.com)

Mexican-owned, these two sister resorts share some facilties, such as swimming pools and restaurants.

Rhumba Heavens (☎ 562-6725, fax 562-0660, www.coralhotels.com)

This resort was comparatively mediocre, but has been undergoing renovations. Stay tuned.

Villas Doradas (☎ 320-3000, fax 320-4790, www.hotetur.com)
Fairly small for Playa Dorada, Villas Doradas is considered a decent value. The Chinese restaurant breaks up the monotony of the buffets.

West of Puerto Plata

■ Costambar

This beach area just west of Puerto Plata has a few condos and beach accommodations, but, except for its year-round residents and vacation homes, has recently become largely deserted. Much of the action has moved farther west.

■ Cofresí

A mile or so farther west of Costambar is Cofresí, a small, quiet community with a handful of *pensións* and two outstanding resorts. The downside, however, is that the water can get rough. Cofresí is also home to the slick new Ocean World Adventure Park (see *Family Activities*, above).

Sun Village Beach Resort (☎ 970-3346, www.sunvillagebeachresort.com) $$$$

This recently opened and very elegant resort on Cofresí Beach offers both all-inclusive and more limited pricing plans. You can sign up for accommodations only; modified American plan (includes breakfast and dinner); three-, five-, and seven-day food and beverage plans; or a "twilight" plan that includes dinner, beverages, and nightly entertainment. Choose from among five restaurants (most of them beachside), eight bars, and six pools, including a three-tier pool with cascading waterfalls, Roman tubs, children's pool, and two swim-up bars. The spacious rooms come with furnished balconies or terraces; many have ocean views.

Hacienda Resort (☎ 586-1227, fax 970-7100) $$$-$$$$

The 750-room Hacienda is actually four resorts in one. The beachfront **Hacienda Tropical** is a deluxe property, the **Hacienda Suites** are spacious and family-oriented, the **Garden Club** is more budget-priced, and the village-like **Karisma Villas del Mar** offers privacy, with 67 individual villas, each with its own pool. The resort totals five restaurants and eight bars; the level of access to them varies by type of accommodation.

■ Bahía de Maimon

About six miles west of Puerto Plata, this little bay hosts the Riu Resorts complex.

ClubHotel Riu Mambo (☎ 320-1212, fax 320-1118, www.riu.com), **ClubHotel Riu Bachata** (☎ 320-1212, fax 320-1118, www.riu.com), and **ClubHotel Riu Merengue** (☎ 320-4000, fax 320-5555, www.riu.com) $$$$

Located adjacent to each other along the beach on the bay, these three all-inclusive resorts share some facilities such as a disco, a tikki bar, and a shopping complex with spa. Some amenities differ, however: the Riu Merengue has just one pool (with children's section), while the other two have two pools, as well as a children's pool (and the pools at the Bachata are much larger). Restaurants, snack bars, and the usual assortment of pool and beach bars are scattered throughout the complex. If you aren't staying at one of the resorts, you can get a day-pass that includes three meals and drinks for US$50.

■ Luperón

Luperón Beach Resort (☎ 571-8303, fax 571-8080) $$$

Beautiful Luperón Beach may be the best part of this resort, which is tattered around the edges, but you will find a pool, disco, and nicely landscaped tropical grounds here. And the beach is a great place to get away from it all.

Places to Eat
Puerto Plata

Note that the *motoconcho* noise can be unbearable in Puerto Plata so, with few exceptions, dining is best kept to the Malecón and around the Rotunda near the baseball stadium by Avenida Hermanas Mirabal. You'll still get *motoconcho* noise there, but not as much as in "downtown" Puerto Plata, where the noise bounces off the buildings.

Acuarela Garden Café (Calle Professor Certad 3 between 30 de Mayo and 27 de Febrero, ☎ 586-5314) $$-$$$

This elegant dining room bills its menu as "Cocina Creativa" – typical Dominican dishes (with emphasis on seafood) done up with significantly more pizzazz than at the local *comedor*. It's one of the few off-resort restaurants in the area where you can dine on food that meets high international standards. It's located about four blocks south of the Malecón, east of the Old City limits.

Aquaceros Bar & Grill (Malecón 32, ☎ 586-2796) $$

Seafood, steaks, and Dominican specialties are the fare at this lively waterfront favorite, a good value.

Café Cito (Highway 5 Km 3.5, 1/4 mile west of Playa Dorada main gate, ☎ 586-7923) $$

Puerto Plata's top off-resort bar, this Canadian-owned hangout draws a steady stream of both expats and travelers. The steaks, lobsters, burgers, and wings are reasonably priced, the music is a refreshing change – jazz, blues, and rock & roll – and you can buy top-flight cigars, too. The surrounding grounds resemble a romper room of sorts with splash pool and trampoline intended for adult enjoyment.

Above: Monte Cristi on the northwest coast

Below: The southwest coast

Above: Barahona

Below: Laguna de Oviedo

Jamvis Seafood & Steakhouse (Malecón 18, ☎ 320-7265) $$

Pasta, pizza, steak, and seafood served by the water – it sounds like a broken record in these parts, but Jamvis "plays" it with harmony.

Pizzeria Internacional (Rotunda, in front of the baseball stadium, off Av. Hermanas Mirabal, ☎ 586-4740) $$

Pasta, pizza (baked in a wood-burning brick oven) and seafood are served here in an open-air setting. It's a nice place to grab a bite before a baseball game in winter.

Sam's Bar & Grill (José del Carmen Ariza 34, ☎ 586-7267) $-$$

Located in the Hotel Castilla (see *Places to Stay*, above), Sam's is open from 7 am to 11 pm and serves American-style breakfast, lunch and dinner. But the main attraction here is the atmosphere, fueled by a clientele of world travelers and local expats.

Playa Dorada

Hemingway's Café (Playa Dorada Plaza, ☎ 320-2230) $$-$$$

Amid the Hemingway memorabilia here, this comfortable air-conditioned café serves standard pub fare as well as the usual seafood and steaks. Open seven days a week from lunch time to the wee hours of the morning, Hemingway's is a popular warm-up spot before hitting the club circuit.

Cheers Bar (Playa Dorada Plaza, second level, ☎ 320-2811) $$

Don't expect the cozy neighborhood bar atmosphere popularized by the TV show of the same name. This is more your typical resort bar, filled with tipsy tourists – many of them young, half-naked, tattoo-clad, and on the prowl. Almost as an afterthought, Cheers serves up burgers, sandwiches, and, of course, lots of liquor to accompany a blaring big-screen TV for showing sporting events.

Cofresí

Le Papillón (Playa Cofresí, ☎ 970-7640 after 5 pm, www.le-papillon.de) $$-$$$$

A longtime German expat operates this well-run restaurant, which features five-star service in a casual airy setting. Choose from the smoked or fresh catch of the day. The seafood platter (US$18) is very popular, as is a four-course lobster dinner for two (US$38 per person) – done by special order. Chateaubriand is also available.

Chris & Mady's (Playa Cofresí, ☎ 970-7502, www.chrismadys.com) $$-$$$

Colorfully located in a large circular thatched *bohio* (a hut in traditional Taino style) facing the beach, Chris & Mady's is wildly popular both with resort guests and local expats (some customers drive in from Puerto

Plata and even Sosúa). Steaks, seafood, hamburgers, and tropical drinks are on the menu, and a satellite TV broadcasts sporting events.

Nightlife & Entertainment

Puerto Plata

 Puerto Plata's Malecón and Av. Hermanas Mirabal (south of Long Beach, on the Malecón's eastern end) are loaded with bars and nightspots, but they are often thick with prostitutes.

Puerto Plata Pub Crawl (☎ 586-7923 after noon, www.popreport.com/PubCrawl/)

Organized by Café Cito (see *Places to Eat*, above), this tour of the most popular area nightspots stretches all the way east to Cabarete. It starts at sunset for cocktails at the Colonial-era Fort San Felipe along Puerto Plata's Malecón, stops at a Dominican car wash (a traditional beer-drinking gathering place in the DR), and visits Café Cito for beer and food. It then moves on to Sosúa, where the group prowls the merengue bars, British pubs, and sidewalk cafés along Pedro Clisante in El Batey. It concludes in Cabarete, where the pubs are literally on the beach. Transportation is by air-conditioned bus – complete with bar – which returns to Puerto Plata-area hotels at 12:30 am (though some skip the ride back to continue partying in Cabarete). The price is US$45 per person, but drinks at private establishments are extra. The Pub Crawl sets off every Wednesday and Saturday night in high season. Don't make plans for early Thursday/Sunday.

Playa Dorada

There are a number of discos within the complex; ask around to see which is the "hottest" of the moment. The action tends to get going after midnight. Both Hemingway's Café and Cheers Bar (see *Places to Eat*, above, for both) can get noisy and even rowdy with late-night revelers.

■ El Castillo

Orientation

 Aside from the ruins of nearby La Isabela (see *Historic Sites*, above) there isn't much else to attract visitors to El Castillo, or at least to keep them hanging around after their visit. Though the setting is peaceful and scenic, the town itself is little more than a handful of homes and one good hotel along a dirt road cutting into the side of a hill. In fact, most visitors come with guided groups and never set foot in town at all, simply entering the ruins at the town's entrance. But if you're making the time-consuming trip on your own, you may want to stay overnight there.

Getting Here

Getting to El Castillo either by driving or by public transportation is no easy task. **Caribe Tours** does not service the town, leaving rental cars or informal *guaguas* your only alternatives for transportation. Approaching El Castillo from Puerto Plata, you will first have to take a *guagua* (or drive west on Highway 5) to Imbert. From Imbert you take another *guagua* (or drive north on Highway 30) to Luperón. From Luperón you will then have to hop a *motoconcho* (RD$100) or drive to El Castillo.

Places to Stay

Rancho del Sol (Carretera Las Américas, ☎ 543-8172) $$$

For tourist-class accommodations, this apart-hotel is the only game in town. Rooms are basic but comfortable, and the on-site restaurant, which specializes in whatever fresh seafood is hauled in that day, is a big plus.

Places to Eat

There are two options for eating in El Castillo, the slightly upmarket restaurant attached to Rancho del Sol (above) or the down-home **Comedor Milagro** next door to the Rancho, where you can get tasty Dominican standards.

■ Punta Rucia

Orientation

Punta Rucia stretches a mile and a half along the sand, with the town occupying one side of the road and the ocean the other. The main road leading north into town ends at the beach and splits two ways, with most of the village lying to the east and the few accommodations that there are to the west. This fishing village was once a happening little tourist town with its own repeat clientele. But then the main hotel in town, the Ocean Breeze Resort, closed its doors, and the tourist industry here has yet to regenerate. The former resort, which consisted of four multi-level buildings and a set of bungalows, has now been taken over by a number of individuals, who use part of it as an informal hotel and part as a base for tour staff. Local families now live in the bungalows. Still, the beaches here are as enticing as ever, and the reef diving can be spectacular.

Punta Rucia has no tourist services – no ATM, no calling station, nothing – so be sure to carry sufficient funds. If you need to make a phone call, check with Rainer Angermann at Coral Reef Tours (see below). To the east, just beyond Comedor Tata (see below), is a *colmado* where you can get bottled water, snacks, and other little necessities. If you're driving and need gas, try the fish shack/gas shack, where gas is often on display in plastic containers. For all its simplicity, Punta Rucia does see a lot of action in early mornings and again in late afternoons, when busloads of tourists from Puerto Plata pass through en route to Cayo Arena, the beautiful nearby island.

Getting Here & Getting Around

Punta Rucia is located at the end of a wide dirt path about a 45-minute ride north of Highway 1 (Autopista Duarte) from Villa Elisa, a small agricultural town an hour northwest of the city of Santiago. Caribe Tour buses pass Villa Elisa en route to Montecristi, but it's not an official stop, so tell the driver in advance that you want to get off there. Once in Villa Elisa, you will be met by an eager set of *motoconcho* drivers offering to take you to Punta Rucia. The fare is RD$130 per person, even if you share the *motoconcho* with others.

Places to Stay

Punta Rucia Sol (☎ 471-0173) $$

A longtime favorite of backpackers, Punta Rucia Sol – a couple of cold-water bungalows with a restaurant run by aging hippies – has a good reputation, but has recently undergone major renovations. Check to see if it's back up and running.

No-Name Hotel/Coral Reef Tours (☎/fax 656-0200, angermannskeet@hotmail.com) $$

This is dubbed the "No-Name Hotel" simply because it has no name. It's one of the four-story buildings that at one time formed part of the Ocean Breeze Resort. It is now occupied by German expat Rainer Angermann and his Dominican wife, who jointly run a dive operation from the first floor. All of the large basic rooms feature two queen-size beds and a balcony overlooking the beach. While there's no air conditioning or even fans, Punta Rucia's climate tends to be comparatively cool and breezy. There are, however, much-needed mosquito nets to keep out the area's notorious sandflies. The RD$800 room rate includes an excellent breakfast at the Cayo Arena Tours office just a short walk down the beach.

The building directly to the east also operates as a no-name hotel and is somewhat cheaper, but lacks a back-up generator – so if electric power is important to you, it's worth paying the extra RD$200 at Angermann's.

Places to Eat

Damaris (no address, no phone) $$

Since it caters mostly to the crowds of daytripping tourists, Damaris often closes when business is down, but when it is open it offers a slightly upscale spot to enjoy fresh-caught fish, lobster, and oysters pulled from local waters. It's located a short walk east of the town entrance.

Cayo Arena Tours (on the beach) $

This outfit caters mostly to daytrippers as well, but is the regular breakfast spot for those staying at the "No-Name Hotel"/Coral Reef Tours (see above). All others pay RD$80 for three eggs prepared to order, a plate of excellent meats including pâté and prosciutto, a bread basket with preserves and butter, coffee, and fresh-squeezed orange juice.

Comedor Tata $

Just across the very narrow road running along the beach, Tata is little more than a shack with a single table out front that accommodates about six people at a time. Many of the village men congregate here for their meal after a day's work. The delicious helping of fresh-caught fried fish, served with an enormous green salad and a healthy portion of fried green plantains, is just RD$80, which has to be one of the best deals in the DR.

■ Montecristi

Orientation

 Montecristi is as far northwest as you can get in the Dominican Republic. This remote, mostly arid region near the Haitian border is well worth a visit for the national park that surrounds the town of the same name (see *Eco-Travel*, above, for details).

Five centuries old, settled in 1533 by 60 families from the Canary Islands and having experienced a series of booms and busts ever since, Montecristi has retained the look and feel of an old and rather well preserved pioneer town, from the Victorian mansions scattered about (some now abandoned) to the turn-of-the-century post office. Once a major exporter of mahogany and tobacco, Montecristi is now dependent on the salt trade.

The town is built on a grid and easily navigated. Most of the action is centered around three streets: **Calles Mella** and **Benito Munción**, running from east to west, and **Avenida Duarte**, which runs north to south and leads to nearby beaches and the national park. Avenida Duarte also runs by the parque central – which, unlike in most Dominican towns, is not the center of the action. The park's most interesting feature is an Eiffel Tower-looking clock in the center that was donated by France. Off the park is a charming neo-colonial church.

Just about anything you'll need can be found on Avenida Duarte: an ATM, a currency changer, the post office, and a general store. If you wander this street, stop in at #44 and say hello to local artist Leonardo Batista. The doors to his enormous Victorian home are always open, and you will usually find him sitting at his easel painting the day away, while his elderly mother looks after his two young sons. Back on Benito Munción and next door to Hotel Chic is a Verizon calling station and a carpeted romper room for kids, complete with swings, slides, and monkey bars.

Getting Here & Getting Around

 The **Caribe Tours** bus depot is on Calle Mella. It has connections to Santo Domingo, Santiago, and Puerto Plata, via Highway 1. If you're driving, Highway 1 is a well-paved road; once you get there, though, some of the area roads in the national park can be rough going. Taxis and *motoconchos* are available to take visitors to the beaches and attractions in the national park, while boat captains make trips to the offshore islands.

Places to Stay

 Cayo Arena (Playa Juan de Bolaños, ☎ 579-3145, fax 579-2096) $$$

HOTEL PRICE CHART	
Rates are per room based on double occupancy.	
$	Under US$20
$$	US$20-$50
$$$	US$51-$100
$$$$	Over US$100

This apart-hotel occupying a neat two-story building directly across from the beach has the best facilities in Montecristi. Each unit has a kitchenette, air conditioning, pool, and balconies facing the garden.

Los Jardines (Playa Juan de Bolaños, ☎ 579-2091, www.elbistrot.com, hotel.jardines@verizon.net.do) $$

This charming set of bungalows by the sea is next door to Cayo Arena (see above). The management speaks both English and French, and will arrange for boat excursions, Jeep trips, and bike rentals.

Don Gaspar Hotel (Pte. Jiménez 21, ☎ 579-2477, fax 579-2206) $

The Don Gaspar offers similar but fresher and brighter accommodations than its competitor, the Hotel Chic (see below), and at the same rate. The staff is friendly, English is spoken, and the rooms come with cable TV. The on-site restaurant, though rather dark and dreary, is also popular with the local crowd. The Don Gaspar tends to get full on the weekends, so it's best to call in advance if arriving on a Friday or Saturday.

Hotel Chic (Benito Munción 44, ☎ 579-2316) $

Because of its central location within walking distance of the Caribe Tours bus depot and next to the Verizon calling station, this is one of the most popular hotels in Montecristi. The restaurant attached to the hotel (see below) is also the place where the monied Dominicans about town go for a night out. The 50 rooms are a little dank and nothing to rave about, though for RD$350 you do get a private shower, cable TV, phone, and fan (a room with air conditioning is an additional RD$150). A drawback is the *motoconcho* noise from town and the blare from the impromptu rehearsal studio for the local *perico ripiao* band across the street – charming enough until you're ready to go to sleep. Ask for a room on the south or east side, which should be a bit quieter.

Places to Eat

 The two informal food counters nestled between Hotel Chic and the Verizon calling station are good places to grab a quick burger, chicken, or fish sandwich. Also available are snacks, cold drinks, and good *batidas*. More formal restaurants are the following.

DINING PRICE CHART	
Price per person for an entrée, not including beverage or tip.	
$	Under US$2
$$	US$2-$10
$$$	US$10-$20
$$$$	Over US$20

El Bistrot (Calle San Fernando 26, ☎ 579-2091) $$$

Run by the same owners as Los Jardínes Hotel, El Bistrot serves excellent Dominican cuisine with French accents in a lovely courtyard setting. An assorted seafood menu features lobster, octopus, *lambi* (conch), and fresh fish.

Hotel Chic (Benito Munción, ☎ 579-2316) $$-$$$

With both the most extensive and one of the more expensive menus in town, the hotel restaurant offers a variety of dishes including chicken, meat, soups, and salads, plus the usual array of seafood that's ubiquitous in Montecristi. There's a pleasant patio for people-watching, too.

Coco Mar (entrance to Playa Juan de Bolaños, ☎ 579-3354) $$

This lively beach bar stands at the entrance to Playa Juan de Bolaños. It's a good place to grab a casual lunch of a fried fish sandwich and a beer before or after the beach.

Don Gaspar Restaurant (Pte. Jiménez 21, ☎ 579-2477) $-$$

The food is good (try the fried crab) but the restaurant is tucked away and the dark and dreary interior is severely lacking in atmosphere.

North by Northwest

Cordillera Central – The Dominican Alps

With its pine-covered mountain terrain, comparatively cool climate, and European village atmosphere – including narrow streets and cabin-like architecture – the heart of the DR's vast Cordillera Central mountain range has become known as the "Dominican Alps." Bordered roughly on the east by Highway 1 (which cuts north-south through the center of the country) and rippling west toward Haiti through two big, mountainous national parks, the Dominican Alps is a far cry from the usual tropical stereotypes. While you won't see any snow-capped mountains here, you will find temperatures that often dip near the freezing point and an unmistakable frost in the air. Understandably, it's become one of the areas of choice for Dominican weekend homes, as residents of Santo Domingo, especially, try to escape the searing urban heat. The area has two huge draws for adventurous visitors. The first is a pair of adjoining mountain national parks, **Armando Bermúdez** and **Carmen Ramírez**. They're best known for harboring **Pico Duarte** – the highest summit in the Caribbean – as well as the next three highest peaks in the Antilles. Pico Duarte itself lures upwards of 3,000 trekkers in some years, and, since it requires no technical climbing, is accessible to most anyone in good shape who's willing to rough it a bit. The second big lure is the massive **Río Yaque del Norte**, which provides scenery-studded opportunities for whitewater rafting at both novice and experienced levels, depending on water level.

But don't overlook the area's other compelling natural attractions. The mountains offer plenty of opportunities for day-hikes and scenic drives. Remote waterfalls provide a variety of sometimes challenging adventures, including canyoning, cascading, rock climbing, and swimming in pristine natural pools. Horseback riders can enjoy trail rides along rivers and through pine forests. Hang gliders, in turn, head to scenically stunning Constanza, a town perched in a fertile high-elevation valley that was carved by the crash of an ancient meteor.

The town of **Jarabacoa**, which lies along the Río Yaque del Norte in the northeastern stretches of the Cordillera Central, is the base for much of the adventuring in the region. Outfitters use it as the jumping-off point for river-rafting trips, and it also serves as a gateway for the most popular trail to Pico Duarte. The Jarabacoa area hosts a number of thundering waterfalls and other natural wonders as well. **Constanza**, larger but more isolated and less developed for tourists than Jarabacoa, is the other top resort area in the Dominican Alps. While Constanza doesn't boast as many organized activities or notable sights as Jarabacoa, its magnificent valley setting ringed by mountains, rivers, and forests is reason enough to come – whether to get active with day-hiking, hang gliding, and horseback riding, or simply to kick back and breathe in the cool mountain air.

History

Christopher Columbus himself ventured into the northeastern fringes of the Cordillera Central as early as 1494, near what is now the industrial city of La Vega, 18 miles northeast of Jarabacoa. The explorer founded a settlement there now known as La Vega Vieja, which was destroyed by an earthquake in 1562. Some of the old foundations and other remains can still be toured in what has become a national historic park.

The mountain town of Constanza, which was essentially cut off from the rest of the country until a crude road there was built in the late 19th century, was the scene of two unusual events during the 1950s. The then-dictator Rafael Trujillo, who was constantly trying to transform the economy of the DR throughout his reign, imported about 200 Japanese families to work the fruit and vegetable fields around Constanza and improve the agricultural output of the region. The old Colonia Japonesa – now mostly a collection of tumbledown shacks – can still be seen there, though most of the Japanese who remained have moved to more upscale dwellings. The year 1959 brought a bizarre invasion by Cuba, when the then-new Castro regime tried to overthrow Trujillo in an attempt to bring a more Cuba-friendly government to the DR. A Cuban force landed in Constanza only to be routed by Trujillo's forces; most of the Cubans were later executed.

Ironically, perhaps, the past few decades have indeed seen a revolution in the mountain area's economy – based on adventure travel. For those who like to experience adventurous activities that go beyond the tropical standards of sand and sea, the Dominican Alps have become ground zero in the DR.

Getting Here & Getting Around

■ By Air

The nearest major airport, **Santiago International Airport**, is near the country's second largest city. **American Airlines** (☎ 800-433-7300, www.aa.com) flies there from New York City, and there are domestic flights from around the country via **Air Santo Domingo** (☎ 800-359-2772, www.airsantodomingo.com). Rental cars and taxis are available at the airport. Travelers could also fly into Puerto Plata's **Gregorio Luperón International Airport**, or into Santo Domingo's **Las Américas International Airport**. All have good highway connections to the region.

■ By Bus

Caribe Tours serves Jarabacoa daily from Santo Domingo, Santiago, and various north coast resorts via the town of La Vega, which is 18 miles to the northeast along Highway 1. For Constanza, Caribe Tours serves the town of Bonao, easily reached from Santo Domingo, Santiago, or the north coast along Highway 1; at Bonao, transfer to a *guagua* for Constanza (ask the driver to drop you at the *"parada para Constanza"*). The 40-mile route to Constanza from Highway 1, while narrow and curvy at times, passes through lush rural landscapes, some of the most scenic countryside in the DR.

■ By Car

Take Highway 1 (a four-lane highway also known as Autopista Duarte) from Santo Domingo or Santiago to either the Constanza exit or the Jarabacoa exit. Both are well-marked; if coming from Santo Domingo, the exit for Jarabacoa is about a half-hour farther north along the highway after the exit for Constanza.

Tip: Some hotels in Jarabacoa offer guided tours to Constanza; ask at the desk.

It's also possible to drive directly between Jarabacoa and Constanza without going back to Highway 1, but you have to follow a very rough and

Cordillera Central

bumpy road – albeit extremely scenic — that cuts over a high mountain. Unless you have a four-wheel-drive vehicle and are experienced in using one, this alternative is not recommended – it's better to backtrack a ways and go via Highway 1. If you're willing to let someone else do the driving, however, you can catch a *concho* over the mountain; cars leave Jarabacoa when full from in front of Comedor Lopez at Paseos de las Profesoras and Calle Carmen.

> **Inside advice:** If you do take a *concho* between Jarabacoa and Constanza, expect a crowded ride, squeezed into a car with four or five other people, bobbing up and down on the craggy mountain road for a good hour or so. The views are hard to top, however. Fares are about RD$70 per passenger. Since *conchos* leave sporadically, especially from Constanza, this form of transport works best for those with flexible schedules.

Festivals

Carnaval in La Vega. While the modern city of La Vega isn't known for much else of touristic interest, it puts on one "hell" of a Carnaval show in the February pre-Lenten season – not least because the elaborate costumes and masks that celebrants wear are meant to represent the devil. Daily parades that draw up to 50,000 people during the lively and sometimes rowdy festivities have made La Vega's Carnaval one of the most famous in the country. (Alas, accommodations are extremely basic and limited here, and pressed to overflowing during the festival, but you can visit on a day-trip from the north coast, Santiago, or even Santo Domingo.)

Fiesta patronal in San José de las Matas. Early in August, this town 25 miles southwest of Santiago honors its patron saint, San José.

Information Sources

■ Tourist Offices

Constanza: Carretera Las Auyamas, ☎ 539-2900.
Jarabacoa: Plaza Central (no phone).

Adventures

■ On Water

Whitewater Rafting & Kayaking

Río Yaque del Norte

 Starting at 8,500 feet in the Cordillera Central mountains and running for more than 150 miles down to the Bahía de Montecristi on the northwest coast, where it empties into the sea, the Yaque del Norte is the most important and impressive river in the Dominican Republic. Adventurous travelers know it as the most popular venue in the country for whitewater rafting. Depending on the time of year and how high the river is, rapids here range from mild class II to more wild-and-woolly class IV.

The village of Jarabacoa is the only entry point for rafting expeditions, though tour operators will pick you up at your hotel in resort towns along the north coast (or even Santo Domingo) in the early dawn hours and return you there by early evening. The actual river trips themselves last from four to five hours. Highlights include drops such as the "Mike Tyson" – so called for the way rafts dizzy around after being punched by particularly intense water surges – and the "Toilet," created by whirling cascades of water. These waterborne rollercoaster rides are led by experienced guides who also have the job of keeping rafters focused on the task at hand – getting down the river – and not distracted by the stunning tropical scenery on both sides of it.

Three of the top rafting outfitters are **Caribbean Bike & Adventure Tours** (☎ 571-1748, http://www.caribbeanbiketours.com/ws_whitewater_rafting.htm), **Iguana Mama** (☎ 571-0908, fax 471-0734, www.iguanamama.com), and **Rancho Baiguate** (☎ 574-4940, www.ranchobaiguate.com). No prior experience is necessary but age and fitness requirements vary among the outfitters (Rancho Baiguate, for example, has a minimum age of 12, while 14 is the minimum for Caribbean Bike & Adventure Tours). Trips run about US$75, including lunch.

Ríos Jimenoa & Baiguate

Smaller than the Río Yaque del Norte, these two tributary rivers in the Cordillera Central offer a more intense challenge than the Yaque for technical kayakers, with frequent class V runs.

Rancho Baiguate (☎ 574-4940, www.ranchobaiguate.com), the biggest tour operator in the area, and its affiliate, **Get Wet** (☎ 586-1170), which operates along the north coast, run extreme kayaking adventures here. Excursions average about US$65.

Swimming

La Confluencia

La Confluencia is where the Río Yaque del Norte and Río Jimenoa meet, near the town of Jarabacoa. The area is a bit scrubby looking, with the grass overrun by weekend visitors (usually local families picnicking and barbecuing on Sunday afternoons, and, unfortunately, not very diligent about properly disposing of trash). Still, you can swim in the *balneario* (swimming hole) here or explore the river banks either on foot or on horseback (see *On Horseback*, below). There's no admission fee to the area. To get here, take Avenida La Confluencia all the way to the end from the town's entrance (as you come in from La Vega); you'll see the marked sign for it.

> **Tip:** At one point the two-lane road eventually turns rough, so don't be afraid to drive on the opposite side of the road if the potholes get too daunting – everybody else does. (That's both the good and the bad news, but typical of driving behavior in the DR.)

Canyoning & Cascading

These adventurous sports involve climbing up and then leaping off or sliding down waterfalls – or rappelling down canyon walls – into deep pools or rivers below, then swimming downstream to an exit point and hiking back to do it all over again. While definitions differ, generally canyoning involves using safety equipment like ropes, harnesses, helmets, and wet suits, while cascading does not.

Rancho Baiguate (☎ 574-4940, www.ranchobaiguate.com) and **Get Wet** (☎ 586-1170) offer canyoning and cascading trips on Ríos Jimenoa and Baiguate. Salto Jimenoa I (see *Waterfalls*, below), is a popular staging spot.

Waterfalls (Saltos)

The following three falls are near Jarabacoa.

■ Salto Jimenoa I

Tumbling down nearly 250 feet, Salto Jimenoa I is one of the highest waterfalls in the region – and so spectacular that it appeared in a scene in the movie *Jurassic Park*. Getting to it, however, can seem just as big a feat. Those who succeed – and not all that many even try – must traverse a steep dirt path and then scramble over a parcel of boulders to reach the base of the falls. But a reward awaits for all the effort: the magnificent sight of water crashing down from high above, sending spray and mist rising from a big pool of water below. (Adventure operators sometimes use a ledge high up the falls as a launching point for adventures in canyoning; proceed at your own risk.) To get there, take the Carretera Constanza about 4½ miles south of Jarabacoa, where a sign points the way down a path. If you reach the point where the road becomes suitable only for four-wheel-drive, you've gone too far.

> **Tip:** If you can't get to the falls on your own, check with **Rancho Baiguate** (☎ 574-4940, www.ranchobaiguate.com) for bike tours there.

■ Salto Jimenoa II

While not as dazzling as Jimenoa I, Salto Jimenoa II (sometimes also called Lower Salto Jimenoa) is quite a bit easier to get to, and is therefore a bigger draw for visitors. In fact, crowds can be something of a problem here, especially since 1998's Hurricane Georges damaged the landscape and left only a small patch of ground available for stretching out and gazing at the falls – or perhaps catching some sun after a swim in the deep pool at its base. About five sunbathers can be accommodated, uncomfortably, at one time. Most visitors tend to hang out on an often-crowded viewing platform, posing for pictures with the cascading water as a scenic backdrop.

Still, it's fun to get there. First, you cross a suspended foot bridge that runs from the main road to the falls, then climb a set of small steps carved into the rocks to reach the viewing platform. To get to Salto Jimenoa II, take the road from Jarabacoa north toward La Vega for about 2½ miles until you reach the Escuela Nacional de Foresta. Turn right and follow the signs pointing the way to "Salto Jimenoa." After a short drive you'll come to a dead-end gravel-covered road with parking off to your right. Park there for free and then walk across the suspended bridge ahead of you. Admission is RD$60.

■ Salto Baiguate

This nearly 200-foot-high salto is hidden among a thick mix of pine and tropical foliage and has a natural pool at the base so blue and serene you may think you've stumbled onto a set for a Tarzan movie.

To get there on your own, take the Carretera Constanza by the Shell gas station on the southern edge of Jarabacoa until you see the "Salto Baiguate" sign pointing down a side-road. This road will take you through a modest village before it turns into a path that ends right before the salto. You'll know you've arrived when you see an abandoned concrete structure and, possibly, a Politur (tourist police) officer hanging out under the big, shady tree. Park your car and walk the path for a few yards before descending a steep set of steps cut into the rocks and leading to the base of the falls. But first, stop to admire the picture-perfect setting. There's no admission charge if you come on your own.

> **Tip:** You can also visit by horseback through **Rancho Baiguate** (☎ 574-4940, www.ranchobaiguate.com).

■ Aguas Blancas

A fourth waterfall to visit is in Constanza. At a towering 492 feet, Aguas Blancas is the mother of all Dominican waterfalls, and the only real tourist attraction in Constanza. Surrounded by pine forests, it drops majestically in three separate stages into a natural pool far below.

To get there, take Carretera Constanza and turn onto the dirt road marked by the sign "Colonia Japonesa" (the old Japanese settlement); it's on the left-hand side of the road as you leave Constanza. It's another rough, potholed six miles from there, but the beauty of the falls and the natural surroundings makes it worth the effort. If you don't have a suitable four-wheel-drive vehicle, consider joining a guided group — hotels in either Jarabacoa or Constanza offer tours. If you can get there on your own, there's no charge.

■ On Foot

Rock Climbing

 The steep rock faces around the Ríos Jimenoa and Baiguate offer opportunities for climbing and rappelling. Contact **Rancho Baiguate** (☎ 574-4940, www.ranchobaiguate.com) or **Get Wet** (☎ 586-1170).

Hiking & Trekking

Jarabacoa & Constanza

 There are a number of good day-hikes around both Jarabacoa and Constanza. Just set off into the mountains or contact **Rancho Baiguate** (☎ 574-4940, www.ranchobaiguate.com) for guided walks.

Armando Bermúdez/Carmen Ramírez National Parks

These two adjacent and almost identically sized national parks together protect more than 1,500 square miles of mountain territory and the flora and fauna within. They are also home to the four highest peaks in the Caribbean, topped by Pico Duarte (10,128 feet or 3,087 meters) and its nearby "twin tower," La Pelona, just 16 feet or so shorter at 3,082 meters. La Rucilla (10,000 feet or 3,049 meters) and Pico Yaque (9,053 feet or 2,760 meters) follow behind. A dozen of the country's biggest rivers have their headwaters here as well.

■ Climbing Pico Duarte

Five established trekking routes lead up Pico Duarte, typically ranging in length from three days to six, and in distance from 28 miles to 67 miles roundtrip. Some of the longer treks are arduous, but most hikers in decent shape can reach the summit via the most popular three-day, 28-mile-roundtrip route. And help is available: you can hire mules to carry your gear – or yourself, if necessary. (Even if you aren't concerned about your hiking ability, the mules provide insurance in case you are injured along the way.) A gear-carrying mule is most useful in any event, since you'll need to pack all your camping equipment – tents, sleeping bags, food, cooking utensils, etc. – for use at the campsites en route.

> **Be warned:** The two parks contain a total of 14 campgrounds, each with a plain wooden cabin and space for sleeping out under the stars. The cabins hold at least 20 people and are first-come, first-served, with no fee for use. They have no beds, no tables, and few other amenities (some have pay phones or drinking water available). Restroom facilities are primitive at best.

Weather along the way can be unpredictable. The routes begin in sub-tropical climate and gradually turn cooler with the rising elevations, getting downright cold at night. Prime time to make the climb is between November and Easter week, because the weather is most stable then – you're less likely to encounter rainstorms and lightning. Warm clothes and rain gear are essential (see *What to Bring*, below), but no technical climbing skill is required – if the weather gets too nasty, guides simply won't take you up at that time.

Along the route you'll be treated to plenty of bird sightings – you may spot trogons, Hispaniolan parrots, and palm chats – and possibly wild boar and the indigenous hutia. Moss-covered pines, ferns, and crystal-clear rivers – some of which you'll cross by foot or bridge – add to the pristine and magical surroundings. Waiting at the rocky summit is a

Wild boar

statue of Juan Pablo Duarte, father of the country, who gave his name to the mountain, a Dominican flag, and spectacular views – though clouds often obscure the panorama below. Duarte's nearby twin peak, La Pelona (whose summit is also reached on some routes), often looms above the clouds.

You can either make all the arrangements yourself or go as part of an organized tour. All hikers, however – whether traveling independently or with a group – must be accompanied by a guide certified by the National Park Office. The purpose is twofold: to keep hikers from getting lost on the trails and to bring money into the local economy. If going on your own, you can hire guides at the national park offices nearest the trailheads. As a rough estimate, figure about RD$250 per day for a guide, RD$150 per day per mule, and an additional amount for food and gratuities. It's customary to pay for the food for your guide as well. It costs an additional RD$100 to enter the park.

> **Warning:** The local guides do not speak English, so bring a Spanish phrasebook – it's essential to establish in advance whether you or your guide is going to buy the food, and who is going to bring utensils, cutting implements, and the like. Guides often do the shopping and cooking, so don't forget a generous tip for services performed.

DID YOU KNOW?

Pico Duarte was first climbed in 1851 by the British explorer and then-consul in the Dominican Republic, Sir Robert Schomburgk, who called it Monte Tina and estimated its height at 10,300 feet (3,140 meters). Later it was renamed Pelona Grande (with neighboring La Pelona being Pelona Chica) and then renamed again Pico Trujillo during the Trujillo regime. At that time, an overzealous surveyor – no doubt trying to please the dictator – raised the peak's estimated height to 3,175 meters (10,414 feet), which is still commonly listed on maps and many other sources. With Trujillo's demise, and using more scientific instrumentation, the peak's official elevation has been lowered to 3,087 meters, leaving it just a few meters higher than La Pelona. And as of 2004, in a bizarre twist due to a legal technicality, Pico Duarte has now officially been renamed Pico Trujillo again. But everyone still calls it Pico Duarte. Stay tuned for future developments.

If you're joining a guided tour group, be sure to shop around, since rates can vary significantly (sometimes as much as US$300) for essentially the same service. Also try to hook up with other hikers – the per-person cost sometimes drops with larger groups. The price should include guides, equipment, mules, food, drink, and transport to and from your base. All you need to bring is your clothing and personal gear. Besides convenience, another benefit to going with a guided group is that the trip leader will in all likelihood speak English. Families can also benefit by joining guided tours geared to kids' paces and interests; **Iguana Mama** offers an excellent one-week trip (see *Tour Operators*, below).

> **Tip:** You can also take other hikes in the national parks, as long as you hire a guide to go with you. One particularly scenic trek is through the gorgeous Valle del Tetero, which also figures in some routes to Pico Duarte.

■ Pico Duarte Tour Operators

Camping Tours (☎ 563-9401, www.campingtours.net). Four- to five-day trips follow the Mata Grande route (see *Pico Duarte Trails*, below). Rates start at US$100.

Caribbean Bike & Adventure Tours (☎ 571-1748, www.caribbeanbiketours.com/home.htm). Three-day, two-night "express" hikes are US$357, while four-day, three-night "normal" hikes are US$475; five-day, four-night expanded hikes that include the Valle Del Tetero are US$787.

Iguana Mama (☎ 571-0908 or 800-849-4720, www.iguanamama.com). Rates are US$425 per person for three days, $950 for seven days (the latter is for a leisurely family trek; children under 17 are $750 each). Groups are a minimum of four people.

Metro Tours (☎ 809-544-4580, www.metrotours.com.do). Metro's hikes are popular with Dominicans who go up over the Christmas and Easter holidays. Rates start at US$100.

Rancho Baiguate (☎ 574-4940 or 574-6890, www.ranchobaiguate.com). Rates range from US$270 to $755, depending on the length and number of people in the group.

■ Pico Duarte Trails

These are the five established routes, though you can also "mix and match" a bit, since several of the routes cross or join each other at various points. Some campgrounds are shared by climbers following different routes.

La Ciénega – three days, 28 miles (46 km) roundtrip

This route is sometimes dubbed "Pico Duarte 101" – the least difficult, best developed, and by far the most trammeled of the five trails. (It would be a mistake, though, to think of this trail as a "gut" course – it's still a challenge.) The route approaches the peak from the east, starting about two miles from the ramshackle pueblo of La Ciénega, which is about 15 miles southwest of Jarabacoa. All the major tour operators depart from

Cordillera Central

here. If you're not with an organized group, you'll need to go to the National Park office in La Ciénega at least a day in advance to register and hire your guide so that he can make arrangements for your hike – lining up needed permits, food, mules, and the like. Don't leave this task for the day you want to depart. You can return to Jarabacoa to spend the night in your hotel if you want, or roll out your sleeping bag and stay at the informal campground in La Ciénega, where there are no formal lodgings.

> **Tip:** When you go to the national park office, bring a photocopy of the name page from your passport to serve as ID.

On the first day, hikers are typically on the trail for five to six hours and log about 11 miles with a 6,500-foot elevation gain, following a river up into the mountains. After spending the night at the high-altitude La Compartición campground (which tends to get very crowded, so get there as early as possible), most hikers shove off at 4:30 in the morning. The object is to reach the summit of Pico Duarte to catch the sunrise – a three-mile, two-hour climb. The hike down then begins, returning to La Ciénega by the following afternoon.

> **Warning:** If going on your own, don't miss the last *guagua* from La Ciénega back to Jarabacoa, which leaves at 4 pm.

Mata Grande – five days, 56 miles (90 km) roundtrip

This strenuous trek, which approaches Pico Duarte from the north and has an elevation gain of about 7,350 feet, is the second-most popular after the La Ciénega route. Along the way you'll climb La Pelona, the Caribbean's second-highest peak, as well as Pico Duarte. The national park station and trailhead are in the pueblo of Mata Grande, about 13 miles southeast of the town of San José de las Matas, which most hikers use as a base. (The road from San José de las Matas isn't paved, but *conchos* make the run.) On the first day, trekkers typically hike about 12½ grueling miles – including a steep uphill stretch toward the end – before spending the night camping at Río La Guacara. The second day is relatively easy – a 7½-mile hike along the Bao River through a beautiful high-mountain valley before reaching the Valle de Bao campsite. The third day begins early, a trudge of eight miles first to the top of La Pelona and then onto the summit of Pico Duarte. You can either return via the same route, or continue down to La Ciénega for all-new scenery and make your way back to your base from there.

Los Corralitos – six days, 53½ miles (86 km) roundtrip

On this often difficult, sparsely used, but dramatically situated trail, you'll use Constanza as a base. Los Corralitos, site of the park station and trailhead, is five miles west. Guides and mules are available there. The first day takes you along rivers and over hills some 12 miles to a set of cabins at Los Rodríguez campground. The second day brings the toughest climb, 11 miles to the 5,000-foot-high Tetero Valley, where you can spend the night in a cabin at the scenic Valle del Tetero campground. On the third day, you'll hike to Pico Duarte via the La Ciénega trail, before beginning the trip back down. Total vertical ascent is more than 5,000 feet.

WHAT TO BRING (IF HIKING ON YOUR OWN)

- Backpack or daypack (the latter if using a mule for gear; you'll need a daypack for easy access to small items along the trail).
- Food/plates/utensils.
- Matches/lighter fluid.
- Bottled water (you can boil/purify river water as needed for drinking and cooking, too).
- Sturdy, waterproof hiking boots and hiking socks.
- Warm sleeping bag (waterproofed) and tent.
- Flashlight.
- First aid kit.
- Insect repellent.
- Sun block, sunglasses, and lip balm.
- Toilet paper.
- Warm clothing (including a waterproof jacket, hat and gloves).
- Rain poncho or other rain gear.
- Swimsuit.
- Small Spanish-English dictionary to help you communicate with the guides.
- Walking stick or pole (optional, but very useful for descents or on soggy trails).
- Camera/film/extra battery (optional).
- Binoculars (optional).

Sabaneta – six days, 60 miles (96 km) roundtrip

On this arduous trek, you'll climb both Pico Duarte and La Pelona. Elevation gain over the course of the three-day hike up is more than 8,000 feet, but with all the ups and downs, the total climb is more like 12,000 feet.

The city of San Juan de la Maguana makes a good base for this trek. From there, you'll travel by *guagua* or *concho* to the Ramírez national park station at Sabaneta, where you can hire your guide and mules and camp out the night before you set off. The first day is a tough 7½ miles,

Cordillera Central

with a 3,300-foot elevation gain that leads to a mountain cabin at Alto de la Rosa. The second day is longer – almost 14 miles – but with a climb of "only" 2,000 feet to another cabin at Macutico. The third day covers another 8½ miles and leads to the top of both La Pelona and Pico Duarte before beginning the three-day descent.

Las Lagunas – six days, 67 miles (108 km) roundtrip

This route is longest in terms of distance and a test of endurance. Use San Juan de la Maguana as your base for this trek, too, before proceeding by *concho* to Las Lagunas, where you'll find the park station, guides, mules, and trailhead. The first day's hike leads to El Tetero, where you can camp for the night. The following day, a 10-mile hike climbs to a 7,000-foot summit and then drops some 2,000 feet into the beautiful Valle del Tetero (Tetero Valley), where you can spend the night in a cabin. The third day, you join with the La Ciénega trail, which leads to Pico Duarte. The final three days are descent.

WATCH OUT FOR CIGUAPAS!

According to local mythology, Ciguapas – lightning-fast Taino women with blue skin, waist-length black hair and hoofed feet that face backwards – fled to the Cordillera Central some five centuries ago to escape the conquistadors, and have remained there ever since. They are reputed to seduce young men after dark and lure them to their deaths in the forests. The moral? When you're staying overnight in the mountains, keep to your cabin or tent.

■ On Horseback

Rancho Baiguate (☎ 574-4940, www.ranchobaiguate.com) runs horseback trips to Salto Baiguate near Jarabacoa.

At La Confluencia near Jarabacoa, where the Río Yaque del Norte and Río Jimenoa meet, local men on horseback might approach you for rides on their *caballos* (horses). Expect to pay about RD$200 for an hour's ride.

In the Constanza area, two lodgings, **Rancho Guaraguao** (☎ 508-3333) and **Alto Cerro** (Carretera Constanza, ☎ 530-6192) offer horseback riding excursions.

■ On Wheels

Mountain Biking

Rancho Baiguate (☎ 574-4940, www.ranchobaiguate.com) has two-hour, nine-mile bike tours to either Baiguate Falls or Jimenoa Falls near Jarabacoa. Excursions average about US$65 and include a buffet lunch at the ranch.

Iguana Mama (☎ 571-0908, fax 471-0734, www.iguanamama.com) runs periodic (and strenuous) nine-day Dominican Alps bike trips that begin in Cabarete on the north coast, wind down to Constanza through the mountains and then up to Jarabacoa to visit waterfalls and go river rafting. The tours then return to Cabarete via Santiago, for a total distance of 162 miles. Cost is US$1450.

Quad Bikes

Rancho Baiguate (☎ 574-4940, www.ranchobaiguate.com) runs four-wheel motorbike tours (US$65) through the rugged countryside around Jarabacoa, leading across rivers, through woods, and to waterfalls. You must be at least 16 years old to join in.

■ Eco-Travel

Reserva Científica Valle Nuevo

This protected alpine forest situated on a high plateau near Constanza is noted for a stone pyramid marking the exact center of Hispaniola (about 18 miles south of Constanza). It's also known for good bird-watching, including sightings of striped-headed tanagers and Antillean siskins. Vegetation includes many species endemic to Hispaniola, including Creole pines and Dominican magnolias.

The road leading south into the reserve from Constanza (just off Carretera Constanza) is a little difficult to pin down so it's best to have a local point it out to you. From there the road – which quickly deteriorates into a washed-out, potholed mess – cuts south through the reserve before ending in the town of San José de Ocoa, a total of about 55 miles.

> **Warning:** The poor condition of this road can't be overemphasized. Do not attempt this drive in anything less than a sturdy four-wheel-drive vehicle – with an extra tire or two as well as extra gas. (Intrepid mountain bikers might have better luck avoiding the gaping holes.) The view over the Cordillera Central is breathtaking, however, and there's no admission fee when (or if) you get there.

Reserva Científica de Ebano Verde

This protected cloud forest reserve situated atop Casabito mountain (en route to the Constanza Valley) protects the green ebony tree and the more than 600 other species of plants and 60 species of birds (a dozen endangered) that thrive in this area. While hiking here, you may spot a Hispaniolan emerald, or possibly even el zumbadorcito, the world's second-smallest bird.

Zumbadorcito

Just to the right of the park entrance is a sign marking a four-mile trail that winds down into the reserve.

■ In the Air

There's no more thrilling way to view the stunning Constanza Valley than from the vantage point of a hang glider. One outfitter providing packages and services is **Caribbean Free Flying** (JulianSV@CaribbeanFreeFlying.com, www.caribbean-freeflying.com). A five-day package runs US$65 per day and includes accommodations, transfer to and from the airport, transport to and retrieval from flying/landing zones, flight planning and radio assistance. **Vuelo Libre Dominicano** (www.vuelolibredominicano.com.do) offers similar services.

Historic Sites

■ Parque Historico La Vega Vieja

This small national historic park about 20 miles northeast of Jarabacoa commemorates the La Vega settlement founded here in 1494 by Christopher Columbus, who ventured inland in search of Taino slaves. Not much has survived beyond the ruins of a fortress – some walls remain intact – along with scattered ruins of some houses and a church. (The original settlement, which prospered with the discovery of gold nearby and the growing of sugar cane before being destroyed by an earthquake in 1562, is said to have contained the New World's first bishopric, first mint, and first brothel, among other notable sites.)

Nearby and overlooking the ruins is **Santo Cerro** (Holy Hill), where a famous miracle is said to have occurred that helped Columbus and his men defeat the Tainos in battle. As the story goes, Columbus had planted a wooden cross during the battle, which the Tainos attempted to destroy. At that moment, a vision of the Virgin Mary appeared above the cross, sufficiently frightening and distracting the Tainos for the Europeans to emerge victorious. The hole where the cross is said to have stood is en-sconced within a church (**Iglesia Las Mercedes**), where the faithful come to pray every September 24. A reputed centuries-old descendant of the tree used to make the cross stands behind a fence nearby. Even if you don't believe in miracles, you'll find excellent views looking out over the Cibao Valley.

The site is about three miles north and east of the present-day city of La Vega. Taxis are available in town, or, if you're driving yourself, look for the marked turnoff along Highway 1.

Bases for Exploration

■ Jarabacoa

Situated along the Río Yaque del Norte, Jarabacoa is a pleasant town of 40,000 that's well equipped to host adventure travelers.

Like most Dominican villages, Jarabacoa is easy to navigate. The main road entering town is Avenida Independencia. (It's one-way until you enter the town, and then becomes a two-way street.) The centers of activity in Jarabacoa are the main crossroads and around the parque central, where you will find restaurants, entertainment (there's a popular pool hall) and a bank with a 24-hour ATM. On the busy corner to your right as you're leaving town to the south is a convenience store where you can get good coffee, pastries, and fresh fruit, along with the local (Spanish-language) newspapers. The Shell gas station opposite the convenience store marks the start of the bumpy road to Constanza and the route to many of the area attractions and accommodations outside of town.

THE PARQUE CENTRAL

Every Dominican city or town has a parque central ("central park"), which marks the center of town and the heart of activity. It's a promenade of sorts – usually a green space that's typically in front of the town church or cathedral. Sunday afternoon is a popular day for sitting and hanging out in the parque central.

Several towns in the DR are known more for their central parks than perhaps any other feature. Some of the more famous parks in the country are in San José de Ocoa, which many compare to an enchanted forest; Las Matas de la Farfán, a lush stretch of greenery with a Victorian gazebo; Constanza, whose pine-encircled park has a gorgeous mountain backdrop; and San Juan de la Maguana, known for its large shaded promenade directly in front of a pretty church.

Cordillera Central

Places to Stay

■ Jarabacoa

Brisas del Yaque (Avenida Luperón, ☎ 574-4490) $$

This clean, newish hotel is your best option if you don't have your own vehicle, since it's within walking distance of the town center, restaurants and entertainment. Rooms are on the small side but come with air conditioning and TV.

HOTEL PRICE CHART	
Rates are per room based on double occupancy.	
$	Under US$20
$$	US$20-$50
$$$	US$51-$100
$$$$	Over US$100

Rancho Baiguate (Carretera Constanza, ☎ 574-4940 or 574-6890, fax 574-0000, hotel@ranchobaiguate.com) $$$

This self-contained camp lies on several wooded acres containing hiking trails, rivers, and an unheated swimming pool. The 27 large rooms all have two double beds and enormous bathrooms with very hot water. Rates include three daily cafeteria-style meals except on Tuesday nights, when guests are shuttled over to a sister restaurant in town. The rancho is a good 30-minute walk from town on an unlit dirt road so, unless the management is running a nighttime shuttle service, you'll need your own vehicle or will have to hire a *motoconcho* driver to take you into Constanza and back at night.

Gran Jimenoa (Avenida La Confluencia, ☎ 574-6304, fax 574-4345, hotel.jimenoa@verizon.net.do) $$

You can sit on the terrace of this cozy lodge overlooking the Río Yaque del Norte outside town and watch the rafters go by, perhaps contemplating your own river trip. For an otherwise posh place, the tacky room décor is a bit of a letdown, though rooms are large and have TV. There's a pool with hot tub here, too. Prices include breakfast on the weekends only, when it tends to fill up with Dominicans escaping the city.

Piñar Dorado (Carretera Constanza, ☎ 574-2820, fax 687-7012, pinardorado@verizon.net.do) $$

Often used to house package travelers, this hotel has an old Catskills resort feel to it, from the dining room that serves up group à la carte meals to the active lounge/bar that occasionally erupts with spontaneous entertainment resembling "Talent Night" at Sunny Oaks. Owned by the Rancho Baiguate group, the rooms are a little more upmarket than the Rancho itself, with TV, air conditioning, and private balconies. It's also a bit closer to town than the Rancho.

Places to Eat

La Herradura Independencia
(Corner of Duarte and
Independencia, ☎ 574-4795)
$-$$

DINING PRICE CHART	
Price per person for an entrée, not including beverage or tip.	
$	Under US$2
$$	US$2-$10
$$$	US$10-$20
$$$$	Over US$20

Somewhat resembling an old-time sa-
loon – complete with a (perfectly serious) sign asking patrons to check their
guns at the door – this popular restaurant and night-time hangout has an Old
West feel to it. The extensive menu features fish, meat, seafood, pork, and
chicken, prepared *criolla*, *plancha*, or *con limón*-style. Try the fowl in
wine, a delicious Dominican specialty. The soups and sandwiches are also
excellent.

> **Did you know?** It is legal for Dominican citizens to
> carry unconcealed, loaded firearms, as long as they have a
> permit to do so. Men who carry guns usually tuck them
> into the waist of their trousers.

Restaurante del Parque (Parque Central, ☎ 574-6749) $

A casual, open-air spot located on the quieter side of the park, this popular lunch place serves up pizza and *comida criolla* as merengue music
plays at an unusually quiet level in the background. If you're traveling
with kids, you can take them to the secure playground in the rear after
the meal.

El Rancho (Calle Independencia, ☎ 574-4557) $$-$$$

The most formal dining establishment in town, this sister establishment
to Rancho Baiguate (see *Places to Stay*, above) serves excellent Dominican cuisine (the shrimp *asopao* is delicious), steaks, and pizza. Guests of
the Rancho eat here on Tuesday nights when the cafeteria there is closed.
Try the berre soup (a leafy green similar to kale) if it's available.

Don Luis (Colon and Duarte, ☎ 574-4878) $$

This long-established restaurant on the parque central serves Domini-
can specialties along with steaks and seafood.

Nightlife & Entertainment

The **Galaxia Pool Hall** above the Don Luis Restaurant is a
popular gathering spot any night of the week. La Herradura
has a live band on weekends that will take requests, including
American pop tunes. **Antillas Independencia** at the town's

entrance is good any night of the week for merengue and a local version of *bachata* that has an odd country-western ring to it.

Constanza

Situated at nearly 4,000 feet in a high valley formed by an ancient meteor, Constanza is still largely undeveloped for tourism.

The main route into town is a long, narrow two-way road leading from Highway 1, cutting straight through a flat valley with acre after beautiful acre of fertile farmland on either side. Carretera Constanza eventually turns into Avenida Luperón, the busiest strip in this otherwise sleepy town. At its center is one of the most beautiful central parks in the country, set placidly among thick pine trees with a mountain backdrop that gives it that Swiss Alps feeling.

If you stay in Constanza, you will likely take most of your meals at your hotel, since restaurants are few and far between. There are, however, a few exceptional lodgings in the area, whose dining rooms serve dishes made from fresh local ingredients.

> **Tip:** Banks and ATMs are in short supply in Constanza, so it's prudent to carry along sufficient cash.

■ Places to Stay

Rancho Constanza (off Carretera Constanza, ☎ 539-3268, ranchoconstanza@hotmail.com) $$-$$$

The Rancho has 14 fully equipped modern villas set on a hillside amid a bountiful garden. An adjacent cluster of modest cabins offer more basic, but nonetheless charming, "Swiss"-style accommodations. There's a good restaurant, and the extremely attentive staff can also help with stocking your refrigerator, preparing meals, and coordinating adventures. To reach it, go right off the Carretera Constanza (as you're heading into town) at the Colonia Kennedy sign.

Alto Cerro Villas (Carretera Constanza, ☎ 530-6192, fax 530-6193) $$$

These 20 self-contained villas are situated a little farther down the road from Rancho Constanza. You'll also find camping facilities, horseback excursions, bike rentals, a restaurant, and a large veranda used for outdoor barbecues on weekends.

Rancho Guaraguao (☎ 508-3333 in Santo Domingo, ☎ 539-3333 in Constanza, fax 508-1212, www.ranchoguaraguao.com/home.html, rguaraguao@verizon.net.do) $$$$

With 30 fully appointed two- and three-bedroom cabins, the Rancho Guaraguao spreads across several acres in the Las Neblinas mountains. The cabins come with cable TV and telephone, and some have fireplaces. The common area features a restaurant, thermal pool, small gym, nightly entertainment, and a barbecue area. Rental horses and four-wheel drive vehicles are available for excursions.

■ Places to Eat

 Most visitors to Constanza eat in their own or at other hotels. The restaurants at Alto Cerro and Rancho Constanza are popular dining options. Outside the hotels, restaurants in Constanza are few and basic but usually serve good Dominican fare.

La Montana (Calle Salome Urena, ☎ 539-2518) $

You can get excellent *comida criolla* here, particularly the roasted guinea hen, a local specialty.

The Southwest & Along the Haitian Border

Part-mountain range, part-desert, part-coastline – the Dominican Republic's great southwest is the most geographically diverse region on the island. And for adventurous travelers, it can be the most exciting part of the country to visit. The mountain range, the Sierra Bahoruco, is the DR's second-largest, covered with dazzling flora and lush virgin forest. The semi-arid desert is home to terrific opportunities for bird-watching and reptile-spotting. The coastline is stunning, harboring some of the island's most gorgeous

beaches. There are also chances for arduous yet awe-inspiring off-road exploring, both in the deserts and the mountains. Yet the region remains largely unknown and undiscovered, especially by foreign visitors, making it an ideal destination for backpackers and well-heeled travelers alike – or for anyone who prefers an off-the-radar spot to a "wherever-the-pack-is-heading-this-season" kind of place.

Starting west of Santo Domingo and stretching for a few hundred miles along a peninsula to the Haitian border, the southwest is a wide-open naturalist's playground. It contains the country's largest protected zone, and includes three national parks and two sizeable lagoons that are habitats for well over 100 bird species, some of them among the most colorful in the tropics. You can also visit a desert-like island in the middle of a vast and striking saltwater lake, which will bring you up close to one of the largest wild American crocodile populations in existence. And, after working up a sweat exploring the desert or mountains, you can relax at idyllic, mostly unpopulated Caribbean beaches, right out of a photo spread in a travel magazine.

Because of its relative scarcity of tourists, the southwest doesn't have much in terms of fancy accommodations or to-die-for restaurants. Except for the region's major tourist base, Barahona, and a few resorts along the coast to its south, most of the facilities catering to visitors are eco-minded operations that provide somewhat rustic lodgings. However, you will find an occasional splash of elegance or gourmet cooking, which becomes all the more appreciated in these surroundings.

In this chapter you'll also find recommendations for exploring the areas along the border with Haiti, which extend from the far southwestern to the far northwestern sections of the country, as well as tips for crossing into Haiti. These far western border areas are among the most remote, undeveloped, and intriguing in the country. Exploring the border towns and backroads will bring you into close contact with another culture as well as offering expansive scenery – if you're equipped (and game) for some challenging drives.

A long-standing rumor has it that the government plans to turn parts of the coast into another all-inclusive haven. But local environmentalists have persistently lobbied to preserve the area much as it is, and the battle over development continues. The best advice: see it sooner rather than later.

History

 Evidence of pre-Columbian history dates back thousands of years in the region, with the discovery of various Taino archeological sites, including caves with pictographs, dating from the time of Christ or before.

Though it's now among the most remote parts of the Dominican Republic, the southwest was one of the first areas settled by the Spanish after the arrival of Columbus in the late 15th century. **Azua de Compostela** (now usually just called Azua), one of the industrial towns along Highway 2 that leads from Santo Domingo to Barahona, was founded in 1504 and served as home for a time to such future conquistadors as Diego Velasquez (who conquered Cuba), Hernán Cortés (who conquered Mexico), and Juan Ponce de León (who later went off in search of the Fountain of Youth in Florida).

The cities of **Bani** and **San Cristóbal**, also situated along the route from Santo Domingo to Barahona, date from the early colonial days as well, as does the more northerly city **San Juan de la Maguana** and the far smaller and more remote villages of **Sabana Real** and **Banica** along the Haitian border. San Cristóbal later served as the site of the signing of the nation's first constitution in 1844 and as the birthplace of the ruthless 20th-century dictator Rafael Trujillo, who had mansions built for himself (now mostly in ruins) throughout the region. If you stop in San Cristóbal, you can visit Trujillo's home and one of his palaces (which he never occupied) as well as the palace where the constitution was signed. But for the most part, these centuries-old cities along the highways to the southwest have retained little of their historic heritage, and don't have much to offer modern-day sightseers.

The southwest has seen its share of strife over the centuries, often fueled by fierce rivalries between the people of what would become modern-day Haiti and the Dominican Republic. For centuries after the Spanish arrived, the areas near the border that now separates the two countries were mostly wild and untamed, and the two peoples often moved freely back and forth across the quite flexible lines of demarcation. In the 19th century, Haitians under the leadership of General Toussaint L'Ouverture frequently attacked and pillaged Dominican settlements in the region. L'Ouverture founded the city of Barahona in 1802 to serve as a port during the time of Haitian rule here.

Long-strained relations between Haitians and Dominicans remain wary to this day, as Dominican police and military jealously patrol the border areas, searching for smugglers and illegal entrants. Still, the border remains porous in many of the more remote areas, and a good many Haitians continue to enter the DR illegally, usually to work as sugar cane cutters for paltry wages under deplorable conditions. Away from the cane fields, the most visible Haitian presence in the DR today is in the border-town markets, where Haitians come to sell or barter goods ranging from household utensils and gym shoes to fruits, vegetables, and knock-off designer clothing items. Dominicans sometimes journey from as far away as Santo Domingo to pick up bargains.

In the 20th century, Rafael Trujillo (who was assassinated in 1961 while en route to San Cristóbal) transformed the economy of much of the southwest – and added much to his own wealth – by ordering the planting of vast fields of sugar cane, many of them in the coastal areas between Santo Domingo and Barahona. Sugar cane still plays an important role in the region's economy, though the industry has encountered hard times since the Trujillo heyday.

Over the years, the region has also met destruction from hurricanes, earthquakes, floods and other natural disasters. One quake destroyed the original colonial city of Azua in 1751, while in 1998 Hurricane Georges led to flooding that wiped out entire villages in the mountains. It now remains to be seen whether the promise of tourism can resurrect the fortunes of this often beautiful but scarred region.

Festivals

Carnaval Cimarron. In the town of Cabral, this pre-Lenten carnaval celebration is one of the most colorful in the country, with celebrants wearing masks and elaborate costumes. It takes its name from the *cimarrones*, escaped African slaves who settled the region in colonial days.

Semana Santa. Colorful Holy Week celebrations are held in Elias Piña on the Haitian border, San Juan de la Maguana (a city east of Elias Piña along Highway 2), and others.

Espiritu Santo. Held about two months after Semana Santa, this fervid religious celebration is marked by a long procession from the countryside into San Juan de la Maguana.

Fiestas patronales. Patron saint festivals are held at various times of the year in San Juan de la Maguana, Azua, and many other towns throughout the region. One of the biggest religious processions honors the Virgin de la Altagracia, held January 21 in San Juan de la Maguana.

Getting Here & Getting Around

■ By Air

From Santo Domingo, Barahona is a 3½-hour bus ride via **Caribe Tours** or a 30-minute flight via **Air Santo Domingo** (☎ 683-8020) into the **Aeropuerto Internacional María Montéz**, named for a Dominican film star of the 1940s.

A LOCAL FILM LEGEND

The Barahona airport is named for native daughter María Africa García Vidal, who grew up to become María Montéz – a huge box-office draw for Universal Studios during World War II. After a half-dozen forgettable films, she won the lead role in *Arabian Nights* – Universal's first all-color film – in 1942. Her alluring face, figure and copper-toned hair mesmerized audiences, who flocked to see her films – *Ali Baba and the Forty Thieves*, *Gypsy Wildcat*, *White Savage*, *Cobra Woman*, and *Sudan* – lavishly photographed formula melodramas. Co-starring handsome John Hall and set either in the desert, on a tropical island, or some other exotic locale, these escapist films earned her the title "Queen of the Technicolor" and made her the box-office champion throughout the war years.

■ By Public Transport

Public transport around the region is comparatively limited, so renting a car is your best bet for exploring the area independently and efficiently. However, *guaguas* do serve the routes between Barahona and Pedernales and Barahona and Lago Enriquillo, with chances to stop at various national park points and beaches along the way. So, if you have plenty of time, a flexible schedule, a sense of adventure – you may have to overnight in some very basic accommodations – and if you want to get around cheaply, they are an option. (Look for *guaguas* around the parque central in Barahona.) You can also take taxis from Barahona to points down the coast or over to Lago Enriquillo.

■ By Car

While backroads through the southwest and along the Haitian border are notably rough and suitable mainly for rugged four-wheel-drive vehicles, the major regional highways are (for the most part) well paved and in good shape. **Highway 2**

(known locally as Carretera Sanchez) is the chief road connecting Santo Domingo to the southwest region. It begins just west of the capital and continues west through the towns of San Cristóbal, Bani, and Azua before turning north through the rural Valle de San Juan and ending in the hardscrabble town of Elias Piña at the Haitian border.

When Highway 2 turns north, **Highway 44** begins its 120-mile journey through the far southwest, first continuing west and then heading south down the coast to Barahona and beyond. The coastal stretch southwest of Barahona makes a particularly beautiful drive, where lush mountains framed by splashing rivers and cascading waterfalls plunge down to the sea. When Highway 44 reaches the village of Oviedo, near the far southern tip of the Pedernales Peninsula, it swings northwest through remote countryside to the frontier coastal town of Pedernales on the Haitian border, where it ends. Most of this latter section of Highway 44, where there are no roadside services, forms the northern boundary of huge Parque Nacional Jaragua, which occupies much of the bottom part of the peninsula.

Two other highways, **48** and **46**, also serve as key corridors through the southwest. Extending west from Barahona, they form a rough loop around Lago Enriquillo, one of the major sightseeing destinations in the region.

One possible alternative to driving yourself is to join a guided tour to one or more of the adventure spots listed below, which you may be able to arrange through your hotel. Check when making your reservation to see if your hotel offers this service.

Orientation

 Beyond **Barahona**, the outpost town of **La Descubierta** at the northwestern edge of **Lago Enriquillo** serves mainly as a jumping-off point for trips to the lake and **Isla Cabritos**, an island in its center that's the focal point of a national park. **Jimani**, a hot, dusty border-crossing town, is another potential destination in that area (if only to cross into Haiti or to spend time amid the border bustle). Jimani has a Haitian market in the no-man's land between the two countries where residents from both sides of the border buy and sell clothing and household items.

In the far southwest, the town of **Pedernales** serves as an entrance to nearby **Parque Nacional Jaraqua**, as well as a border crossing for Haitians. The rest of the Pedernales Peninsula is primarily a scattering of pueblos (small villages) inhabited by extremely friendly locals.

The Southwest

Accommodations & Tourist Services

 Most hotels in the southwest that are set up to receive foreign travelers were established by expatriates who now call the area home, helping to develop a small and informal tourism industry that survives largely on word of mouth. You'll find little in the way of group tourism – no tour buses, no cruise ship day-trippers – or, for that matter, much of a tourist infrastructure of any kind.

Barahona has a variety of services – a bank ATM, a long-distance calling center, and pharmacy, all around the parque central – but such services are sorely lacking elsewhere. Except for the larger towns along Highway 2, well away from most attractions of interest to visitors, there are no banks or even ATMs outside of Barahona (although you can receive a cash advance on a credit card at the Barcelo Bahoruco Beach Resort on the coast south of Barahona). And, except for roadside stands that sell fuel in plastic bottles, there are few places to buy gas outside of Barahona or Pedernales. (The gas station on the Malecón a little less than half a mile south of Barahona is the last opportunity to purchase unleaded fuel until Pedernales, some 80 miles away.)

> **Caution:** Keep in mind that the climate in much of the southwest is very hot, especially in the far southern reaches of the peninsula. Carry plenty of water and sunscreen when you travel.

Trip Planning

When planning a trip to the southwest, and assuming you're traveling by car rather than *guagua*, allow at least three days just to hit the highlights. Lago Enriquillo will take one day, Laguna de Oviedo and Bahía de las Aquilas another, and relaxing on one or more of the peninsula's splendid beaches a third. Or, you can see much of the region at a more relaxed pace in about a week. Spend two nights in or around Barahona (with sidetrips to Lago Enriquillo and nearby points) and then consider another two nights in Pedernales, which you can use as a base for visiting the Bahía de las Aguilas and Jaragua National Park. While traveling between Barahona and Pedernales, stop at one or more of the lovely beaches along the coast and explore the Laguna de Oviedo, a habitat for birds and turtles. You'll probably need additional time if you want to take one or more of the off-the-major-road trips along the Haitian border.

Information Sources

■ Tourist Offices

Pedernales: Calle Duarte, ☎ 524-0409.

Adventures

Here are the top sights and activities to take in during your stay in the southwest. Many of the sites are well-marked with National Park signs, so, while remote, they are still reasonably easy to locate.

■ On Water

Diving & Snorkeling

While there are some good snorkeling and diving spots along both coasts of the peninsula, there aren't many outfitters working in the region. **Coral Sea Divers** (Malecón 6, Barahona, ☎ 223-1070, fax 419-828-5381) runs trips to the **Bahía de Neyba**, just northeast of Barahona. Some divers have spotted manatees in the bay.

Windsurfing

The place to go is **Las Salinas**, a laid-back windsurfing haven on the Bahía de Ocoa. Las Salinas offers the same great windsurfing as Caberete on the north coast, but without the crowds and the heavy pick-up scene.

Beaches

A few miles south of the village of Bahoruco, you'll find three of the most popular attractions on this side of the peninsula: the lovely playas of San Rafael, Paraiso, and Los Patos. They're situated one after the next along the coastal highway, framed by mountains and forests to the west. There's no admission charge to any of them. You can usually find makeshift lunch-counter operations nearby grilling up fish and selling drinks to visitors.

> **Tip:** You'll find the beaches to be less crowded on weekdays than on weekends, when Dominican families like to come here to cool off.

Playa San Rafael

Besides a stony beach, San Rafael's added attraction is a waterfall that tumbles down the side of a mountain to form a cool, refreshing sweet-water pool (called a *balneario*) and a popular swimming and picnic area. Public showers and bathroom facilities have helped to turn this into a somewhat informal campground where campers pitch their tents wherever they find a space.

Playa Paraiso

Farther down the road is Paraiso, an immensely popular stretch of sandy beach serving the town that edges the shoreline. Though it's the least scenic of the three playas, it's a good place to hang out if you want to mingle with locals. You can also have a good Dominican lunch at one of the comedors lining the road.

Playa Los Patos

The third of the three beaches, Los Patos, is probably the most beautiful. Here you'll find an enchanted forest-like setting framed by a thick healthy mangrove swamp and a crashing waterfall. Another natural wading pool has formed here as well, a big draw for local families.

▪ Eco-Travel

Lago Enriquillo & Parque Nacional Isla Cabritos

 Lago Enriquillo, a massive saltwater lake that stretches for 26 miles near the Haitian border, was once part of an inland channel that connected the Bahía del Neyba near Barahona to the bay of Port-Au-Prince in Haiti. (You might spot ancient bits of coral and seashells along the shoreline here.) Today, it roughly forms the boundaries of the Parque Nacional Isla Cabritos, named for the largest of the three islands that lie within it. Occupying a desert valley between two mountain ranges, the Sierra Barohuco to the south and the Sierra Neyba to the north, Lago Enriquillo is the lowest point in the entire Caribbean, some 140 feet below sea level.

Six-mile-long Isla Cabritos (Little Goats Island) is the centerpiece of the national park – a flat, arid, cactus-studded sanctuary in the middle of the lake that serves as a habitat for thousands of colorful tropical birds. You can see a host of flamingos here, along with herons, burrowing owls, Hispaniolan parrots, roseate spoonbills, West Indian nighthawks and other species. And there's much more: Hundreds of American crocodiles inhabit the lake as well, swimming to the mouths of freshwater rivers by day and spending their nights on the island, where they also lay their eggs.

Two endangered endemic species, Ricord iguanas and rhinoceros iguanas, are among the thousands of other reptiles on the island. The mostly tame iguanas often approach visitors in hopes of being fed.

Touring the Lake

Lake tours depart at around 7:30 am, 8:30 am, and 1 pm, but the morning departures are far preferable if you can make it, since you're much more likely to see crocodiles in the cool earlier hours than in the heat of midday (and also far less likely to roast yourself in the sun). The 2½-hour boat excursions can cost up to RD$1,000, which includes a boat and guide for up to five or six people. (If you're traveling by yourself or with one or two others, the boatmen will usually wait a few minutes for more people to arrive). While the guides speak enough English to get you in the boat and out onto the lake, don't expect too much in the way of in-depth commentary along the way. But the remarkable spectacle of colorful birds, crocodiles, and iguanas speaks volumes by itself.

> **Be sure** to carry water and sunscreen and wear sturdy, closed shoes for the walk around the island.

Directions

You can visit the lake and Isla Cabritos by boat with an authorized guide from the National Park Station in the town of La Descubierta, located along the lake's northwestern shore. To get there, take Highway 46 west from Barahona, in the direction of Neyba. (It's a good idea to fill up with gas before you start.) After about an hour's drive you will come to a fork in the road marked by a huge statue of the legendary Taino rebel leader Enriquillo, who once took refuge from the Spanish on Isla Cabritos.

You now have two choices. If you bear right (north) toward Neyba, you can drive to La Descubierta via Highway 48 along the northern and much cooler side of the lake. If you take the road to the left, you will have a more scenic – but longer and much hotter – drive to La Descubierta along the southern side of the lake via Highway 46. The northern route is about 30 miles, while the southern route is 40 miles, since you have to drive north several miles to loop back around the lake at the end. You should be able to complete either drive from Barahona within two hours at a comfortable pace. The National Park Station is just east of La Descubierta – look for the bright yellow and green park sign indicating the entrance.

Historic Interest

The lake was named after the legendary Taino cacique (chieftain) Enriquillo, who from 1519-1533 resisted the Spanish by hiding out and conducting raids with his men in the mountains of the Sierra Bahoruco – where he established his own mini-state – and the caves and islands in the area of what is now Lago Enriquillo. (The lake, perhaps fittingly, has now become a wildlife sanctuary.) Enriquillo eventually won a peace treaty from the Spaniards, but died of smallpox a few years later. Also taking refuge in the southwestern mountains and remote regions near the Haitian border were the *cimarrones*, escaped colonial-era slaves who turned to farming for a livelihood; their descendants still populate the area today.

> **Tip:** If you have a few minutes either before or after touring Lago Enriquillo, you can stop at the **Cueva de las Caritas**, just a mile or so east of the National Park Station in La Descubierto. It requires a short but fairly steep climb up from the road, but you'll be rewarded with a look at some carved Taino petroglyphs as well as good views of the lake. The Taino rebel leader Enriquillo himself is said to have used the cave as a hideout from the Spanish.

COOLING OFF

Want a chance to cool off in a natural pool (*balneario*) after a hot morning on Lago Enriquillo? If so, then you have a few options, depending on how you return to Barahona from the lake.

The first is right in La Descubierto, a cold sulphur spring called **Las Barias**; ask one of the locals for the exact location.

If you drive back east toward Barahona along the northern shores (Highway 48), you can head for **Las Marías de Neyba**, a huge tree-shaded *balneario* about 1½ miles east of the town of Neyba (a big sign there points in the direction of the pool). If you choose to return via the southern route (Highway 46), you can aim for the pueblo of La Zurza, which is located shortly beyond the town of Duverge and just past the pueblo of Ven a Ver ("Come and See," where the residents are appropriately friendly). A sign on the left-hand side of the road (as you head east) marks the turn for La Zurza. Inside is a small freshwater swimming hole with incredibly blue water, where you can soak off the morning heat.

Duverge is also near one entry point for Park Nacional Barohuco, which you can access via a dirt road that heads south from Duverge to the mountain village of Puerto Escondido, a hot spot for bird watching (see *Parque Nacional Bahoruco, Puerto Escondido*, above, for more information).

Laguna Rincón Reserve

This lagoon reserve, also known as Laguna Cabral or the Cabral Scientific Reserve, serves as a habitat for native freshwater turtles and several species of shallow-water wading birds, including flamingos and herons. The nation's largest freshwater lagoon, it's roughly 10 miles northwest of Barahona and about three miles from the center of the town of Cabral on Highway 46. From the National Park Station on the north end of Cabral, you can take a 2½-hour guided boat tour, which will run about RD$800 plus a RD$50 park entrance fee. Few of the guides, though, speak enough English to provide in-depth answers to any questions.

> **Tip:** You can also drive out to the lagoon and then hike a ways to view it from the water's edge, though the route, which leads through the pueblo El Penon north of Cabral, is somewhat confusing. Ask a local to point out the dirt track that leads west from El Penon to the lagoon.

Parque Nacional Jaragua

At the tip of the Pedernales Peninsula lies the Dominican Republic's largest protected area, Parque Nacional Jaragua, a hot, arid, cactus-laden region that stretches over nearly 600 square miles. The park, named after a famous Taino cacique, is mostly inaccessible except for the wildlife-rich Laguna de Oviedo and Bahía de las Aguilas, a bay with a long swath of deserted beach. Two small islands, Isla Beata and Isla Alto Velo, are also part of the park and can be reached by boat from the town of Pedernales.

> **Warning:** Don't forget to stop at the national park office near the town of Oviedo to pick up permits (RD$50) before setting out.

Laguna de Oviedo

 This scenically stunning six-mile-long saltwater lagoon in Parque Nacional Jaragua encompasses at least a dozen small islands and is considered one of the top bird-watching spots in the entire country. Along with the DR's largest year-round population of flamingos, Laguna de Oviedo serves as a habitat for herons, roseate spoonbills (shown at left), white-crowned pigeons, and brown pelicans among some 130 species of birds, representing more than two-fifths of all those in the Dominican Republic. The area is also home to several species of turtles and the indigenous rhinoceros and Ricord iguanas.

There are two ways to visit the lagoon. The first is to join a guided group. One of the best outfits is **Tody Tours** (Calle José Gabriel García 105, Zona Colonial, Santo Domingo, ☎ 686-0882, www.todytours.com, kate@todytours.com), run by Kate Wallace, a former US Peace Corps volunteer and naturalist from Massachusetts who remained on the island to live and work. As part of her four- to-five day tours from Santo Domingo into Parque Nacional Jaragua and the Sierra Bahoruco, which specialize in endemic birds of the Dominican Republic, she offers early-morning boat tours of the lagoon that cost an additional US$50 for a boat (holding up to eight people) and local guide. Because the lagoon is too shallow to run a motor, the boatman gets out and wades, pushing the boat silently and enabling bird-watchers to get quite close to flamingos and other wading birds. You might also see iguanas. The full tours cost US$150 per person per day (US$75 for the second person of a couple) for her guide services, not including transportation, food, or lodging.

You can also visit the lagoon independently, either traveling on foot along the water's edge or hoping to find a local boatman who will take you out onto the lagoon for two or three hours of bird-watching. If you want to visit Laguna Oviedo on your own, you will need to stop at the National Park Station first to get an entrance permit (RD$50). Watch for the park signs at the left of the entrance to the lagoon outside the town of Oviedo, which is about 40 miles south of Barahona (and the last sign of life until you reach the town of Pedernales on the Haitian border).

Bahía de las Aguilas

If you have your own four-wheel-drive vehicle and you've gotten an early start from your base at either Barahona or Pedernales, you may have time to visit both Laguna de Oviedo and the beautiful Bahía de las Aguilas in the same day. The latter is located west of Oviedo and southeast of Pedernales; turn south at the marked turnoff along Highway 44 about seven miles east of Pedernales. (You'll need to pay a park fee of RD$50 at the National Park Station when you turn off the highway.)

The dirt road turns rough (thus the need for four-wheel drive), but the scenic payoff is breathtaking. The sand skirting the bay stretches on uninterrupted for miles. On one side it is bordered by intensely blue sea water; on the other is lovely desert terrain that attracts hundreds of migratory birds. All this pristine wonder may change if the Bahía becomes the site of a future all-inclusive resort complex – stay tuned for future developments, or lack of same.

> **Tip:** Along the way to the Bahía is the impoverished little community of **Las Cuevas**, where the residents have settled in nearby caves and sell fresh fried fish to passersby for about RD$80.

Islas Baeta & Alto Velo

These two uninhabited islands, the third major – though little visited – attractions of the Parque Nacional Jaraqua, lie off the southernmost point of the Pedernales Peninsula. (Alto Velo is the southernmost point in the country.) On the south coast of Baeta are a number of caves filled with Taino rock art, while both islands are habitat for flamingos, burrowing owls, and Ridgeway's hawks.

Watchable wildlife: On Alto Velo you might spot (with a pair of very sharp eyes) the *Sphaerodactylus ariasae*, a miniature gecko just two centimeters long – the smallest reptile known to man.

Because it's something of an ordeal and an expense to get there – three or more hours by boat, over often choppy seas – the islands are well off most visitors' radar screens. To go, you will need to pay the RD$50 fee at the park station on the highway. You can then hire a small fishing boat with captain in Pedernales for about RD$2,000 to take you to one or both of the islands, but plan for a long day on the water.

Parque Nacional Sierra Bahoruco

The highlight of this vast protected area is its cloud-covered, forested mountain range and the wide variety of bird life inhabiting it. Among some 50 species here are white-necked crows, narrow-billed todies, Hispaniolan trogons, and Hispaniolan parrots (left) and parakeets – some found only in the Dominican Republic. Climbing to heights of more than 7,700 feet near the Haitian border, the park contains wide-ranging pine forests and fields of broad-leafed plants and orchids (more than 160 species of the latter). But because of its remoteness and its mostly rough roads that require rugged four-wheel-drive vehicles, it's one of the least-visited parks in the country.

Hoyo de Pelempito

A recently built viewing stand known as Hoyo de Pelempito, situated along a paved road that runs about 20 miles into the mountains north of Highway 44, offers the easiest access to the Sierra Bahoruco National Park as well as breathtaking vistas of the entire peninsula. About seven miles east of Pedernales, watch for the turnoff going north from 44 – it's directly opposite the turnoff south to Bahía de las Aguilas. Park admission fee is RD$50, payable at the national park station on Highway 44.

Puerto Escondido

This mountaintop village on the northern fringes of the Sierra Bahoruco is a popular spot for birdwatching. From Barahona, take Highway 46 northwest to Duverge (on the south side of Lago Enriquillo). From there it is another seven or eight miles south through the mountains via a marked dirt road turnoff from Duverge. An RD$50 park fee is payable at the park station inside the village. Ask at the park station for directions to lookout points.

> **Tip: Tody Tours** (Calle José Gabriel García 105, Zona Colonial, Santo Domingo, ☎ 686-0882, www.todytours.com) includes Puerto Escondido in its multi-day bird-watching tours of the southwest.

■ Off the Beaten Path

Jimani & the Haitian Border

The often-broiling-hot frontier desert town of Jimani lies just southwest of Lago Enriquillo, near the Haitian border. You may want to hop out of your car here and amble amid the border-crossing chaos for a bit.

> **Caution:** Unless you want to spend the night in Haiti, where there are no nearby hotels, be sure to be back at the border by 6 pm or whenever the guards say it's closing that day. (For border crossing details, see *Crossing Into Haiti*, below.)

There's a big, bustling Haitian market here that operates most days between the two countries. The chain cordoning off the border entrance is to keep out vehicles, but you can stroll in if you want, and possibly even continue on into Haiti. This is one of two official border crossings for foreigners between the Dominican Republic and Haiti (the other is at Dajabon to the north). Port-Au-Prince, Haiti, lies about 30 miles west.

> **Tip:** If you're interested in just getting a quick look at the other side, you can do so here by catching a *motoconcho* or taxi to **Etang Saumatre**, a saltwater lake a few miles away. Much like Lago Enriquillo, only a bit smaller, it's also a haven for flamingos and crocodiles. (The two lakes were once joined, perhaps a million years ago.)

Larimar Mines

Larimar is the semi-precious turquoise-colored stone found only in the Dominican Republic and used in making jewelry. Before you head off in search of them, be aware that the mines are hardly more than holes in the ground, and getting there can be a chore. The road is extremely rough (especially after a heavy rain) and not recommended unless you have a sturdy four-wheel-drive vehicle. Still, the mines are a novel place to visit, and may be worth the rough-and-tumble hour's journey from Barahona if you value buying a souvenir piece of larimar directly from the source. (While there's no shop there, you can usually buy pieces from the miners for around US$10 each.)

How to Get There

Take the coastal road south from Barahona about seven miles until you get to the village of Arroyo. Ask a local to point out the dirt road that leads to the mines, which winds several miles up the mountains through thick forest.

Historic Interest

Before the mines were discovered, the blue pebbles of larimar would wash down the mountain after a heavy rain and come to rest on the coast several miles away, where local people would collect them. One day, or so goes the story, a man decided to follow the trail of pebbles up the mountains and came across their source at what would become the mine site. It's said he named the blue stones "Lari" (after his daughter Larissa) and "mar" (Spanish for the sea, because of their color).

Polo Magnetico

Is it a freak magnetic phenomenon or an optical illusion? You'll have to decide for yourself. This otherwise forgettable slope in the road south of the town of Cabral has long been the subject of debate. Here's all we can say for sure: If you stop here and put your vehicle in neutral, it will feel as if it's moving uphill. The locals claim the phenomenon is caused by magnetically charged ore in the earth. Student surveyors from the Santo Domingo Catholic University, who have made a scientific study of the matter, say it's all an optical illusion – that what appears to be moving uphill is actually moving downhill due to the eye-fooling cut of the gradient. Whichever interpretation is correct, it can be fun just trying to figure it out. (Pack your carpenter's level, if you happen to have one.)

Perhaps the most remarkable aspect of the whole experience is that no one has figured out how to make money from it – yet. The Polo Magnetico is free of charge (free of an admission fee, that is – we're not taking sides on the magnetic charge debate). To reach it, follow the Carretera Polo south of Cabral about 10 miles. The mysterious spot is marked by a billboard north of the pueblo of Polo.

■ On Wheels

Haitian Border Road Trips

 Three exciting road trips ply the Dominican/Haitian border and make for some outstanding scenic drives. These rough-and-tumble roads will take you high into the Sierra Bahoruco, through vast pine forests and strawberry and orchid fields, and then north over the Sierra Neyba and Cordillera Central mountain ranges, providing glimpses into rural Haitian life along the way. Each leg is at least five hours of tough driving, so you may want to consider spending the night in or near the town where each day's drive ends rather than try to return to your previous base. Keep in mind, though, that accommodations are extremely limited along the way.

Driving along the border roads you will be privy to often lush landscapes – at least on the Dominican side. Much of Haiti has been stripped dry by years of deforestation, the result of rampant coal-making practices. You will come across some of the most remote settlements in the country, especially in the Sierra Bahoruco, whose inhabitants include descendants of *cimarrones* who fled to the area in colonial days to escape slavery. You will encounter bustling Haitian markets in the border towns, where cheap kitchenware items mingle with counterfeit designer-label fashions and smuggled rum. At some points you will be able to look directly into Haiti, where you will see brightly painted homes with voodoo figures intended to ward off evil spirits, or catch a glimpse of women doing laundry in the river. You will also spot a number of armed guards in military towers, providing a stark illustration of the tense relations between the two neighboring countries.

Caution: Public transportation to the remote areas in the Southwest is much less available than to other remote *campos* across the island. Therefore you're likely to encounter a number of hitchhikers along the roads. Be very careful about whom you give rides to – particularly when traveling east along Highway 46 from the border town of Jimani and on Highway 2 leading east from Elias Piña, where the Dominican military has set up several checkpoints in search of illegals and contraband coming out of Haiti. You must stop at these checkpoints. Unless you did cross the border into Haiti, just say *"no conozco Haiti"* (I don't know Haiti) when asked. Otherwise, you will have to show your passport and may be subject to a search.

PREPARING FOR A HAITIAN BORDER TRIP

Most drivers make these trips in sturdy four-wheel-drive vehicles, although some daredevil types have successfully negotiated them with 125cc motorbikes. Assuming you aren't auditioning for daredevil school, however, here are some tips to help you make it back safely:

- **Carry maps**. Don't attempt any of these drives without a detailed road map. Berndtsen & Berndtsen produces a detailed map of the Dominican Republic's primary and secondary roads, while also highlighting the country's many natural attractions. The map is usually available at hotel sundry shops; you might also check your local bookstore before leaving home. The National Parks Department in Santo Domingo also produces an outstanding topographical map that you can have for the asking – if it's in stock. If you speak Spanish, it's best to call first (☎ 472-4204, ext. 247, Spanish only). The office is open Monday-Friday, 9 am-2:30 pm, and is located north of Santo Domingo off Avenida Máximo Gómez and the intersection of Avenida Ovando (just before the overpass). Turn left onto the steep incline leading up the office. Their website is www.medioambiente.gov.do.

- **Fill 'er up**. Start out with a full tank of gas and carry a back-up supply as well, since there are no gas stations along these roads.

- **Bring food**. Restaurants are also non-existent outside the towns, and scarce even then, so pack a lunch unless you're willing to wait to eat until you reach the next major town – which may be hours away.

- **Wake up with the roosters**. Get an early start so you can complete the drives during daylight hours.

- **Watch the weather**. Don't set out on these roads after a heavy rain – no matter how rugged your vehicle.

- **Carry your papers**. If you want to cross into Haiti, you'll need your passport and other documentation along with some cash. See *Crossing Into Haiti* box, below.

- **Act responsibly**. Remember that you will be entering an extremely fragile environment with machines capable of doing extensive damage should you go off road. Inform yourself about how to enjoy and preserve these natural wonders. The non-profit organization **Tread Lightly, Inc.** (www.treadlightly.org) offers responsible recreational tips on everything from ATV riding to watersports.

Sierra Bahoruco Border Road

Beginning in Pedernales: This is the toughest of the three border road trips, passing some 18 miles up a steep, rutted mountain road – if you can call it a road – through the clouds to Loma del Toro, the Sierra Bahoruco's highest point at 7,766 feet. From there, you can enjoy an impressive view north to Lago Enriquillo – appropriate, since the great Taino rebel leader himself once used these very mountains as a hideout while attacking the Spanish. The track next cuts through orchid fields and several miles of rainforest before turning east through deforested hilly desert and reaching the isolated village of Puerto Escondido.

Watchable wildlife: Set on desolate terrain, **Puerto Escondido** is nonetheless a prime site for bird-watching. Ask about good spots to go at the National Park Station in the village. (You'll need to pay the RD$50 park entrance fee there.)

The road then descends for eight more desolate miles before ending in the town of Duverge to the north. From here it is a fairly short, easy drive along Highways 46 and 48 to La Descubierta on the opposite (western) side of Lago Enriquillo, where you can spend the night before starting out again the next morning (see *Bases for Exploration, La Descubierta*, below).

Tip: If you aren't planning to continue north along the border the next day, you can return to Barahona for the night instead of staying in La Descubierta.

Sierra Neyba Border Road

Beginning in La Descubierta: This often steep and winding rock and gravel path/road (also known as Highway 47) runs between La Descubierta on the northwest side of Lago Enriquillo and the border town of Elias Piña about 50 miles to the north. On this adventurous drive through the Sierra Neyba mountains you'll be privy to expansive views of a rainforest, as well as pass through one of the oldest villages in the entire country, Sabana Real.

Did you know? You may come upon a beautiful bell-shaped red and yellow flower called *mata de campaña*. Don't be tempted to pick one; this flower is considered a drug and possession of it carries a jail term of up to one year.

At the end of this trip you can either spend the night in dusty Elias Piña, where the accommodations are extremely basic, or in the town of Las Matas de Farfan, about 13 miles east of Elias Piña along Highway 2, which has better hotels and whose shaded parque central is often rated the most beautiful in the country. (See *Bases for Exploration, Las Matas de Farfan*, below, for lodging suggestions.) The next day you can either continue north along the Haitian border or head back east along Highway 2 to Santo Domingo, about 145 miles from Las Matas. That road will take you through the largest city in the region, San Juan de la Maguana, where there are plenty of tourist services (ATMs, gas stations, restaurants and lodgings) though not much to see.

> **Elias Piña** does have a Haitian market on Mondays and Fridays that's worth seeing, and you can also enter into Haiti there for a few hours, if you're so inclined; otherwise, the town is easily skippable.

■ Directions

To bypass Elias Piña altogether, and avoid a particularly treacherous stretch of the border road, you can cut over to Las Matas de Farfan by a different route. When you reach the village of Hondo Valle on Highway 47, head east (rather than north) and drive about 12 miles along Highway 50 to the village of El Cercado. From there, go north on 50 about 10 miles to Las Matas.

Carretera Internacional

From Las Matas de la Farfan or Elias Piña: Head either west or east, respectively, along Highway 2 a few miles to the village of Matayaya, where you can drive north to the border on Highway 45 or Carretera Internacional, as it's known. The Carretera Internacional is unpaved for about 25 miles. When it reaches the village of Villa Anacoana, it turns into a paved highway, with smooth driving all the way to Monte Cristi on the country's northwest coast.

In the village of Restauración (shortly after the highway becomes paved), you might be stopped and directed to a small office on the roadside where you will be required to obtain a road permit. The permits are free and the process is quick and painless. At this point your tires might also be disinfected, on the suspicion that you have entered Haiti and your vehicle could be carrying airborne diseases from the other side. (For whatever reason, they don't disinfect people.)

Along the Carretera Internacional is the village of Banica, which was founded in 1504 and boasts a recently restored Spanish colonial-era church dating from 1514, well worth a look. Some local residents believe St. Francis of Assisi was born in a nearby cave, and mark the event each October 3 with a religious parade.

While the unpaved part of the road is rough (and murder on tires), it also provides fascinating glimpses into Haitian culture. Several of the border towns have Haitian markets, and farther north, along a better stretch of highway, you can enter into Haiti itself if you wish. The town of Dajabon is one of two official border crossing towns for foreigners in the DR (the other being Jimani), and is probably the number-one entry point for land visitors into Haiti.

Fort Liberté: Though you aren't allowed to drive a rental car across, once over the border you can find a *motoconcho* or taxi to take you the 12 miles into Haiti's Fort Liberté, a town with an old French fortress overlooking a scenic bay (see *Crossing into Haiti*, below, for more details). The town itself isn't much, however.

CROSSING INTO HAITI

To enter Haiti you will need your passport and the tourist card you purchased when you initially arrived in the Dominican Republic. After paying the US$20 departure tax to the DR border authorities, you will then need to buy Haitian gourdes in the equivalent of US$10 to buy that country's tourist card. And when you re-enter the Dominican Republic, you'll have to pay another US$10 to purchase a new DR tourist card. (You might even have to grease a few palms on both sides of the border to speed up the process.)

The two official border crossings for foreigners are at Jimani toward the south and Dajabon in the north, though you can usually cross unofficially for a few hours in either Pedernales or Elias Piña, especially if you tip the border guards. At the latter crossings, there will be no Haitian officials to stamp your passport, so it's not advisable to stay too long on the other side. (It's a good idea to report your presence to the local police station in Haiti in any event.)

If you're driving a rental vehicle, you'll have to park it on the Dominican side, and, once in Haiti, hop a *motoconcho* or taxi to where you want to go, or simply walk around for a while. Official border stations are open from 8 am to 6 pm, though the crossings at Pedernales and Elias Piña may close earlier. Be sure to ask, so you can return in time, unless you're planning to spend the night in Haiti (where there are few if any hotels near the border).

■ History

The Carretera Internacional and other border roads were first built by the American military during the eight years the US occupied Hispaniola around the time of World War I. The crude roads were intended to serve as the first distinct boundaries between Haiti and the Dominican Republic, a reasonable goal in and of itself. But when dictator Rafael Trujillo later came to power, he put those new boundaries to appalling use. With an eye toward reducing the Haitian presence and influence in the Dominican Republic, Trujillo ordered his secret police in 1937 to round up any Haitians they could find on the Dominican side of the border. He then had the Haitians brutally massacred by the thousands.

Bases for Exploration

The Southwest doesn't usually see many visitors – except on weekends and particularly on holiday weekends, when Dominicans often flock to Barahona to enjoy the beach and nightlife. Considering the limited options for good accommodations in the area, it's best to consult the introductory section for the complete list of Dominican national holidays. At those times, especially, be sure to secure lodging reservations well in advance.

■ Las Salinas

Orientation

Known for its great windsurfing – but far more quiet and laid-back than the country's other top windsurfing haven, Cabarete, which is on the north coast – Las Salinas is at the southeastern tip of the lovely Bahía de Ocoa, about 80 miles west of Santo Domingo and an hour east of Barahona. Of the many beach communities along the coast between Santo Domingo and Barahona, Las Salinas is the nicest. And since it's just a few miles south of Highway 2, the main artery leading west from Santo Domingo, it makes a good stop en route to the southwest. From the town of Bani on Highway 2, follow Carretera Las Calderas about 12 miles southwest to Las Salinas. On the way, you'll pass the dunes of the Bahía de Calderas, the largest sand dunes in the Caribbean.

Places to Stay & Eat

Salinas Hotel & Restaurant (Puerto Hermosa 7, ☎ 470-6646, salinas@hotelsalinas.com) $$$

This small, independent all-inclusive hotel (also known as Salinas High Winds Center) comes complete with an excellent on-site seafood restaurant, specializing in locally caught lobster. There's also a swimming pool, bar, and disco, making it both a fun and convenient place to stay. It caters mostly to a very hip Dominican set who escape the city on weekends to take in windsurfing on the scenic Bahía de Ocoa.

■ Barahona

Orientation

There's nothing particularly alluring about this big, noisy seaside city of around 100,000 people, which was founded just over two centuries ago by Haitian general Toussaint L'Ouverture and has since become a center of the sugarcane industry and for various mining operations. The public beach isn't much to speak of – small, often dirty, and plagued by jellyfish in the water. Yet Barahona does provide a handy and popular base for exploring the natural wonders around much of the southwest. The city is also known for a notoriously rowdy spring break-like nightlife scene that attracts university crowds from Santo Domingo.

Arriving in Barahona, you'll find that most everything you need – bank ATM, Verizon calling station, pharmacy – are located around the parque central near the Malecón. You can also find *guaguas* in this area to take you down the coast and over to Pedernales at the far end of the peninsula by the Haitian border, as well as to Lago Enriquillo to the west. Most of the better accommodations and restaurants are found along the Malecón or on the coast south of town.

Places to Stay

Costa Larimar Hotel (Malecón, ☎ 524-5111, fax 524-4115) $$$

This multi-story, 108-room deco-style hotel (formerly the Riviera Beach) is situated right on the water on the southern fringes of Barahona. Comfortable rooms come with air conditioning, TV, and phones, and have been freshly redecorated by new management. There's an on-site restaurant as well.

Pontevedra Apart Hotel (Carretera Costa del Mar, ☎ 341-8462) $$$

A sparkling complex about a 15-minute drive south of town, the Pontevedra features both a good beachfront and two pools. Breakfast and dinner are included in the rates. Because of its location, however, you need a car, taxi, or *guagua* (heading toward Pedernales) to reach it.

Guarocuya Beach Resort (Malecón, ☎ 524-4121) $$

This once-grand resort was *the* place to stay in the region back in the days of the Trujillo regime, but the decades have taken their toll and it's now showing its age. Still, it is well-situated on the waterfront (and near

Barahona's notorious nightlife) and the rates are quite reasonable, considering its former stature. All rooms have air conditioning, cable TV, and phones. You'll find an on-site restaurant here, too.

Hotel El Quemaito (Km 10 Carretera Costa del Mar, ☎ 223-0999, http://stodomingo.cjb.net) $$

This small Swiss expat-run hotel is set in well-tended grounds on a cliff overlooking the sea and a pebbly beach, about six miles south of the city. The large and basic rooms have queen-size beds and air conditioning, and, with half-board included, offer prime value for the money (rates go up slightly during the Christmas season).

Los Hijos de Dindo Hotel (30 de Mayo 39, ☎ 524-5510) $

Dead-smack in the middle of town, this hotel with basic rooms and cold showers is very popular among the budget options, so it fills up fast – particularly on weekends when the university crowd heads to Barahona looking for action.

Places to Eat

Brisas del Caribe (Malecón, ☎ 524-2794) $$

This excellent seafood restaurant has a great location on the waterfront, with service to match. You can dine exceptionally well here on shrimp, lobster, or kingfish, reasonably priced for the quality.

Costa Sur (Malecón, ☎ 524-3828) and **El Laurel** (Carretera Central 1, ☎ 524-6352) are both good for seafood. $$

Restaurant Domino (Km 10 Carretera Costa del Mar, ☎ 471-1230) $$

The restaurant at the El Quemaito Hotel serves good Swiss cuisine with Caribbean ambience, right by the swimming pool.

Nightlife

The parque central area also serves as Barahona's party district. A number of informal bars and clubs border the park where you can cut a few dance moves or sip on a beer. **Lotus** is the most popular, with **Legends** running a close second. The classiest among your options, though, is **Costa Sur**, a dance club on the Malecón.

■ Bahoruco

About 10 miles south of Barahona along the coastal highway, the seaside village of Bahoruco has no facilities to speak of except for its beach resorts and a few modest pueblos inhabited by friendly villagers.

Places to Stay & Eat

Barcelo Bahoruco Beach Resort (Km 17 Carretera Costa del Mar, ☎ 800-227-2356 or 524-1111, fax 524-6060; www.barcelo.com) $$$$

This all-inclusive four-star, 105-room resort, about 20 minutes' drive south of Barahona along the coastal highway, is situated amid beautifully landscaped grounds with stunning views of the coast. Amenities include three swimming pools (one for kids), Jacuzzi, beach bar, clay tennis court, and a beautiful sandy beach. Except for a modest fishing village near the entrance of the hotel, it stands in splendid isolation, one of the top resorts in the entire southwest.

Barahona Coralsol Resort (Calle Uruguay 4, Barahona, ☎ 233-4882 or 301-774-6231 in US, fax 524-3929, www.coralsolresort.com, diazfranju@aol.com) $$$-$$$$

Although billing itself as the Barahona Coralsol Resort, with an address in Barahona, this hotel is actually about 12 miles down the coast, a couple of miles south of Barohuco. The separated cottages here are simple but tastefully done, and are all perched on a hillside overlooking the water. There are no phones, TV, or air conditioning, but there is an excellent on-site restaurant with open-air grill, a bar, and two swimming pools (one with seawater). The US$50 per-person rate is based on double occupancy and includes breakfast and dinner – a bargain. The resort offers excursions into the Sierra Bahoruco and to Lago Enriquillo as well as bird-watching packages and car rentals.

Casa Bonita (Km 16, Carretera Costa del Mar, ☎ 565-7310, www.casabonitadr.com) $$$

This elegant colony of rustic thatched-roofed villas is set on a hill with a beautiful pool area overlooking the Caribbean, while mountains form a backdrop to the west. All rooms are tastefully furnished, have water views, air conditioning, and fan. Breakfast is included in the rates. Non-guests can also dine at the hotel's restaurant (☎ 696-0215), which features Dominican cuisine prepared with flair.

■ La Descubierta

This outpost along the northwestern edge of Lago Enriquillo serves mainly as a jumping-off point for trips to Isla Cabritos National Park (see *Adventures*, above) and to Jimani, a dusty Haitian-border crossing town. It also makes a convenient place to spend the night if you're traveling north along the Haitian border (see *Haitian Border Road Trips*, above). There's a sulphur spring here that's popular for swimming, and a Taino archeological site, La Cueva de las Caritas.

The Southwest

Places to Stay

Hotel Padre Billini (Calle Billini, ☎ 696-0327) $

There's nothing fancy about this hotel, but you can get a clean, comfortable, fan-cooled room with private bath here, for not much money.

Places to Eat

Brahaman's (Calle Deligne, no phone) $

On the parque central, Brahaman's serves basic Dominican food for a pittance – and, for that matter, is the only real restaurant in town.

■ Pedernales

The farthest southwest town in the DR, Pedernales is a fishing village right on the Haitian border, at the end of Highway 44. It has a nice public beach and makes a handy base for exploring the Parque Nacional Jaragua, the Bahía de las Aguilas, and parts of the Sierra Bahoruco, though accommodations are generally spartan. While there's no Haitian immigration office at the border here, you can usually get permission to enter Haiti from here for a few hours if you want to (this may include a small monetary token of your appreciation to the guards). The Haitian fishing village of Anse-à-Pitres is on the other side, where you should report to the police station to make your presence known. A Haitian market is held on Mondays and Fridays in the no-man's-land between the two border posts.

Places to Stay & Eat

Sur Caribe (Calle Duarte, ☎ 524-0106) $$

With a location just off the public beach, a swimming pool, and air conditioning and hot water in the rooms, Sur Caribe is the best choice in town. Some of the more spacious rooms come with small kitchenettes. The hotel restaurant, which specializes in seafood, is as good as it gets around here.

■ Las Matas de Farfan

When traveling along the Haitian border, this town makes a nice stopover since it has better accommodations and more services than the border town of Elias Piña to its west. Along with gas stations, ATMs and a calling station, Las Matas has what is often said to be the nicest parque central in the country, a large square of lush greenery with shade trees and a gazebo.

Places to Stay

Hotel Independencia (Calle Independencia, ☎ 527-5439) $

This is the best bet for accommodations here. Nothing fancy – it has cold-water baths and ceiling fans – but it's clean and safe and near the parque central.

Places to Eat

Restaurant Gloria (Calle Independencia) $

This is pretty much it for restaurants in town, but you can eat decent Dominican food here in an outdoor courtyard near the Hotel Independencia.

Dominican Spanish Glossary

■ Pronunciation Guide

Unlike English, with Spanish pronunciation what you see is what you get. In other words, pronunciation is pretty much phonetic once you know the rules. Every letter is pronounced (with some exceptions pointed out below). Spanish also differentiates between genders. Masculine nouns end in O and feminine nouns end in A. Vowels always sound as follows:

A – as in "alone"

E – as in "fetch"

I – sounds like an English E as in: "easily"

O – as in "oh!"

U – as in "*uber*"

C is soft before E and I; elsewhere it is pronounced K as in "kay"

G sounds like a guttural H before E and I and is pronounced "higante" as in "*gigante*"; otherwise it is a hard G at the beginning of a word as in "gum"

H is always dropped when it is at the beginning of a word, with stress placed on the vowel following the H; "*hielo,*" however, sounds more like yellow

J sounds like an English H, so "*jamon*" is pronounced "hamon"

LL is pronounced as a Y at the beginning of a word, as in "llama," and elsewhere as an English J, as in "*calle*"

N is pronounced as in English unless it has a tilde accent over it making it more like NY, as in "*mañana*," which is pronounced "manyana"

QU is pronounced as an English K

RR is heavily stressed with a roll

S is generally not pronounced unless it is at the beginning of a word

V sounds more like B

Z is pronounced the same as a soft C

■ Spanish Words & Phrases

The words and phrases listed below will help you to "get by" in Spanish if you don't already speak the language. The phrases are written in the informal *"tu"* form which is how the Dominicans you are likely to meet will speak to you. Several phrases are also expressed as Dominicanisms (not all are grammatically correct) as opposed to universal and more formal Spanish.

The Basics

Yes – *Sí*
No – *No*
Please – *Por favor*
(No) thank you – *(no) gracias*
You're welcome – *A su orden*
Can you help me? – *¿Puede ayudarme?*

Greetings & Responses

Hello – *Hola*
Welcome – *Bienvenido*
Goodbye – *Adiós*
Good morning – *Buenos días, buen día, (saludos)*
Good afternoon – *Buenas tardes, (saludos)*
Good evening – *Buenas noches*
How are you? – *¿Como estás? (¿Como ta tu?)*
I am fine, thank you – *Muy bien, gracias a Dios*
What is your name? – *¿Que es su nombre?*
My name is – *Mi nombre es*
Nice to meet you – *Mucho gusto*
Where are you from? – *¿Donde eres?*
I am American – *Soy norteamericano/a*
I am Canadian – *Soy canadiense/a*
Do you speak English? – *¿Hablas inglés?*
I don't speak Spanish – *No hablo español*
See you later – *Hasta luego*
Go safely – *Te vaya bien*

Useful Terms for Asking Questions

Where – *Dónde*
When (at what time) – *Cuando, (a qué hora)*
What – *Qué*
How much does it cost? – *¿Cuanto cuesta?*

This, that – *Este/a, ese/a*
These, those – *Estos/as, esos/as*

Useful Statements

Excuse me – *Con permiso, perdón*
Do you have small change? – *¿Tienes menudo?*
I don't know – *No se*
I (don't) like it – *(No) me gusta*
I (don't) understand – *(No) entiendo*
I'm thirsty – *Tengo sed*
I'm tired – *Estoy cansado/a*
I'm hungry – *Tengo hambre*
I'm ready – *Listo/a*
I'm sorry – *Lo siento*
I'm cold – *Tengo frío*
I'm hot – *Tengo calor*

Expressions & Swear Words

Abre sus ojos – when someone says this to you they are telling you to be careful, to keep your eyes open for thieves and pickpockets.
¡Anda el Diablo!, ¡Coño!, ¡Diablo!, ¡Mierquina! – used interchangeably to express, anger, indignation, and surprise.

Referring to Time & Place

Here (right here) – *Aquí (aquí mismo)*
Over there – *Alli, p'alla*
Move forward – *Sigue p'alante*
Move to the back – *Sigue p' atra*
Now (right now) – *Ahora (ahora mismo)*
Later – *Ahorita*
Today – *Hoy*
Tomorrow – *Mañana*
Yesterday – *Ayer*
In the morning – *En la mañana*
In the afternoon – *En la tarde*
In the evening – *En la noche*

Shopping

Open – *Abierto/a*
Closed – *Cerrado/a*
Size – *Tamaño*
Small – *Pequeño*

Medium – *Mediano*
Large – *Grande*
Cash – *Efectivo*
Credit card – *Tarjeta de credito*
Discount – *Descuenta*
Shop/store – *La tienda*
How much does it cost? – *¿Cuanto cuesta?*
It's too expensive – *Es demasiado caro/a*
Do you have anything cheaper? – *¿Tienes algo más barato/a?*

Numbers

1 – *uno*	11 – *once*	30 – *treinta*
2 – *dos*	12 – *doce*	40 – *cuarenta*
3 – *tres*	13 – *trece*	50 – *cincuenta*
4 – *cuatro*	14 – *catorce*	60 – *sesenta*
5 – *cinco*	15 – *quince*	70 – *setenta*
6 – *seis*	16 – *dieciséis*	80 – *ochenta*
7 – *siete*	17 – *diecisiete*	90 – *noventa*
8 – *ocho*	18 – *dieciocho*	100 – *cien(tos)*
9 – *nueve*	19 – *diecinueve*	500 – *quinientos*
10 – *diez*	20 – *veinte*	1,000 – *mil*

■ Ordinal Numbers

First – *primero/a*
Second – *segundo/a*
Third – *tercero/a*
Fourth – *cuarto/a*
Fifth – *quinto/a*

Days of the Week

Monday – *lunes*
Tuesday – *martes*
Wednesday – *miercoles*
Thursday – *jueves*
Friday – *viernes*
Saturday – *sabado*
Sunday – *domingo*

Getting Around

How do I get to ...? – *¿Por dónde se va a...?*
Can you show me ...? – *¿Puedes ensenarme ...?*
Where is ... – *¿Donde esta ...*

  ... the bank? – *el banco?*
  ... the bathroom? – *el baño?*
  ... the bus station to (Santo Domingo)? – *la parada a (Santo Domingo)?*
  ... a calling center – *un centro de llamada?*
  ... the entrance to ...? – *... la entrada a...?*
  ... the nearest hotel? – *un hotel más cercano de aquí?*
  ... the supermarket? – *... el supermercado?*

How far? – *¿Qué distancia?*
Left (left-hand side) – *Izguierda (mano izquierda)*
Right (right-hand side) – *Derecha (mano derecha)*
Straight ahead – *Derecho*
I would like a round-trip ticket to ... – *Quisiera una boleta ida y vuelta a*
What time does it leave – *¿A que hora sale?*
What time does it arrive in ...? – *¿A que hora llega en ...?*

Accommodations

■ The Basics

Do you have ... – *¿Hay ...*

  ... a room? – *un habitación?*
  ... with two beds? – *con dos camas?*
  ... with a double bed? – *con una cama matrimonial?*

There is/are – *Hay*
It is for ... – *Es para ...*

  ... one person – *una persona*
  ... two people – *dos personas*
  ... one night – *un noche*
  ... one week – *una semana*

It's fine, how much is it? – *¿Está bien, cuánto es?*
It's too expensive – *Es demasiado caro/a*
Do you have anything cheaper? – *¿Tienes algo más barato/a?*
Can one camp here (near here)? – *¿Se puede acampar aquí (cerca)?*

■ Useful Terms & Phrases

I have a problem – *Tengo una problema*
Air conditioning – *aire condicionado*
Bathroom – *baño*
Bed – *la cama*

Hair dryer – *secador*
Iron – *plancha*
Ironing board – *mesa de la plancha*
Key – *llave*
Pillow – *almohado*
Towel – *toalla*
TV – *televisión*
Shampoo – *champu*
Shower – *la ducha*
Soap – *jabón*
Swimming pool – *piscina*

Eating & Drinking

■ The Basics

Waiter – *camarero*
Waitress – *camarera*
A menu, please – *Un menú, por favor*
Give me – *Dame*
I'd like – *Quisiera*
I want – *Quiero*
I'm a vegetarian – *Soy vegetariano/a*
The bill, please – *La cuenta por favor*
Join us (in our meal) – *A bien tiempo*
Enjoy your meal – *Buen provecho*
Cheers! – *Salud!*
Breakfast – *desayuno*
Lunch – *almuerzo*
Dinner – *cena*
Knife – *cuchillo*
Fork – *tenedor*
Spoon – *cuchara*
Cup – *taza*
Glass – *vaso*
Plate – *plato*
Napkin – *servilleta*
Salt – *sal*
Pepper – *pimiento*
Ice – *hielo*
Tip – *propina*
Tax – *impuesto*

■ Useful Terms

A little – *un chin*
With – *con*
Without (sugar) – *sin (azucar)*
Very cold (plenty of ice) – *bien fría*
Dominican cuisine – *comida criolla*
Garlic sauce – *ajillo*
Baked – *asado/a*
Tomato sauce – *criolla*
Barbecued – *barbecue*
Fried – *frito*
Roasted – *horneado*
Stewed – *guisado/a*
Grilled (meat) – *plancha*
Grilled (fish) – *parrilla*

■ The Menu (El Menu)

Breakfast (*Desayuno*)

Conflai – cereal
Huevos – eggs
Huevos interno – fried eggs
Huevos revuelto – scrambled eggs
Huevos herido – boiled eggs
Mangú – mashed plantain with oil and onions
Mantequilla – butter
Marmalada – jelly
Pan – bread
Queso (frito) – cheese (fried)
Tocineta – bacon
Tosatado – toast

Soups (*Sopitas*)

Asopao – soupy rice with chicken, shrimp, or octopus
Mondongo – tripe stew
Sancocho – hearty soup made with five different kinds of meat and a variety of indigenous tubers
Sopa de pescado – fish soup

Meat (*Carnes*)

Aletas – chicken wings
Bistec – steak
Carne – pieces of meat
Chicharron – pieces of fried pork
Chivo – goat

Chuletas – pork chops

Cerdo – pork

Guinea – fowl in wine

Jamón – ham

La Bandera – rice and beans with chicken or meat and a side salad

Longaniza – sausage made from pork, tripe, garlic, and oregano

Monfongo – mashed roasted plantain with garlic and pork cracklings

Pasteles en hojas – boiled mashed plantain stuffed with meat served in a banana leaf

Pechuga – chicken breast

Pollo – chicken

Seafood (*Mariscos*)

Atún – tuna

Calamar – squid

Camarones – shrimp

Cangrejo – crab

Carite – kingfish

Chillo – red snapper

Almeja – clam

Lambí – conch

Langosta – lobster

Mero – sea bass

Ostra – oyster

Pescado con coco – fish in coconut sauce

Pulpo – octopus

Fruits (*Frutas*)

Aquacate – avocado

Champola, guanabana – soursop

Chinola – passion fruit

China, naranja – orange

Fresas – strawberries

Guineo – banana

Granadillo – pear-flavored fruit

Lechoza – papaya

Límon – lemon

Limoncillo – lime

Mango – mango

Piña – pineapple

Tamarindo – tamarind

Tomate – tomato

Zapote – vanilla/raspberry-flavored fruit

Vegetables (*Verduras*) and starches

Arroz – rice

Batata – sweet potato

Berenjena – eggplant

Cassava – yucca

Cebolla – onion

Ensalada – salad

Gandules – pigeon peas

Habichuelas – red beans

Maiz – corn

Maduro – ripe plantain

Morro – mixed rice and beans

Ñame – yam

Papa (mashed, boiled) – potato (*puree, herido*)

Plátano – plantain

Remolacha – beet

Tostones – fried plantain

Yautía – indigenous tuber

Zanahoria – carrot

Desserts (*Postres*)

Pudin de arroz – rice pudding

Bizcocho – cake

Dulces de pasta – sweet pastes made from a variety of fruits

de coco – coconut

de batata – sweet potato

de leche – sweet milk

de naranja – orange

de pina – pineapple

de guayaba – guava

Flan (*de leche, de maiz*) – custard (milk custard, corn custard)

Helado – ice cream

Drinks (*Bebidas*)

Agua – water

Agua mineral – mineral water

Agua purificada – purified water

Batida – fruit shake

Café con leche – sweetened coffee with milk

Café negro – sweetened, black coffee

Cerveza – beer
Cuba libre – rum and cola
Fru' pon – fruit punch
Jugo – juice
Jugo de china / naranja – orange juice
Jugo natural – fresh squeezed juice
Leche – milk
Limonada – lemonade
Mama guana – home brew made from tree bark, leaves, honey, and rum
Morir soñando – orange juice with milk
Refresco – soda
Ron – rum
Té - tea
Vino tinto – red wine
Vino blanco – white wine

Fast food (*Comida rápida*)
Chimi – roast pork sandwich
Empanda – meat- , chicken- , cheese- , or vegetable-filled pastry
Pastellito – smaller version of the empanada
Fritura – chopped pieces of fried meat with fried plantain
Hamburger – hamburger
Hot dog – hot dog
Mayonesa – mayonnaise
Mustaza – mustard
Cachup – ketchup
Pica pollo – fried chicken with fried plantain
Pizza – pizza
Quipes – cracked wheat and meat fritter

Glossary

águila – eagle
ámbar – amber
apagón – power outage
aeropuerto – airport
avenida – avenue
Arawaks – the first known inhabitants of the island
bachata – twangy ballad music once reviled as the low-culture of ordinary Dominicans, it is now gaining widespread acceptance
bahía – bay
balneario – swimming hole

ballena – whale

bandera – flag, or "la bandera" as a typical meal of meat or chicken with rice and beans is called.

barbacue – barbecue

barrio – neighborhood

batey – a public plaza in the times of the Tainos, now refers to slums inhabited by Haitian migrant workers

bohío – circular thatched-roof huts of the Tainos that are still in use today

la bomba – gas station

buscone – a freelance guide

cabaña turística – motel rooms rented out by the hour

cabrito – young goat

cacique – Taino chief

canoa – canoe carved from tree trunks used by Tainos

calle – street

campesino/a – a person from the countryside

campo – village

Caribes – war-like Arawaks who began arriving on the island a few centuries before Columbus

carretera – highway

carro público – public cars ferrying up to eight passengers at a time along established routes. Also called *conchos*.

casa de cambio – currency exchange house

casa de huéspedes – guest house

casava – bread made from the yucca root that was a staple in the Taino diet and is still in use today

caudillos – Dominican strongmen who held power and influence over a particular region

cemi – Taino idol made of stone that was believed to hold benevolent spirits

chivo – goat

cimarrones – escaped African slaves who terrorized plantation owners from their enclaves in the island's mountain ranges during the colonial era

ciudad – city

Ciboney – a branch of the Ararwaks who arrived in the islands from Venezuela around 3000 BC

Ciguayo – a branch of the Tainos who later joined with the Spaniards to help subjugate their fellow tribesmen

chin – a little bit

ciguapa – mythical Taino women living in the Cordillera Central who had blue skin, long black hair, and hoofed feet turned backwards

club gallistico – cockfighting arena

colmado – a convenience store prevalent in Dominican neighborhoods that also serves as a popular watering hole

comedor – a family-run eating establishment specializing in Dominican cuisine

comida criolla – Dominican cuisine

concho – dilapidated cars ferrying up to eight passengers at a time along established routes. Also called a *carro público*

conuco – a Taino farming method still in use today although not as conscientiously as it once was. It now refers to slash-and-burn farming practiced by *campesinos*

devastaciones – the burning down of north coast villages and forced resettlement of inhabitants in order to stop illegal trade with privateers in the 17th century

encomienda – a reform of the *repartimiento* system wherein the Tainos were to be educated and brought into the Catholic faith as well as paid for their forced labor in the gold mines

extranjero/a – foreigner

fiesta patronal – festival for the patron saint of a town or village

frontera – border land between the Dominican Republic and Haiti

gomero – a tire repair shop

gourde – Haitian currency

gringo/a – foreigner regardless of race

guagua – bus

güira – a folk instrument resembling a grater used in *périco ripiao*

Hayti – the Taino name for the island of Hispanola

hamaca – hammock

Hispaniola – the name given to the island by Christopher Columbus

Huracán – the evil and powerful Taino god from which we get the term hurricane

iglesia – church

Igneri – more advanced branch of the Arawaks known for their superb ceramic artistry

jonron – home run

ladrón – thief

larimar – semiprecious turquoise stone unique to the Dominican Republic

malecón – seaside boulevard, found in many Dominican cities

manatí – manatee

merengue – fast paced national music and dance

motoconcho – motorbikes used both as private and public transportation

motoconchista – a person who operates a *motoconcho*

parque central – the public square in every Dominican town that usually serves as the center of social and commercial activity *pensión* – a private home that rents rooms to travelers

peso – Dominican currency

périco ripao – old-style merengue using the accordion, *tambora*, *güira*, and African thumb piano

pueblo – small Dominican town

puta – prostitute

Quisqueya –the island as it was called at the time of Columbus' arrival

repartimiento – the forced apportioning of Tainos to colonists

río – river

ruta – route

sanky panky – gigoló

sierra – mountain range

tiburón – shark

son – Cuban music form especially popular among the Congolese descendents in Villa Mella north of the Santo Domingo city center

supermercado – supermarket

Taino – predominant inhabitants of the Dominican Republic at the time of Columbus' arrival

tambora – a lap drum carved from a tree trunk that is common in old-style *merengue*

taxi – taxi

tigeré – a thug

todo incluido – all-inclusive

yanguí – an American

yola – hazardous boat used by Dominicans to illegally emigrate to Puerto Rico via the Mona Passage.

Index